PHILOSOPHY IN GERMANY
1831–1933

PHILOSOPHY IN GERMANY
1831–1933

Herbert Schnädelbach

translated by Eric Matthews

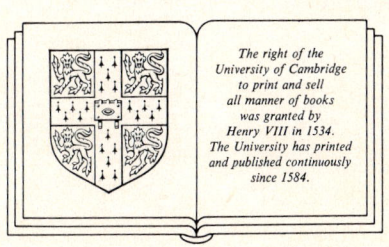

Cambridge University Press

Cambridge
London   New York   New Rochelle
Melbourne   Sydney

Published by the Press Syndicate of the University of Cambridge
The Pitt Building, Trumpington Street, Cambridge CB2 1RP
32 East 57th Street, New York, NY 10022, USA
296 Beaconsfield Parade, Middle Park, Melbourne 3206, Australia

© Cambridge University Press 1984

First published 1984

Printed in Great Britain at the University Press, Cambridge

Library of Congress catalogue card number: 83-20944

British Library Cataloguing in Publication Data
Schnädelbach, Herbert
Philosophy in Germany 1831–1933.
1. Philosophy, German
I. Title
193   B2743
ISBN 0 521 22793 3 hard covers
ISBN 0 521 29646 3 paperback

Contents

	Translator's note	vii
	Preface	ix
	Introduction	1
1	Sketch of an Age	12
2	History	33
3	Science	66
4	Understanding	109
5	Life	139
6	Values	161
7	Being	192
8	Epilogue: Man	219
	Notes	235
	Select bibliography	257
	Index	260

For Jürgen Habermas

Translator's note

A number of points about the translation require some comment. First, the German word '*Wissenschaft*' is notoriously difficult to translate in a way which does not mislead. I have generally translated it simply as 'science' (though occasionally as 'scholarship'): but although this translation has much to be said for it, it is far from perfect, since the German word covers any organized and systematic academic study, while the English word always tends to carry overtones of *natural* science. For this reason, such expressions as 'historical science' may convey misleading connotations if the imperfect equivalence between the German and English terms is not borne in mind. Secondly, the term 'historicism', though often used in philosophical English in a way more or less equivalent to the German *Historismus*, has acquired some misleading associations from its usage by Popper and his followers. As used in the present translation, it does *not* refer to the Popperian bogy of a belief in 'Laws of Historical Destiny' but, as the text makes clear, to an emphasis on the historical character of thought. Thirdly, I have used the somewhat awkward terms 'life-philosophy' and 'nature-philosophy' for *Lebensphilosophie* and *Naturphilosophie*, in order to avoid the possibly misleading associations of 'philosophy of life' and 'philosophy of nature'. (The exception to this is that I refer to Hegel's *Naturphilosophie* as his 'philosophy of nature', because of the relative familiarity of that expression in the Hegelian context.) Finally, I have usually translated the word '*Geist*' as 'spirit' for the sake of consistency, except where some other translation, such as 'mind', seems obviously required by the context. In this and other cases, where there seems any real danger of misunderstanding, I have resorted to placing the German word in brackets after the English.

I have tried throughout to reduce to a minimum the use of capital letters.

Nothing contributes more to the wrong impression gained of German philosophy in the English-speaking world than the spattering of capitalized words ('Spirit', 'Reason', etc.) across translations. Exceptions to this rule are, first, that terms which have a specific use in a philosophical system, different from their normal use, have been given capital letters (e.g. Absolute, Idea in Hegel; Being in Heidegger); similarly, names of philosophical systems which also have a non-philosophical use have been capitalized (e.g. Idealism, Realism); and names of philosophical movements which are based on proper names have been similarly treated (e.g. Kantianism, Marxism). I hope I have been reasonably consistent in sticking to these rules.

All translations from German-speaking authors are my own; most have been specially done for the present work. The exception is that translations from Max Weber are taken, wherever possible, from *Weber: Selections in Translation*, edited by W. G. Runciman and translated by Eric Matthews, Cambridge, 1978.

I am grateful to Professor Schnädelbach for his consistently helpful and friendly comments and criticisms. I should also like to thank my friend and colleague Dr Paul Gorner for his help on a number of points.

Aberdeen, January 1983   Eric Matthews

Preface

This book is an experiment. It attempts to present a century in the history of German philosophy in such a way that it becomes clear what was of particular concern to the philosophers of that time in Germany and how much of these concerns still have actuality for us even today. From the outset, therefore, all pretensions even to approximate to a complete presentation of the authors and intellectual tendencies of the age must be renounced. The procedure of concentrating on the history of problems, which suggests itself as an alternative, is however itself not without problems, since the selection of the themes which are supposed to be representative of a period of time always has about it something of the contingent and contestable. I hope I have made my selection in such a way that it illuminates what is essential: the identity-crisis of German philosophy after Hegel, which still continues even today. All the same, many will feel the lack of several things, e.g. a chapter on ethics. This seemed to me dispensable, because what is characteristic of the German discussion is dealt with in the chapter on 'Values', and what was not affected by this theme was not essentially different from the usual West-European modes of thought. As for a chapter on aesthetics, I have foregone that because the philosophy of art at that time – insofar as it did not simply continue along the paths marked out by Hegel – was above all historical and psychological in tendency; it was only through Hermann Cohen's *Ästhetik des reinen Gefühls* (Aesthetics of Pure Feeling) of 1912 that the 'beautiful' became once more a specifically philosophical theme. A chapter which I had originally planned to include on 'Thought', in which Frege's and Husserl's critique of psychologism in the foundations of logic and its consequences were to have been discussed, I decided to leave out since both authors are also sufficiently familiar in the English-speaking world and continue to be influential there through their intellectual successors. Anyone who feels the lack of any discussion of social theory may reflect that it was more or less immediately after Hegel that sociology emerged as an independent discipline which from the beginning reserved the theme of 'society' for itself alone. Social scientists of all tendencies at that time placed no value on being regarded as philosophers; rather, philosophers presented themselves as sociologists, like Georg Simmel, Othmar Spann, Ferdinand Tönnies, Alfred Vierkandt and many others. Besides, most philosophers felt themselves competent to deal with the social only from an ethical point of view. No one should infer from the lack of a chapter on 'society' in this book that its author does not regard society as a subject for philosophy: simply, it was not normally so regarded at that time.

Anyone who writes for a public with which he is not familiar does well to assume that nothing he writes about is familiar to it. Hence, I have done no research into English-language accounts of the period and have made use only of German literature. Not once have I written in the language of those to whom my account is directed, but in German. This book owes its leap over the language-barrier to Eric Matthews, who permitted me to share in the process of translation and thus made it plain to me how much patience, conscientiousness and care this task required of him; I should like to thank him above all. It is not possible for me to thank all those who have assisted my work by their criticism and encouragement. I should like at least to mention my colleague Dr Josef Meran M.A., who has read the whole book with care and made many helpful comments. I am grateful to Frau Karin Benda (Hamburg) for her conscientious preparation of the manuscript, which was completed in Autumn 1981.

Hamburg, December 1982   Herbert Schnädelbach

Introduction

To attempt to give an account of the history of German philosophy between the end of the Idealist period and the first stirrings of the philosophy of our own time is to enter largely unexplored territory. In academic teaching, this period is thought of as an age in which 'great philosophy' was in decline, even moribund, only to revive, according to most accounts, in the twenties of the present century. It is true that contemporary philosophy has been decisively shaped by a number of works published at that time: Ludwig Wittgenstein's *Tractatus logico-philosophicus* (1921), Georg Lukács' *Geschichte und Klassenbewusstsein* (History and Class-Consciousness) (1923) and Martin Heidegger's *Sein und Zeit* (Being and Time) (1926). But these three works, the most influential philosophical writings of this century, originated from, and defined themselves in relation to, certain traditions which they themselves brought to an end. Earlier writers are generally known only from the references to them which appear in these same books, which makes it only too easy to accept a picture of them which is predigested and polemically distorted. Thus, neo-Kantianism, for instance, which is alleged to have reduced philosophy to the theory of knowledge, is still frequently dismissed as 'outmoded' even today, for no other reason than that the leading figures of modern philosophy, from the neo-positivists of the Vienna Circle by way of the critical theorists to the new ontologists, have defined their new positions primarily by differentiating them from that once dominant tendency in academic philosophy. A similar fate threatened to befall Edmund Husserl's phenomenology: if one were to believe such writers as Max Scheler, Nicolai Hartmann and Martin Heidegger, we owe to Husserl only a philosophical method which once again makes metaphysics possible, and this would have remained the 'judgment of history', had not Husserl's late philosophy had its own, often remarkably complex, influence on subsequent history. In general, it seems to be the fate of most philosophers between Hegel and Heidegger to spend their afterlife as either *epigoni* or *precursors* – to the extent that they are not forgotten altogether. The original questions which they posed, and the situation of their thought, which they regarded quite differently from their successors, seem no longer to have any actuality for us.

For Karl Marx and Friedrich Engels, Søren Kierkegaard and Friedrich Nietzsche, of course, this does not seem to be the case: they are well known, and their lives belong to the period to be considered here. It would also be impossible to dispute that their thought has much more significance for the philosophy of our own time than that of their numerous contemporaries. But to give it the central place in a historical account of the philosophy of that time would be simply anachronistic.[1] Marx the philosopher is a discovery of the twenties, connected with the publication of his early writings. The same is true of Kierkegaard, whose general influence began to be felt only with the philosophers of existence (above all Karl Jaspers) and the Protestant dialectical theologians (Karl Barth, Paul Tillich, Friedrich Gogarten and others). The philosophical influence of Nietzsche was confined, until well into the present century, to a small group and to life-philosophy: academic philosophy accepted his work only long after his death. All three authors – and the name of Sigmund Freud ought also to be added to the list – revolutionized traditional thought. Present-day philosophy is unthinkable without them. They are present to us, but in their own day they were – seen from the point of view of the history of philosophy – out of their time. They were not philosophers in the traditional sense of the word – nor did they generally want to be – and their historical influence in philosophy did not coincide with their life-history. If one does not want to limit oneself to asking about the present-day significance of the philosophical thought of that time, but seeks to become acquainted with it in its own place and in its own present, then it is wrong to give special preference to those famous names.

The usefulness of such an undertaking is not simply that it fills in gaps in knowledge or does historical justice. Nor can it be a matter of representing the much maligned philosophy of the nineteenth century, contrary to the general view, as a newly discovered period of intellectual brilliance. If it is the case that we are indeed familiar with the beginnings of present-day philosophy, but only in a remarkably unhistorical manner – that is, as responses or reactions to something with which we are not acquainted – then the roots of the present situation lie in obscurity. If we pay attention to them, we shall discover something about ourselves, for the conditions of our own philosophical activity were not determined by those fathers of modern philosophy who are still actual for us: they themselves were already reacting to them. Our concern is thus with the immediate prehistory of that which we regard as the philosophical present, and we shall not understand that as long as we do not understand its antecedents.

1 The boundaries of periods

The dates by means of which we define the period to be considered here have a symbolic character. The year 1831, in which Hegel died, has often been linked with what is known, somewhat melodramatically, as the 'collapse of Idealism'.[2] The same cholera to which Hegel succumbed drove Arthur Schopenhauer from Berlin, putting an end to his academic career: thus, the year 1831 also symbolizes the departure from the University of those elements in the philosophical thought of the time which still have a direct influence in our own day. Ludwig Feuerbach, Marx, Engels, Kierkegaard, Nietzsche – not one of them was any longer a professor of philosophy in the way that Kant, Fichte, Schelling and Hegel had been. In 1832 Goethe died, thus ending the 'Age of Goethe', which embraces not only German Idealism, but also German classicism and romanticism, and which is generally regarded as a period of relative cultural uniformity spanning the decades between 1770 and 1830. It is only in the thirties that the nineteenth century really begins in Germany, if that expression is used to refer to a cultural period: this was the beginning of the age of science, of historical culture, of realism and 'disillusionment'; but it was also the beginning of the crisis of European humanist civilization, the true extent of which was first revealed by the two World Wars.

When the nineteenth century in Germany ends is much harder to determine. The year 1900 does not mark any kind of turning-point. Much more significant is the year 1918, when, because of the military defeat, all the revolutionary tendencies of the time in Germany were enormously intensified. Under the Weimar Republic many things came to an end and there was a change of direction, recognizable even in philosophy, in that the great controversies which provide the framework for our present discussions all go back to those years. It is certainly sensible to treat the twenties as the final phase of the nineteenth century in philosophy. The year 1933, however, is again a symbolic date: the beginning of the 'Third Reich' marks the beginning of the end, not only of the political unity of Germans in the German national state, but also of the cultural identity which they had enjoyed up until that time, which was much more seriously disturbed by the abomination of National Socialism and the sufferings of the war than by the political and ideological division of the country. After Auschwitz almost everything in Germany was different from before: it was necessary to assimilate afresh the elements in German tradition which had not led in that direction.

2 On method

In so far as any general accounts of nineteenth century philosophy exist at all, they present their object either in terms of the 'great thinkers' or by grouping the numerous authors and their works into 'schools' or main tendencies. In this book, a quite different approach will be adopted: I shall attempt to give an account based on the *history of problems*. Such a procedure itself involves problems: there is the possibility of arbitrariness in the selection of the principal problems to be presented, and the difficulty that the real historical connexions may become stylized and idealized, as if it were a matter of presenting pure chains of argument. The crux for problem-based history is the excessive emphasis on systematization, but one can justify this procedure by its aim. A strongly systematic emphasis is in place in approaches to the history of thought in which historical completeness is *not* the principal consideration. In what follows the aim will be philosophically to assimilate the thought of the nineteenth century: that is, the primary concern will be our present-day self-understanding. There is at work here an implicit preconception of what constitutes contemporary philosophy for us: to make this explicit in the form of questions posed to the past and to verify it by means of the answers could be regarded as the most important philosophical aspect of a work on the history of philosophy. The pragmatic purpose of giving an account of philosophy in Germany requires in addition concentration on specifically German themes. We have to ask what it was that occupied the foreground of the philosophical consciousness of the time in Germany and what were the subjects of debate. Thus, we shall apply ourselves to considering the 'mainstream' of thought and set in their proper context of problems those 'peaks' of the period which were out of their time or belonged to another country. The question of what, in all this, is still important for us today must recede into the background. Since we thus allow the period to speak for itself about its own problems, we must moreover take account of the fact that our own scale of importance is being changed. Above all, our aim is to enquire into the original philosophical achievements of the period, so as to counteract the popular clichés about epigoni and precursors.

The main question in the following investigations is this: what, in a post-Idealist age, is philosophy, and how is what bears that name possible? This was a vital question for all those who sought to be philosophers after Hegel (who had asserted that all philosophy is Idealism) and who saw through the vulgar manoeuvre of proclaiming the 'end of philosophy'. That the 'collapse of Idealism' plunged philosophy into a profound identity-crisis which has persisted up until the present day may be seen in the fact that the question 'Whither philosophy?' has since become a constant theme in philosophical inaugural lectures. To enquire into the causes of this identity-crisis and the possibilities of overcoming it is the philosophical aim of the following studies in problem-based history. It is this which ultimately determines also the choice and arrangement of the set of problems to be discussed.

3 'Idealism'

The word 'Idealism' has many meanings. In philosophical contexts it refers as a rule to an epistemological position, but educated speech and intellectual small talk have also assigned to it several other meanings. If we discuss philosophy after Idealism, this can only mean *Absolute* Idealism, which is defined in terms of the systems of Fichte, Schelling and Hegel and whose downfall brought about the identity-crisis of philosophy already referred to. This crisis is so characteristic of the German scene only because it was at one time almost completely dominated by Absolute Idealism. This also explains the fact that in other countries, especially Britain, there has been no similar division into epochs in the history of philosophy. The philosophy of Immanuel Kant, incidentally, does not belong to Absolute Idealism and this is what made it such an attractive basis for a general rehabilitation of philosophy after the end of Idealism.

The nature of Absolute Idealism may be elucidated by three theses defended by those who uphold this position – illustrations are taken from the philosophy of Hegel: (1) the unity of being and thought in the Absolute; (2) the unity of the true, the good and the beautiful in the Absolute; (3) the science of the Absolute as the philosophical system.

(1) Absolute Idealism does not need to deny what everyone knows,

namely, that being and thought are distinct, since it conceives of their unity as a *dialectical* unity: as 'identity of the identity and non-identity'[3] of being and thought, though this is admittedly supposed to be explicable only in the context of the Absolute. According to Hegel, the Absolute is the Idea, and

the Idea can be conceived as reason (this is the proper philosophical meaning of reason); it can be thought of, further, as the subject-object, as the unity of the ideal and the real, of the finite and the infinite, the soul and the body, as the possibility which has its actuality in itself, as that whose nature can be grasped only as existing, etc.: because in it are contained all relations of the understanding, but in their infinite return and identity to itself.[4]

In the domain of the understanding, on the other hand, which Hegel defines as that of finitude and of the ordinary view of the world, it goes without saying that what in the Absolute is dialectically united is separated. It is from this perspective, according to Hegel, that we get

the explicit teaching and corresponding refutation ... that the subject is distinct from the object, as likewise is the finite from the infinite, etc., as if the concrete spiritual unity were without determinations in itself and did not itself contain in itself the distinction; as if anyone were unaware of the difference of the subject from the object, the infinite from the finite, or philosophy, caught up in its scholastic wisdom, had to be reminded that there is wisdom outside the Schools, to which that distinction is familiar.[5]

The most famous version of this thesis is Hegel's dictum, 'What is rational is real; and what is real is rational'. The provocation contained in this sentence has determined the character of the argument with Hegel right up to the present day, and one could write a sound history of this argument by following the guiding thread of the history of the exposition of this sentence. To be sure, if one takes account of what 'reason' and 'reality' mean in the context of Hegelian philosophy itself, one will no longer interpret it as nothing more than a philosophical justification of the status quo, as has often happened: the sentence is primarily an affirmation of Absolute Idealism, not of conservative ideology.

(2) Hegel's Absolute Idealism, as a philosophy of the Absolute Idea, sees the unity of thought and being, reason and reality, subjectivity and objectivity, as also a unity of the true, the good and the beautiful. Leaving aside Hegel's philosophy of art, in which the beautiful is defined as 'the sensuous appearance of the Idea', one can regard Absolute Idealism as rehabilitating the Scholastic dictum, *ens et verum et*

bonum convertuntur. Hegel identifies what truly is with the theoretical Idea, and the good with the practical Idea, and states in transition to the Absolute Idea,

The truth of the good is thereby posited, as the unity of the theoretical and the practical Idea that the good in and for itself attains – the objective world is thus in and for itself the Idea, as it also eternally posits itself as a goal and through activity brings about its reality. This life which has returned to itself from difference and finitude is the speculative or Absolute Idea.[6]

This makes it clear at the same time that even the famous dictum from the Preface to the *Philosophy of Right* has both a descriptive and a normative aspect. Consequently, one who holds such a position cannot accept as the last word in philosophy the distinction between 'is' and 'ought', which he also recognizes; rather, on this view, metaphysics and ethics, theoretical and practical philosophy, are integrated into one system, and furthermore make one and the same claim to absolute knowledge.

The thesis of the unity of the true and the good in the Absolute Idea has in addition the important secondary implication that in virtue of it we can understand what we apprehend as true as being at the same time meaningful, where the understanding in question is primarily a matter of grasping purposes and purposiveness, not of interpreting meaning in the hermeneutic sense. The true as the good, as what corresponds to the absolute purpose, is at the same time the meaningful and the intelligible. Hegel defines this relationship also as a relation between objective and subjective-cognitive reason, and the congenial relationship between the two is what is expressed in the terminology of post-Hegelian hermeneutic philosophy as 'understanding' in a not exclusively subjective sense. As a consequence of that unity of facticity and meaning in the world, which only the identity of reason and reality varies, Hegel rehabilitates teleology in the explanation of nature and history and so takes up a position opposed to the dominant understanding of science in his time. The philosophical loss of the real, as what is rationally intelligible, then had the consequence, however, that all reality was reduced to a facticity which is devoid of meaning or purpose. What Hegel criticized as the 'atheism of the ethical world' and believed it possible to localize in the historical domain was then felt as the experience of nihilism, which lent philosophical weight to the dominant nineteenth-century problems of understanding and of values in general.

(3) A philosophy which has placed itself at the point of absolute unification of thought and being, subject and object, truth and good-

ness, can present its knowledge only in an absolute whole, that is, one which encompasses everything in itself, and which, for the sake of maintaining the scientific character of the knowledge, must be not a mere summary, but a *system*. 'A philosophy without system cannot be scientific'. This systematic character alone is sufficient to mark out a philosophy as Idealist: 'System, the form of presentation of a totality to which nothing remains external, sets thought absolutely over against each of its contents and evaporates the content in thought: idealistically, before all attempts to argue for Idealism.'[7] Thus the Hegelian philosophy also imposes the obligation to present all available knowledge, which it is bound to classify in the first instance as 'finite' and prephilosophical, as comprised in the absolute system and for that very reason rationally intelligible. Hence, the two parts of the system, the 'philosophy of nature' and the 'philosophy of spirit', need to present all knowledge belonging to the special sciences scientifically, for philosophy is nothing but 'the scientific knowledge of reality'. This implies, however, on the other hand, that Hegel's philosophy recognizes no knowledge as scientific which is not set in the context of the absolute system. It is hardly to be wondered at that this claim was soon felt by contemporaries to have a hybrid character: reinforced by the impression which they must have gained from Hegel's philosophy of nature, it merely increased the universal disgust for philosophy which had come, long before Hegel's death, to characterize the intellectual scene.[8] What was often called the 'collapse of Idealism' was in fact nothing but a general tendency of the time, after some disputes over the Hegelian succession between 'Right-' (or 'Old-') Hegelians and 'Left-' (or 'Young-') Hegelians, to turn away from philosophy and to pursue science in a post-Hegelian sense of that word. Idealism lived on for some time undisturbed – above all in the academic world – but it was forgotten rather than supplanted. It was an indication that the conception of science had changed that Hegel's philosophy was regarded as scientifically discredited. A disproportionate part in all this was played by Hegel's reputation as the Prussian official philosopher of the period of the Restoration, before 1848, for which Hegel himself must admittedly bear some of the blame. His Preface to the *Philosophy of Right* is a text which could only be interpreted as a political pamphlet by a public in which no intimate knowledge of his system could be presupposed. Its publication, through which Hegel himself seriously impeded a just reception of his philosophy of right, can only be described as a publishing disaster: *it* has formed the principal basis for liberal and liberal-inclined criticism of Hegel, right up to our own time, rather than the political theory of the work itself.[9] Thus, the

Hegelian system soon came to be discredited on political, as well as scientific, grounds, and this intensified the alienation from 'philosophy', which was above all identified with Absolute Idealism.

4 Survey of themes

The examples of types of problem which have been chosen to illustrate the following account of philosophy in Germany between 1831 and 1933 have been selected in such a way that a description of them will also make it possible to keep in mind the situation of philosophy in general in a post-Idealist age. Although there was a general movement of consciousness away from Absolute Idealism in the name of science, thus precipitating a profound identity-crisis for philosophy, the explicit revision of the Idealist concept of science was historically preceded by the impact of Hegel's philosophy of history. The Young Hegelians and the young Marx opposed Hegel in the name of 'real' history, but held firm at first to the concept of science as the systematic presentation of the knowledge of the whole. This is also true to a certain extent of the Historical School (Ranke, Droysen, etc.), although it was the source of the most effective opposition to Hegelian thought; it too insisted, as against the philosophy of history, on the knowledge of 'how things really were', but remained in thrall to the Idealist conception of system at least to the extent that it thought of history in general as *world*-history and subordinated its scientific efforts to this goal. The alienation from Absolute Idealism in the name of history was thus the prelude to the general revolution in the concept of science: indeed, one might go further and see it as a special case of this revolution itself. Hence, we shall discuss first the set of problems connected with 'history' (Chapter 2) and only then those connected with 'science' (Chapter 3).

The transformations in the concepts of history and science after Hegel had the consequence that the unity of the historical and the systematic which Absolute Idealism had proposed broke down. Without the philosophical guarantee that the history of reason revealed at the same time reason in history, the problem of the accessibility of the historical to knowledge arose: the problem of 'understanding' (Chapter 4). The importance of the much older hermeneutic problem for the philosophical consciousness of the nineteenth century – an importance which can scarcely be overrated – is not simply a consequence of the fortuitous emergence of the human sciences: it is not a merely methodological problem, but that of the possibility of unity between a historically and culturally alien reason and one's own, that is, philosophically speaking, the problem of the unity of reason in general, which must be such as to be manifest in understanding.

A further characteristic of the situation of philosophy after Absolute Idealism is that it no longer gives a complete systematic interpretation of reality which could justifiably make claims to scientific status. The need for such an interpretation cannot be satisfied by science: it is taken over by world-views. World-views are accounts of the world from the perspective of a contingent life-situation: 'life-views' was another term which soon came into use. The catchword 'life' (Chapter 5) indicates that the concept of life is the only concept of *totality* of which thought, after the abandonment of the Idealist concept of the Absolute, believed itself to be the master. This is the explanation of the extraordinary influence exerted by the life-philosophies, which is today merely a matter of history: in them, the whole was still conceived of as thought, though of an essentially irrational kind. Before this is dismissed, in the manner of the critique of ideology, as mere 'irrationalism', it would be better to enquire into the internal philosophical pressures which drive a post-Idealist philosophy in this direction.

Along with the Hegelian concept of system, the newly claimed unity of the true and the good, the theoretical and the practical, also came to grief. 'Is' and 'ought' once again came to be distinguished, as in Kant. Following their criticism of over-simplified reductions, of the kind which would nowadays be called 'naturalistic', of the *bonum* to *ens*, philosophers responded to this situation by developing a philosophy of 'value' (Chapter 6). The value-theories which were projected, however, were intended not merely as foundations for an 'ought' which was understood in ethical terms and so as an antidote against the irrationalism of pure will or abstract decision: primarily, they were seen as attempts to make philosophical repairs in the post-Idealist breach between the facticity and the meaning of the world. Their opponent was what Nietzsche diagnosed as 'nihilism': the spectre of metaphysical meaninglessness. Only secondarily did the philosophy of value understand itself as a foundation of ethics and a philosophy of culture in a scientific age.

In the context of Idealist philosophy, however, the problem of the good refers back to the true. Under the heading 'Being' (Chapter 7), we shall consider discussions of the question, in what sense can that which is, which has come to belong to the domain of the sciences, be an object of philosophical knowledge. This problem of the philosophical knowledge of being is the problem of metaphysics under post-Idealist conditions. Thus, towards the end of the period to be considered here, the 'rebirth' of metaphysics as ontology was generally proclaimed.

Finally, in an epilogue, 'Man' (Chapter 8), there will be an analysis of the consequences which the post-Idealist identity-crisis of philosophy has had for the image which philosophers form of themselves. The fact that, at the end of the period, there arose the kind of philosophical anthropology which is so characteristic of the German scene and which combines the purposes of life-philosophy and philosophy of value with a concern for empirical science, must be interpreted as an effort to resolve the identity-crisis of philosophy by means of a new definition of its tasks of a sort which would simultaneously make it possible to overcome the resulting crisis of the traditional Western conception of man. The earlier history of philosophical anthropology, which stretches back into the eighteenth century, also belongs to the history of the aftermath of Absolute Idealism.

1

Sketch of an Age

In this chapter I have no results of original research to offer. My remarks on political and social history are drawn from recent accounts and are intended simply to draw attention to the background conditions for German cultural, educational and scientific history, of which the history of philosophy represents only a part.

1 On political history

In 1831, Germany consisted of thirty-nine separate states (including four free cities), which since 1815 had been united in the 'German Confederation' (*Deutscher Bund*): it existed as a nation only in the cultural sense. Constitutionally, the German Confederation was a very loose federal structure; its political character was determined by the double hegemony of Prussia and Austria, in which, however, Austria was dominant. The policy of Restoration followed in those years is still linked, even today, with the name of Prince Metternich, who in external policy too sought to make it the basis of the first European peace-system through the 'Holy Alliance' of Austria, Prussia, Russia and later most of the European monarchies. Prussia had not yet become a constitutional monarchy: it was a military and bureaucratic state, centrally ruled by the royal cabinet, and without political participation by the bourgeoisie, except at the communal level. The character of internal politics was determined by the Carlsbad Decrees of 1819, through which the states of the Confederation attempted to repress all democratic and national aspirations by such measures as banning the *Burschenschaften* (student associations), persecuting 'demagogues', censoring the press, and so on. Numerous intellectuals were persecuted (for example, the 'Göttingen Seven') and driven into exile (Georg Büchner, Heinrich Heine, Ludwig

Börne, Karl Marx and others). 'Democracy' and 'nation' were the political themes of a politically immature bourgeoisie, which had been mobilized to resist Napoleon in the so-called Wars of Liberation essentially by the promise of national unification and democratic reforms.

In 1848 there occurred a bourgeois revolution, which in Germany resulted in the defeat of the national and democratic forces. In 1849, the Prussian King, Friedrich Wilhelm IV, declined the German Imperial crown which was offered to him by the first German Parliament, meeting in the Paulskirche in Frankfurt: to him it seemed 'tainted with the carrion-stench of the Revolution'. The most important political cause of the 'defeat of the bourgeois Estate' was the incompatibility of the goal of national unity with the real configuration of power in Europe, which was in turn determined essentially by the political weakness of the German bourgeoisie: it was not emancipated or united enough to be able to realize democratic demands on the national scale.

The subsequent foundation, by Bismarck in 1871 and under Prussian leadership, of a 'Little-German' Empire (that is, one which excluded the Germans of Austria) was preceded by a long period of reaction to 1848, marked by the imposed constitution of 1850 in Prussia and neo-absolutism in Austria, and by the period of what Prussian official history described as 'wars of unification' – the conflicts with Denmark (1864), with Austria and its allied South German states (1866) and with France (1870–1). As a result, Bismarck was able to have the Prussian King proclaimed as German Emperor in Versailles and without participation by the bourgeoisie. German unity was not established in the sense of the political demands of the years before 1848. The German national state was a result of a policy imposed from above, a policy, in Bismarck's words, of 'blood and iron', and this was also one reason for the rejection by many intellectuals of this solution of the national question.[1] For the most part, the bourgeoisie made its peace with this 'Little-German' or Prussian Empire, which represented, constitutionally speaking, a compromise between absolute monarchy and the principle of popular sovereignty: the Imperial constitution was more democratic in several respects than the constitutions of the German Confederation, for instance in regard to universal suffrage.

Both constitutionally and in relation to the national question, the German Empire of 1871 represented a compromise between opposing forces, which began to crumble as a result of the defeat in the World War of 1914–18. The grievances associated with that defeat – the traumatic Versailles thesis of war-guilt, the prohibition on union with the Austrian Germans, the separation of Alsace and Lorraine and the ineffectiveness of the political system of the Weimar Republic in comparison with that of the Empire – weakened any real will to defend the new state against anti-democratic activities. All this was made worse by the economic consequences of the inflation and the world economic crisis, which many attributed to the former enemies and to the political system.

Hitler's seizure of power was the end of democracy in Germany and the beginning of the end of its national unity. The consequence was that, after 1945, Germany ceased to exist as a nation even in the cultural sense.

2 On social history

In 1831, Germany was still essentially an agrarian society; there existed only a numerically weak bourgeoisie, which looked to culture for its sense of identity and upheld cultural ideals of a mainly individualistic and apolitical character. In Prussia, the member of the German Confederation which became in the decades which followed more and more the motor of social and economic development, it was not the bourgeoisie but the state bureaucracy which was emancipated after 1815: the bureaucracy introduced a 'revolution from above', making use of administrative measures to develop a liberal economic system and to establish a Prussian national state. It effectively removed power from the monarchy without constitutional reform and, together with the military, took over all the central political and social functions. The break-up of the traditional economic order, with the replacement of the guild-system by freedom to exercise a trade, and the agrarian reforms, which strengthened the landed estates at the expense of many peasants, brought about a redistribution of property on a vast scale; it was accompanied by the pauperization and proletarianization of large parts of the rural population, which could not yet find employment in industry. This process was intensified by the liberal external trade policy of Prussia, which up until the 1870s exposed the weak domestic industry to competition on world markets. (This was one of the causes of the weavers' revolt of 1844, made famous by Gerhart Hauptmann.) There was internal movement of population from east to west on a large scale, and the great movement of emigration to America began. One of the social preconditions of the 1848 revolution was that in the period before 1848 an already capitalistic agriculture and a socially largely rootless 'free' rural working class stood opposed to each other, with the result that the large landowners could combine the benefits of the government's liberal economic policy with the privileges of their social position. The revolution revealed also the socio-political dilemma into which Prussia had fallen: it had produced a social change 'from above', without having the political and constitutional means to cope with its consequences for the traditional order. The constitutional question was increasingly overlain by the 'social question', and the administration was made increasingly responsible for the negative consequences of the upheavals which it had caused. Reinhart Koselleck says,

> Even in 1848, the capitalist mode of economy followed by the landowners and the system of free labour-contracts for rural workers were already so far developed that all revolutionary demands – whether by the landowners for a written constitution or by the rural poor for land, social security and democratization of the administration – were a consequence of the liberal economic policy followed by the Prussian state and a response to its abuses.[2]

The events of 1848, which were followed by a new wave of emigration, were not yet a consequence of industrialization: that began in Germany only after 1850, and intensified to an extraordinary degree in the period of foundation of the Empire, which continued up to the late 1870s. In Prussia, old and new land ownership formed the basis of Prussian conservatism, which dominated political life (Bismarck was Prime Minister in 1861) and was highly privileged as a result of the three-class electoral system which prevailed from 1850 to 1916. In association with the bureaucracy, this social stratum created the conditions (such as the German Customs Union after 1834) for rapid capital accumulation, which was then achieved in alliance with the bourgeoisie. Thus the bourgeoisie, which was largely excluded from politics and had so far found its identity in culture, found new fields of activity in the economy. This coalition of 'property and culture' was reinforced by the common dread of the labour movement, which arose in the course of industrialization; it led to the beginnings of an *embourgeoisement* of the nobility and to the feudalization of the upper bourgeoisie: the old boundaries between the classes began to become blurred. The Bismarckian Empire was characterized by the alliance of state and civil society against the Fourth Estate: in it the bourgeoisie, which had made its peace with the system after 1848 and regarded the economy and culture as its special domains, was identified with a state which was still essentially bureaucratic and military in character and based on the old aristocracy. From the point of view of social history, the German Empire may be interpreted as a 'ratification of the defeat of the bourgeois Estate',[3] which was further accelerated and confirmed by the labour movement.

It was only after 1871 that the 'Industrial Revolution' took place in Germany; the shift in population from rural and agricultural to urban was completed only after the turn of the century. The integration of the working class into society could begin only after the repeal of the Socialist laws in 1890. As for the bourgeoisie itself, already around 1914 there were definite signs of extreme fragmentation according to economic, social and cultural interests: a bourgeoisie based on property, a cultural bourgeoisie, a petty bourgeoisie and, not least, the newly emerging stratum of clerks and other employees can be fairly clearly distinguished from each other as separate social groups.

Perhaps these indications from social history show how precarious was the relation of state and civil society in Germany, in contrast to Britain and France. What was defeated in 1918 and annihilated in 1945 was not a bourgeois state in the sense of a state dominated by the bourgeois 'class', but an alliance for a common end, largely economically motivated, between pre-bourgeois state traditions and a bourgeoisie which was essentially a product of this state itself. This alliance was cemented by the danger of a proletarian revolution. The bourgeoisie, which found its identity after 1848 in the economy which the state had set free, perceived that state, which was not its own, essentially as the expression of force. The limited possibilities for identification with a state which could legitimate itself in their eyes only through its political and social achievements for the bourgeoisie explains also why the Weimar Republic, as the state of the defeat and of the economic difficulties, found so few defenders: it was impossible in these circumstances to make up for the failure to integrate the national state and bourgeois democracy in the nineteenth century. The events of 1933 thus had essentially social roots which extended far back into the past.

3 Commentators on German culture

Of the many writers who have participated in and commented on the cultural development of Germany in our period, a few will be quoted here: they represent the beginning, the middle and the end of the period.

In 1835, Heinrich Heine published his essay, written for French readers, 'On the history of religion and philosophy in Germany' (*Zur Geschichte der Religion und Philosophie in Deutschland*). In it, he brought to the attention of the French, proud of their revolutionary past, after the July revolution of 1830, the fact that there had at the same time occurred in a Germany which was politically powerless, divided and subjugated by Napoleon, another revolution of whose radicalism they had no suspicion – the philosophical revolution.

It is said that the spirits of the night are alarmed when they catch sight of the executioner's sword: how then must they be alarmed when they are confronted by Kant's *Critique of Pure Reason*! This book is the sword with which deism was put to death in Germany. Frankly, in comparison with us Germans, you French are tame and moderate. You have at most been able to kill a king, and he had already lost his head before you beheaded him. And in doing so you had to beat the drum and shout and stamp your feet so much that it made the whole world shake. Really it is honouring Maximilian Robespierre too much to compare him with Immanuel Kant[4] . . . Immanuel Kant has stormed . . . heaven, he has put the whole crew to the sword, the Supreme Lord of the world swims unproven in his own blood.[5]

– he is the Robespierre of the philosophical revolution. Fichte is compared with Napoleon, Schelling's nature-philosophy with the French reaction; Hegel, finally, is extolled as the one who completed the philosophical revolution. Then Heine says,

Germany philosophy is an important matter, which concerns the whole human race, and only our last descendants will be able to decide whether we are to be blamed or praised for the fact that we first worked out our philosophy and afterwards carried out our revolution. It seems to me that a methodical people such as ours had to begin with the Reformation, was able only after that to concern itself with philosophy and could go over to the political revolution only after the philosophical one was completed. This ordering I find quite rational. The heads which philosophy has made use of for reflection can subsequently be diverted by revolution to any goals it chooses. Philosophy, however, would never have been able to use heads which had been diverted by revolution if this had preceded it. But do not be timid, you German republicans: the German revolution will not turn out any gentler or milder because it was preceded by the Kantian *Critique*, by Fichte's Transcendental Idealism or even by naturephilosophy. Through these doctrines revolutionary forces have developed which await only the day in which they can burst forth and fill the world with terror and admiration . . . If you then hear rumblings and clankings, take care, you neighbour's children, you Frenchmen, and do not get mixed up in what we are accomplishing in our own house in Germany. It could be the worse for you. Take care not to fan the fire, take care not to put it out. You could easily burn your fingers on the flames. Do not smile at my advice, the advice of a dreamer who warns you about Kantians, Fichteans and nature-philosophers. Do not smile at the visionary who in the realm of appearances expects the same revolution which has taken place in the domain of the spirit. Thought comes before the deed, as lightning comes before thunder.[6]

This reversal of order of the political and the philosophical revolutions was then interpreted by Karl Marx, in the spirit of the critique of ideology, as a phenomenon of compensations:

> As the ancient peoples experienced their earlier history in imaginative form, as mythology, so we Germans have experienced our subsequent history in the form of ideas, as philosophy. We are philosophical contemporaries of the present, without being its historical contemporaries. German philosophy is the ideal extension of German history. What in the advanced nations takes the form of a practical conflict with the conditions of the modern state, in Germany, where these conditions themselves do not yet exist, primarily takes the form of a critical conflict with the philosophical reflection of these conditions[7] . . . In politics, the Germans have thought what the other nations have done.[8]

The idea that the flowering of German literature and philosophy was closely related to the political and social backwardness of Germany was widespread in the literature of the time: Heine, and Marx who followed him in this, merely propounded this idea in a particularly effective way.

In the second book of his *Geschichte des Materialismus und Kritik seiner Bedeutung in der Gegenwart* (History of Materialism and Critique of its Present-day Importance), one of the most influential works of philosophy in the nineteenth century, Friedrich Albert Lange looked back from the vantage-point of 1875 at the watershed of 1830 and interpreted his own time against the background of the cultural changes which had begun then:

> The breakdown of German Idealism, which we date from the year 1830, turned gradually into a struggle against the existing authorities in state and church, in which philosophical materialism mainly played a merely subordinate role, while the whole character of the time began to incline towards materialism. It would be possible to see German poetry as ending in 1830 – very little of real significance would be missed. Not only was the classical period over, but the romantics had also sung their last; the flowering of the Swabian School was already past, and even in the case of *Heine*, who exercised such a significant influence on the new period, almost everything with any tinge of the ideal comes before that turning-point. The famous poets were dead or silenced or had turned to prose: what was still produced bore the mark of artificiality. No more telling proof of the inner connexion of speculation and poetry could be required than the manner in which this change in philosophy was reflected. *Schelling*, once the most conscious exponent of the idea of the age, an exuberant apostle of production, produced nothing more. Genius, with its quickly ripened fruits, was past, like a tidal wave which has retreated on the ebb. *Hegel*, who seemed to dominate the age, sought to confine the Idea in ossified for-

mulae. In his system indeed the influence of the great period of Idealism on the younger generation still continued at its most decisive, but with what transformations! Most of all, sympathy for *Schiller* was lost, as is shown by the applause which greeted Börne's heartless criticism among the public at large.

Gervinus, who articulated in a very definite fashion the thought that our age of poetry had temporarily come to an end, cherished the opinion that there must now follow a period of *politics*, in which Germany, under the leadership of a political Luther, would be raised to a better form of existence; but he forgot that a regeneration of the kind he had in mind had always been accompanied by a new impetus of Idealism and that, for the realist period which was now beginning, *material wellbeing* and the development of *commercial activity* were in the front rank. Certainly, the preference was to look towards 'realistic' France, even in matters of politics. But what made the July Monarchy and French constitutionalism so particularly beloved in the circles which now became fashionable was its position with regard to the material interests of the property-owning classes. Now, for the first time in Germany, it was possible for a tradesman and founder of joint-stock companies such as *Hansemann* to become the spokesman for public opinion. *Trade associations* and similar organizations mushroomed at the beginning of the thirties; in the domain of education, *polytechnic institutes*, further education colleges in commercial subjects and commercial schools were founded by the citizens of the more prosperous towns, while the indisputable shortcomings of the *Gymnasien* and the universities were subjected to microscopic and hostile scrutiny. Governments sought, here to restrain, there to anticipate, but by and large they were clearly in the grip of the same mood. A characteristic minor feature is that *physical education*, which had been abandoned on account of its Idealist tendencies, once more became acceptable on *grounds of health*. The most important governmental activity was in the field of *transport*, and the most significant socio-political creation of the whole decade was the German *Customs Union*. In later years, to be sure, the *railways* were to become even more important, with the major commercial cities competing with each other, from the middle of the decade onwards, in railway-building. At exactly the same time, interest in the *natural sciences* finally took root in Germany, and the leading role in this was played by a science which was particularly closely associated with practical interests, namely *chemistry*. Once Liebig in Giessen had set up the first laboratory in a German university, the dam of prejudice was breached, and when one excellent chemist after another came out of the Giessen school, the other universities felt compelled to follow the example thus given.[9]

Lange here establishes a clear connexion between the general 'realism' of the age, of which the philosophical materialism which he attacks forms a part, and what the elder Toynbee, at almost the same time (1880), called the 'Industrial Revolution'. He saw in that the beginnings of a thoroughgoing change in traditional German culture, and he pointed out the associated change in the function and structure of education in a scientific direction, which was to be thoroughly analysed only much later.

Finally, in the years 1934-5, Helmuth Plessner, as an émigré in Groningen, delivered a course of lectures on 'The fate of the German spirit at the end of its bourgeois period' (*Das Schicksal deutschen Geistes im Ausgang seiner bürgerlichen Epoche*), which were published in Zurich in 1935. In 1959, they were republished with a new Foreword and given the title, 'The Retarded Nation: on the political seducibility of the bourgeois spirit'. Plessner undertook to expose the roots of the German ideology of the 'Third Reich', to indicate the reasons for its demagogic influence, and to do this in the framework of an 'intellectual history of German nationalism'. The new title of the book refers to the central thesis: the problems which, for historical reasons, the Germans have with their national identity are the cause of the ideology of a 'racial' (*völkisch*) protest against West European political humanism in 1933.

The essential difference between the Germans and the peoples of the old West, who had found their basis in a national state in the sixteenth and seventeenth centuries and are able to look back to a 'golden age' in a way which we cannot do, lies in this temporal dislocation, which has impeded the establishment of any internal connexion between the influences of the Enlightenment and the formation of the national state.[10]

Thus began a

specific decline, to which are owed those revolutionary energies which became evident in distorted form in German nationalism . . . As the nation which came on the scene too late, referred from the outset to models which were the opposite of theirs, the German people distances itself from the norms of latinity and urbanity which it nevertheless feels to be authoritative, while in its own *élan* it gives priority to spontaneity and originality, and thus also inner depth: that is, it flatters itself that it is like a volcano, erupting in extravagance and wildness.[11]

Without a democratic basis of legitimacy, the German Empire was 'a power-state without any idea of the state', but also, from the point of view of the history of ideas, the period of national unification came at a time when the influence of the ideals of humanism and Enlightenment was flagging, so that it was all the easier then, in the prehistory of that 'racial' protest, for German nationalism to transform itself into an ideology of merely physical self-assertion, later given a racial interpretation. The national state, thus interpreted, consequently came to be seen as a 'power-state without the need for humanistic justification. The reality of the race (*Volk*) was considered sufficient'.[12] Plessner interprets this renunciation by the state of democratic and ideal legitimation as one of the causes, also, of the politicization of German culture, for which, besides, there was no longer any place in the economic sphere. The regression of culture to ideology was the counterpart to the practical materialism which prevailed in economics and power-politics: it led to a romanticization and privatization of German culture, which drove the cultivated almost inevitably into 'capitulation in the face of politics'.

4 University – Culture – Science

The years between 1831 and 1933 were the century in which German-speaking science, which is essentially university science, won undisputed worldwide acceptance. The institutional preconditions for this had been prepared by the German university-system of that time: under the name of the 'Humboldt-University', it gained worldwide recognition and imitation. At the same time, this age may be described as the century of *Bildung*, of 'culture' in the specifically German sense of that word, and of the cultivated bourgeoisie, which did not come to an end in 1918. It was only in 1933 that the decisive turning-point came, marked by such things as the restriction of the autonomy of the colleges in the Nazi state, which attempted to remodel the Humboldt-University in order to make it the embodiment of the Nazi view of the world – Ludwig Curtius speaks of the 'destruction of the character of the German universities by National Socialism'; the expulsion of the Jews and many other unpopular groups, which brought in its train an enormous reduction in the intellectual potency of German science; and, finally, the 'failure' and the 'guilt' of the German universities themselves, which allowed the Nazi state to overwhelm them without any resistance worthy of mention. This is merely one aspect of the 'capitulation' of German culture and the German cultivated bourgeoisie 'in the face of politics', that is, of the humanistic ideals of culture in the face of the principle of national power, to which the field was left open in the domain of public affairs.

i. *The Humboldt-University*

The Friedrich-Wilhelm University, founded by Prussian royal decree in Berlin in 1809, became the model for German universities throughout the nineteenth and twentieth centuries, until the reforms of the 1960s. This model was given the name of the 'Humboldt-University', because its structure and the tasks assigned to it were principally formulated and put into effect by Wilhelm von Humboldt, who held the office of 'Chief of the Departments of Religion, Public Instruction and Health', with the rank of Privy Counsellor. The establishment of Berlin University had been preceded by the programmatic writings of Schelling, Fichte, Schleiermacher, Steffen and others, and Humboldt's conception may be regarded as a creative synthesis of the ideas contained in them. Berlin University, whose first Rector was to be Fichte, was not a reform of an existing institution, but a genuine new foundation, which was plainly possible only in the general climate of reform resulting from the collapse of Prussia in 1806-7. When one considers that Humboldt resigned his office as early as 1810, on account of the effective removal of his power as a result of a reform of the cabinet,[13] and how quickly the forces of Restoration in Prussia regained the upper hand, it becomes clear how short was the creative moment in which the Humboldt-University could be born.

The fundamental principles of the Humboldt-University were academic freedom and the unity of research and teaching. If these principles, which nowadays seem to have degenerated into empty phrases, are to be properly understood, then one must bear in mind what it was that the Humboldt-University opposed. The 'opponent of the day before yesterday' was the medieval guild-university, which had long come to be regarded with contempt in the century of Enlightenment. The 'opponent of yesterday' was the utilitarian conception of the university of the age of Enlightenment and absolutism, according to which the university was established for state and socially useful purposes: this was the aim of the new foundations of that time, such as Halle (1694) and Göttingen (1733), but it was first achieved by Napoleon in 1806, in his creation of the Imperial University for the whole of France. This Napoleonic model found numerous supporters in Germany also, with whom Humboldt had to argue, and this shows the extent to which what was then called academic freedom had been discredited as a result of the decay of the traditional ivory-tower conception of the university: it was thought of as a dusty relic, long-since compromised both by the abuses of the corporations and by its scientific and pedagogic ineffectiveness – indeed, it was regarded as a deliberate fraud on the part of the privileged. There was no noticeable expression of regret at the numerous closures of universities during the Napoleonic Wars. In the accounts of the Humboldt-University given by its supporters, its conception was extolled time and time again as a happy mean between the English and the French models of a university. In Oxford and Cambridge, learning was pursued by an essentially aristocratic élite in a way which was divorced from practical considerations, and there was no effort at anything worthy of the name research. They continued to be medieval guild-universities under High Church government; their mode of life (the college-system) was monastic and there was no principled recognition of the freedom of learning. Research, on the other hand, was a matter for the bourgeoisie, which it privately financed and published, or a concern of the Academies, such as the Royal Society. In France, by contrast, the 22 former universities of the country had been reduced since 1806 to the level of technical schools, which were directed and controlled by the coordinating institution known as the 'Imperial University'. It was no longer 'teaching science, but the instructing state'[14] which propelled the universities. Research was excluded from the universities in favour of state-controlled courses of training and was kept for the Academies. This French model had already, under the influence of Leibniz, been introduced into Russia by Peter the Great at the beginning of the eighteenth century and still affects even today the Soviet and East European conception of a university; the fact that Leibniz preached it is further evidence of how little the cultivated of that time expected from the university. The university as an instrument of domination, as a producer of officials, as a recruitment-factory – that, in the eyes of Humboldt's contemporaries and numerous opponents, was the only rational meaning which could still be given to this dusty old establishment. The fact that at least in the new foundations of the eighteenth century the principle of freedom of teaching had been introduced was thus considered to be of very little importance. On the other hand, Humboldt himself accepted only after long hesitations the name 'university' for the 'teaching institute' which he had conceived, and in that respect he had to give in to the traditionalists. The Humboldt-University sought to achieve a creative compromise in all respects: academic freedom alongside responsibility for the requirements of state and society; vocational training combined with the pursuit of knowledge for its own sake.

ii. *The institutional regulations*

German university scholarship is 'bureaucratic scholarship',[15] that is, the state guarantees the leisure which, according to Aristotle, alone makes knowledge possible by making the scholars into bureaucrats, while the scholars, for their part, form a 'republic of learning' in the faculties within the general framework of their duties as state officials. 'Academic freedom', in this context, means the right to self-government under the legal supervision of the state; keeping one's own house in order; the right of the faculties to fill their own vacancies, limited by the minister's right of appointment (above all, by means of the institution of proposals of appointment and the 'habilitation', associated with the granting of the *venia legendi*, or permission to lecture, which led to the system of *Privatdozenten*, teachers independent of the state administration); the separation of the state examinations from the academic examinations independent of the state; freedom of teaching for the Professors and *Dozenten* and freedom of access for the students, limited only in a formal sense through the requirement of the *Abitur*, or school-leaving certificate. The 'unity of research and teaching' was to be secured by means of the principle that the university teacher must also engage in research and the freedom of students to attend any lectures they chose, in explicit contrast to the *Gymnasien*; through the institution and form of teaching of the seminars (the 'seedbeds' of scholarship); through the close links established between the universities and the continuing academies and other research-institutions which soon arose within the framework of the universities themselves.

As early as 1919, Max Weber spoke of the fact that the old university structure had become 'inwardly as well as outwardly . . . a myth'.[16] The idea of the scholar engaged in teaching and research had been turned into a bourgeois career-goal; the seedbeds of scholarship had changed, especially in the fields of medicine and natural science, into institutions in the manner of 'state-capitalist' enterprises; the quasi-industrial organization of research had produced 'an extraordinarily wide gulf, outwardly as well as inwardly, between the boss of such a great capitalistic university enterprise and the ordinary professor in the old style'.[17] Weber recognized that industrialization had caught up even with the universities and with scholarship. The alteration in role of the old type of university teacher corresponded to an alteration in the institutions, which became clear in the foundation of the Kaiser-Wilhelm-Gesellschaft (now the Max-Planck-Gesellschaft) in 1909: the unity of research and teaching was no longer to be preserved within the framework of the Humboldt-University, and industry, the economy, state administration and scientific institutions worked together in order to make up by institutional means the ever-growing deficit in research. Another attempt to achieve this was the foundation and extension of Technical High Schools, which were intended, within the traditional academic framework, to develop research-based teaching of technology; but it was only in the Weimar period that the Technical High Schools gained equal academic status with the universities. The fact that research has continued to migrate from the universities and that the latter have continued to be limited to the tasks of teaching and training – indeed, that both these processes have constantly accelerated – confirms that Weber's diagnosis still holds good even now.

iii. *What is meant by 'the unity of research and teaching'?*

To answer this, one must start from the function of teaching in the medieval and in the absolutist university. Teaching in these cases meant the transmission of an essentially static body of knowledge, preserved in compendia and in the works of recognized authorities: creativity was not required of the university teacher, indeed was frequently considered undesirable. Even Kant in Königsberg was still obliged to give lectures based on other people's text-books. Because, according to the scholastic and rationalist understanding of knowledge, truth is something already settled and recognized, to acquire truth is simply a matter of learning. This was reinforced by the strict definition of the purpose of the kind of knowledge taught in the 'higher' faculties: theology, jurisprudence and medicine had to serve the 'eternal', the 'civil' and the 'corporeal' good of men. Kant further emphasizes in his sombre account the close link of teaching in those faculties with authority: indeed, he makes just this the principle of division of the faculties themselves:

> According to established usage, they are divided into two classes, one consisting of the three higher faculties and the other of the one lower faculty. It is plain to see that this mode of division and these names serve the interests, not of the learned professions, but of the administration. For the higher class includes only those in which the administration itself has an interest in the question whether their teaching ought to be so or otherwise constituted or publicly expounded; and on the other hand the faculty in which only the interests of scholarship are at stake is called the lower, because it can deal with its propositions in any way it thinks fit. The government, however, takes most interest in that by which it can achieve the strongest and most enduring influence on the people, and such are the objects of the higher faculties. Hence it reserves to itself the right to sanction teaching in the higher faculties: that in the lower it leaves to scholars' own reason.[18]

The philosophical faculty, on the other hand, which embodied the heritage of the *artes liberales*, was, as the 'lower' faculty, also at the same time the free faculty.

> There must be one faculty belonging to the commonwealth of learning in the whole university, which in view of its teaching, which is independent of the commands of the government, has the freedom, not to give commands, but to evaluate all which may be given, which has to do with the interests of scholarship, that is, with those of truth, where reason must obviously be

entitled to speak: because without such a faculty the truth would not come to light – to the injury of the government itself. But reason, by its very nature, is free and accepts no commands to hold anything as true (no *crede*, but only a free *credo*).[19]

Here reason, independent of authority and interested only in the truth, and the ideal of rational critical and theoretical science are central and the description of this faculty nevertheless as 'lower' cannot be understood, in the case of Kant himself, without the hint of irony: of the higher faculties, bound up with the authority of statutes, he says,

Hence the biblical theologian (as a member of the higher faculty) derives his teaching not from reason, but from the Bible, the jurist not from natural law but from the law of his own country, the medical man his published methods of treatment not from the physiology of the human body but from the medical handbook. As soon as one of these faculties ventures to introduce some element borrowed from reason, it offends against the authority of the government which rules through it and comes into the domain of the philosophical, which removes from it all the glamour of those borrowed plumes without exception and deals with it on a footing of equality and freedom. Hence the higher faculties must take care most of all not to get entangled in a misalliance with the lower, but to keep themselves well apart at a respectful distance from it, so that regard for their statutes should not suffer damage through the free sophistry of the lower faculty.[20]

At all events, in the Humboldt-University the philosophical faculty had taken over the leadership. The institutional consequences of this were in accordance with the Kantian notion that everything put forward in the 'higher' faculties with a claim to science must be able to justify itself before the principles of the 'lower' faculty. The philosophical faculty embraced not only theology, jurisprudence and medicine, but all *theoretical* disciplines, even the natural sciences.[21] It embraced them as *rational* (in the Kantian sense – the opposite of 'positive') disciplines, which included a reference to the 'equality and freedom' of all involved. Seen in this way, the principle of rational science coincides with that of critical: the critical consists precisely in knowledge which is reflective and accompanied by the scientist's own reason and autonomous activity. In regard to teaching, this conception rules out all forms of authoritarian communication of knowledge. According to Humboldt, there are no reasons either for authoritarian constraints on science, since 'in the internal organization of the higher scientific institutions everything is based on the maintenance of the principle that scientific knowledge should be treated as something which has not yet been completely discovered and which will never be entirely discovered, and that it should be unremittingly pursued as such'.[22] The university was 'to treat science always as a problem which has not yet been entirely resolved, and hence should be constantly engaged in research',[23] where 'research' means simply the pursuit of truth and the acquisition of knowledge for their own sake. According to Humboldt, it is also committed to this principle in teaching, once all connexions with external authority and the idea of a finally fixed body of knowledge have been severed: it must think only of the process of research itself as what is to be taught, not of 'the' truth: it is in this that the 'unity of research and teaching' consists. In this sense all the members of the university are to be researchers – teachers and students are 'both there for science' – and the university institutions were conceived by Humboldt in such a way that they were to unify under one roof all those involved in the business of research.

Later, 'research' took on a new meaning: it was equated with the process of scientific and technical innovation in general. It was thus conceived of in an objectivist sense, depersonalized and thought of as independent of the researcher as a subject: it was then possible to 'serve research' like any other 'objective goal'. This difference in meaning between the modern and the Humboldtian concepts of research is all too easily overlooked when the idea of the 'unity of research and teaching' is nowadays abandoned as antiquated.

iv. *From 'culture through science' to 'science as a vocation'*

Humboldt's concept of science and the university is part of a more general concept of culture, which also points in the direction of a political programme in the cultural field.

As soon as one ceases to pursue science in the proper manner, or fancies that it does not need to be created from the depths of the spirit, but is the product of extensive accumulation, then everything is lost, irretrievably and for ever: lost for science, which, if this process continues for long, escapes to such an extent that it even leaves behind language like an empty husk, and lost for the state. For only that science which stems from the inner and can take root in the inner also transforms the character, and the state has as little concern as does humanity in general with knowledge and talk: its concern is with character and action . . .[24]

University study had to combine objective science with subjective cultivation, which at the same time was defined as intellectual *and* moral cultivation. General cultivation – in contrast to specialist – was the process of the autonomous unfolding of all the powers of the individual, even his moral powers, and hence cultivation through science, according to Humboldt, was at the same time the *moralization* of human beings: it was expected that the philosophical self-reflection of truth in its universality would also bring human action closer to the right. Although Humboldt thinks of this process essentially in terms of the individual, he is no individualist in regard to culture: the principles of 'solitude' and 'freedom' are rather presuppositions for the optimal fulfilment, through the process of cultivation so conceived, of the claims of the community on the scientifically cultivated.

The state must treat its universities neither as *Gymnasien* nor as specialist schools, and must not make use of its academy as a technical or scientific committee. On the whole, it must demand of it nothing which refers immediately and directly to the state, but must cherish the inner conviction that, if it achieves its own purpose, it also fulfils the state's purposes, and indeed from a much higher point of view – one from which much more may be included and quite different powers and methods may be applied from those which the state could set in motion.[25]

It is precisely from the 'useless' activities of science that the results needed by the state for the fulfilment of its political tasks are expected.

Humboldt's ideal of culture, to which his concept of science and the university conform, is the image of the enquiring spirit of man, which brings itself through its own activity to the highest understanding and moral perfection: culture, for him, is the process of self-development of the individual, who embodies in himself a true and moral world. There is conclusive evidence that this concept of culture is theological and mystical in origin: Helmuth Plessner in particular refers to the quasi-religious function assigned to culture in a secularized Protestant society: culture was seen as the individual's self-redemption from natural limitations.[26] Friedrich Schlegel says, 'Every good man becomes more and more God. To become God, to be human, to cultivate oneself – all these expressions have the same meaning.'[27] The reinterpretation of this process of cultivation in world-historical terms has, since Lessing and Herder, been a basic image of Idealist philosophy in general.

In Max Weber, on the other hand, quite a different picture is to be found: the connexion of culture and science is dissolved, and a professionalized 'science as a vocation', which has come to be a role for highly specialized experts, is opposed by 'personality' and 'experience', the new 'idols' whose 'cult' is to be encountered everywhere. 'Both are closely associated: it is a modish idea that the latter constitutes the former and belongs to it. There is an agonized pursuit of experience – for that is part of the way in which a personality should conduct a life appropriate to his standing – and if it does not succeed, then one must at least act as if one had this gift of grace'.[28] Max Weber counters this view by saying, '"Personality", in the realm of science, belongs only to the man who devotes himself purely to the matter in hand'.[29] The principle of personality, which was once the basis for cultivation through science, is here replaced by the principle of 'objectivity' (*Sachlichkeit*) and Weber explicitly rules out the notion of cultural self-realization of the person in science. In so doing, he affirms that culture and science have moved apart: culture has largely become ideology, and science, now pursued for its own sake by 'experts' in a professionalized spirit, must be protected from encroachments by demands, connected with the idea of personality, for meaning and values. This is the background in the philosophy of culture to the famous requirement of value-freedom, which Weber himself elucidates in terms of cultural history. Modern science, which is to find its meaning only in the process of its own advancement, is simply a 'segment' of the Western 'process of intellectualization', the 'intellectualist rationalization' of our world through 'science and scientifically orientated technology': it is part of the 'disenchantment of the world', which reduces that which is to mere facticity, without immanent meaning and without normative force. The science which studies this facticity, also, is incapable of adopting any meaningful or evaluative stance towards it, that is, it cannot be a matter of cultivation in the Humboldtian sense. Questions of meaning and value themselves can be answered only on the basis of ultimately personal and person-related value-positions, and hence can be answered only *for* persons and not scientifically. To the question why, in a world of value-anarchy, precisely this ethos of value-free science, rather than some other 'god', ought to be followed, Weber answers by alluding to 'intellectual integrity', which, according to Weber himself, is to be seen as a subjective aspect of the Western process of rationalization, though not for that reason normatively grounded. Despite all its decisionistic elements, the ethos of 'science as a vocation' in Weber has a material foundation in the philosophy of culture.

v. *On the 'failure' of the German universities, culture and science*

What is meant is the general weakness of the resistance of German culture to National Socialism: why did the 'German spirit' put up such a feeble defence? The answer lies in the direction indicated by Max Weber. The elimination of all cultural elements from science is only one aspect of German cultural history in the nineteenth century: nevertheless it had an extraordinarily disproportionate influence on the whole process, because the culture of this period understood itself fundamentally as a scientific culture. It was essentially characterized by the process of the increasing formalization, privatization and ideologization of culture. Formalized culture is culture as a mark of social standing, of the 'academic' and hence of the 'cultivated bourgeoisie', associated with relatively uniform expectations of conduct and social advancement. By 'privatization' is to be understood the process of forcing culture away from the domain of the publicly relevant and into the realm of the inner and the aesthetic – a process already mordantly diagnosed by Nietzsche in his *Unzeitgemässe Betrachtungen* (Untimely Meditations).[30] Abstention from politics thus became the obvious standard of conduct for the cultivated: this is to be understood only in terms of the history of ideology, against the background of the specifically German situation of a defeated bourgeois class, which left open to the bourgeoisie, in a pre-bourgeois state 'without an idea of the state', only the possibility of an apolitical culture, wrapped up in the cult of inwardness.

Thus it becomes intelligible how the vacuum of meaning and orientation necessarily left behind by modern science in a fundamentally scientific culture could, in the specific conditions of German cultural history, so easily be filled by a thinly veiled ideology of power. Friedrich Paulsen remarks on the subject of this vacuum in his representative work of 1902 on the German university:

> there are a number of auguries of a counter-current against the development which has taken place thus far, an undercurrent hostile to the preoccupation with science in our universities in recent times. Something like disillusionment can be felt: scientific research does not seem to have fulfilled the promises which were made for it – of a comprehensive and absolutely certain view of the world and a philosophy of life firmly based on necessary conceptions. Religion and theology gave these things to earlier generations. Its place was taken in the eighteenth century by its heir, philosophy; with what joyful hopes did the generation of Voltaire and Frederick the Great look in that direction! The last in the lineage of pure reason was Hegel. Then a new generation, mistrustful of reason as an earlier generation had been of faith, turned to science: exact enquiry was to secure the ground beneath our feet and give us an accurate picture of the world. But science does not achieve that: it becomes ever more clear that it does not lead to a view of the world which encompasses the whole and satisfies the imagination and the heart. It produces only a thousand fragmentary pieces of knowledge, in part tolerably certain, above all in the natural sciences, which at least give technology a foundation, in part eternally debatable, eternally subject to revaluation, as in the historical sciences. The consequence is a feeling of disillusionment: science does not appease the hunger for knowledge,

it does not even fulfil the desire for personal development; it requires the pledging of all one's powers and gives only meagre fruits in reward. This feeling of disillusionment is widespread: those who follow in Nietzsche's train are mainly united by their lack of faith in science – times when faith is lacking are always the times when quacks flourish. But even from the circles of science itself there is occasionally to be heard a note of resignation, for example in the concluding remarks in Harnack's *Geschichte der Berliner Akademie* (History of the Berlin Academy) (I. 791, 977). Is it, as some think, the bankruptcy of science which is coming to light, its abdication in favour of belief in authority? Or is it rather the natural desire for concepts, the long repressed yearning for philosophy, which is stirring again and is merely not yet sure of the way and the goal?[31]

When politics and culture, 'power and spirit', move apart, and culture itself becomes sufficiently depoliticized, it is not surprising if even cultivated people long for a leader and are aesthetically fascinated by power. Ludwig Curtius confirms this picture in his memoirs; in the context of a comparison with the character of British and French culture and their social function, he says of the German university,

... it resembles a vast barrage, built and supported by enormous resources, whose water for the most part evaporates on its own surface. Hence it came about that in the Germany of Wilhelm II and in the Republic it was possible to find everywhere excellent, supremely honourable, industrious, painstaking, dependable professional men in the civil service, among the judges, in industry and trade, from the upper echelons right down to the commissionaires, bank clerks and industrial workers, but men of character, spiritually cultivated in the higher sense of having a philosophical world-view, were so seldom encountered among them. If one recognizes, however, that in the case of many people, above all among the Protestant population of the Empire, religion had quite ceased to have any influence, but had not been replaced by any new philosophical spirituality produced by the universities, then one can well understand the vacuum which could be filled by National Socialism with its all too easily accessible theories of race and national self-glorification. To the credit of the philosophical faculties of the German universities, it must be said that by far the greater part of their members resisted this terrible disintegration of the German spirit. But because each university on its own did not constitute a corporate spiritual entity, not to mention the totality of German universities, the individual scholar who upheld the freedom of the spirit was completely defenceless and powerless. And because, as we saw, the nation had no connexion with the universities, neither through tradition, nor through the personal gratitude of individuals, nor through any living spiritual relationship, it sat back and watched the spectacle of their destruction, in fact scarcely understood what was happening. Indeed, there were in the universities themselves numerous teachers whose unspiritual specialist pursuits were not disturbed, and who subsequently found that basically very little had changed because of National Socialism.[32]

In another place Curtius says, 'The German universities achieved distinction in the training of scholars, but they failed in their task of spiritually educating the nation'.[33]

Finally, Hermann Heimpel, in his famous address of 1954, 'Obligations and Tasks of the University' (*Schuld und Aufgabe der Universität*), sees the responsibility for this failure as lying in the identification of science with culture in general. He thus answers Ortega y Gasset, according to whom Humboldt was to blame for everything: university research, on account of the process of specialization and professionalization which necessarily accompanied it, had systematically destroyed culture in the sense of spiritual awareness of one's time, or self-knowledge in respect of the forces which determine one's own time.[34] As in Max Weber, it becomes clear in this criticism that it was not the relation of research and teaching, but that of research and culture, in view of the change of meaning of 'research' since Humboldt's time, which was the main problem for the Humboldt-University. Heimpel confirms this indirectly through his attempt to find a justification for research: *it* was not the problem, but the cultural relations of science, which had remained, after the age of Hegel, an unsolved question. To that it should be added that a science and its institutions without cultural connexions tend to abandon all culture outside themselves to its own devices, and this applies above all to political culture, if political abstinence is recognized as a necessary price for the freedom of science.

2

History

Nineteenth-century consciousness as a whole achieved its emancipation from Idealism in the name of science and history. In order for this to be possible, the words 'science' and 'history' had to change their meaning, so that they acquired a sense opposite to that which they had had, for instance, in Hegel: the change can be expressed in slogan form by saying that now it was 'science *instead of* a philosophical system' and 'historical science *instead of* a philosophy of history'. Hegel himself had already been faced with such, for him, absurd oppositions, and had engaged in repeated polemics against them. For him, science could only be systematic, and German Idealism was not the first to regard being philosophical as a fundamental condition of the scientific character of science. Evidently, there had been even during Hegel's lifetime a far-reaching change in the understanding of science, which itself first made possible opposition to the philosophy of history in the name of a scientifically revealed 'real' history. Nevertheless, in Germany the explicit rejection of the Idealist conception of science came historically later. At first, it was the science of history (in the modern sense) which took the lead in the struggle against German Idealism and at the same time, in so doing, brought about an implicit revision in the prevailing concept of science: only much later was it joined by the philosophers and theoreticians of science. Professional discussion amongst philosophers continued until well into the 1860s to be conducted within the framework of late Idealism, and this lack of historical contemporaneity among professional philosophers of the time makes it impossible to confine a discussion of the topics of 'history' and 'science' mainly to those authors of the period who were, in the narrower sense, philosophical: the primary influence on thought was the conception of history and science held by precisely those writers who were fundamentally critical of philosophy.

The young science of history took over after Hegel not only the leadership in the field of scientific opposition to Idealism: it became for a time also the leading cultural force, and thus assumed the traditional role of philosophy.[1] Historical culture and historical consciousness based on a scientific approach to history – in the dawning age of science these came to be the highest forms of culture and consciousness in general. Droysen was simply playing a variation on a widespread theme of the time when he wrote, 'History is the way in which humanity becomes and is conscious of itself. The epochs of history are ... the stages of its self-knowledge, its knowledge of the world, its knowledge of God ... History is humanity's awareness of itself, its self-consciousness.'[2] Only very much later, in the climate of materialism and the realist movement in culture in the late fifties and sixties and after, did history lose this leading position in culture. 'Culture through science', in the age of Humboldt, Ranke and Droysen, meant culture through scientific history, and it was only with Nietzsche's second 'Untimely Meditation' in 1876, after Schopenhauer's scepticism had remained unheeded for decades, that the problems in this concept were effectively brought to light. This was also an astonishing example of conceptual change. Whereas for Kant what was cultivated only in the historical sense had remained on the periphery of genuine culture, in the nineteenth century (after a radical change in the meaning of the word 'historical') it was precisely the man who was historically cultivated who was regarded as the only genuinely cultured person, and even Nietzsche does not absolutely reject historical culture, but merely doubts the compatibility of history and culture in a scientific age: the problem of how it is possible for historical culture to be scientific leads him to raise the sceptical question of the scientific character of the cultural force known as 'history' itself.

The age of historical culture and of historical consciousness is also regarded as the age of historicism, and a brief consideration of this phenomenon of 'historicism', so particularly characteristic of the German scene, is necessary if one wishes to understand how, in the period after Hegel, the historical could become a leading cultural force.

1 Historicism

Although the term 'historicism' may be traced back to very early in the nineteenth century, it first came into general use around the beginning of our own century: like many 'isms', it was first used to denounce – it signified something to be overcome, something which was in crisis, something outmoded. Later, neutral and even positive uses of the expression are also to be found. At best, historicism is characterized as a position which makes 'history into a principle'. Long before it was called 'historicism', it existed as an opposition to ahistorical thinking and an attempt to introduce historical approaches in all fields of culture. The expression 'historicism' first gained more general circulation at the moment when historical thought began to lose its cultural prestige: why this happened will be suggested by a brief typology of concepts.³

i. *'Historicism'*

The first sense of 'historicism' (historicism$_1$) is positivism in regard to the human sciences: the value-free accumulation of material and facts without distinction between what is and what is not important, which nevertheless makes a claim to scientific objectivity. 'Historicism$_1$,' thus refers to a particular kind of scientific *practice*, characterized by a purely contemplative attitude and abstinence from practical considerations: questions of relevance and practical political problems are set aside with a good conscience based on the conception of science. Used in this way, 'historicism' is an expression of scorn, which makes it all too easy to forget what we owe to the much maligned historicists – the immense labour of collecting source-materials, making texts accessible, compiling handbooks, and so on, of the nineteenth century.

In another use, 'historicism' refers to what can be regarded as the theoretical justification of historicism$_1$: historicism in the sense of historical *relativism* (historicism$_2$), that is, a philosophical position which, on the grounds of the historically conditioned and variable nature of all cultural phenomena, rejects, indeed classifies as crude, all claims to absolute validity – be they of a scientific, a normative or an aesthetic kind. Historicism$_2$ thus faces us with the alternatives of being either barbarians with convictions or refined relativists. Culture on this view rests on the only thing which the scientific approach to history in a scientific age can furnish: historical facts and connexions which, for the sake of scientific objectivity, may only be stated – normative orientations are not to be expected from it. In reality, it is historicism$_1$ which gives so much persuasive power to historicism$_2$ as a philosophical position, even though the latter is the only basis for the legitimacy of that scientific practice itself. Here again we can see that change in the concept of science after Idealism which also underlies the view that scientific history must be founded on a value-free account of the facts. Historicism$_2$ consequently simply makes visible the dilemma of culture through science in a post-Idealist age. If evaluative and normative viewpoints can no longer be justified as scientific, then equally no normative force can any longer be derived from the objects of such a science. No moralizing effect on someone who occupies himself with the knowledge of such objects is any longer to be expected: relativism thus becomes the last word of a culture which understands itself as scientific.

Historicism$_2$ is the form of historicism which still requires to be 'overcome': it is historicism in crisis, which suggests that there must be a more comprehensive meaning of the word, that which refers to the position of which it was said above that it makes history into a principle. Historicism in this sense (historicism$_3$) is the view that all cultural phenomena are to be regarded, to be understood and to be explained as historical. It is an essentially culturalist position, which is opposed to naturalism.[4] The world of human life, according to this view, is not nature, but the product of human action: hence it also has a history, which itself should not be conceived of as a process of merely natural development. Historicism$_3$ arose in Germany towards the end of the eighteenth century, in opposition to the allegedly ahistorical rationalism of Enlightenment philosophy.[5] A philosophy is rationalist, as opposed to 'historicist', when it looks upon all that is human as conditioned and determined by essentially invariant principles of reason, in particular in a normative sense. The unchangeable human reason as the supreme standard is the normative foundation of the Enlightenment critique of culture and tradition, of the revolutionary theories of natural rights and emancipation, against which historicism can set always only what has historically come-to-be at any given time and the value of tradition itself. This is also the explanation of the fundamentally conservative, indeed traditionalist, character of historicism$_3$, which made it possible for it to become, long after its emergence in the conditions of a post-revolutionary situation in Germany, the leading current of thought. Its principal exponents were the 'Romantic School', following Hamann, Herder, Friedrich Schlegel and others, the 'Historical School' of legal theorists (above all von Savigny), and also the 'Tübingen School' of theologians.[6] The principal object of criticism in all fields was ahistorical dogmatism, whether in the domain of art, of the theory of culture, of law or of religion. The enemies were Enlightenment aesthetics and the uniform rationalistic picture of man, the doctrine of natural rights and orthodox theology. From the point of view of the history of science, this was the beginning of the historicization of those disciplines which were later to be called the '*Geisteswissenschaften*' or 'human sciences'.[7] The *Geisteswissenschaften* – an expression which first came into general use as a result of the work of Wilhelm Dilthey – may be characterized in their early phases as those disciplines which adopt an essentially historical approach to what in Hegel had still been a theme for the 'philosophy of spirit': the philosophical theory of subjective, objective and absolute spirit was replaced by interpretative psychology and historical anthropology, the history of law and the science of history itself, as well as the histories of art, religion and philosophy. Historicism₃, in the sense of the application of historical thought in all fields of culture, has been described by Friedrich Meinecke as the specifically German achievement, to be set alongside the application of naturalism by the West European Enlightenment. It must be agreed that he is right also in that all the important intellectual tendencies of the first half of the nineteenth century had a share in this achievement, and this is true, despite all their criticisms of romanticism and the newly emerging historicism, even of Hegel, the Young Hegelians and Marx.

The fact that 'historicism' came to be a term of abuse, indeed came into general circulation as a term of abuse, can be explained only by saying that the phenomena characterized above as historicism₁ and historicism₂ were really decadent or degenerate forms of historicism₃, which nevertheless were definite logical consequences of it.

ii. *Historicist Enlightenment and historical consciousness*

This process is associated with the total history of the historicist Enlightenment.[8] Enlightenment and historicism₃ are not simple opposites: historical and culturalist thought was already widespread in the Enlightenment philosophy of the eighteenth century. Indeed, the argument with naturalism, as with ahistorical rationalism, was already being carried on at that time,[9] even if it was only later, in the German situation already outlined, that it led to an open breach between the two positions. But even then historicism remained an Enlightenment movement, in so far as it brought into play the arguments of Enlightenment philosophy itself against those Enlightenment positions which were ahistorical, and then turned them against the Enlightenment movement in general: it brought enlightenment to bear on the Enlightenment, and in its critique of the Enlightenment it was not simply a counter-Enlightenment, in that its criticisms operated in an enlightening way. The most important achievements of historicism were the historicization of history and the historicization of man. By the 'historicization of history' is meant the transition to the modern understanding of history and its liberation from models of the development or progress of the historical process which were themselves unhistorical. The idea that even the historical is merely an exemplification of general features of being or of laws such as 'eternal recurrence', progress, decadence, etc., was abandoned in favour of the principle of historical individuality and individual development. Hence the science of history could no longer be a science of essences or laws. The specifically Enlightenment aspect to the achievement of historicism, however, concerns the other form of historicization: that of man, that is, of the very foundation of Enlightenment philosophy. Thereby, the natural endowment of man, previously treated as ahistorical and cross-cultural, and human reason, as that which makes man human, were themselves interpreted historically and hence inserted into the historical process, and this was done by means of Enlightenment arguments, such as that one can treat as unhistorical only that of whose origin one does not know.[10] Once history had been historicized, there were no longer available any supra-historical models to offer an a priori guarantee of the rationality or even simple intelligibility of that process. The historicization of man was in reality the reduction of reason to history: through it, man himself became a historical theme, and competence in systematic philosophical reflection was no longer sufficient to determine what man is. The human sciences took their first steps away from systematic philosophy as historical disciplines, and only much later began in consequence to reorganize themselves as empirical disciplines on the model of the natural sciences.

The result of the historicist Enlightenment was the historical consciousness in the double sense that the cultivated consciousness of the historical at the same time grasped itself as something historical. This reflexive structure it shared with enlightened consciousness in general, for we speak of Enlightenment only where knowledge of the world at the same time also involves this knowledge itself. As consciousness of the historical and consciousness of itself as something historical, the historical consciousness locates itself in the process of history, which, after the historicization of history, it can no longer confidently regard as being commensurable with our current conditions of interpretation and understanding. Historical consciousness is thus at the same time consciousness of its own finitude and limited autonomy in the face of the superior force of history as a whole: this explains the character of historicist thought – sceptical, inclined to relativism, indeed frequently resigned – which was bound to appear, from the traditional Enlightenment point of view, as intellectual feebleness or practical defeatism.

iii. *Two stages of historicism*

If it is asked why the historicist reduction of reason to history was not immediately generally seen as a victory of relativism and as a loss of all the reference-points of obligation, the question can be answered only by reference to the fact that at first history itself was given the role of normative foundation for our thought and action. History was to achieve what was no longer expected from reason alone. Thus, the Historical School did not limit itself to the mere description of connexions in the history of law, but claimed to be able thereby to discover the correct, appropriate, obligatory law, which could be opposed to the Code Napoléon with its rationalistic foundation in the theory of natural rights. Hence the historical account itself, formulable in scientific statements, was taken as the norm of correct law, rather than any absolute 'Reason', which was unmasked as an ahistorical abstraction favoured by uncultivated propagandists of revolution;[11] still less was natural law so regarded – only someone who understood nothing of the history of law could believe that *that* was natural or rational. This ascription of a normative role to history also explains why the transition from practical and political philosophy to scientific history and historically orientated sociology,[12] from normative aesthetics to the history of art, literature and music, indeed from philosophy to the history of philosophy, was not thought of as a radical break. Almost all the intellectual tendencies of the time were involved in it. A belief in the normative force of the historical is as much a premise of the Historical School as of the newly emerging Marxism. When Droysen writes, 'Ethics and historics are, as it were, coordinates. For history reveals the genesis of the "postulates of pure reason", which remained undetectable to "pure reason" ',[13] he formulates a fundamental proposition of the philosophy of history implicitly accepted by the Historical School as a whole, which also justified its moral and political commitment. The socialism of Marx and Engels based its claim to be 'scientific' essentially on the use of historical methods, and both found formulations which, by reference to history, make discussions of ethical goals in general appear superfluous.

The theoretical propositions of the communists do not in any way rest on ideas, on principles which have been invented or discovered by this or that reformer of the world. They are merely general expressions of a class-struggle which already exists, of a historical movement which is proceeding under our eyes . . . It is not a matter of what this or that proletarian or even the proletariat as a whole for the moment sets before itself as a goal. It is a matter of what it is, and what it is historically compelled to do in accordance with what it is.[14]

In so far as Marxism still, even today (as Kautsky once maintained) believes in the dispensability of normative ethics, and believes that it can be replaced by, or at least based on, a theory of society, it is no more than a solidified form of the first phase of historicism, in which an attempt was made to oppose the revisionists by restoring to validity the principle of the historical Enlightenment.

The fact that the revisionists of the Second International felt the lack of an ethic in the structure of the Marxist world-view and undertook to close the normative gap in its foundations by going back to Kant indicates that they had noticed the problem of historical relativism which is an essential feature of the second phase of historicism. It was the result of the insight that no normative claims can any longer be associated with a scientifically objective approach to history (and in a scientific civilization no other approach can be considered as generally obligatory). Max Weber formulated this point in the course of the contemporary dispute about value-judgments in the social sciences, in the context of his well-known requirement of value-freedom. 'Intellectual honesty' demands that one accept that history based on the use of scientific methods is simply an account of the bare facts, which implies no general directives about meaning or action: the earlier belief in such directives was evidently the result either of projection or of a *petitio principii*. Anyone who from now on believes in the normative force of historical facts is either being dishonest or bringing into play without noticing it his own subjective ideas about value, wrapped up in a scientific disguise. Although it was precisely this conviction which first released positivism in the human sciences (historicism$_1$), it is difficult to deny that it was the result of a further advance of Enlightenment, where 'Enlightenment' simply means the elimination of naïvety. Historicism$_2$, in the sense of historical relativism, is for that reason itself a product of the historicist Enlightenment, which Friedrich Nietzsche described as the experience of nihilism (see Ch. 6, Sect. 1. iii): all those objective values, by means of which even historical culture still believed it possible to find ultimate guidance, proved themselves, precisely as a result of historical criticism, to be a *nihil* or nothing, mere projections of subjective valuations. This experience was the basis of that 'crisis of historicism' which was so much complained about, which was really the identity-crisis of the historical consciousness itself. The second phase of historicism was for that reason characterized by a simultaneous and constantly accelerating withdrawal from history and by a weakening in its claim to cultural leadership, which has been frequently lamented by philosophers and historians ever since. In this sense, too, one has to speak of a crisis of historicism.

2 '. . . above all not a philosophy of history'

In this half-sentence Jacob Burckhardt[15] speaks for a whole age: history, which has successfully contended with philosophy for its traditional leading role, interprets itself as a *science* of history, and that seems to exclude the philosophy of history. The post-Hegelian opposition of 'philosophy' and 'science' also applies to historical knowledge. However, that should not conceal the fact that the scientific mode of thought and study of history which was at that time contrasted with 'the' philosophy of history (it was almost always Hegel's which was meant) did not rule out an 'implicit' philosophy of history: it even presupposed it, if by 'philosophy' one means the prior material understanding by a discipline of its object-domain, together with the totality of methodological and practical norms which it follows in dealing with its objects. This implicit philosophy of history, which takes its essential character from the understanding of history and science accepted in the Historical School, has exercised an influence on the historical consciousness in Germany which it would be hard to over-estimate and which can still be felt in the historical books and controversies of the present; it, rather than the pronouncements of philosophy professors on the subject of 'the philosophy of history', was for a long time the real philosophy of the historical consciousness and the basis of historical culture. It can be shown that academic philosophy of history regained credit only as a result of the 'crisis of historicism', though certainly it should not be overlooked that in the meantime the concept of philosophy itself had acquired a meaning completely different from that which it had had for Hegel.

It is astonishing to see how close this implicit philosophy of history of the Historical School remained to the Hegelian position, despite all attempts at differentiation. Although it is impossible here to make a really thorough comparison, it should nevertheless become clear that this philosophy of history is a form of historical Idealism, and that it differs from Hegel's Absolute Idealism only in that it regards as impossible, both on methodological grounds and because of the very nature of the case, Hegel's claim to achieve an absolute synthesis of the historical and the systematic. To show this, we must first ask just what is the 'philosophy of history' which is supposed to be resisted and excluded from the study of history.

i. *The critique of the philosophy of history*

In the lectures 'On the study of history' which Jacob Burckhardt regularly gave in Basel from 1868 onwards, and which appeared in book form only after his death, with the title *Weltgeschichtliche Betrachtungen* (Reflections on World History), Burckhardt collects together all the important objections to Hegel's speculative philosophy of history which were current in the Historical School, to which he, as a pupil of Ranke's, himself belonged. For him as for his contemporaries, Hegel's system represented the philosophy of history in general. The tradition of the Historical School appears in Burckhardt in an idiosyncratic form, marked above all by the assimilation of Schopenhauer's influence, but one which nevertheless leaves untouched the common opposition to Hegelianism. Burckhardt says,

We do not wish to give an introduction to historical study in the academic sense, but only some hints on the study of the historical in the various regions of the intellectual world. Furthermore, we reject all attempts to be systematic: we make no claim to 'world-historical Ideas', but are content with observation; we make cross-sections through history, and in as many directions as possible; above all, we do not provide a philosophy of history. That is a centaur, a *contradictio in adjecto*: for history, that is, coordination, is not philosophy, and philosophy, that is, subordination, is not history.[16]

By referring to the 'study of the historical in the various regions of the intellectual world', Burckhardt clearly distinguishes himself from the mainstream of the Historical School, which does not talk of 'the historical', but always sticks to speaking of 'history' in the singular, meaning by that world history in the sense of the history of political events; Burckhardt is here advocating the broader and richer concept. His exclusion of 'world-historical Ideas' also distinguishes his conception from that of Humboldt, Ranke and Droysen, who use the expression 'Idea' throughout in a positive, if also intuitionistic and empirical, sense, distinct from that which it has in Hegelian usage. On the other hand, the rejection of system and the emphasis on sensory observation are important and characteristic of the Historical School in general. The exclusion of subordination in favour of coordination fits in with this. What Burckhardt means by 'subordination' is made clear by his accompanying critique of Hegel. He briefly cites Hegel's *Lectures on the Philosophy of World History* and criticizes Hegel's assumption that reason rules world history, going on to attack the conception of the philosophy of history as a theodicy and the doctrine of the ultimate goal of history towards which everything historical necessarily strives, and finally the doctrine of progress in general, which suggests the idea that everything up to now has existed only for the sake of the present. For Burckhardt, subordination is the subjection of the historical material to such preconceptions, which form the prior basis for the study of the historical, rather than resulting from it. Hegel's doctrine is merely an example of those 'chronologically applied philosophies of history' which 'claim to be following a world-plan, and in so doing, since they are incapable of approaching their material without presuppositions, are coloured by ideas which the philosophers have imbibed since the age of two or three'.[17] Philosophy of history, therefore, rests on obvious preconceived ideas, and Burckhardt argues against Hegel's premises like a philosopher of the Enlightenment arguing against dogmatic theology: he thus exemplifies what was called above the 'historicist Enlightenment'.

ii. *On the philosophy of history of the Historical School*

The rejection of subordination is the core of the methodological critique of Hegelianism which Jacob Burckhardt shares with the whole of the Historical School. It rules out any scientifically defensible doctrine of teleology in regard to the historical process, and also any univocal use of the concept of progress which makes the characteristic and individual value of historical phenomena relative to some ultimate value to be found in the goal of history in general.[18] The result is a rejection of a priori constructions – be they laws of the historical process or value-hierarchies – under which the historical data were only subsequently subsumed, so that history was reduced to a mere 'collection of examples',[19] and this is done in the name of observation and the understanding of the historically individual in its individuality at any given time. This does not exclude the discovery of connexions, indeed it requires it, since observing and understanding are possible, according to this tradition, only if one can exhibit how things have come to be as they are.[20] Even the 'cross-sections through history, and in as many directions as possible' which Burckhardt promises serve the same end. All that is required is that such connexions between historical individuals should result from historical observation itself – they are admitted as, at best, explanatory hypotheses – and that they should not be insinuated as something which is already established and has prior existence: that is liable to the charge of preconceived ideas. This principle of observation is the essential distinction between the scientific approach to history and speculative philosophy of history. Droysen's further definition of this historical observation as understanding (*Verstehen*) (see Ch. 4, Sect. 3) was meant to stabilize the other front, where the opponent was the natural sciences, which at that time saw themselves as advocating a similar empirical and inductivist model against the speculative nature-philosophy of the Romantics and the German Idealists. *Understanding observation* is the fundamental concept in the theory of science current in the Historical School.

That Jacob Burckhardt even rejects the chronological approach in favour of the 'cross-section', indeed, that he uses the word 'history' only as a way of characterizing a certain kind of material, which can be arranged and analysed in almost any direction one chooses and from the most diverse points of view, is a clear demonstration of how widely his conception diverges from that of Hegel, and how close he has already come to Max Weber's conception of science. Moreover, the overtones in his thought of a fundamental scepticism about the scientific character of his model of a 'study of the historical' should not be ignored. Burckhardt himself plainly does not fear the reproach of subjectivism which he, in common with the Historical School, makes against the Hegelian conception. This is quite different from the representatives of the mainstream of the Historical School who, since Niebuhr, have sought to base the objectivity of historical knowledge fundamentally on the scientific character of the way in which historical knowledge is acquired, that is, on the method of scrutinizing and criticizing sources. This set of tools, first developed amongst classical philologists, was taken by Hegel himself, paradoxically, as a reason to object to the developing practices of the Historical School on the grounds of subjectivism. 'Critical' historiography was for Hegel a case of reflective history, a characteristic of which was that it brought to bear general points of view, which did not arise from the historical material itself but were those of the modern student, in interpreting and explaining this material. The method of source-criticism, first applied in a thoroughgoing way by Niebuhr in his *Römische Geschichte* (Roman History), he criticizes on the grounds that it is not history, but

> history of history and a judgment of historical narratives, a judgment of their truth and credibility . . . The extraordinary element which is to be found in this, indeed which ought to be found in it, consists in the sagacity of the writer, who manages by haggling to extract something from the narratives, not in the material itself . . . With us the so-called higher criticism has taken possession both of philology in general and of the history books (where the very basis of history, cautious historical study, has been abandoned, leaving room for the most arbitrary ideas and combinations). This higher criticism has then been obliged to justify the admission of all possible unhistorical abortions of a frivolous imagination. This too is a way of bringing the present into the past.[21]

The extent of the opposition between Hegel and the Historical School, in which there was also a strong element of university politics,[22] can be judged when one considers that Hegel rejected as superficial subjectivism precisely what his opponents saw as the basis of the scientific character of historical science; he did this against the background of his own conception of philosophical history, to which the other side in turn could object only that it was merely subjective. In reality, this dispute concerned the understanding of science in general, and the controversy among historians discussed here represents only an aspect of it.

It should not be overlooked that this exchange of polemics was but an episode in the history of historicism, in which Hegel himself was only partially involved; only through Droysen, who had studied under Hegel, was Hegelianism introduced to a greater extent into the mainstream of historicism. Moreover, the bitterness of the polemics between the parties should not conceal how close to each other they nevertheless were, particularly in the area of material presuppositions of the historical in general. For Hegel as for the Historical School, history is *spirit*, that is, a domain of reality which is in essence *not* nature, but depends on freedom, on action which is capable of becoming conscious and creative individuality, and hence is *intelligible* to the individual knower. Furthermore, historical knowledge, on account of the fact that the knowing subject belongs to the object-domain, is essentially defined as self-knowledge on the part of this subject. Taken together, these two things are the basis for the great significance of the hermeneutic problem for the theory of history after Hegel: this is not just a methodological problem, but concerns the constitution of historical objects and their accessibility.[23] In its emphasis on the principles of individuality and freedom in history, the Historical School reaches back far beyond Hegel into Romanticism. Observation and coordination are the methodological maxims which exactly correspond to those principles, since a priori construction and subordination – whether in the form of subsumption under generalizations as 'a case of . . .' or of deduction from general causes – would reduce the individual to the general and, by making it something completely explicable, annihilate it in its freedom. It is understandable that, in contrast to this, the Hegelian conception was bound to seem like a repetition of rationalistic metaphysics, and that it was believed that it was necessary to resist Hegel in a way analogous to that in which Hamann, Herder and Novalis had once resisted Enlightenment theories of history and all attempts to make history into a science based on general principles.

A further shared characteristic of the opposing parties is the conception of history as *objective* spirit. In this context, 'objective' means not only that the objects of historical knowledge, being spiritual, possess an objectivity of their own, but in particular that history has a preordained relation to the subject of this knowledge. This preordination means, first, that historical knowledge itself has ineliminable historical conditions and so is always limited knowledge; the historical consciousness, in the twofold sense already explained, is finite, not absolute, consciousness. The emotional force of this sense of finitude increases the methodological weight of the principle of historical observation, but then also comes to be the basis of the concept of history as *enquiry*: the historical consciousness, on account of its finitude, cannot grasp history as a whole all at once, but can only approach it by finite steps. The idea of the objectivity of the historical is also formulated as the idea that history cannot be produced: the pull towards the contemplative, to abstinence from practice, which is especially marked in Ranke and Burckhardt, finds in this its philosophical basis.[24] It is also the reason for the quasi-natural conservatism of the historians of the Historical School, right up to our own day. The objectivity of history further comes to mean in many much the same as the normative force, the objective obligatoriness of whatever precedes the individual as *his* history; at all events, this idea was widespread among historians and philosophers belonging to the first phase of historicism.[25] History as objective spirit chiefly means, however, the history of historical individualities, which are themselves an objective universal; the 'holistic' approach is as characteristic of Hegel's philosophy of history as of the view of history current in the Historical School. Popular spirits (as in Herder), nations, states, ethical forces (as in Droysen), cultures, and later also classes, populate historical space, and individuals are historically significant only to the extent that they actively embody a universal.[26] Such totalities are the true actors on the stage of world history: they are the source of all the creative powers of humanity. The concept of action and the notion of collective subjects of historical action suggest, from the point of view of the theory of science, the concept of a history of political events based on the principle of the primacy of external policy. Whereas in Hegel this holism is dialectically modified by his theory of subjectivity as the principle of the modern period, in much of the work of the Historical School there is in the conception of history a romantic organicism which tends towards irrationalism. The objective historical totalities are indeed conceived and described, not primarily as spirit, but in terms of biological metaphors, as living structures or organisms. It then appears to be no more possible rationally to understand history than it is life itself. The possibility of associating anti-individualistic and anti-rationalist aspirations with this conception is plain to see: the individual's insistence on his own reason can only endanger the unity and vitality of the 'collective organism'. The principle of individuality which nevertheless underlies this concept of the objective universal in history also provides the basis for the principled rejection of cosmopolitanism and the scepticism about a universalistic morality which infringes the individuality of the 'ethical forces';[27] this, however, is precisely the way in which the Historical School prepares the ground for historical relativism (historicism$_2$), even though this is far from being what it originally intended.

iii. *Unity of history?*

Erich Rothacker has very felicitously characterized the implicit 'universal philosophy of spirit and history' current in the Historical School by means of the following conceptual scheme: he speaks of the ultimate

> valuations of the living and concrete, of the organic and manifold, natural and authentic, original and ethically persistent, of the ancient and venerable, of what has freely grown and historically developed, the popular, the national, the sensuously vigorous and intuitive, the prudent and clearheaded, of a harmony of the parts with the whole, the content with the form, and so on, together with the corresponding aversions.[28]

This needs to be supplemented by a clarification of the role allotted to the objective universal in historical knowledge. This universal, which is not merely invented, constructed or arbitrarily producible, is, as that in which the abundance of the historical individualities is to find its synthetic unity, at the same time to make possible the knowledge of this individuality. Anyone who can knowingly put himself in the place of that universal gains understanding of the chaos of the historical manifold, since he sees it in the perspective of that on which it ultimately depends; at the same time, he also thereby comes to know himself, for he himself belongs to that universal as an element of the whole. From this it is only a step to the thesis that only a practical and political identification with this universal can put historical knowledge on the right track.[29]

Hegel does not fundamentally differ from the Historical School in regard to the epistemological aspect of this construction; his dispute with it is sparked off by the question of how the objective universal is to be introduced into science. For Hegel, this is the task of philosophy:

> I want first of all to remark, in regard to the preliminary concept of the philosophy of world history, that, as I said, the principal objection to philosophy is that it comes to history with thoughts and treats it according to thoughts. The only thought which it brings with it is, however, the simple thought of reason, that reason rules the world, and so that world history also

proceeds rationally. This conviction and insight is presupposed in the consideration of history as such and in general. In philosophy itself this is not a presupposition: there it is demonstrated through speculative knowledge that reason ... is the substance, and the infinite power, itself the infinite material of all natural and spiritual life, and also the infinite form, the activity of this its content ... That such an Idea is the true, the eternal, the simply powerful, that it reveals itself in the world and reveals nothing in the world except itself, its majesty and its glory – this it is which, as I said, is proved in philosophy and is here presupposed as proved.[30]

The philosophy which believes itself to be master of this Idea of the Absolute and so of the Absolute Idea in speculative knowledge is Absolute Idealism: the unity of being and knowing, of the true and the good, and also of the all-embracing totality of the system, is for it also the only philosophical perspective involved in the study of history. From the point of view of the historian who makes no claim to speculative means of knowledge, all this is bound to appear like an arbitrary presupposition, not to be justified by the methods of historical science alone, as indeed Hegel himself concedes. That does not mean, however, that the historians of the Historical School did not themselves make assumptions which are very close to Hegel's Absolute Idealism. For them, too, history is that which embraces both the historical objectivity and the subject who knows it, as the double sense of 'historical consciousness' indicates. History embodies for them, too, a value-laden, meaningful and normatively obliging account of the facts; above all, they too held firm for a long time to the idea of the unity of history, though in a narrative sense as opposed to Hegel's rigid systematization. What in Hegel is the Absolute Idea, representable in philosophical terms, appears in his opponents only as an object of surmise, of religious conviction, of faith: it is no longer an object of science in the post-Hegelian sense. In terms of their methods, the totality can be allowed to function only as a working hypothesis, a regulative Idea, an ideal goal of scientific history. After the divorce of philosophy and science, there were no longer any conceptual means available for a thoroughgoing integration of the historical facts into an ideal whole. The tension between the historically individual and the unity of history, which in Hegel it still seemed possible to resolve by means of dialectical logic, thus persisted to its fullest extent in the Historical School: it simply overstepped the bounds of what they were still prepared to defend as science.

This was pure gain for historical science itself. If the universal in history ceases to be scientifically intelligible and so becomes sufficiently vague, then one gains 'elbow-room for the empirical':[31] it is no longer necessary to relate each separate individual to the totality in order to be able to comprehend it, indeed it is strictly speaking impossible to bring it into relation with the totality (on account of the methodological difference between the scientific guarantee of the empirical by means of source-criticism etc. and a theory of the historical universal). In this way, again, history becomes more and more scientific and independent of the philosophy of history, and if all ideas of the objective universal in history come to be seen as scientifically dispensable, what was characterized above as historicism$_1$ is achieved: the history which is a record of singular facts, with all interpretative or evaluative positions and all attempts at systematization regarded as merely subjective trimming. Hegel's historical Idealism, and that of the Historical School, are thus reduced to a merely private concern of the historian, which has no place in the science itself. To be sure, this has not prevented this Idealism from having a widespread influence, until well into our own century, as a *cultural* property, on the consciousness of historians, but still it has affected their private, not their professional consciousness. The need for a universal, where it is felt, can in a scientific age ultimately be satisfied only by scientific means, and if this cannot be done by historical science, it is natural to turn to other sciences: this is why political economy, the theory of evolution, psychology and anthropology have come to be accepted as foundation sciences for history. It is important, however, that historians in the mainstream of the Historical School have stubbornly opposed this procedure, and continue to do so even now: this has always been because of their apprehension that the importation of such theories will destroy the special character of history. Such attempts to introduce other sciences have therefore been made in Germany, up until the fairly recent past, only by minorities.

This is not the place for a historical sketch of the alterations in the picture of the objective universal within the Historical School.[32] It should be made clear only that the tension between this universal and the scientifically describable particular in history, which later broke down in historicism$_1$, is simply the tension between the systematic and the historical in historical science itself, which can no longer be overcome by the methods of this discipline because of the dominant conception of science. As a result, systematization in history itself becomes a scientific problem. Out of the problem of the unity in history comes that of the *unities* in history: the identity of its objects, their identifiability and capacity for coordination, and hence their intelligibility and explicability. This problem of systematization ultimately concerns the historical consciousness itself, which indeed has its own identity in the unity of its history: what, according to Hegel and the Idealism of the Historical School, is the foundation of the historical consciousness and the historical culture? Such problems, which cannot be solved by the methods of scientific history, suggest that we should turn once again towards the formerly abused philosophy of history, which, to be sure, cannot any longer take the form of Hegelian speculation about history: philosophy of history becomes the *critique of historical reason*.

3 The critique of historical reason

The expression 'critique of historical reason' originated in Wilhelm Dilthey, and appeared in 1888 in the subtitle of his *Einleitung in die Geisteswissenschaften* (Introduction to the Human Sciences). The allusion to Kant is completely intentional and has a programmatic purpose. Dilthey, like many of his contemporaries, was convinced that in the philosophy of history too only 'the critical way [was] still open'.[33] *Critical* philosophy of history, that is to say, an investigation of our concepts of and modes of interpreting the historical, has consequently to precede all material theses on the nature and development of the historical process. The epistemological turn in the philosophy of history, to be outlined in this section, became visible after the middle of the nineteenth century; through it, this subdivision of philosophy took its own part in the post-Hegelian rehabilitation of philosophy as epistemology (see Ch. 3, Sect. 3), and the strong tendency towards the reduction of philosophy in general to the theory of knowledge makes it seem as if there could be a philosophy of history nowadays only in the framework of logic and methodology. But even where the philosophy of history is understood in this way, there still remains the doctrine of historical knowledge as always accompanied or determined by a prior material understanding of the object of such knowledge, which is at least implicitly co-represented, and which may be regarded as the covert metaphysics of history of such meta-theorists of the historical. For the rest, criticism of the reduction of philosophy to the theory of knowledge is a widespread theme in the literature of the time, and it is found even in those who usually tend to be criticized for such reductionism.

The epistemological turn in the philosophy of history was, however, also motivated by the development of the historical sciences themselves. The Historical School saw its scientific identity in method, and it was to this that it appealed when it began to differentiate itself in general from the philosophy of history. Attempts to systematize these methods of historical science into a methodology, however, which Droysen then called 'historics', led necessarily to more general questions of epistemology, if, that is, it is a matter of also giving a foundation to the methodology of the historical sciences and defending it against Hegelianism. In addition, there was also the necessity to defend the science of history, and later the human sciences as a whole, against the claim to universality made by the natural sciences and their methodology. The need to maintain this double front, against philosophy *and* the natural sciences, which was especially characteristic of the historical consciousness in Germany, gave a considerable impetus to epistemological reflection among historians, and explains also the strong, if also often indirect, influence of writers such as Droysen, Dilthey or Rickert on the way in which the human sciences understood themselves. In this connexion, it is possible to observe how the problem of the demarcation of the human from the natural sciences gradually came to overlay that of differentiating them from philosophy. Droysen, who had studied under Hegel, already had a much less polemical attitude to his system than the first generation of the Historical School: indeed, numerous elements of doctrine from Hegel's philosophy of spirit can be found, in a slightly modified form, in Droysen's 'historics' (*Historik*). This shift of attention can be explained by the fact that, in most people's minds around the middle of the century, philosophy seemed to be generally discredited, and was therefore no longer an opponent to be taken seriously, and it was the natural sciences to which one appealed if one regarded philosophy as superfluous: this was why the natural-science front became so important.

The question of how historical knowledge is possible and which rules it must follow as a scientific discipline was, however, forced upon the historians by an internal problem of their science: namely, the problem of systematization outlined above, which became more and more pressing because of the increasingly scientific character of history. Philosophy of history, in the sense of the critique of historical reason, is the attempt to overcome this complex of problems by epistemological means. The aim was to locate the ground of the unity, the special character and the independence of history in our mode of conceiving the historical. At the same time, it was hoped that the gain in precision to be expected as a result of this procedure would also assist the disciplinary demarcation and secure identity of the historical and human sciences *vis-à-vis* speculative philosophy and the natural sciences.

In what follows, three projects for theories, all representative of the epistemological turn in philosophy of history, will be briefly outlined; for the rest, reference should be made to the extensive literature.[34]

i. *Droysen's 'historics'*

Johann Gustav Droysen (1808–84), a famous and also politically active historian of his time, delivered, beginning in 1857, a lecture (which he gave altogether eighteen times in twenty-five years), *Enzyklopädie und Methodologie der Geschichte* (Encyclopaedia and Methodology of History): as early as 1858, he had printed a brief *Grundriss der Historik* (Outline of Historics) to accompany this lecture. Although this 'outline', because of its concise formulations, is almost unintelligible without interpretation and the complete text of the lecture was printed only in 1936, Droysen has exercised a strong influence, which still persists even today, on historians' understanding of themselves, above all in the direction of internal professional traditions. His 'historics' contains the first really thoroughgoing attempt to reflect on the method practised in the Historical School, and undertakes in regard to it to ground this method on the implicit philosophy of history of that tradition, which had in the meantime been further developed, and which is on this occasion also explained. Hence, 'historics' in Droysen's sense is not merely methodology, but an epistemology of the historical sciences, which, however, is not achieved without elements of a material philosophy of history, as will be shown.

Droysen says of historics, 'Historics is not an encyclopaedia of the historical sciences, nor a philosophy (or theology) of history, nor a physics of the historical world, and least of all a poetics of historiography. It must set itself the task of being an organon of historical thought and enquiry.'[35] Droysen differentiates it from universal history, the philosophy of history, Comte's sociology and the kind of literary history, very popular at that time, of the type found in historical novels: he gives a positive characterization of the 'organon' in another place as 'theory of science in relation to history'. It 'includes the methodology of historical enquiry, the systematics of what can be historically investigated, the topics of the accounts of what has been historically investigated'.[36] The fundamental proposition of the methodology states that 'the essence of the historical method is *understanding through enquiry*'.[37] The word 'enquiry' still belongs completely to the Humboldtian tradition in which the talk was of 'research', but, as the context of 'methodology' shows, it is already given a strong tinge of empirical science: the competition of the natural sciences compels even Droysen to emphasize more strongly than Humboldt had the empirical character of history. The concept of understanding, on the other hand, was meant to take care of the methodological distinctiveness of historical knowledge; Droysen thus takes over the whole hermeneutic tradition derived from Schleiermacher, F. A. Wolf and Boeckh; the momentous task of integrating historics and hermeneutics was essentially Droysen's work.

The justification of this methodology is suggested in the sentence, 'The method of historical enquiry is determined by the morphological character of its material';[38] that is, the theory of historical science in Droysen is affected by a prior material conception of the historical, which cannot itself be obtained by application of the historical method. This prior conception of the 'morphological character' of the historically given involves a reference to the implicit philosophy of history of the Historical School to which Droysen belonged. It is important that Droysen seeks to undertake this philosophical anticipation of history, not directly in an ontological way, but critically – starting, not from the object of knowledge, but from knowledge of the object. 'Nature and history are the broadest concepts under which the human spirit comprehends the world of phenomena.'[39] 'History' is not a name for a domain of beings, but a category in Kant's sense. Droysen's position is chiefly distinguished from Kant's transcendental philosophy, however, by the fact that the basis of these 'broadest concepts' is no longer an ahistorical 'consciousness in general', but historical consciousness, which has interpreted *itself* already in the light of prior material conceptions of the historical. 'Historical enquiry presupposes the reflection that even the content of our ego is something mediated, something which has come to be, a historical result.'[40] History is thus seen as what makes men men, as their essence: '. . . instead of the species-concept, they have history.'[41] The consequence of the double sense of 'history' as a category and as an essential determination of the knowing subject himself, to whom such categories refer, is in Droysen the characteristic interlacing of transcendental philosophy and an ontology of history, which at first sight looks like a defect in construction. In fact, however, what is asserting itself here is the historicist Enlightenment and historicism$_3$, which will no longer allow the subject of historical knowledge to exclude himself from the principle of the historicity of everything cultural. The influence of hermeneutics then suggests that this interlacing of subject and object be itself interpreted hermeneutically, rather than dialectically, now that Hegel's instrument of thought seems, along with his whole system, to be discredited. The 'hermeneutic circle', which at first concerned only the structure of understanding a text, has thus already become here (rather than first of all in Heidegger) an *ontological* conception. The understanding of history is consequently always at the same time self-understanding, and vice versa. It is no longer a question of a transcendental a priori in Kant's sense, 'for all thought and reflection, all the creativity, the will and the capacity of man grow ... out of these lived experiences and achievements, the continuity of which it is the task of history to investigate'.[42]

Certainly, it should not be overlooked that the introduction of the a priori of historical knowledge into the process of history gave an extraordinary impetus to the tendency towards historicism$_2$. Without the notion of a reason of general principles, independent of history, it is only with great difficulty that one can rule out historical relativism or perspectivism: historical knowledge itself becomes a historical fact among other facts, and the question arises whether this can really be the last word of a philosophy of history which has taken the epistemological turn.

ii. *Dilthey's foundation of the human sciences*

Wilhelm Dilthey (1833–1911) saw Droysen's achievement as lying above all in his introduction of hermeneutics into the theory of the human sciences, but objected to him and the Historical School in general on the grounds that there was a lack of a 'philosophical foundation', which he himself undertook to provide. By 'philosophical foundation', Dilthey understood a psychologistic variant of the Kantian programme, a grounding of historical knowledge by means of an 'analysis of the facts of consciousness', in which this analysis is itself understood as an analytic part of a 'critique of historical reason'.[43] It is important that Dilthey does not only criticize reason to the extent that it concerns itself with the historical, but as something historical itself. His programme is conceived, not as a mere completion of Kantian critical philosophy, but as a radical new beginning against the background of the historicist Enlightenment. That historical reason takes the place of pure reason is only one point of difference from Kant; the other results from the objection to Kant and the empiricists that their theory of the knowing subject

> explains experience and knowledge on the basis of a state of affairs which appertains to mere representation. In the veins of the knowing subject which Locke, Hume and Kant construct there flows no real blood, but only the diluted fluid of reason, in the sense of merely intellectual activity. I, however, have been led by a historical and psychological concern with the whole man to the point where I take as the basis, even of explanation and knowledge, this being in the multiplicity of his powers, this willing, feeling, representing being.

He proceeds

from the whole of human nature ... whose real life-process merely has its various aspects of willing, feeling and representing. The question which we all have to address to philosophy cannot be answered by the postulation of a fixed a priori of our cognitive capacity, but only by the history of our development, which proceeds from the totality of our being.[44]

Dilthey wishes to provide a philosophy of the whole man, to grasp him in the totality of his psychological and historical reality: thus in him psychology, developmental history and transcendental philosophy enter into a characteristic association.

Dilthey's central thesis is that the human sciences (*Geisteswissenschaften*) must be grounded in the connexion of lived experience (*Erleben*), expression (*Ausdruck*) and understanding (*Verstehen*). 'Lived experience' is the basic concept, and it is very felicitously chosen, since it appears to be able to take on a variety of functions of mediation. In lived experience, first, subject and object are still undivided: if one speaks of what one has experienced, one must speak at the same time both of the experienced object and of the subjective experience. Thus, the difference between the physical and the psychological is also still not clearly marked, for it is only as a physically involved being that one can experience anything. Above all, however, what is meant by 'lived experience' embraces 'willing, feeling and representing', and thus the 'willing, feeling, representing being' as a whole: it is plainly to affirm that experiences always concern the whole man. It is important, furthermore, that lived experience always already belongs in a lived context and is only possible and intelligible in such a context: it is not in the end the etymological connexion of the expressions which makes it plausible to set the theory of lived experience in the context of a life-philosophy (see Ch. 3, Sect. 1).

The interpretation of lived experience must attach to the expression of experience, in which what is experienced and the way in which it is experienced are manifested in a sensuously perceptible form. It can proceed along two different paths: to the 'outside', in the sense of an objectification of the content of experience involving elimination of the subjective qualities of the experience, and to the 'inside', that is, the exposition of just these subjective aspects of the experience itself, which, according to Dilthey, are essentially expressive qualities. The first path is for him the way in which the natural sciences are constituted, the second is that of the human sciences. Interpretation of the qualities of experience as expressive qualities – that is what Dilthey means by

'*Verstehen*' or 'understanding'. He defines it essentially as understanding of expressions, and, because in the understanding of experience he who understands and that which is to be understood belong to one and the same context of life, the triad, 'lived experience, expression and understanding', in reality designates the process of the self-interpretation of life. This life which interprets itself, however, Dilthey calls 'spirit' (*Geist*), and the sciences which methodically investigate this process he calls '*Geisteswissenschaften*' (sciences of spirit or human sciences). The transition to historical science is then effected by Dilthey's definition of history (in imitation of Hegel) as 'objective spirit', in the sense of an epitome of all the objectifications of a self-interpreting life.

If we grasp the sum of all the achievements of understanding, then there becomes visible in it, in opposition to the subjectivity of experience, the objectification of life. Besides experience, the observation of the objectivity of life, its externalization in manifold connexions, becomes the basis of the human sciences. The individual, the communities and the works into which life and spirit have been transferred form the outward kingdom of the spirit.[45]

The essential difference from Hegel's philosophy of objective spirit consists in the fact that in Dilthey the spirit is embraced by life, whereas for Hegel life is a deficient mode of spirit (see Ch. 5, Sect. 1. i). The basis of the critique of historical reason in a philosophy of life in Dilthey is, however, even if one disregards the problem of irrationalism, a precarious foundation for the theory of the historical sciences, which are themselves 'objectifications of life' and are an element in all the alterations which life experiences. The historical consciousness, a psychological analysis of which Dilthey has put in the place of the Kantian theory of 'consciousness in general', is also inserted into the stream of life which objectifies itself in history, and the facts of this consciousness seem necessarily to be subject to permanent change in this stream of life. Once again we must ask, therefore, whether perspectivism or relativism is the last word. The finite subject, in his experience and understanding dependent on history, is moreover already an object of psychology and of history, that is, of disciplines which were first of all to be grounded by the critique of historical reason. Dilthey's philosophy thus becomes entangled, not only in all the difficulties of historicism, but also in those of psychologism.

iii. *Transcendental philosophy of history*

An attempt to find a basis for historical knowledge in a strictly transcendental philosophy in Kant's sense, which would avoid the difficulties in

Dilthey's project, was made by the 'South-West German' School of neo-Kantians, above all by Wilhelm Windelband (1848–1915) and Heinrich Rickert (1863–1936). 'Strictly transcendental philosophy' means that no prior material conceptions of the object are employed in the theory of knowledge – such conceptions were regarded by the neo-Kantians as suspiciously metaphysical or as a circular borrowing from the special sciences; it is only formal points of view, having to do with the logic of concept-formation and the formation of judgments, which are admissible into the theory of knowledge. What was called in Kant 'pure reason' is then seen as nothing but the object of a strictly formal logic of knowledge.[46] Windelband's Rectoral Address, *Geschichte und Naturwissenschaft* (History and Natural Science) (1894) can be considered a classical text for this. In it, he first of all attacks the idea that the problem of the classification of the sciences can be resolved in the way suggested by the expressions 'sciences of nature' and 'sciences of spirit' (*Geisteswissenschaften*): namely, by starting from the concepts of 'nature' and 'spirit'.[47] Above all, the emergence of modern psychology as a 'natural science of the spirit' shows that the material principles of classification do not in any way necessarily coincide with the structures of modes of knowledge. Instead, Windelband hopes for 'a purely methodological classification of the empirical sciences, to be based on secure logical concepts'; the 'principle of classification' must be 'the formal character of their cognitive goals'. Windelband continues,

> Some seek general laws, others particular historical facts: expressed in the language of formal logic, the goal of the one is the general apodictic judgment, that of the others the singular assertoric proposition ... Thus we should say: the empirical sciences seek, in their pursuit of knowledge of reality, either the general in the form of laws of nature or the particular in the form of what is historically determined; they study on the one hand the permanently identical form, on the other hand the once-for-all and completely determinate content of the real event. The one kind of science is concerned with laws, the other with events; the one teaches what always is, the other what once was. Scientific thought, if new and artificial expressions may be permitted, is in the one case '*nomothetic*', in the other '*idiographic*'.[48]

This opposition of the concepts 'nomothetic' and 'idiographic' has since been taken up from many sides, in particular by some theoreticians of the historical sciences who had otherwise earlier stood apart from neo-Kantianism. The reason for this is that Windelband seemed with his thesis to have given a rigorous grounding in the logic of knowledge for a basic conviction of historicism in general – namely, the doctrine of the irreducible individuality of the historical and the necessity of individualizing methods. It is frequently overlooked even today, however, that Windelband merely wanted to provide a rough typology of scientific modes of procedure, which is not directly suitable for demarcating actual disciplines from each other. Thus, although historical knowledge for Windelband is idiographic, nomothetic elements may, according to his conception, be readily compatible with historical science: conversely also it is possible to conceive of idiographic aspects of natural science.

Windelband also suggests an idea which was later systematically developed by Heinrich Rickert in his influential works *Die Grenzen der naturwissenschaftlichen Begriffsbildung* (The Limits of Concept-Formation in the Natural Sciences) and *Kulturwissenschaft und Naturwissenschaft* (Cultural and Natural Science) (published in several editions, beginning in 1899): namely, that a decision on the mode of knowledge of the given which we are to pursue depends, not on the objects themselves, but on our value-attitudes towards such objects. Where we take an evaluative interest in something, we also have an individual interest in that thing, and we will approach it idiographically. Rickert then develops this theorem into a theory of the constitution of individual objects subject to the value-relevance through which objects first become cultural objects and the concern of cultural science. The world, seen as the totality of objects which are relevant to *values*, is *culture*; the world as the totality of objects which are related to *laws* is *nature*. The expression *Geisteswissenschaften* is rejected on account of the metaphysical or psychological connotations of the concept of spirit. Rickert thus, on account of his detailed categorial analysis, expounds a transcendental philosophy of culture, which comes very close to the Kantian model, and of which the philosophy of history is only a part: nevertheless, this view still remains dependent on a prior material conception of the historical, as the partial concepts 'value' and 'culture' indicate. For the reference to values which is constitutive for the method of cultural science is not necessarily a reference to the values which the knower himself accepts as valid: the problem of relativism in regard to values, which indeed no one has analysed more acutely than Rickert himself, is here posed yet again. It can be resolved, according to him, only by means of a non-relativistic philosophy of values, which would then also make possible a material philosophy of history. However, this philosophy of values remains, as far as he is concerned, merely a programme. We shall return to Rickert in the chapters on 'Understanding' and 'Values'.

4 The rejection of history

The leading role of history in culture, which characterized the age of historicism, was never undisputed. If at first it was principally in the name of pre-historicist traditions that the dominance of the historical sciences was put in question – by means of such arguments as that there could be no science of history, which was simply the aggregate of individual events[49] – the 'crisis' of historicism, which became acute after the end of the century, led to a profound disgust with history. The much-discussed problem of relativism makes it clear that it is, in Plessner's phrase, a 'god who is not above suspicion', and that a culture needing orientation needs *other* orientations. At the same time, the cult of the historical consciousness was always subject to the competitive pressure of naturalism, which was generally idolized, on account of the undeniable successes of the natural sciences, as a scientifically founded world-view. This was intensified by the general pressure to be scientific, from which, in a scientific age, even historically orientated culture could not escape. But as far as progress towards scientific status was concerned the natural sciences anyway appeared to have an unbeatable lead. Moreover they themselves offered something which was quasi-historical and so very attractive, in the form of Darwinism, whose influence precisely in philosophy it would be hard to overestimate. As historicism descended further and further into crisis, it seemed sensible to look around for other forces to play the leading role in culture, and ultimately to dethrone history. Whatever took its place – life, evolution, values, Being – the philosophy of history took a subordinate place, and so the age offers a spectrum of positions which, after the end of Idealism and the dominance of the Historical School, stretches from social Darwinism to the ontology of historicity (as in Heidegger).

i. *Schopenhauer's attack on historical science*

In the famous thirty-eighth chapter of the second volume of *Die Welt als Wille und Vorstellung* (The World as Will and Representation), which is entitled 'On History', Arthur Schopenhauer (1788–1860) disputes, first, whether history can become a science. The opposition later cited by Jacob Burckhardt between subordination and coordination appears in the argument, as well as the reference to the lack of that systematic character without which no science is conceivable. History, for Schopenhauer, is

> certainly knowledge, but not a science. For nowhere does it know the particular by means of the general, but must directly grasp the particular and so, as

it were, creep forward on the ground of experience; whereas the real sciences hover over it, in that they have acquired comprehensive concepts by means of which they gain mastery of the particular and, at least within certain limits, conceive the possibility of the things belonging to their domain, so that they can also think calmly about what is perhaps still to be added. The sciences, since they are systems of concepts, speak always of species: history, of individuals. It would accordingly be a science of individuals: which implies a contradiction.

The only general object to which history could attain is

merely a subjective one, that is, such that its generality arises only from the insufficiency of the individual awareness of things; but not something objective, that is, a concept in which things would be really already thought.[50]

In the next chapter, 'Science', it should become clear that Schopenhauer is here still defending the classical Aristotelian concept of science, which was replaced by another conception only after Hegel. It is important for the moment only that Schopenhauer is using precisely the argument in whose name emerging historicism had broken free from the philosophy of history – namely, the principle of individuality – as an objection *against* the scientific status of historical knowledge. The Historical School had long allowed such objections to have little effect on it, especially since its conception of its scientific character had a different basis. This changed, however, as soon as Schopenhauer's historical influence began really to be felt, that is, after the middle of the century, when his metaphysics of the Will seemed almost to have become the articulation of the cultural atmosphere of the age and was beginning to influence life-philosophy (see Ch. 5, Sect. 1). It was only against *this* background that scepticism about the cultural dominance of the historical sciences was again reactivated: but it was no longer based on the traditional arguments from the theory of science alone, which anyway had little chance of being heard in view of the fact that the academic and scientific study of history was so firmly established.

Schopenhauer's fundamental argument is that history remains on the surface, that it does not penetrate to the essence of the world, to the thing-in-itself, and in that respect lags behind even art.

A real philosophy of history should not therefore, as they all do, study that which (to use Plato's language) is always coming to be and never is, and consider this as the real essence of things; rather, it should keep before its eyes that which always is and never comes to be or passes away. It consists, therefore, not in elevating the temporary aims of men into something eternal and absolute, and in constructing artificially and in imagination their advance to it through all complexities; but in the insight that history, not only in its execution but already in its essence, is mendacious, in that, while speaking of well-known individuals and particular events, it pretends always to be relating something else; while from beginning to end it always repeats only the self-same thing, under other names and in other guises. The true philosophy of history consists, that is to say, in the insight that, in all these endless changes and their disorder, one is yet confronted always only with the same, identical and unchangeable essence, which has the same concerns today as yesterday and always: it should therefore recognize the identical in all events, of ancient as of modern times, of the Orient as of the Occident, and, in spite of all differences in the special circumstances, of costume and of customs, everywhere discover the same humanity. This identical element, which persists amid all change, consists in the fundamental qualities of the human heart and head – many bad, a few good. The motto of history in general should read: *Eadem, sed aliter* [the same, but differently]. If someone has read Herodotus, he has, for philosophical purposes, already studied enough history. For everything which makes up subsequent world history is already to be found there: the striving, doing, suffering and fate of the human race as it proceeds from the qualities just mentioned and its physical destiny on the earth.[51]

Thus seen, history is certainly little suited to say what man in reality is, for 'what history relates is in fact only the long, hard and confused dream of humanity'. These remarks are accompanied by Schopenhauer's usual polemics against Hegel, though this does not prevent him from adopting a position very close to Hegel's in determining the positive value of history. 'What reason is to the individual, that history is to the human race.' According to Schopenhauer,

> History is to be regarded as the rational self-consciousness of the human race ... In this sense, history is therefore to be regarded as reason, or the rational consciousness of the whole human race, and takes the place of a self-consciousness directly shared by the whole race, so that only by virtue of it does the race really become a whole, a single humanity.[52]

What distinguishes Schopenhauer here from Hegel and even from Droysen is the rejection of the thesis that humanity in its historical self-consciousness at the same time knows what it *essentially* is; man is not merged in his historical reality, because all spatio-temporal reality according to Schopenhauer is merely an appearance of a being which does not itself appear, that is, of the Will. Droysen's formulation, 'instead of the species-concept, they have history', is not accepted as valid for man by Schopenhauer; his historical self-consciousness is for him only a subjective universal, a universal of the *idea*. The thesis that it was not historical knowledge, but only art, which was ranked higher than history, which is master of the true essence of the world, later also inspired the Schopenhauerian Richard Wagner to turn aside from historical opera and to set his interpretation of the world in a total work of art in the realm of timeless myth.

ii. *Nietzsche's critique of historical culture*

Friedrich Nietzsche (1844–1900) celebrated 'Schopenhauer as educator' (the third of his *Untimely Meditations*) and, like Jacob Burckhardt and Richard Wagner, was attracted not so much by the pre-historicist, but by the romantic and irrationalist elements in his system. Schopenhauer's critique of progress, of optimism and of the Idealism of absolute reason, and his depreciation of history in the name of philosophy and art, created the cultural climate of a whole age, in which there was a steadily growing counter-current against historicism. Schopenhauer's and Nietzsche's critiques of historicism are different, despite a number of similarities, because of the character of their opponents. Whereas in Schopenhauer it is principally Idealist historical speculation against which his polemics are directed, Nietzsche, in his second 'Untimely Meditation', 'Of the advantages and disadvantages of history for life' (1876), is already dealing with a historical culture, proud of its scientific character, which he cites before the tribunal of the positively active Schopenhauerian Will, that is, of life. This change was the beginning in essence of what was later called 'life-philosophy'. Nietzsche's polemic, however, was itself the first document in the critique of historicism from the point of view of life-philosophy: it already contains the most important arguments, and through its influence accelerated the repudiation of history.

Nietzsche says of his essay, 'These thoughts are also untimely because I seek to understand something of which this age is justifiably proud, its historical culture, as the wound, the infirmity and the blemish of the time, because I even believe that we all suffer from a historical fever and at least ought to recognize that we are suffering from it.'[53] The *Leitmotiv* is that history is a sickness, and the remedy that is prescribed is that we should restrict our contact with history to the degree which is advantageous to life. 'Life' is itself the criterion: 'There is a degree to which history may be promoted, and a valuation of it, at which life shrivels away and becomes debased'.[54] Nietzsche first points out, by setting out a typology of ways of dealing with history – the monumental, the antiquarian and the critical varieties of history – the boundaries between the life-enhancing and the life-destroying, but he does not confine himself to phenomenology, giving it again and again a normative application. Life is not only the criterion for the distinction between sickness and health, but also the norm and the goal of our dealings with history. 'Only in so far as history serves life do we wish to serve it.' 'If we could only learn better and better to harness history to the purposes of life.' In a later passage, he speaks of the requirement 'that man should learn above all to live, and use history only in the service of the living thus learned'.[55] With his notion of 'hygiene of life', Nietzsche was already laying the foundations of his ethical life-philosophy (see Ch. 5, Sect. 2. iii), a title we can also give to his metaphysic of the 'will to power'; the factual priority of life to history, that is, the fact that all history factually stands in a context of life and is also capable of distorting it, becomes in him the source of the normative superiority of life to history. Thus history loses its monopoly in giving direction to culture: 'the unhistorical and the historical are equally necessary for the health of an individual, a nation and a culture'.[56] This cultivated acceptance of the unhistorical as an 'antidote' was bound to appear to the historical consciousness like an invasion of unculture, indeed an invitation to barbarism, and all the more so because Nietzsche himself took historical culture severely to task. He objected most of all to the increasingly scientific nature of the approach to history, which for him was a process of objectification, and so of isolation from life as it is really lived.

History, thought of as a pure science and become sovereign, would be for humanity a kind of closing and settling of the account with life . . . History, in so far as it is in the service of life, is in the service of an unhistorical force and thus will never be able – nor ought it to be able – to become, while it is thus subordinated, a pure science in the way that, for example, mathematics is.

Nietzsche then undertakes a reinterpretation of the concept of historical objectivity which makes the scientific ideal of objectivity look like a eunuch's virtue.

Only from the utmost vigour of the present ought you to interpret the past; only in the most intense exercise of your most exalted qualities will you divine what in the past is worth knowing and preserving and is great. Like through like! Otherwise you drag the past down to your own level . . . The historian must have the energy to re-coin what is universally familiar so as to make it into what was never heard before and to proclaim the universal so simply and so profoundly that one forgets the simplicity in the profundity and the profundity in the simplicity.[57]

In such objectivity there can be felt the human

artistic impulse – but not its impulse to truth or fairness. Objectivity and fairness have nothing to do with one another. It is possible to conceive of a way of writing history which contained not a single drop of ordinary empirical truth and yet could make claim in the highest degree to the predicate of objectivity.[58]

Nietzsche thus brings into play against the scientific concept of objectivity one which is (in the Aristotelean sense) *poetic*, and one which measures itself against the normative scale of life, as the standard of all standards. From here it is only a step, which others after Nietzsche have taken, to the political reinterpretation of the ideal of objectivity and the warrant which followed from it to 'objectify' history more and more in the sense of a factual power.

iii. *'Farewell to the philosophy of history'?*

After Hegel, the philosophy of history was repeatedly pronounced dead. The Historical School attacked it, without, to be sure, itself renouncing it altogether. Nietzsche's escape from historicism in the name of the philosophy of life seemed to have sealed its fate, and yet brought in its train an abundance of theories of history based on life-philosophy (see Ch. 5, Sect. 2. ii). The increasingly scientific character of academic history, and above all the emergence of sociology, made it possible for that which had once been a theme of the philosophy of history – the origin, course and goal of history as a whole – to become to a large extent a question to be posed in terms of empirical science; the transformation of the philosophy of history into the logic of history or theory of the historical sciences was thereby accelerated. Besides, a rival had appeared to these former monopolists in the field of theories of man – a rival which was at once philosophical and a branch of empirical science, in the form of philosophical anthropology (see Ch. 8). The very fact of its appearance, towards the end of the period to be discussed here, shows that philosophers were not ready to come to terms with the simple choice between empirical history and social science and a metatheory of the empirical sciences. Philosophical anthropology, which claims to be a natural science and hence seems more scientific than the human sciences, which traditionally had a more historical orientation, participates in other respects in the widespread effort to use more radical questioning in order to get in under the guard of the philosophy of history and degrade history to the status of an epiphenomenon. In the same way that Nietzsche makes life prior and superior to history, philosophical anthropology makes it into an essential characteristic of man to be 'open to the world' and to have a history. In a parallel way, Martin Heidegger locates human history in the existential domain of the historicity of *Dasein*.[59] The thread of philosophy of history was really taken up only by the neo-Marxists in the twenties.

The publication of the early writings of Marx and Engels, so close in spirit to Feuerbach and to Hegel, whom Feuerbach attacked, led to the discovery of the philosophical Marx, who had been lost sight of behind the social scientist and economist. Georg Lukács' *Geschichte und Klassenbewusstsein* (History and Class-Consciousness) of 1923 introduced – also under the strong additional influence of the neo-Kantian and life-philosophy traditions, to which Lukács as a pupil of Georg Simmel belonged – a 'rephilosophization' of Marxism, which had its strongest impact on the critical theory of the Frankfurt School. It brought about a situation in which political economy, which had been an element in the 'silenced orthodoxy',[60] again receded behind the philosophy of history. Critical theory's return to the early, Young Hegelian, Marx became particularly clear in its principal work, the *Dialectic of Enlightenment* of 1944. Here was to be seen the process of Enlightenment, portrayed as a destiny of the world and encroaching upon all specific social formations, exemplifying simply the law of development of our civilization, and even determining the Marxian dialectic of productive forces and relations of production. The extraordinarily polemical positions which the authors of critical theory took up towards Heidegger should not be allowed to conceal how close the two sides are in their endeavour to give a philosophical interpretation, in the light of an ahistorical substructure, to what the empirical sciences can say about man and his history. Even critical theory's dialectic of Enlightenment is not a genuinely historical model of the process, once one assumes the historicist historicization of history: it is no more so than the later Heidegger's 'destiny of Being (*Seinsgeschick*)', which is what became of the existential notion of 'historicity'. Does not the neo-Marxist renaissance of the philosophy of history, therefore, really only confirm its end?

Philosophy of history in competition with the empirical sciences of man, or as a super-science of man itself, has already been for a long time a thing of the past. Its limitation to a theory of knowledge or a theory of science for the historical sciences could satisfy no one. Perhaps its future lies in what Kant reminded us of, and what several recalled even in the days of historicism: in its function as an appendix to practical philosophy,[61] that is, as a reflection on the imperative and realizable goals of human action in the perspective of world history. In this form, philosophy of history will not so quickly become obsolete.

3

Science

Historicism was not the only distinctive feature of the period between 1831 and 1945 in Germany: it was rather, above all else, a century of science. The term 'science', in this context, has to be understood in a sense which is fundamentally different from 'philosophy', since contemporaries were convinced that they could win the right to label their age as scientific only by a process of liberation from the philosophy of German Idealism and resistance to its monopolistic claims to being scientific. The pioneering influence in this regard of the emergent human sciences with their idea of historical culture has already been mentioned on a number of occasions. In this chapter, I shall attempt to describe in broad outlines the change in the function and structure of science after Idealism – a change already represented by the human sciences themselves. It is as impossible to do this simply in terms of the internal history of philosophy as it was in the chapter on 'History'. In the period which we are considering, we have to do with a culture which understood itself as scientific; but the equation of philosophy and science which had been traditional from Aristotle to Hegel had been abandoned – that is, the philosophy which was available was no longer the model of a scientific approach in general. The result was that the philosophers also forfeited their monopoly over definitions of the 'scientific': suddenly, they had to face questions about whether their occupation was of the sort that can be accepted as scientific in a scientific culture. The history of 'science' as a philosophical theme after Hegel is thus essentially a history of philosophical reactions to the factual and normative transformations in the world of science, a world which was external to philosophy; our theme must be the implicit theory of science inherent in a scientific practice which was non-philosophical or anti-philosophical, the understanding of science of the leading scientists, and not what the professional philosophers of the time said about science.

Hegel's death did not only mark the end of the age in which philosophy could make credible its leading role in the world of the sciences – ironically enough, although this role had first been institutionalized in the Humboldt-University. After Hegel, even scientific reactions to philosophical impulses became more and more rare and usually came about only in an indirect fashion. Above all, however, philosophical foundations in science, or for science in general, suddenly came to seem dispensable; even in the normative sphere, it now seemed, the sciences could look after themselves. Philosophy was thus in the unfortunate position of having constantly to demonstrate its indispensability, or even its right to exist. The repercussions on philosophy itself of this new pressure to prove its legitimacy, which gradually took the form of an obvious crisis of identity, and the various attempts to counter it, will also be outlined in this chapter.

1 The change in the function of science

The central fact about the social context of science between 1831 and 1933 is that it was between these dates that the first Industrial Revolution took place in Germany. It forced a social change of a tempo and violence which we today can conceive of only with difficulty. In a century, it transformed Germany from a backward and particularistic agrarian society into the strongest industrial state on the continent; moreover, it forced the 'retarded nation' (as Plessner called it), which had always been based on essentially feudal political traditions, to find its way after 1918, without any preparation worthy of the name, into a bourgeois mass democracy, and after a global defeat at that. Attention has already been drawn in Chapter 1, Section 2 to particular aspects of this change; under the heading 'From "culture through science" to "science as a vocation" ' (Ch. 1, Sect. 4. iv), there has also been some discussion of its consequences within science, for the professionalization of science referred to there is simply one of the changes in function undergone by the system of science in the wake of industrialization. In modern industry, science, as fundamental enquiry and technology, has itself become a productive force: this in turn is possible only because modern science, as opposed to the older conception, is inherently technologically applicable. The social and cultural effects of this process may be described as the transformation of the life-world by science. 'Science', the structure of action and interaction which had been so successful in industry, began to permeate all the social and cultural spheres of life. The pre-industrial traditions of the life-world, already weakened by the social change, became further enfeebled by the advance of science, and it now came to be expected that science itself would perform the tasks of orientation and organization which had once been the responsibility of familiar traditional practices. This is certainly the real basis for the global scientism to be found in both East and West – the quasi-natural belief in the universal competence and normative force of science in its modern form, in the face of which philosophical criticism seems to have become so impotent and so irrelevant.

The scientific transformation of the life-world, which was as influential in the fields of production and organization as in those of culture and education, but which, because of its ideological consequences, left science as evidently the only remaining unquestionable source of legitimacy, did not even stop in the face of science itself. In this sense, we have to speak of a scientific transformation of science itself. What this means is that the scientific transformation of the life-world which resulted from industrialization embraced and determined science as one of the most important determinants of industrialization. Helmuth Plessner, at the end of our period, analysed this process under the heading 'the industrialization of science',[1] and made it clear that the professionalization of science sketched by Max Weber, which brought about the transition from 'culture through science' to 'science as a vocation', was only one aspect of the wider process of industrialization. Professionalization was one of the conditions for the productivity of science, which was basically utilized as an element in industrial production. Other conditions were the division of labour, that is, specialization in science, and its organization into institutions of a quasi-industrial sort: above all, in vast institutes, which burst the bounds of the Humboldt-University and the unity of research and culture – Max Weber had also referred to this. Plessner attempted a sociological analysis of the conditions of this change in the function of science, already noted by Weber and others. He pointed out first of all the 'connexions, intelligible at the level of meaning' between types of science and types of society, which were discernible as soon as one raised the question of their mutual 'causal or intentional influence'.[2] According to Plessner, the West has produced three types of social form: the hierarchic and feudal society of the Middle Ages, the absolutist society of the seventeenth and eighteenth centuries, with its conceptions of natural law, and the evolutionary democratic society of the nineteenth and twentieth centuries. The first two types represent 'closed social forms of a static and cyclical character'; the Church and the centralist national state are their highest points of reference. Plessner continues,

> The medieval world's relation to time was defined by the Church's transcendence of time, while that of the absolutist world of natural law was defined by the timeless validity of the principles of reason and the divinely ordained nature of the relations of social dependence. The associated forms of knowledge have corresponding properties. In both systems, truth is materially secure, as a store of supranatural revelation or as laws of being which are immanent to reason, the successive clarification of which in the course of enquiry is part of a closed order which is given once for all. Incapable of either addition or diminution, the system of knowledge requires precise presentation and defence against objections. The problem of criteria is solved either by means of the principle that our understanding should conform to the teachings of the Church or by that of immanent necessity. Empirical confirmation does not play any significant role, although the classification of the material is guaranteed by means of the material principles of being. These presuppositions form the basis of the scholastic method, in the narrower and also in a wider sense, which was reflected in the great systems of the seventeenth to nineteenth centuries.[3]

The rationalist conception of reason is described by Plessner as a result of the secularization of the divine *noûs*: reason becomes the union of what is evident in itself, without authorities, as when Leibniz defines *raison* as the place of innate ideas; this reason, as the constant factor of man's being which is accessible to every individual, opens up at the same time through its use the approach to true knowledge of nature and successful mastery of nature. Reason in this sense becomes, from the philosophical and psychological point of view, the principle of 'objectivity (*Sachlichkeit*) as an expression of an inner-worldly attitude to existence'. Plessner then describes the consequences of the formalization of this conception of reason, which can be looked on as a further step in secularization. Reason is then no longer itself a source of understanding, but only a *formal* principle of procedure; thus it comes to be the basis of 'quantifiability', that is, the mathematization of the world and organization of our dealings with it in terms of quantifiable means–end relations. The achievement of such a formal rationalization of our dealings with the world by scientific means guarantees in turn, for the first time, the uniformity of nature, which first and foremost makes possible the instrumental and economic domination of nature. It is the basis 'for the curious mutual harmonization of objective world-view and business maxims, and for the symmetry of progress in an interest-free science, pursued for the sake of truth, and in the purposive exploitation of life by means of science'.[4]

The form of science associated, in a way which is 'intelligible at the level of meaning', with the evolutionary democratic type of society is described by Plessner in these terms:

Objectivity as an expression of an inner-worldly attitude to existence means, considered from the logical point of view, a uniform objectification of the natural fullness of life in terms of material domains of a structure which is in principle intelligible. All non-objective principles remain out of play, and an immanent classification and definition of material is established. Groups of material are segregated from each other, in accordance with the meaning of their objective content, into homogeneous domains, and the corresponding activities are separated into specialist areas with particular methodologies, that is, in accordance with the criteria of a learnable and checkable discipline. The specialist areas become professions, the rationally abstract form of activity of which gives work and the possibility of profit to a relatively large number of persons. For ultimately it is perceptually detectable success, in any form, which is the criterion of all forms of rational activity: action and inaction, capacity and deficiency on anyone's part are subject to public check, and to a certain extent society continuously supervises itself. As a result of the increasing competition in every specialism the individual is forced to seek new fields and thus creates new specialities. Narrower and narrower groups of material and more and more new forms of combination of materials are proclaimed as autonomous and made into specialized fields, that is, into sources of income. Thus there results finally, alongside the continuous creation of new modes of activity in the ideal coexistence of specialization, as its meaningful complement the uninterrupted transformation of work in the ideal succession of progress. Scientific labour, divided in the process of specialization and progress, itself fits in in a professional way to a society which is professionally articulated. These essential features of objective labour can be identified in every activity of contemporary European and American society, except where the profession itself (as for instance in the case of the clergy) prevents their full effect from being felt.[5]

The 'mechanization, methodization, depersonalization (along with total dedication to individual achievement!) of the process of producing . . . economic and spiritual goods' alters the internal structure of science as well as the role- and personality-structure of the scientist. The evolutionary character of science under the principle of progress is ascribed by Plessner to the 'essential infinity of autonomous fields of material', which resulted from the formalization of reason. (Reference should also be made here, for completeness' sake, to the pressure of technical and industrial innovation, which has had a direct influence on the structure of science only in the present day.) This change of structure will be discussed in the next section under the heading of the 'dynamization of science'; a science which is committed to innovative research itself becomes a research-science, which finds its identity no longer in its content – which is anyway constantly liable to be overtaken – but only in its procedures or methods.

This 'mechanization' or 'methodization' of science corresponds, on the side of the researcher, to what Plessner calls 'depersonalization': research which is rationalized, in the sense of rigorously methodical, promises success only when the individual scientist precisely does not bring his own individuality into play in any essential way and when he strictly follows the ethos of pure 'objectivity'.

> The modern researcher brings to bear in his work all his powers, but excludes his personality, and to the extent that he does so he is in his discipline an impersonal question; in individual cases, he may perhaps have the inestimable value of genius, but nevertheless as an individual he is in principle replaceable. The logic of the development of problems keeps his science in motion in the same way that a production-plan does for an enterprise.[6]

What Plessner calls 'depersonalization' could also be described as a process of increasing anonymity. Science, on this view, is neither what is contained in the knowledge of a particular man, nor essentially the work of nameable individuals, as is now suggested by the collective singular 'research'. What is achieved by Peirce's 'community of inquirers' must have a validity which is independent of persons and be universally available: thus research itself must also in principle follow rules which are independent of persons. No individualistic cultural ambitions of a Humboldtian stamp, therefore, can any longer be associated with a research-science which has become a subsystem of an evolutionary democratic society; only capacities and knowledge which can in principle be acquired by anyone are demanded, not the great 'personality of the enquirer'. (It is significant that in German the word *Forscher* (enquirer, researcher) is beginning to become obsolete, but not the word *Forschung* (enquiry, research.) Scientific training (*Ausbildung*) is supplanting culture (*Bildung*) through science, just as research and culture themselves parted company (see also Ch. 8). The principle of 'replaceability in authorship', which goes along with the 'internationality of science', and which Plessner explicitly relates to the egalitarian premises of the modern interpretation of democracy, requires moreover an ethos of attitudes and intentions, which is essentially related to the form of rational behaviour in the face of constantly changing requirements. Here Plessner appeals to Max Weber: the remarkable harmony between the ethic of research and the 'work-ethos of the modern world' is for him merely the subjective complement to the relation between the industrialization of science and the 'rationalization of social life' in general.

2 The change in the structure of science

The expression 'dynamization' has already been used to refer to the essential feature of the internal change in the structure of science, which, according to Plessner, does not have a directly causal relation to industrialization, but is connected with it 'at the level of meaning'. The new type of science based on research, which he associates with the 'evolutionary democratic world of the nineteenth and twentieth centuries', and which is primarily defined by its innovative and impersonal procedures, must be understood as a result of the dynamization of the conception of science which was accepted from Aristotle to Hegel. The two most important components of this change are the *empiricization* and *temporalization* of science,[7] where both expressions are to be taken as referring both to the object-domain and to the form of scientific knowledge. To make it possible to clarify this point, we shall need first of all to consider some facts about the history of science.

i. *On the history of science*

What has here been called the 'dynamization of science' was experienced by contemporaries, at least around the middle of the century, as a constantly accelerating advance, indeed as an explosion of the material of knowledge. Up until the end of the 'Age of Goethe', an educated man could still get an overall view of available knowledge and follow the development of science. Goethe himself and even Hegel, so much maligned by natural scientists, were supreme in their time as far as scientific knowledge was concerned. Then this universal scientific culture began for the first time to be gradually modified into the objectively necessary specialization, which must be divided into professional and methodological specialization. An all-embracing scientific 'world-picture' became as a result a matter for dilettantes and the popularizers of science who wrote for them. To meet the needs which a specialized and professionalized science could no longer satisfy there sprang up a constantly increasing supply of world-views, which promised to provide what the scientists could no longer provide and which for the most part claimed to be scientific themselves.

a. *The structure of scientific disciplines*

Scientific specialization means, in the first instance, an internal diversification of the sciences, and this can be seen even in the development of the faculty structure of the universities. The university in Hegel's time had four faculties: philosophical, theological, medical and legal. In the sixties, the faculty of natural science split off from the philosophical faculty; later there emerged faculties of political science, economics and social science, for the most part as offshoots of the law faculty. The increasingly academic character of the Technical High Schools (*Technische Hochschule*) led to the creation of a series of faculties of technology. The Pedagogic High Schools should also be mentioned here as proto-faculties of educational science, although it was only much later that they were integrated into the universities. (Chairs of Education in the philosophical faculty had existed since the early nineteenth century.) In all these faculties there was a continual increase in the departments belonging to them, especially in the fields of natural science and medicine. But even the philosophical faculty was affected by this. The historicization of what in Hegel had belonged to the philosophy of spirit created a whole series of new historical disciplines: the histories of law, art, religion and philosophy. Germanistics was the prototype of the 'new philologies', which first appeared in the form of linguistic sciences, but later merged with the historical disciplines. Sciences of literature, music, art and religion arose on the model of the integrative 'science of classical antiquity'; they were also called 'philologies' in a wider sense, although their natural tendency was more in the direction of cultural sciences than in that of a science of 'words'. All these new departments copied the integration of philological and historical methods which had made it possible for history at an earlier stage to constitute itself as historical science.

In Germany, however, the most important consequences followed from the emergence of sociology and psychology in the modern sense, since they called in question just that new structure of the scientific world which had now become consolidated. From that point of view, sociology and psychology are irritatingly integrative sciences: sociology combines philosophical, historical, economic, juristic and (through its French tradition) what are claimed to be natural-scientific points of view, while psychology is presented as a 'natural science of the spirit'. In fact, however, these new disciplines did not so much result from the reintegration of an earlier departmental specialization, as respond in an integrative way to the methodological specialization due to the duality of natural and human sciences. The idea of using the methods of the natural sciences to study 'objective' and 'subjective spirit', which was constituted as the object of the human sciences by means of the specific methods of the human sciences, was at the heart of the provocation offered by sociology and the new type of psychology, which seems to have lost none of its force even today. 'Interpretative' psychology and sociology on the model of the human sciences was a specifically German response to this problem, which remained, despite all its later consequences, merely an episode.[8]

The rise of a psychology modelled on the natural sciences, which began as a 'psychology without the soul' and soon developed into a pure science of behaviour, also had considerable effects on the human sciences themselves, since psychology was for a long time considered to be their basis.[9] The later opposition to such 'psychologism' and efforts to find a new foundation for a depsychologized science of culture in hermeneutics or the theory of values would be inconceivable without the threat to identity posed by the rise of experimental psychology. This was a threat to identity because it made it evident that the Diltheyan, interpretative, route 'inwards' could not on its own any longer lead to an adequate self-understanding of the human spirit; despite all attempts at resistance, directed against Freud as much as against behaviourism, the interpretative science of reflection ultimately had to surrender its exclusive claim to be a human science. This was one of the root causes of the significance attached in Germany to philosophical anthropology (see Ch. 8). The debate about foundations in the field of logic and mathematics also had its origins in this: psychology, considered as a science of reflection, is not essentially distinct from philosophy; it was only the 'new' psychology, considered as a strictly empirical science, which led to the well-known problems of circularity created by 'psychologism' in logic, which Husserl and Frege analysed and which led them to look for foundations elsewhere.

b. The natural sciences

The paradigmatic significance of the natural sciences in the scientific situation of the period makes it necessary here to sketch in some of the main features in their development. The fundamental tendency can be described as one of unification of theories and methods combined with a simultaneous explosion of experimental knowledge. Whereas in the thirties of our own century quantum theory had already been formulated as the basic theory of all the natural sciences, in 1830 there could as yet be no thought of a unified natural science. The classical mechanics of Galileo and Newton, which for Kant represented the fact of 'science', along with mathematics and geometry, was far from being the whole of physics. Mechanism, as a total explanation of nature, was either a mere programme or a philosophical dogma: the actuality of science looked different. The theory of heat, optics, magnetism and the theory of electricity were largely independent divisions of physics. The young science of chemistry (after Lavoisier) and even more biology, still a science largely concerned with classification or comparative morphology, did not make use of mechanistic models of explanation. After 1830, however, optimism about a unification of theories and methods under the banner of mechanism first began to gain ground, helped by, for example, the discovery of Brownian motion in 1827, which finally seemed to provide empirical confirmation of the kinetic theory of heat. Particularly important, however, was the formulation of the first law of thermodynamics by Robert Mayer and Helmholtz in 1846, which had been prepared for by Joule's investigations of the relations between mechanical work and heat. Helmholtz still supported this mechanistic optimism in a university address in 1869, seeing his faith in it confirmed by the principle of the conservation of energy, which he formulated as a principle of the conservation of force. 'If, however, motion is the unchanging basis which underlies all other changes in the world, then all elementary forces are forces of motion, and the aim of science is to discover the motions and their motive forces which underlie all other changes, that is, to be reduced to mechanics.'[10] The principle of the conservation of force was also interpreted, and accordingly celebrated, by adherents of a materialistic world-view as a confirmation of mechanism and thus of their own position. But even Helmholtz attacked the equation of mechanism and materialism.[11] The interpretation which Robert Mayer had given to the first law of thermodynamics, which was purely in terms of energy-theory and ignored the significance of any 'forces', also made it possible, moreover, to loosen the Helmholtzian connexion of this law with mechanism; it thus prepared the way for the later 'energetics', which was a rival of the mechanistic view up until our own century and which became, once elaborated into a world-view, an important source of life-philosophy. The antagonism between the mechanistic and 'energetic' views then came to be superfluous as a result of Einstein's relativistic physics and modern atomic physics.

In physics after 1830, the most important innovations were the result of integration: the integration of magnetic and electrical phenomena by Ørstedt led to the theory of electromagnetism, which Faraday connected with mechanics and Maxwell and Hertz with optics; the new electrodynamics became the foundation of many previously separated subdisciplines of physics. From it also there developed Einstein's Special Theory of Relativity, as the title of his original paper of 1905 shows: 'On the electrodynamics of moving bodies'. But this innovative integration transcended the limits of physics itself. Volta had already sought to discover connexions between chemical and electrical phenomena. Now there emerged physical chemistry. Chemistry itself, which found a first theoretical completion in the periodic table of the elements, also encroached on the domain of biology, in the form first of organic chemistry and later of biochemistry. Biology in its turn was given a new theoretical foundation in the form of physiology, which arose as a result, principally, of the application of chemical analysis to the processes of life: this led biology gradually away from its classificatory and morphological phase. Physiology also became the basis for modern scientific medicine, and this confirmed the tendency, identifiable throughout the whole of the nineteenth century, towards the integration of human and natural sciences. Reference has already been made to the effects of Darwin's theory: these too are examples of innovative theoretical integration, of a kind which occurred in various fields, but above all they led to changes in the scientific picture of man himself.

The history of science between 1831 and 1933, however, can also be described as a history of crises, meaning both crises of identity for traditional specialisms and foundational crises. Frequently the one became the other. For instance, the crisis in the foundations of mathematics caused by the antinomies of number-theory compelled a new definition of the relations between mathematics and logic, as a result of which the traditional understanding of both disciplines was fundamentally altered. The development of non-Euclidean geometries and of the theory of relativity brought about a revision of the traditional understanding of geometry, and also the end of the monopoly of classical physics. Many of the changes in the relation between physics and chemistry and between chemistry and biology may also be interpreted in terms of this model. Psychology should also be mentioned here: in the form of psychophysics and of physiological psychology,[12] it entered into similar combinations, the most relevant feature of which for present purposes is their effect on the identity of psychology.

c. An excursus: the Romantic and Idealist nature-philosophy

The scientific consciousness of the post-Idealist period was underpinned in Germany mainly by the attacks which became commonplace after 1830 on the Romantic and Idealist nature-philosophy. Hegel's nature-philosophy in particular was generally regarded as a horrible example of the aberrations of philosophical speculation, and was taken as a motive for affirming that it was now finally time to leave philosophy in general well alone and to pursue the advance of science. Although the origins of the historical and the scientific consciousness here ran in parallel – the rejection of Hegel in both cases had a paradigmatic significance – nevertheless the second process was the more far-reaching and the more thoroughgoing. Hegel's philosophies of law and history were attacked principally on the grounds of accommodation with Prussia, the philosophical justification of the status quo, the hypostatization of the present, optimism about progress and so on, that is, with moral and political arguments. The scientific doubts felt by historians played only a subordinate part in the public debate, and that is the explanation of the importance which Hegel's *Philosophy of Right* nevertheless came to have for scientific history and which even some of his opponents acknowledged.[13] In the case of the nature-philosophy, on the other hand, Absolute Idealism seemed to have brought itself into scientific disrepute, and hence this part of Hegel's system was not even discussed except as an arsenal of bad and ridiculous examples. Hegel's pupils retreated very quickly after his death: thus Michelet pleaded, on the occasion of the publication of Hegel's nature-philosophy, simply for coexistence between the different approaches to nature and thereby abandoned the position of superiority to empirical natural science which Hegel himself had claimed for his nature-philosophy.

If one were to rely only on this picture, one would gain the impression that it was only after Hegel that empirical scientific enquiry about nature in Germany had been freed from the clutches of vain speculation and had generally taken on its modern form. The reality was different. Certainly, as elsewhere, so in Germany, there was in the 'Age of Goethe' no unified science of nature, but the effective influence of the Romantic and Idealist nature-philosophy on the actual practice of science at that time was greatly overestimated in later decades. German natural scientists took part, relatively untroubled by philosophical impulses, in the mainstream of Western scientific development. Friedrich Albert Lange says, 'It should . . . not be forgotten that the cultivation of the positive sciences remained cosmopolitan, whereas philosophy in Germany followed an isolated course which corresponded to the general mood.'[14] However, it is also important not to *underrate* this influence; the interrelations between nature-philosophy and recognized natural enquiry, even at a later stage, were numerous, and the boundaries between the two were fluid. Alexander von Humboldt was close to the Goethean conception of natural science, but was nevertheless a scientific authority of the first order.[15] Goethe's own morphology of plants and animals was accepted as pointing the way forward up until the acceptance of Darwin's theory,[16] and there were motifs from Schelling's nature-philosophy which influenced both Ørstedt in his formulation of electro-magnetism and Johannes von Müller in the conception of his physiology. The co-founder of psychophysics, Gustav Theodor Fechner, was a pupil of Schelling, and he did not allow either his own researches or his later polemics against philosophy in general to hinder him from advocating a mystical hylozoistic cosmology which has every conceivable Romantic and Idealist feature.[17] Finally, mention should be made of Ludwig Büchner and Jakob Moleschott themselves, those two propagandists of materialism in the name of exact natural science, who have been convincingly shown by Lange to be epigoni of the Idealist nature-philosophy.[18]

The boundaries between nature-philosophy and natural science in the 'Age of Goethe' are blurred, however, not only because of the lack of unity in the practice of science and the theoretical tendencies on the side of natural science, but also because nature-philosophy itself was not a unified whole: Goethe, the Romantics and Hegel represented clearly distinguishable conceptions. Besides, 'philosophy' and 'science' had not yet been conceptually separated. It was only as a result of the polemics on behalf of the empirical and mathematical investigation of nature and against speculation about it, which was not entirely unencumbered from the philosophical side (contemporaries spoke time and again about the philosophers' 'arrogance') that the fronts were stabilized, and 'nature-philosophy' and 'natural science' came to be contrasted in the way familiar throughout the whole nineteenth century. This contrast at the same time generally confirmed a fundamentally changed post-philosophical understanding of science. Thus the notion arose that around 1830, after a period of 'conceptual Romanticism', the normal situation of 1780 had been re-established. Nature-philosophy thus appeared, like the Leibniz-Wolffian system in Kant's time, to be empty metaphysics, against which empiricism ultimately had to defend once again the cause of Enlightenment and of scientific progress.[19] It should not be overlooked that the internal process of theoretical and methodological unification within natural science also contributed to this polarization. Above all, however, reference must be made to the radical change in ways of thinking which set in around 1830 and which led to a move away from the Idealist and neo-classicist ideals of personal cultivation and culture towards a new realism in all fields, towards anti-Romantic attitudes, the politicization of the educated classes in the period before the 1848 revolution, but also the growth of popular materialism as the world-view corresponding to that new realism. In terms of social history, this process combined with the first thrust of industrialization to produce the 'realist movement in culture'.

Admittedly, from an international point of view, German nature-philosophy was a purely German episode. Its roots are to be sought in the reaction of the *Sturm und Drang* movement and the early Romantics to French materialism in the style of Holbach, which was widely equated with French Enlightenment philosophy in general. Because it was taken (like the form of materialism which Lange was later to oppose) for a necessary consequence of classical mechanics and mathematical physics in general, there was a search for alternative sorts of natural science which would in their turn furnish a vindication of the anti-materialist concepts of nature-philosophy. Kant's critique of reason first opened up the possibility of divorcing classical mechanics from materialistic dogmatism; at the same time, the *Critique of Judgment* also provided the possibility of positive points of contact for an anti-mechanistic conception of nature. Heine, on the other hand, attributed the influence of Schelling to young people's boredom with Fichtean transcendental abstractions:

Fichte is merely a philosopher, and his power consists in dialectic, and his strength in demonstration. This however is Herr Schelling's weaker side, he is more intuitive, he does not feel himself at home in the cold heights of logic, he is happy to slip over into the flowery valley of symbolism, and his philosophical strength consists in construction. The latter, however, is a mental capacity which is found in mediocre poets as often as in the best philosophers. After this latter suggestion it becomes intelligible that Herr Schelling remains and must remain merely a blind follower of Fichte in that part of philosophy which belongs simply to transcendental Idealism, but that he is bound to blossom and radiate in full force in the philosophy of nature, where he conducts his business amidst flowers and stars. This direction is thus followed by preference, not simply by him, but also by his congenial friends, and the turbulence which made its appearance in this regard was likewise merely a poetic reaction against the earlier abstract philosophy of spirit. Like schoolboys let out of school, who have groaned all day under the burden of words and numbers, the pupils of Herr Schelling dashed out into nature, into the fragrance and sunshine of the real world, and rejoiced and turned cartwheels and made a great spectacle. The expression 'the pupils of Herr Schelling' should also not be taken here in its ordinary sense. Herr Schelling himself says that he wanted to form a school only in the manner of the ancient poets, a poetic school, where no one is bound by a definite doctrine and a definite discipline, but where everyone obeys the spirit and everyone manifests it in his own way. He could also have said that he was founding a prophetic school, where the inspired begin to prophesy at their pleasure and according to their humour and in any form of speech they choose. This was what the young men actually did, provoked by the master's spirit: the narrowest minds began to prophesy, each in a different tongue, and there was a great Pentecost of philosophy.[20]

It is only the ironic tone in which Heine, in 1834, speaks about nature-philosophy as a whole which confirms the change in ways of thinking referred to above, for which his whole work stands.

Typologically, it is possible to distinguish in 1800 between scientific, transcendental and metaphysical nature-philosophy. The scientific variety essentially consists of methodology and flows into the mainstream of what was later called 'theory of science'. Kant's transcendental nature-philosophy takes as its theme the formal a priori of all natural knowledge, and from it there arises, as a result of the objective turn which Schelling gives to the Fichtean notion of intellectual intuition, a new metaphysical nature-philosophy which retrospectively constructs the material a priori of our natural knowledge, that is, which constructs a priori the natural genesis of the spirit.[21] Goethe's natural science, on the other hand, remains on the approaches to transcendental thought: it is a variant of the scientific type on the basis of metaphysical, that is, principally Spinozist beliefs. Hegel's nature-philosophy,[22] finally, is materially dependent on Schelling and Goethe, but seeks its philosophical foundation in a metacritique of the Kantian critique of reason (his *Science of Logic* can also be read in this way); it thus claims to integrate what has gone before into itself and attempts furthermore to remain consistent with the empirical investigation of nature. Thus Hegel keeps his critical distance from the Romantics, from Schelling and Goethe, despite all his points of agreement with them. He accuses the Romantics of the fanciful perversion of nature-philosophy, which has contributed to the general contempt for philosophy.[23] (Hegel thus himself uses the point later made against him, of the way in which philosophy had been discredited by nature-philosophy.) He does not confine himself, however, to criticizing the bowdlerization of Schelling's conception, but attacks directly – admittedly without mentioning Schelling by name – his principle of intellectual intuition, which is responsible for everything, and opposes to it the work of the concept: nature-philosophy is 'thinking knowledge of nature'. Hegel is closest to Goethe in his nature-philosophy: especially in the theory of colours, Hegel takes Goethe's part against the Newtonians. Nevertheless, he also feels the absence in him of the thought that one cannot 'philosophize on the basis of intuition', and Goethe declines to ascend to the level of the concept. The theory of metamorphoses was taken over by Hegel, but given a new interpretation, for 'metamorphosis belongs only to the concept as such, since only alteration in it is development'. He also uses this argument to attack on grounds of principle all theories of evolution, which for him was merely a 'clumsy idea both of older and more recent nature-philosophy'. It must of course be added that the doctrine of the fixity of species was generally accepted at that time and was first really displaced by Darwin.

The rejection of the Idealist metaphysical nature-philosophy later led to the belief that it was possible to despise not only transcendental nature-philosophy, but nature-philosophy in general, that is, even methodological reflection, and it is worth noting that it was natural scientists who attempted to rehabilitate it (see Ch. 3, Sect. 3. iv), if only in a scientific and transcendental form. Metaphysical nature-philosophy, on the other hand, was no longer taken seriously from the scientific point of view: it became (as, incidentally, did the seemingly anti-metaphysical materialism) a mere world-view and survived at best in sects, sometimes founded by reputable scientists.[24] The Romantic and Idealist type of nature-philosophy experienced something of a renaissance around the turn of the century as a result of neo-Romanticism and neo-vitalism, in which several eighteenth century objections to mechanism and mathematization re-emerged.[25]

ii. *The dynamization of science*

The meaning of dynamization, as the core of the structural change in science, can be explained only against the background of the classical conception of science, which was accepted from Aristotle to Hegel. Its fundamental elements are universality, necessity and truth. Up until the modern era, these properties were given an ontological interpretation: science is knowledge of the universal (of essence, of the grounds, causes, principles of the particular), of the necessary or what eternally is and of truth in the sense of true being. Scientific method had to measure itself against this standard: science uses universal concepts and makes universal judgments; it is a connected system of judgments, which is constituted by valid rules of inference, and it consists not of suppositions, but of knowledge, that is, of genuinely demonstrable judgments. In Descartes, on the other hand, universality, necessity and truth came to be fundamental features of scientific judgments, both in regard to their structure and their acceptability, and defined what a scientific object is: mathematics was the guiding model. This substitution of a gnoseological for an ontological characterization of science was at the heart of Kant's statements about science. 'Any theory is termed a science if it is supposed to be a system, that is, a totality of knowledge organized in accordance with principles'.[26] Universality was guaranteed by means of the theoretical character, necessity by means of the systematic character and truth by means of the cognitive character of knowledge. The Cartesian way of fulfilling these requirements, by means of the mathematization of knowledge, was also followed by Kant: 'I affirm, however, that, in every particular branch of natural knowledge, there can be found only as much genuine science as there is mathematics.'[27] Classical mechanics thus came to be the paradigm case of science in general, which, for example, chemistry or indeed history vainly strove to emulate. Hegel too continued to regard universality, necessity and truth as the distinctive features of science, though his use of these concepts looks, from a Kantian perspective, like a re-ontologization. When he specifies the aim of his 'philosophical endeavours' as 'the scientific knowledge of truth', the term 'truth' is not interpreted simply as a quality of judgments: philosophy has truth as its object. The true is the Idea, as absolute unity of concept and objectivity, that is, of true understanding and true being. True understanding makes it impossible to remain at the level of intuition, even if it is Schelling's intellectual intuition, since it cannot comprehend the universal. Necessity, on the other hand, is to be secured only by means of the systematic character of knowledge: 'The true form in which truth exists can only be the scientific system of truth.'[28] Hegel, however, criticizes the idea that this systematic character can be secured by means of the recourse to mathematics. Hegel says on this point,

Philosophy, inasmuch as it is to be a science, cannot ... borrow its method in this regard from a subordinate science such as mathematics, any more than it can rest content with categorical assurances of inner intuition or make use of reasoning on the basis of external reflection. It can be only the nature of the content which is at work in scientific cognition, inasmuch as it is at the same time its own reflection of the content which itself first fixes and engenders its definition ... This spiritual movement which in its simplicity gives itself its determinateness, and in the latter gives itself its identity with itself, which therefore is the immanent development of the concept, is the absolute method of cognition, and at the same time the immanent soul of the content itself. On this self-constructing path alone, I maintain, is philosophy capable of being an objective, demonstrated, science.[29]

This conception of science, defined in terms of the features of 'universality', 'necessity' and 'truth', fell victim to the dynamization of science and was replaced by a new guiding model. This process was also the reason for the separation of philosophy and science, and for the compulsion felt by philosophy to rethink its own position in relation to the new understanding of science.

a. Empiricization

By 'empiricization' is meant the process by which empiricism came to be the defining characteristic of real science: if one disregards the so-called formal sciences, that is, mathematics in a formalistic interpretation, 'science' is synonymous with 'empirical science'. But it is not every experience which is suitable for marking out a type of knowledge as scientific: it must be a matter of *scientific* experience. It is impossible, however, to define what is meant by 'scientific' in this context by reference to examples of science which have to be shown to be such in terms of this notion of experience. Thus it is not science itself, in the sense of a system of assertions or an aggregate of knowledge, which makes it possible to qualify the experience as scientific; only the procedure for acquiring and testing knowledge, a procedure which is already understood as scientific, can achieve this. The essence of this procedure is research, and science characterized procedurally in this sense is fundamentally *research-science*. A characterization of science in such procedural terms is itself unavoidable when the direction of definition changes and it is no longer science which qualifies an experience as scientific but experience itself which is seen as the criterion of science.

What this implies may be seen in Hegel's remarks on the relation between nature-philosophy and natural science:

Not only must philosophy be in accord with the empirical study of nature; empirical physics is a presupposition and condition for the establishment and formation of philosophical science. But the process of establishing and preparing a science is one thing, the science itself is something else: the former can no longer be seen as a foundation in the latter, since that function is here to be fulfilled rather by the necessity of the concept. It has already been mentioned that, apart from the fact that the object is to be specified in accordance with the definition of its concept in the philosophical process, the empirical phenomenon corresponding to it is also to be named, and it must be demonstrated that the latter in fact corresponds to the former. Nevertheless, in relation to the necessity of the content, this does not involve any appeal to experience.[30]

The empirical is here seen as the genetic source of science, with which it must remain in accord; but the 'foundation' of science, according to Hegel, is the 'necessity of the concept' or of the 'content', which is explained in the *Science of Logic*, and it is to *this*, not to experience, that appeal must be made in science. On the other hand, it has to be demonstrated that the empirical phenomenon is in accord with the concept, not vice versa.

Nature-philosophy takes the material which physics prepares for it on the basis of experience to the point to which physics has brought it, and transforms it without basing itself on experience as the ultimate confirmation; physics must thus work to assist philosophy, so that the latter may bring the rational universal thus transmitted to her to the level of the concept by showing how it is derived from the concept as a totality which is in itself necessary . . . Since the method of physics does not satisfy the concept, an advance is made beyond it.[31]

The unwillingness of the physicists to fulfil the role of assistants to philosophy assigned to them by Hegel is not a mere fact in the sociology of science: its significance from the point of view of the theory of science is that 'the concept' or the 'necessity of the content' were no longer accepted as criteria of the scientific character of scientific experience. If it is the procedural rules recognized by empirical physicists themselves which define what is scientific about science, there is equally no longer any necessity to transcend physics for the sake of the 'scientific knowledge of truth' and to pursue nature-philosophy. The positions which Hegel takes up in relation to Kepler and Newton, to the theory of colours or the theory of evolution, as well as his numerous attempts to define natural phenomena, may look at first sight like evidence of empirical error or ignorance, but in reality they demonstrate dissent from the empirical natural sciences on the level of conceptual foundations. What Hegel refers to as merely the 'rational universal' is, from the point of view of the natural scientists, concept and theory enough: the Hegelian 'concept' on the other hand is bound to appear to them as a dispensable and unscientific fiction.

Hegel's position on the relation of theory and empirical observation may appear shocking to us today: in fact he was simply playing variations on certain traditional themes which had been part of the common property of the theory of science since Aristotle. Science and experience were regarded as totally different, and even if science arises for human beings from experience, as Aristotle taught, nevertheless experience cannot itself become science. Science is knowledge of what is universal and necessary, experience is knowledge of what is particular and contingent: there is no science of the singular.[32] How then is science to be able to appeal to experience? Is not 'empirical science' a *contradictio in adjecto*? Even Kant is in this regard closer to Hegel than is commonly assumed: 'Only that whose certainty is apodictic can be called genuine science; knowledge which is capable of merely empirical certainty is only so called in an improper sense.' It follows that there can be a natural science in the strict sense of the word only 'if the natural laws which are its basis are known a priori, and are not merely empirical laws'. Everything else is only 'natural science improperly so called'.[33] Thus Kant too reduces what seems to the modern understanding of science to be the best element in science – empirical knowledge – to 'knowledge which is only improperly so called'. The rediscovery of Kant in the nineteenth century was in his role as an 'epistemologist', not as the author of the *Metaphysical Principles of Natural Science*. His apriorism, which was distinguished from Hegel's position in essence only by the fact that the latter substituted the 'science of logic' for mathematics, was later regarded as refuted by non-Euclidean geometry, by logicism in mathematics and by the theory of relativity.

From the point of view of the theory of science, the idea that experience was the criterion of science and the awkward notion of 'empirical science' as a guiding model signified the breakthrough of empiricism, which became a leading doctrine in Germany only after Hegel. At first, its principal advocates were natural scientists, not professional philosophers, who, in so far as they were not Hegelians, continued to be marked by German Idealism to the extent that they regarded empiricism in general as a subordinate philosophical position: altogether it was not refined enough for cultivated people.[34] In the Germany of the nineteenth and twentieth centuries, empiricism has been a philosophy for natural scientists; in this form it has since Comte also been called positivism, and it is only in the wake of the rise of scientism as a dominant world-view, which was accelerated by the crisis of historicism, that it has also become a part of general culture.[35] At first it was the inductivist version of empiricist thought which held the field: an important part in this was played by the influence of John Stuart Mill's logic.[36] 'Inductive' became the key-word of post-Idealist philosophy and science; 'inductive science' was regarded as the science of reality *tout court*, and philosophy attempted to assimilate it to itself as 'inductive metaphysics'.[37] From the point of view of inductivism, the Kantian a priori, along with all concepts, law-statements and theories, was the result of empirical generalization; its chief proponent in the theory of science was at first Heinrich von Helmholtz (1821–94), whose numerous addresses were widely read, and whose almost unassailable authority as a famous natural scientist enormously increased their influence. For him, 'true science is . . . nothing but a methodically and deliberately completed and purified experience'. 'Completion' refers to the inductive inferences, 'purification' to experiment. In its logically precisified and experimentally disciplined form, inductivism has become, even in Germany, the dominant ideology of the natural sciences and of the scientific consciousness which takes its direction from them.

The deductivist version of empiricism, which in England was principally advocated by Whewell in opposition to Mill, has on the other hand found far fewer supporters: the most prominent of them was Heinrich Hertz (1857–94), who says in the Preface to his *Prinzipien der Mechanik* (Principles of Mechanics) (1894):

It is the next, and in a certain sense the most important, task of our conscious knowledge of nature to enable us to predict future experiences, so that we can organize our present action in accordance with this prediction ... The procedure which we constantly make use of in order to derive the desired prediction, however, is this: we make for ourselves inner phantoms or symbols of the external objects, and we make them of such a kind that the necessary consequences in thought of the images are always in turn the images of the necessary consequences in nature of the objects thus depicted.[38]

If it is possible to make the necessary consequences in thought coincide with those in nature, then prognosis is also possible, and the aim of science is achieved. The influence of this model on Wittgenstein's picture theory is well known; its influence on Popper is much more indirect.[39] The a priori and the universal in science, on this view, is an interconnected system of hypotheses: its significance for the system of propositions called 'science' is that it has a *hypothetico*-deductive structure, rather than the categorico-deductive structure attributed to it in the classical model.

Empirical science on the empiricist interpretation generally implies the elimination of metaphysics, to the extent that 'metaphysics' is taken to mean, as in Kant, synthetic knowledge which is independent of experience. At first, this was directed only against Idealism, but around the middle of the century, as a result of the debate about materialism, the alleged natural ally of the empirical sciences, materialism, also came under the cross-fire of criticism: it too was felt to be suspect on the grounds of being metaphysical. What is correct in this is that our empirical dealings with nature tell us nothing about its 'inside', about its essence in itself: the universal can only ever be a result of our generalizations or a partially confirmed hypothesis, so that assertions about the essence of nature are necessarily ruled out. The exclusion of metaphysics from natural science thus necessarily leads to the rejection of essentialism (as Popper argues) and to de-ontologization: what matter is itself becomes a problem for empirical science. Consequently, materialism cannot any longer be defended as a metaphysic, and it is thus presented in Lenin essentially as a theory of knowledge: in this way he too takes part in the rehabilitation of philosophy as theory of knowledge (see Ch. 3, Sect. 3. iv). De-ontologization, however, means first that physics confines itself strictly to what is given, and what is given are phenomena, which it is a matter of describing. De-ontologization means, secondly, that all concepts of essence and substance, and even the concept of force, are eliminated from science, and that the only concepts which are used are those which make it possible to express *functional* connexions between the given. (Ernst Cassirer has given an account of this change in his classical work *Substanzbegriff und Funktionsbegriff* (Substance and Function) of 1910.) As a result of this de-ontologization, a post-materialist, indeed a post-mechanist, interpretation of physics came to prevail in Germany, which can be called a descriptivist or *phenomenological*[40] view. According to this view, physics consists in nothing but the most precise description possible of the observable phenomena, in which the so-called laws of nature have as their only function to make descriptive economy possible. This idea was then elaborated by Ernst Mach and Richard Avenarius into a principle of intellectual economy.[41] According to Aristotle, science consists in the knowledge of the causes and grounds of what exists; for consistent empiricists, however, such causes and grounds are mere constructions on the basis of what is empirically given: like the laws of nature, they are results of our formulations of the connexions between phenomena which we have observed and not such that they can legitimately be projected into the 'inside' of nature itself. Thus it seems plausible to give a descriptive interpretation of the laws of nature themselves and to conceive of explanation as a particular mode of description. In Ernst Mach (1833–1916) the last remnants of metaphysics in Helmholtz' mechanistic picture of nature were eliminated, and as a result the fundamental role of mechanics in the construction of physics necessarily came to seem a mere 'prejudice'. The phenomenological interpretation of physics, furthermore, was also irreconcilable with the atomic theory; in the famous debate about atomism, in which Ludwig Boltzmann and Max Planck took the opposing side, Mach and others continually attempted to represent atoms as the outcome of a reification of concepts formed for reasons of intellectual economy and the atomic theory as a mere superstition. It was only the indirect experimental support for atomic physics which decided the debate in favour of the atomists.[42] The phenomenological interpretation of physics, without which, for instance, the formulation of the theory of relativity would have been inconceivable, is also important for the history of philosophy because its ideal of science furnished the model for Edmund Husserl's notion of his phenomenology as 'philosophy as a strict science'.[43]

The empiricization of science, however, means above all a dynamization of science: it was not simply a reaction to the explosive growth of empirical knowledge, but gave a significant impetus to this growth itself. If theory is no longer itself the criterion of scientific status, as it still was in Hegel, but on the contrary theories must be measured against the standards of empirical method, now the criterion of scientific status, then this implies the primacy of experience over theory: one is then ready to give preference to experience and in the light of it to revise or abandon theories, since they are, in the empiricist conception, merely results of our systematization of experience. Thus seen, theories are simply intermediate stages on the way to knowledge, on which further progress can be made only by means of experience. The principle of 'experience' thus means a succession of new experiences, and the systematizations must accordingly be constantly subject to revision and supersession: only in this way do they present no obstacle to the new. Innovation thus also comes to be an internal principle of science, since the rules which give its identity to a procedurally defined research-science are themselves essentially rules for innovation. This is also the explanation of the remarkable tendency to give priority in science to asking questions rather than answering them, to which Plessner referred, and in general of the philosophical passion for questioning which was such a particular feature of Heidegger's philosophy. In processes of permanent innovation, what is really important is the innovating, not the outcome, which will anyway soon be superseded: what is valuable is what takes us a step forward, not what allows us to mark time. With empiricization, the modern understanding of science takes its leave of the traditional static ideal of system: the systematization of knowledge is certainly unavoidable, but it is of subordinate significance for a science which is now conceived of as a process.

b. *Temporalization*

The dynamization of science under empiricist auspices, which makes it appear as an innovatory process of research, brings the factor of time into play: science, seen as a totality which is constantly growing and changing as a result of experience, can only be an open system of knowledge, opened to the future. Until well into the eighteenth century, science was regarded as a stationary system of established truths, and innovation was thought of as antipathetic to science in tendency. Hegel still vehemently attacked all attempts to associate the predicates 'old' or 'new', or in general any temporal points of view, with truth. Truth is the permanent and the only thing which it is possible to think of in temporal terms seems to be our awareness of the truth, which is not to be regarded as knowledge simply because it is familiar.[44] Nevertheless, in Hegel himself the temporalization of science was already much further advanced than his extremely traditional argument on this point would lead one to suppose. Whereas Kant, in the concluding section of the *Critique of Pure Reason* entitled 'The History of Reason', instantly turns aside to typological and unhistorical considerations, for Hegel the history of philosophy is the history of thought about the Absolute, which is bound up with the self-unfolding of the Absolute *in* history:[45] it is thus not simply a subjective cultural history or history of knowledge of a truth which is established in itself. The sentence, 'As far as the individual is concerned, everyone is anyway a son of his time: in the same way, philosophy is its time comprehended in thought'[46] has quite a historicist ring. Nevertheless, the Hegelian system has been accused time and time again of insufficient attention to temporality. Its claim to final validity and the assertion that, with it, philosophy has really achieved its goal, 'to be able to lay down its name of the love of knowledge and to be actual knowledge', has been rejected as outmoded *hybris*.[47]

On the other hand, Wilhelm von Humboldt already says in one of the memoranda on educational policy which he wrote at the time of the foundation of the University of Berlin, 'that in the internal organization of the higher scientific institutions everything depends on upholding the principle that science should be treated as something which has not yet been entirely discovered and which will never be entirely discovered, and on unremittingly pursuing it as such'.[48] What it was already possible to say here against Hegel expresses the modern ethos of temporalized science, characterized as it is by the 'yearning for the spurious infinite'.[49] The singular term 'science' is retained; the idea of system is not simply abandoned in favour of process or procedure. The temporalization of the idea of truth anyway creates its own difficulties, since it is no longer possible to distinguish between what is true and what seems true to someone at a particular time. Thus a compromise is reached between statics and dynamics: following the Kantian model, science as a system of true judgments about the world becomes a regulative Idea.[50] The concept of science as a system is thus projected into the future, and is no longer a concept which is constitutive of the reality of science in the present. Science in this sense is not a possession, but something towards which we aspire, an object of constant effort, a sublime aim before us which we all serve. The present of science, on the other hand, is merely a stage *en route*, merely a matter of exertion, of action in accordance with rules which guarantee progress. Anyone who sees matters differently is *unscientific*. Thus the cogent arguments which Hegel advanced against this view no longer find an audience. The thesis that science is something 'which will never be entirely discovered' was interpreted by him as a symptom of the 'fear of the truth' and as obtuseness on the part of the finite understanding,[51] but this too was discredited along with Absolute Idealism.

With temporalization, the modern world's experiences of time have taken over even science. 'Process', 'acceleration', 'replacement of cyclical by progressive thought' and so forth – these are certainly the catchwords by which the idea of progress has passed beyond even the present. Progress is not any longer, as it still was in the Enlightenment models of history, progress towards the present or, as in Marx, towards a conceivable future – for that would still be a kind of present. Progress stretches into an indeterminate future, of which we are nevertheless supposed to have a determinate conception in the regulative Idea. If Goethe permitted himself a certain irony at the expense of Wagner, a believer in science, in his *dictum*, 'And how marvellously far we have gone by now', he also caused his audience at the same time to reflect on how far we have actually come at present. Despite this difficulty, scientific progress was regarded, until Popper, as a great process of induction, in which we gradually approximate to 'the' truth or to the system of true knowledge.[52] The connexion with the inductivist ideology of empiricism is here unmistakable: even if the deductivists give a different interpretation to the individual steps on the 'long march' to truth, the process of knowledge as a whole is conceived of on the model of inductive generalization. On the side of the subject of science, there corresponds to this the replacement of the scholar by the researcher, who 'strives in constant aspiration' and has made the 'yearning for the spurious infinite' into his fundamental ethical attitude. This passion breaks down when even the lofty goal of 'truth' or 'knowledge' falls victim to the elimination of metaphysics. It is suggested that what has anyway, as a result of temporalization, been postponed to an indeterminate future should be exposed as an error which is nevertheless necessary for life or as a fiction.[53] It is not necessary to dispute that it has an important function, in promoting the needs of life and in motivating, but, as for what it is independently of this function, there is nothing more to be said on that score once it has been exposed in this way. Hence, in the theory of science, too, it is equally possible to make the transition to a purely functional characterization of science: science then ceases to be a system of truths or of knowledge, and becomes a system of actions and interactions, which has a definite function to fulfil in the life-process of the human species and which must be assessed in terms of its fulfilment of such functional demands. Truth – even as an 'aim' – then becomes the ultimate myth.

It is important, however, that the temporalization of science also encroaches on its *object*-domain. The empirical pressures felt by the sciences around 1800 as a result of the explosion of knowledge forced them to shift from the inadequate spatial organizational models of the tradition into temporal ones: what was incomprehensible in terms of spatial juxtaposition was organized in terms of temporal succession. This is a convincing explanation for the gradual growth in attractiveness of evolutionary models in natural science, which were not at all unusual, but suddenly became fashionable, and at a date long before Darwin. They were anyway by no means concerned only with the biosphere, like Lamarck's theory; Kant's 'Universal Natural History and Theory of the Heavens' of 1755 was already attempting to offer a scientifically temporalized cosmogony, though one which admittedly still accepted the natural understanding of time found in Newtonian physics. In modern evolutionary theory, by contrast, time is historicized: it is no longer absolutely uniform, but something which is full of vicissitudes, contingently determined and elapsing in various ways – natural history has become the history of nature. When Hegel objected to the very possibility of a theory of evolution on grounds of principle, and when Droysen attempted to reserve the idea of development for the historical world, these were rearguard actions, seeking to keep science at a particular stage of temporalization: the temporalization of philosophy itself has passed that by.

3 Philosophy and science

The dynamization of the traditional conception of science is the most important aspect of the structural change in science after German Idealism: this change can be interpreted in the context of the change in the social function of science, but cannot be derived from that alone. In this process, science was constituted as research-science, that is, as empirical science, to which the formalistic interpretation of the non-empirical disciplines exactly corresponds. It became an open and changeable system of knowledge, indeed one committed to change, in which systematization was subordinated to the ideal of innovation. It was a totality, the identity of which came principally from rules of procedure and standards of testing – which meant that the ideal of system, so long accepted as a regulative Idea, became increasingly dispensable. Finally, it was a system of actions and interactions, whose output, after the rejection of the ideal of system, was to be assessed primarily in terms of its functional achievements for the life of the species and no longer in terms of its degree of approximation to 'the' truth.

These functional and structural changes in science presented philosophy after Hegel with a variety of problems. On the way from 'culture through science' to 'science as a vocation' it had to be on the lookout for new functions, but this affected it, seeing that philosophy in Germany was essentially an academic business within the framework of the Humboldt-University, only on the periphery; the great privateers – Schopenhauer, Kierkegaard, Nietzsche, Marx and Engels –remained the exception, although they were the original thinkers. More important was the general structural change in science which led from a propositionally defined systematic conception of science to a procedurally defined conception of science as research. Philosophy had no active interest in it – which was made clear by the fact that professional philosophers, up until our own century, held firm to the model of science as a system[54] and left it to philosophically inclined natural scientists to formulate the conception of science appropriate to the new understanding of science as research. Thus the history of philosophy in the century of science is in essence a history of philosophical reactions to what was happening in science and in connexion with science in a changed culture. Although Idealistic systematic thought by no means suddenly ended with Hegel's death, as the phrase 'the collapse of Idealism' suggests, but continued for a long time to maintain its own traditions in the form of late Idealism and speculative theism, philosophical activity was forced more and more to take the form of such reactions – not least because of the increasing contempt for philosophy, laments over which became commonplace amongst philosophers from the beginning of the nineteenth century onwards.[55] However, whereas Hegel sought to attribute it to the influence of the Romantics, it became clear later on that it was the perspectives of the new understanding of science which suggested all the talk of the 'poverty of philosophy' (in Marx's phrase). Its seeming inability any longer to compete with science, together with the objections against it in the name of science, intensified the identity-crisis of philosophy already referred to, from which philosophers sought very different ways of escape. In what follows, I shall offer only a very schematic survey of the various attempts which were made to overcome this identity-crisis.

Four sorts of attempt of this kind may be distinguished. First, philosophy may seek to assimilate itself to science and to find a place in the spectrum of recognized research-sciences: it concentrates on historical and hermeneutical research and defines itself as a *Geisteswissenschaft* (human science). A second way leads to the recognition of science itself as the philosophy of the age: the result is scientism in a different form. A third type involves rejection of the traditional model of philosophy and the redefinition of philosophy as critique, which also comes to include a fundamental critique of philosophy. Fourthly, and finally, it is worth glancing at the various attempts to rehabilitate philosophy by finding a new foundation for its tasks and methods. All four methods of dealing with the identity-crisis of philosophy after Hegel still continue, even now, to influence the controversial self-image of philosophers.

i. *Philosophy as a science*

The decline of Idealistic systematic thought after Hegel is detectable in the increasing incongruity between the constantly rising number of philosophical systems on offer, on the one hand, and the claims to scientific character and validity which each of these systems made for itself, on the other. The belief held, up until our own century, by every occupant of a philosophical Chair, that he had to produce a philosophical system was more and more clearly in conflict with what was regarded as scientific in the sciences: namely, that one should apply oneself in common with others and by means of discussion to advancing programmes of research. There is not much of that to be observed in philosophy: it has for a long time remained an interpretative discipline, closely bound up with individual personalities, in which one takes one's bearings by reference to proper names – X's system, Y's philosophy, Z's pupils and so on. Certainly, there are partisan disputes and leaders of schools in other disciplines too, but nowhere is this so marked as in philosophy. It is only after the drive to be more scientific which set in in the train of the 'rehabilitation of philosophy' that it is easier than before to associate philosophers with different tendencies. The existence of philosophy in the form of personal systems claiming to be able to provide a total interpretation of reality is, however, diametrically opposed to the current understanding of science. This even finds terminological expression in the concept of a 'world-view', which always presupposes a 'standpoint' from which one views the world. Talk of 'world-views' came into fashion as a consequence of historical relativism and perspectivism: in interpreting philosophy in general as a world-view and projecting this back on to the philosophy of the past, all claims to scientific status for philosophy were in fact being renounced. World-views simply serve the subjective needs of an individual or a group for orientation, and they are as incomparable with each other as the standpoints of their adherents at any given time. Science, however, is by contrast an intersubjective enterprise.

The privatization of systematic thought in the conception of philosophy as a world-view was accompanied, however, by a contrary tendency which can be called the historicization of philosophy. The first decades after Hegel's death saw a boom in the history of philosophy, initiated by Hegel himself, and it can be said that the work that was done on the history of philosophy represents the greatest achievement of academic philosophy, at least until the end of the nineteenth century. It is generally overlooked that the most important of these historians – Eduard Zeller, J. E. Erdmann, Kuno Fischer[56] – themselves advocated definite systematic positions in philosophy, and did not wish by any means to be merely historians; their positions are nowadays forgotten in the same way as those of the late Idealists who did not follow the trend towards the history of philosophy. It is also important that these great historians of philosophy still proceed in their histories absolutely on the basis of Hegelian ideas of an immanently teleological development in philosophy, but that they increasingly reinterpret this in an empirical historical sense and thus come closer to the historicist understanding of history. The essential point is this: as the history of philosophy, philosophy took part in the development of the Hegelian philosophy of spirit into a *Geisteswissenschaft*, a science of the spirit or human science, and came to conceive of *itself*, to the extent that it saw itself in *scientific* terms, as a *Geisteswissenschaft*. And this had a successful outcome, for in the domain of the history of philosophy it can regard itself also as a research-science, and even the effect of scientific intersubjectivity is produced, since the very same methods are used in this field as in the successful science of history. Debate about the world-view which one may happen to hold at a particular time is bound to be difficult: but there is some prospect of a successful outcome when it is a matter of the fate of Spinoza or the prehistory of the *Critique of Pure Reason*. The attempt to find a way out of the identity-crisis into which it had fallen after Hegel by turning philosophy into a science using the methods of the *Geisteswissenschaften* is a process which even today still influences academic philosophical teaching and discussion: in Germany there is even a *Zeitschrift für philosophische Forschung* – a 'Journal of Philosophical Research'. If it is also true that nowadays historicization is no longer in the foreground, that is because in the meantime a process of philologization has been superimposed on it: it is widely believed today that a basis for the scientific status of philosophy can be found in the scientific, interpretative 'processing' of texts.

Another aspect of the historicization of philosophy is indicated by the numerous revivals of past systems. Many philosophers who do not want to be merely historians of philosophy refer back, in a form of practical renunciation of the traditional ideas of progress which at first still influenced the writing of historians of philosophy, to older philosophers, and in this way give some stability to their own position: they become neo-Aristotelians, neo-Thomists, neo-Leibnizians, neo-Kantians, neo-Fichteans, neo-Hegelians, neo-Marxists.[57] In this list, neo-Thomism and neo-Marxism, because of their close institutional ties with the Catholic Church and the labour movement respectively, reveal very markedly some of the features of world-views. There are almost no historical philosophers who have not been posthumously honoured with a revival, always following the pattern, 'Thus we must go back to X'.[58] There is a neo-Friesian school, but also a neo-Wolffian,[59] not to mention all the implicit references which are not made manifest in the name of current positions: such as 'Immanence positivism',[60] which bases itself on Hume as opposed to Kant, or the philosophy of existence, which rediscovered Kierkegaard. Mention should also be made here of life-philosophy and vitalism, in which there is a revival of Romantic nature-philosophy (see Ch. 3, n. 25). These renaissances are a phenomenon which in the scientific domain is to be found almost only in the field of philosophy, but otherwise is principally confined to the arts, which went through their historicist phase at the same time. This indicates how precarious philosophy's conception of itself as a science had come to be: whereas the sciences were taking their bearings as research-sciences by a unilinear model of progress, philosophers saw their own history as offering an almost inexhaustible reservoir of possible world-views which one could, according to one's standpoint, take over and develop further. The affinity with art in the historicist period, to which, likewise, all art-forms and stylistic principles seemed to have become available, confirms, even from the point of view of content, what the word 'world-view' suggests: the aestheticization of philosophy, as a counterweight to its tendency to become more scientific. Some philosophers even explicitly carried through the artistic analogy.

ii. *Science as philosophy*

A second sort of attempt to overcome the philosophical identity-crisis comes close to what can be called, in Freud's terminology, 'identification with the aggressor'. Philosophy deserts to the very power which is threatening its identity – science. This process can happen in various ways. At its simplest, it is a matter of spreading the word that existing science itself satisfies all philosophical requirements: this can be called scientism. A second, less radical, way is to reinterpret philosophical questions, the legitimacy of which is fully acknowledged, as logical problems or problems of empirical science: philosophy may then live a limited life of its own for as long as this reinterpretation is not yet fully achieved. In this case, scientism is only a regulative Idea. A third possible way of escaping from the philosophical identity-crisis by means of science consists in accepting an established special science as a leading science and subordinating oneself to its methodology and its standards.

The most important example in this period of a consistent scientism is the materialism of Büchner, Vogt and Moleschott, whose names, since Marx and Engels, have always been linked together. This form of materialism, also referred to abusively as 'vulgar materialism', differs from Feuerbach's anthropological materialism and the historical materialism of Marx and Engels in that it simply identifies the natural sciences with science, *qua* empirical science, and takes 'philosophy' to mean nothing but their theoretical or 'thinking' part. Thus, Jacob Moleschott says, 'Philosophy must be absorbed in experience, experience in philosophy.'[61] This form of materialism can also be called *mechanical* materialism, since it is convinced of the practicability of mechanism, that is, of the reduction of all natural forces to inertia and motion. This mechanical materialism appeared in the context of the realist movement in culture, which was formed around the middle of the century as a reaction against Humboldtian neo-humanism and the idealistic cultural ideals of the Age of Goethe, with the claim to offer a comprehensive world-view on the basis of the most advanced science. This is also the explanation of its unexampled success: Ludwig Büchner's book *Kraft und Stoff* (Force and Matter), in particular, appeared in numerous editions and was widely read, especially in petty bourgeois and proletarian circles. This also explains to some extent the extremely intense campaign which Marx and Engels conducted against 'vulgar materialism'. Other tendencies, however, also fed on the fascination exercised by the claim to satisfy all the requirements of a philosophy or a world-view in the guise of popularized science. Mention should once again be made here of Ostwald's *energetism*, which prided itself indeed on having 'overcome' materialism,[62] but which otherwise followed the same pattern as it. A further variant is the view which emerged in the case of Ernst Haeckel as a result of the influence of Darwinism. The scientific theory of evolution was built up by him into a solution of the 'riddle of the world' (*Welträtsel*),[63] and the book of that name was at least as widely read as Büchner's *Kraft und Stoff*. If the latter was the 'Bible' of materialism, Haeckel's *Welträtsel* was the 'Bible' of the freethinkers or of those who were called in the Nazi period, paradoxically enough, *gottgläubig* (believers in a god) and were recognized as a 'third confession' alongside Catholics and Evangelicals. This phenomenon of the formation of sects, which is so incompatible with the idea of science, is in itself sufficient demonstration that the project of a 'scientific world-view'[64] failed to provide a substitute for traditional philosophy.

The other strategy for resolving the philosophical identity-crisis, which consisted in recognizing philosophical problems, but reinterpreting them as problems for the special sciences, can be illustrated by numerous examples taken from the whole of this period. Ludwig Feuerbach was already saying, 'The new philosophy makes man, along with nature as the basis of man, into the one and only universal and highest object of philosophy: anthropology, including physiology, becomes the universal science.'[65] Very much in the Feuerbachian sense, Marx and Engels, in a passage later omitted, discuss the elevation of history into the universal science.[66] The young Marx envisaged a unity of natural science and the science of man, and thought that it was in that area that one should look for the 'solved riddle of history'.[67] In the *German Ideology*, the point was made with lapidary conciseness:

> Where speculation ceases, in real life, there begins, therefore, real, positive science, the description of practical activity, of the practical process of human development. The phrases of consciousness cease, real knowledge must take their place. An independent philosophy loses its medium of existence once reality is described. In its place there can be at most a synthesis of the most general results which can be abstracted from the consideration of the historical development of man. These abstractions in themselves, divorced from real history, have absolutely no value. They can serve only to facilitate the ordering of the historical material and to indicate the sequence of its individual strata. But they in no way furnish, like philosophy, a recipe or schema according to which the epochs of history can be arranged.[68]

From this to a 'philosophy' of Marxism–Leninism, presented as a proletarian world-view and as the ideology of the working class, is a long way.

The reinterpretation of epistemological questions in terms of the physiology of perception, which was inspired above all by the investigations of Johannes von Müller, will be discussed in the section on the 'Rehabilitation of philosophy'. It seemed to provide empirical corroboration of the Schopenhauerian interpretation of the Kantian doctrine, and had that effect – principally via Friedrich Albert Lange – on Nietzsche, whose 'psychological' analyses of the problems of knowledge and value are absolutely full of the anti-philosophical fervour of the modern scientific mind.

> The whole of psychology has so far remained stuck in moral prejudices and apprehensions: it has not ventured into the depths. To conceive in the same way as I have the morphology and theory of development of the will to power – this is something to which no one has yet come near, even in his thoughts: . . . Never yet has a profounder world of insight been disclosed to bold travellers and adventurers: and the psychologist . . . will be entitled at least to demand that psychology be again acknowledged as the queen of the sciences, for whose service, and to prepare the way for which, the other sciences exist. For psychology is now once more the way to the fundamental problems.[69]

Mention should also be made here of the idea that it is possible to purge philosophy by logical means of scientifically insoluble problems: this became the basis of the 'scientific conception of the world' of the Vienna Circle. The idea of 'overcoming metaphysics by means of a logical analysis of language', to employ the title of an essay by Rudolf Carnap, is certainly not a conception which originated from the German-speaking tradition, but it corresponds completely to the model of the transformation of philosophical questions into problems for the special sciences – in this case, mathematical logic. These and many other examples of fruitful reinterpretations of philosophical problems as questions for the special sciences constantly nourished the general sense of optimism of the period that in the long run philosophy could be replaced by science. This was also in accord with the interpretation of philosophy itself as a stage in the history of science that had now become obsolete, or with the more moderate recognition of philosophy as a reservoir of questions which could at some time in the future be made scientific and so solved.[70]

The third way of restabilizing philosophy as a science to be discussed here is less radical than the second, since in this case all ideas of reinterpreting philosophical questions as problems in the special sciences are abandoned; nevertheless, the foundations of philosophical theories are sought in the domain of a special science. Such positions are designated, usually critically, by naming some discipline and giving it the suffix '-ism': psychologism, sociologism, biologism, etc. Psychologism in logic, according to which the structure and validity of the principles of logic are based on the organization of the human psyche, can be regarded as the standard opinion of philosophers from the middle of the last century up until well into our own: Gottlob Frege and Edmund Husserl were fairly isolated in their campaign against it.[71] This even found institutional expression in the large number of double Chairs of 'Philosophy and Psychology', which continued to exist until the thirties.[72] A variant of psychologism is the thesis that psychology is the basis of all human sciences, and so of philosophy also. This conviction goes back as far as Voltaire, but became established in Germany as a general view only as a result of the influence of Mill's logic, and was then defended by Wilhelm Wundt as well as by Wilhelm Dilthey and Georg Simmel. Here, too, Edmund Husserl, with his conception of pure phenomenology, is the great figure on the other side with whose work Max Scheler and Martin Heidegger were associated in the final suppression of psychologism.[73]

Examples of sociologism are mostly to be found in the field of practical philosophy. The notion which has arisen above all in the neo-Marxism of our own century, and which is still occasionally put forward today, that philosophy after Hegel has become, as a result of the work of Marx and Engels, social theory has a long previous history. The best-known parts of this are the discussions in the course of the so-called 'revisionism debate' in the Second International, in which Karl Kautsky chiefly defended the thesis that the supplementation of Marxist theory by an ethic demanded by the neo-Kantian socialists was not necessary because 'scientific socialism', as a theory of proletarian revolution, could give a satisfactory answer to all questions about the right way to act: such a reduction of ethics to social theory must be described as 'sociologistic'. In contrast with dialectical materialism, as conceived of above all by Friedrich Engels and Lenin, which fully acknowledged the legitimacy of philosophy, neo-Marxism tends, like the young Marx, to whom it attaches itself, in general to interpret the rational core of all philosophy in terms of social theory. It certainly has to be said in addition that the type of social theory of which so much was expected in this case is looked on by modern sociologists as 'mere philosophy'. Another example of sociologism is the sociology of knowledge, to the extent that it combines philosophical pretensions with its analyses and explanations; its original was the famous notion of basis and superstructure to be found in Marx and Engels, which it reinterpreted, looking in the case of every form of knowledge and every philosophical position for the social form to which it could be attributed in explanation.

Finally, biologism – the philosophical position which regards biology as the leading science – has developed very different forms in Germany: nevertheless, its influence was so great that Helmuth Plessner could speak of the 'hour of authoritarian biology'.[74] From the physiological foundation for epistemology in Schopenhauer and the first neo-Kantians, already referred to, to a purely biological basis is only a step, and it was explicitly taken by, for instance, Richard Avenarius, the co-founder (with Ernst Mach) of 'empirio-criticism': the title of his major work is *Philosophie als Denken der Welt gemäss dem Prinzip des kleinsten Kraftmasses*, that is, 'philosophy as thought of the world according to the principle of the smallest unit of energy', where the 'principle of the smallest unit of energy' is intended to be taken purely in the sense of energetics as a natural science. This is the difference between Avenarius and Mach, who, despite numerous biological examples in his works, interpreted the principle of 'intellectual economy' in a conventionalistic rather than a biologistic sense. Large parts of life-philosophy are also biologistic: this will be discussed in a special chapter of its own. The way in which biologism was able to become so strong in German philosophy can be explained only by the fact that in Germany the strong influence of Darwin and Darwinism coincided with the crisis of historicism and the 'renunciation of history'. The Idealist and historicist picture of man suddenly came to be regarded as superficial, and it was thought to be 'profound' to seek what was philosophically essential in the physical organization and evolution of the human species. Without this biologism, it would be impossible to understand the history of the influence of Nietzsche in Germany, the extraordinary impact of Oswald Spengler's *Der Untergang des Abendlandes* (The Decline of the West), and above all the 'racial (*völkisch*) realism' and the racial ideology of the Nazi philosophers. Here too there is little to be added to Helmuth Plessner's analyses.

iii. *Philosophy as critique*

The identity-crisis of philosophy after Hegel was also manifested in the fact that, after 1830, the critique of philosophy in general came to be a philosophical topic. In this way, the philosophers made the doubts of outsiders about their subject's right to exist into their own business, and this had the consequence that the internalized critique of philosophy led to a redefinition of philosophy as critique. The general sentence of death on philosophy as an independent field of knowledge was accepted, and it was believed possible to retain the spirit of philosophy only in the form of a critique. This type of attempt to overcome the crisis in philosophy also took many forms. The most important, immediately after Hegel's death, was that of Young- or Left-Hegelianism. In the debate about the position of the philosophy of religion in Hegel's system, there developed a schism amongst Hegel's disciples between Left and Right, which occurred because the 'Left' (D. F. Strauss, Bruno Bauer and others) drew critical consequences from Hegel's philosophy of religion and proceeded to a philosophical critique of Christianity and of religion in general.[75] Ludwig Feuerbach then gave this critique an anthropological twist, as a result of which Idealist philosophy as a whole was itself seen as a form of theology.[76] Marx and Engels then associated themselves with this movement and historicized Feuerbach's critique of religion, with the result that it was transformed into a critique of the existing social relationships on the basis of a critique of political economy.[77] If in the case of D. F. Strauss and Bruno Bauer it is man as a self-conscious being, and in the case of Max Stirner the 'individual', which is the basis for the critique, Feuerbach argues on the basis of the species-being of man, which Marx then interprets historically and economically as the 'ensemble of social relationships'.[78] The common feature of all the Young-Hegelians is that they consider philosophy to have been completed by Hegel's system; in this respect they remain Hegelians – a philosophical advance beyond Hegel is inconceivable. What remains to be done is to realize what in Hegel's philosophy was only thought, and according to them it *must* be realized, since the Absolute which is merely thought is the true in the form of untruth: it is only practical transference into reality which gives the true a true form. The Young-Hegelians remain Hegelians, too, in that they conceive of the true as the whole and of truth as a conformity of concept and reality as a whole. Philosophy can assist in the realization of the truth in making us conscious, through its critique, of the untrue status of the true. The foundation of this critique is again Hegelian, namely, the theory of alienation, which refers the alien character of concept and reality, subject and object to a self-alienation of the whole or of the Absolute. Only this theory is again applied to Hegel himself, whose philosophy is also seen as a form of alienation. With the realization of philosophy, therefore, 'the' philosophy will simultaneously come to an end, and as long as this does not happen, philosophy after Hegel has a right to exist only as critique.[79] Since Georg Lukács' *History and Class-Consciousness* of 1923, this idea has been rediscovered as the basis of an unorthodox Marxist philosophy and has been developed above all in the critical theory of Horkheimer, Adorno, Marcuse and others.[80] The Hegelian version of the model of 'philosophy as critique' was essentially a matter of the period before the 1848 revolution, which lost its attractiveness after the defeat of that revolution. In the history of Marxism, too, this was a decisive turning point. As a result of the influence of political economy and the development by Engels and Lenin of Marxist thought into a closed world-view, there emerged 'scientific socialism', in which the dialectical and critical motif of the Young-Hegelians was increasingly lost sight of in favour of an objectivist process-science, which was to be at the same time a revolutionary science. Neo-Marxism, which recalls that motif in its resistance to Marxist orthodoxy, must therefore be understood at the same time as a renaissance of Young-Hegelianism.[81]

The model of 'philosophy as critique' was, however, also popular outside the Hegelian-Marxist tradition. Kierkegaard's critique of Hegel[82] is not the usual sort of internal philosophical confrontation with another system. Rather, it called in question the customary mode of traditional philosophy in general in favour of a new type of existential thought, which claimed to go beyond what had thus far been regarded as philosophy. This further influenced the philosophy of existence of Karl Jaspers, and above all Martin Heidegger, whose philosophical activity essentially took the form of a critique of Western metaphysics: the foundations for this were laid in his *Sein und Zeit* (Being and Time) of 1926, a work which is indebted to the thought of Kierkegaard even for its terminology. Also worthy of mention here is Schopenhauer's critique of 'university philosophy',[83] which likewise totally questions the traditional form of scientific philosophizing and assimilates philosophy to art and to a personal world-view. Friedrich Nietzsche comes in at this point: in his middle phase, his philosophy is simply a matter of a diagnosis, from the point of view of a moral critique and of psychology, of philosophical attitudes and positions.

It has gradually become clear to me what every great philosophy up to now has been: namely, the self-confession of its author and a sort of unintended and unnoticed *mémoires*; likewise, that the moral (or immoral) purposes in every philosophy constituted the true bud of life from which the whole plant has always grown. In fact it is a sound (and clever) move, in explaining how the most abstract metaphysical assertions of a philosopher have really come into being, always to ask oneself first, what moral does it (does he) intend to point? I do not therefore believe that an 'urge to know' is the father of philosophy, but that, here as elsewhere, another urge has made use of knowledge (and of error!) merely as an instrument. But anyone who considers the basic urges of man with a view to seeing how far they may have played their games precisely here as inspiring geniuses (or demons and goblins), will find that they have all formerly inspired philosophy – and that each of them individually would be only too willing to present itself as the ultimate aim of existence and as the legitimate ruler of all other urges. For every urge seeks domination: and as such it seeks to philosophize.[84]

This text can be read as a preface to Nietzsche's later metaphysics of the 'will to power'. The very widespread revival of philosophical Criticism in the Kantian sense also had its part to play in the definition of philosophy as critique.[85] The Criticist conception of philosophy as critique belongs however in the context of the rehabilitation of philosophy, which will be briefly outlined in the next section.

iv. *The rehabilitation of philosophy*

The phrase 'the rehabilitation of philosophy' refers to the essential features of the attempt to allot to philosophy, in a scientific age, a domain of problems which would be independent of the special sciences. In virtue of the work it did on these problems it could present itself as a science, and in this way it could gain a new foundation. Here too we shall have to content ourselves with a very general survey.

The best known form of the rehabilitation of philosophy is a theory of knowledge which first appeared in the fifties of the last century. It was not the work of the academic philosophers of the time, who were historians of philosophy, in so far as they did not set out to be late Idealists or forerunners of one of the numerous revivals. It was natural scientists who were driven by the success of vulgar materialism to reflect on their own activity and the foundations of their discipline. The materialists' thesis, that their system was merely a systematization of the knowledge gained in the natural sciences and thus had finally put an end to the need for philosophy, was energetically disputed, first of all by Justus Liebig, and then chiefly by Hermann Helmholtz. Their criticisms gained publicity as a result of the debate about materialism which broke out in 1854 at the Göttingen Congress of natural scientists and which caused quite a stir. The address given by the physiologist Rudolf Wagner on 'The Creation of Man and the Substance of the Soul' included an attempt to present the results of science as compatible with the teachings of the Church. Carl Vogt took an opposing view in a biting address which he further developed and had published, still in the same year, in the polemical work *Köhlerglaube und Wissenschaft* (Blind Faith and Science). It is here that is to be found the drastic comparison of the relation of thought and brain to that between bile and liver or between urine and kidney, which, like the dictum 'Man is what he eats', became a commonplace of the materialistic literature of the time. The extraordinary dissemination of materialistic ideas, which, as mentioned before, was part of the realistic movement in the culture of the time and was intensified by the fascination with scientism, compelled those natural scientists who did not wish to be materialists to oppose the monopolistic philosophical claims of materialism. At the same time, they refused to recognize the propagandists of the materialist world-view as natural scientists. They attacked not only their dilettantism, but also the impression created by them that science already knew everything and had at its disposal a closed system of knowledge in the natural sciences. In this way they defended natural enquiry and the new understanding of science as based on research against the materialists' nature-philosophy. At the same time, they affirmed the existence of questions which go beyond the bounds of natural science and which can be dealt with only by philosophical thought.

This is what Hermann Helmholtz says in 1855 in his lecture 'Über das Sehen des Menschen' (On Human Sight), on the occasion of the dedication of a Kant memorial, after apologizing for speaking as a natural scientist on a philosophical occasion:

> The natural sciences rest, even now, on the same fundamental principles which they had in Kant's time – those principles of whose fruitful application Newton furnishes the great example; they have simply been more fully developed and have given their basic principles the support of an ever greater wealth of detailed evidence. But philosophy has changed its position in relation to them. Kant's philosophy did not seek to increase the amount of our knowledge by means of pure thought, since its supreme principle was that all knowledge of reality must be derived from experience. Rather, it sought simply to enquire into the sources of our knowledge and the degree of its justification – a concern which will always continue to be that of philosophy and which no age will be able to avoid with impunity.[86]

Helmholtz's reference to the changed position of philosophy in relation to natural science is an allusion to the Idealism of Schelling and Hegel; Hegelianism above all was responsible for the alienation between philosophy and natural science. The last sentence in the quotation, on the other hand, is critically directed against his own age, in which materialism was becoming more and more widespread: this was not the case at the time when in fact the 'sources of our knowledge and the degree of its justification' were the subject of enquiry. Helmholtz then goes on, in the later part of his address, to indicate how this had to happen. For him, it is the theory of human sense-perception which is the point at which natural science and philosophy in the sense indicated make contact with each other. He therefore presents the results of enquiry in the physiology of perception in such a way that they fit in perfectly in the context of Kantian transcendental philosophy. The dependence established by recent physiology of perception (J. von Müller) of the current content of perception on the subjective conditions of perception is expounded by Helmholtz as a philosophical argument against materialistic dogmatism based on the assumption that empirical natural science recognizes the material essence of the world as a 'thing-in-itself'. This physiological reinterpretation of the Kantian critique of reason then became the basis for the older form of neo-Kantianism, which was founded by Friedrich Albert Lange, to some extent under Schopenhauer's influence: Lange made it familiar, above all, in his *Geschichte des Materialismus* (History of Materialism), which appeared from 1866 onwards. Lange taught in Marburg from 1872 to 1875. His successor, Hermann Cohen, by substituting a strictly logical conception of the Kantian programme for the physiological interpretation, then founded the 'Marburg School' of neo-Kantianism, whose great rival came to be, as a result of the work of Wilhelm Windelband and Heinrich Rickert, the 'South-West German School' of neo-Kantianism.

The slogan 'Back to Kant!' is not peculiar to neo-Kantianism: the idea that it is necessary to go back behind the errors of Absolute Idealism and re-establish links with Kant is a commonplace, to be found in Fries, Herbart and their pupils, in Schopenhauer and in many non-Kantians. Disciples of Hegel also took part in the Kantian movement of the nineteenth century: Karl Rosenkranz arranged an edition of Kant from 1838 onwards, and in 1860 there appeared the first edition of the book on Kant by the Hegelian Kuno Fischer, which went through many editions and influenced the general interpretation of Kant until well into our own century. What was specific to neo-Kantianism was the significance which they attributed to the 'critical way' in giving a fresh foundation to philosophy and a definition of its tasks, and this irrespective of *how* they interpreted this critical way – as a method of enquiry in the physiology of perception, in logic, or, as in the case of the 'South-West Germans', in value-theory. The common catchword was supplied by Eduard Zeller in 1862, in his essay, 'Über Bedeutung und Aufgabe der Erkenntnistheorie' (On the significance and task of theory of knowledge). Theory of knowledge, not formal logic or logic in Hegel's sense, was the basic discipline of philosophy, the one which gave it its foundation: 'How we have to proceed in order to obtain correct representations can be judged only in the light of the conditions with which the formation of our representations is bound up by the nature of our mind: theory of knowledge, however, must investigate these conditions and determine in accordance with them whether and under which presuppositions the human mind has the capacity for knowledge of reality'.[87] For Zeller too Kant is the model which is to be followed:

Wherever there is a continuous development, the need arises from time to time to return to the point from which it started, to recall the original problem and to attempt to solve it afresh in the original spirit, if perhaps with other means. Such a moment, however, seems now to have arrived for German philosophy. The beginning of the sequence of development of which our present-day philosophy forms part, however, was Kant, and the scientific achievement by means of which Kant opened up a new road for philosophy was his theory of knowledge. It is to this investigation that everyone who wishes to reform the foundations of our philosophy will return above all; and it is the questions which Kant posed to himself that he will have to investigate in the spirit of his critique, in order that, enriched by the scientific experiences of our century, he may avoid the mistakes which Kant made.[88]

Neo-Kantianism in all its many varieties (a historian of philosophy distinguishes the physiological, metaphysical, realist, logicist-methodological, value-theoretical, psychological and relativistic versions) rehabilitated philosophy as a whole in the form of theory of knowledge by attributing to this discipline the function of a basis for philosophy and science. The later objection that neo-Kantianism had reduced philosophy to theory of knowledge is on the whole unfair and was rejected by many neo-Kantians themselves.[89] In fact there are to be found in their works also discussions of ethics, aesthetics and philosophy of religion. The debate over revisionism in the labour movement was led on the revisionist side by neo-Kantians. For the rest, it can be shown that the objection on the grounds of reductionism was itself very partisan and was made chiefly from the side of the 'new metaphysics' (see Ch. 7). Nevertheless, this rehabilitation was not a monopoly of the neo-Kantians: the great opposing movement of positivism in its various forms[90] also played a part, and even those who opposed the epistemological orientation in philosophy had to respect this precedent in that they were compelled to preface their discussions with epistemological reflections if they were to be taken seriously. Critical Realism (Külpe, Volkelt), neo-Thomism, even Lenin's dialectical materialism itself could not get by without a critique of philosophical Criticism and thereby indirectly confirmed the very rehabilitation of philosophy as theory of knowledge which they attack.

Another widespread model is the rehabilitation of philosophy as a science with its own special domain. The aim in this case was to provide a basis for the independence and absolute necessity of philosophy by reference to a field of enquiry which belonged to it alone and without it would remain uncultivated. Two examples are particularly interesting in this regard, because they are to be seen in the context of the turn towards theory of knowledge. First, Wilhelm Windelband defines philosophy as a science of 'normal consciousness', that is, of consciousness to the extent that it subjects itself to universally valid norms and values, so that philosophy ultimately coincides with *value*-philosophy (see Ch. 6, Sect. 2). 'Truth' is conceived of as a theoretical value, so that even theory of knowledge, not just ethics and aesthetics, is conceived of as a science of values. The modality of values, however, is not 'being' but 'validity' – as Windelband's teacher, Herrmann Lotze, had already affirmed – so that philosophy as a whole can also be characterized as a theory of validity and philosophical method as reflection on validity. The domain of the valid is consequently the domain of enquiry of a philosophy which is independent of the special sciences. The other influential example of the rehabilitation of philosophy as a science with a special domain is Edmund Husserl's phenomenology. *Philosophie als strenge Wissenschaft* (Philosophy as a Strict Science) operates in a rigorously phenomenological way, that is, it describes only *given* phenomena – reference has already been made to the way in which this is modelled on the phenomenological conception of physics – and it operates in the same field and from the same point of view as introspective psychology, though with an essentially epistemological interest. It is distinguished from the empirical sciences, however, by the *epoché*, that is, by abstaining from assumptions and affirmations of existence with regard to what it investigates in introspection; in this way, a vast field of enquiry, belonging only to 'phenomenological research', is to be opened up, with which philosophy as 'strict science' is to concern itself. Here too philosophy is explicitly endorsing the interpretation of science as based on research in the formulation of which it at first had taken no part.

A third model is that of the rehabilitation of philosophy as a synthesis of knowledge and science. It is essentially associated with Wilhelm Wundt (1832–1920), who began as an assistant of Helmholtz, then took over Lange's Chair at Zurich and in 1875 was called to Leipzig, where in 1879 he founded the first Institute for Experimental Psychology. The synthesis of science is a philosophical programme, the idea of which had already occurred, even if one disregards Karl Marx's *aperçu* cited above, to Lotze and Eduard von Hartmann, but which Wundt was the first explicitly to formulate: it was supposed to achieve a creative bringing together of the results of the sciences on the basis of psychology (in a very wide sense). The outcome was not to be a mere summary, but a *new* form of knowledge, which Wundt characterized as 'inductive metaphysics'.[91]

Finally, the rehabilitation of philosophy as metaphysics belongs essentially to our own century and is to be discussed in a special chapter entitled 'Being'.

4

Understanding

In the century after Hegel, 'history' and 'science' were philosophical problems in a twofold sense: they were a concern of philosophers, and at the same time they had a bearing on philosophy itself, which was compelled, in the age of historicism and research-science, to redefine its own identity. It is not so obvious that 'understanding' is a theme of equal rank: it seems to concern only those who seek to put on a firm footing the independence and scientific status of the *Geisteswissenschaften*, or human sciences. That 'understanding' (*Verstehen*), as a methodological concept, was better suited for that purpose than any distinctions between ontological domains – such as that between nature and spirit or between the physical and the psychic – was a prevalent conviction in a time in which philosophy sought to rehabilitate itself essentially as theory of knowledge and to find a foundation for itself by epistemological means. In the theory of the human sciences too Kant's critical way was generally regarded as the only one still open, although in this area Kant himself had only indicated the path and had not already traced out the route in all its details. In fact, however, the problem of understanding has at the same time a bearing on the possibility of philosophy in general in a post-Idealist age and in the conditions of historical consciousness. Hegel's Absolute Idealism had affirmed the unity of the historical and the systematic on the basis of the Absolute Idea, that is, he had attempted once again to integrate the emerging historicism into a system of comprehensive reason and thus philosophically to neutralize it. If this unity is shattered, and if *reason*, like everything human, must be regarded primarily as something historical, then what does the *unity* of reason consist in? When the historicization of history first released the feeling of the alien character of the historical and undermined the prejudice of the systematic character of one's own traditions, rational intersubjectivity in the historical domain came to be a problem. And since without that there was no longer any unity in 'History', the unity of a reason which understood itself as historical was thereby put at risk at the same time. This unity can thus no longer be presupposed as something which is always already guaranteed, but is at any given time something to be achieved as a result of the work of understanding in establishing rational intersubjectivity. This is the philosophical basis for the philosophical significance of the problem of understanding in the period now under consideration: it is not simply a result of the fact that philosophy here understands itself essentially as a human science.

1 The problem

The numerous uses of the expression 'understanding' may be arranged, basically, in relation to three paradigmatic cases: understanding of a language, understanding of phenomena and understanding of gestures, expressions, texts and so on. 'Understanding of a language' means much the same as understanding what is expressed *in* a language, in so far as knowledge of this language is sufficient for its understanding: such linguistic understanding, which we can think of, following Wittgenstein, as a skill,[1] can here be left out of account. More important, however, is the understanding of phenomena, which has been thought of in modern philosophy as essentially an achievement of the faculty of understanding (*Verstand*). Kant says, 'To understand (*intelligere*) something, that is, to cognize or conceive it by means of the understanding in virtue of concepts'. Only by means of categories or concepts of the understanding, according to Kant, can 'something in the manifold of intuition' be understood, and that is the same as 'to think an object of intuition'. 'Experience is a perception which has been understood. We understand it, however, when we represent it under the title of the understanding.'[2] The relationship, later so much discussed, between understanding (*Verstehen*) and explaining (*Erklären*) is described in Kant as follows: we understand phenomena by means of concepts, but it is only by means of laws that we can explain them.[3] Understanding by means of the faculty of understanding is thought of in Kant, in accordance with a long tradition of thought on this question, as essentially a spontaneously constructive procedure: 'However, we understand nothing correctly except what we could at the same time make, if the material for it were to be given to us.'[4] This idea, according to which only what is made by *human beings* can be understood, also came to play an important role in the theory of the understanding of gestures, expressions and texts, where what is in question is fundamentally an understanding of *meaning*. Understanding of meaning, or *hermeneutic* understanding, in the sense of understanding what is already understood – this is the problem to be discussed in the present chapter.[5]

The origins of the hermeneutic problem are to be sought, historically speaking, in those fields of scholarship in which the interpretation of texts is fundamental: in jurisprudence, but above all in Evangelical theology, which opposes the scriptural principle (*sola scriptura*) to that of tradition and thus bases itself on a foundation which always has to be hermeneutically appropriated before it is capable of bearing any weight. Thus it is above all theologians who have sought, since the Reformation, to formulate rules of method for hermeneutic understanding in the form of 'hermeneutics' and to teach the subject in a systematic way. Hermeneutics are sets of precepts on the *art* of understanding, which are supposed to replace in their hermeneutic function the traditions of understanding, now compromised and expressly abandoned in the name of the scriptural principle, by methodical and controllable interpretative procedures. They prove to be necessary wherever it is a matter of taking up once again and *re-*appropriating interrupted traditions: the obligatory force which the influence of these traditions themselves can no longer provide is to be compensated for by the scientific character of their re-appropriation. As well as theology, the example of classical philology may also be cited: in consequence of the neo-humanist movement in culture in the German Classical period, the task fell to it of making once more accessible, in a binding fashion, the cultural goods of a distant past. Thus Schleiermacher, in his great systematization of hermeneutics, can make contact with the works of two classical philologists, Wolf and Ast.

The history of the hermeneutic problem in its modern interpretation begins at the point at which an emerging historicism had made men conscious of the temporal interval between yesterday and today as a possible qualitative difference and had transformed the very conception of understanding. A classical formulation of the pre-historicist, rationalistic model of understanding can be found in Chladen: 'One understands a discourse or writing completely, if one considers in it all that the words can arouse in us, before our thought, in accordance with reason and its rules of the soul.'[6] 'Reason' and 'the rules of the soul' are considered as unchangeable and supra-historical and thus as the unproblematic *tertium comparationis* between the historical text which is to be understood and the present process of understanding. The universal, ahistorical human reason was also the basis and criterion for rationalistic Biblical criticism from the time of Grotius and Spinoza, through Locke and Reimarus, and up to Kant: it was considered to be 'a principle which was not touched by history'. *History*, by contrast, because of its contingency and lack of perspicuity, was considered as that which has probably disturbed the rational community between author, text and contemporary recipients and confused the clear original meaning. Historicism, on the other hand, reverses, even in the hermeneutic domain, that relationship between reason and history; it treats not only universal human reason as the basis of understanding, but also the original production of meaning and the process of historical transmission as part of the newly understood historical process and teaches that all these factors should be seen, in accordance with the principle of individuality and particularity, as something historical in the modern sense. This development can be called the historicization of understanding. As a result of it, the problem of understanding, which the rationalists thought they had solved in a reductionist fashion, was transformed into a bridging-problem: it was a matter of bridging over the chasm between the Here and Now and a meaning-content which was experienced and respected as alien. The general opposition to the rationalism of the Enlightenment very quickly made it possible for expressions for intuitive and divinatory techniques to come to the fore in the writings of those authors in Germany who concerned themselves with this problem. 'Empathy', 'imagination', 'putting oneself in someone else's position', and so forth, were the watchwords of Romantic hermeneutics, and they determined, indeed encumbered, hermeneutic discussion into our own century as a result of their irrationalist tone. Thus scepticism about such methodological proposals also made itself felt at an early stage.

Historicization of understanding can also be called the development of the conception of understanding as a *process*. Because the static basis of understanding of the rationalist model has become historically fluid, it is no longer possible to count on a momentary act of understanding which excludes all wider problems of comprehension. One cannot rule out the possibility that author, text and interpreter will enter into new historical constellations: thus, understanding is not terminable, indeed it is not even possible to think of it as completed at one time, because no one can survey the 'whole meaning' of what happens with a text when he himself, as an interpreter, is located in the historical dimension of what happens in this way. Schleiermacher speaks of interpretation as an 'endless task' and Droysen of the 'enquiring understanding'; thus there was no longer even a methodological gap between hermeneutics and research-science.

The historicization of the hermeneutic problem also outstripped the solution which Hegel had sought to give of this problem, against the background of his synthesis of the historical and the systematic. According to him, to understanding belongs 'the substantial foundation of the content, which, coming to the spirit as its absolute essence, touches on its innermost being, reverberates in that same innermost being and therein receives evidence of it. This is the first absolute condition of understanding.'[7] This 'absolute essence of the spirit' is the concept which as the Absolute Idea is 'the substance, and the infinite spiritual power, itself the infinite material of all natural and spiritual life, and also the infinite form, the activity of this its content'[8] and consequently 'the concept is the understanding of itself and of the unconceptual form, but the latter does not understand the former in its inner truth'.[9] This hermeneutic asymmetry between the concept, of which the Hegelian philosophy believes itself to be in control, and the 'unconceptual form' is the foundation both for Hegel's philosophy of religion and for his treatment of the history of philosophy. It is also the reason why Hegel was bound to seem to his hermeneutically minded contemporaries like an eighteenth-century rationalist. It makes it clear once again that the hermeneutic problem, in the conditions of the historical consciousness, was essentially a post-Idealist problem.

The step to the universalization of the hermeneutic problem on the basis of historicist presuppositions, however, was taken at the moment when the subjective conditions of understanding in which the interpreter happens to find himself at any given time were recognized as the horizon which always already exists for *every* understandable meaning. In this way the transcendental notion, according to which that which is our object cannot be thought of independently of how it appears to us, was integrated into the theory of understanding. Applied to the problems of understanding, this means that the historical conditions under which *our* capacity for understanding exists have a constitutive significance for what we understand at any given time, and that there is no reason for excluding from history any conditions of understanding – be they those of reason, of intuition or of inspiration. This creates a new theoretical situation to the extent that this insight into the transcendental significance of the conditions of our historical understanding affects the understanding of meaning in general, not just the historical form, and thus applies to all communication-situations. The historicization of the universal human reason no longer admits to the historical consciousness the establishment of any transcendental 'consciousness in general' as a hermeneutic 'normal consciousness' outside history. Rational intersubjectivity in the case of hermeneutic reason must always be achieved and secured in the processes of understanding. Add to this the thesis of the linguistic character of reason,[10] which associates its actuality with the active existence of a language which is actually spoken and so historical: according to this thesis, the understanding of meaning is no longer merely a consequence, but the basis of reason itself. Seen from this point of view, the hermeneutic problem is not simply universal but also fundamental, that is, its solution lies already in the constitutive domain of understanding and reason and so in the approaches to the problem of knowledge, which Kant thought he could approach directly by means of assured concepts of the understanding and reason. If there is in general no reason without an understanding of meaning, the problem of meaning is systematically prior to the problem of knowledge, since in that case in all achievements of knowledge the hermeneutic problems of understanding must be presupposed as already solved. The philosophical importance of the theme of 'understanding' (*Verstehen*) thus lies in the fact that the form of understanding which was universalized and fundamentalized in the conditions of an emerging historicism affects the self-understanding of reason itself and thus necessarily has to be considered in every theory of reason, not just in that of hermeneutic reason. The transcendentalization of hermeneutico-historical reason means at the same time a historicization of transcendental philosophy.

2 General hermeneutics (Schleiermacher)

The credit for taking the first steps along this path belongs to the theologian, philologist and philosopher Friedrich D. E. Schleiermacher (1768–1834), who systematically discussed the hermeneutic problem from about 1805 onwards in his lectures and summarized his fundamental ideas in 1829 in an address to the Academy entitled, 'Über den Begriff der Hermeneutik, mit Bezug auf F. A. Wolfs Andeutungen und Asts Lehrbuch' (On the concept of hermeneutics, with reference to F. A. Wolf's suggestions and Ast's textbook). Schleiermacher says,

> When, twenty-five years ago, I began to deliver exegetical lectures on the New Testament scriptures, I found it essential to render as precise an account as possible to myself of the principles of procedure. There was, to be sure, no lack of instructions on interpretation, and Ernesti's *Institutio interpretis* [of 1762 – H.S.], which was regarded as the product of a sound philological school, enjoyed a considerable reputation; many of the rules proposed therein proved to be very useful, but they were themselves lacking in the proper grounding, because the general principles had not been established anywhere, and I had therefore to

make my own way forward. As, in general, I was in the situation, having very unexpectedly been appointed to an academic teaching post, of having constantly to include immediately in my teaching what I had only just discovered, collected together and brought into some sort of order, there very soon emerged from these investigations my lectures on general hermeneutics.[11]

'General hermeneutics' is Schleiermacher's name for a discipline which, in distinction from the various special hermeneutics, takes the problem of understanding itself as its theme, not just specific techniques of understanding and interpretation. This problem is omnipresent: it touches on every communication-situation and cannot be limited to our dealings with texts,

for I often catch myself engaging in hermeneutic operations in the midst of intimate conversation, when I am not content with an ordinary degree of understanding but seek to enquire how the transition has been made in my friend from one thought to another, or when I track down the opinions, judgments and aspirations with which is connected the fact that he expresses himself precisely so and not otherwise on the subject under discussion. The same facts, which every attentive person will have to give evidence of from his own case, manifest, I thought, clearly enough that the solution of the problem for which we are seeking the theory in no way depends on those situations of discourse which are fixed for the eyes by means of writing, but that it is to be found wherever we have to understand thoughts or sequences of thought by means of words.[12]

A further task of general hermeneutics, as Schleiermacher sees it, lies in the theoretical grounding of those technical rules of interpretation which are merely enumerated in the special hermeneutics: thus it is a doctrine of principles and not merely a matter of teaching the art of understanding. This grounding is sought by Schleiermacher in a transcendental direction of enquiry:

A theory of the art [of understanding – H.S.], however, can arise only when both language in its objectivity and the process of the production of thought as a function of individual spiritual life in its relation to the essence of thinking itself are so completely understood that from the manner of proceeding in the association and communication of thoughts the manner in which one must proceed in understanding can also be described in total connexion.[13]

The presentation of discourse and understanding as functions of the spirit against the background of a theory of thinking can be described, on the analogy of Kant, as the programme of a 'Critique of Hermeneutic Reason'. It has to do, not just with a partial field of application for reason, in dealing with discourse and texts, but with the reality of reason in general, which, because of the indissoluble connexion of thinking, speaking and understanding, is always to be defined as a hermeneutic reason. The basic discipline for general hermeneutics is consequently dialectic, which Schleiermacher defines as an 'account of the fundamental principles for the artistically correct conduct of discourse in the field of pure thought'. It was to this universalized conception of hermeneutics, turned in this way in the direction of transcendental philosophy, that Wilhelm Dilthey explicitly adhered.

In a modification of older hermeneutic terminology, Schleiermacher outlined a general characteristic of understanding with the aid of two pairs of oppositions: 'grammatical–psychological' and 'divinatory–comparative' understanding. 'Grammatical' understanding is the understanding of what is spoken as such, against the background of the total system of a language in a particular historical stage of development; but the comprehension of the coherence and composition of a text in accordance with the sequence of principal and subordinate ideas is also called 'grammatical understanding'. 'Psychological' understanding, on the other hand, relates to the author: Schleiermacher speaks of a 'correct comprehension of the internal course of events involved in the writer's planning and composition', of the 'product of his personal peculiarities in language and in the totality of his situation'. This is given greater precision by the account of discourse 'as an act of continuing production of thoughts' which is to be reproduced by the interpreter in the process of understanding. This thesis of the complementarity of discourse and understanding as psychic processes is the foundation for Schleiermacher's solution of the hermeneutic problem as one of building bridges: because discourse and understanding have a structural correspondence to each other, we can reproduce in the understanding of discourse what occurred in the discourser himself and consequently understand not merely the discourse but him himself. This model continued to have a canonically binding status up until Dilthey and his pupils, but later, on account of its psychological character, brought the hermeneutics of Schleiermacher and Dilthey into disrepute on the grounds that it was 'merely' psychological. What was usually overlooked in such criticism was that Schleiermacher's psychological understanding (and also the grammatical variety) is defined in terms of the *object* of understanding and not intended as a method of understanding. It relates to the understanding of the author himself, to his situation and to what he intended when he said this or that. Many uses of the word 'understanding' are covered by this model and it could be summarized as the understanding of speaker's intentions. In no way is the phrase 'psychological understanding' intended to indicate replacement of hermeneutic methods by psychological.

Understanding is characterized methodologically in Schleiermacher by means of the contrast between 'divinatory' and 'comparative' understanding. 'Divinatory' understanding has constantly been misunderstood as psychological empathy, which amounts to treating understanding as a subjective process and reducing the meaning to be understood to what takes place in the mind of the empathizing recipient; it is then believed that the objectivity of the meaning-structure has to be brought into play as a corrective. The key to a correct understanding of divination is not 'empathy' but the literal meaning of the word – 'to surmise'. Schleiermacher means the attainment of a first, immediate evidence in understanding, with which every process of interpretation always has to begin, and without which there can be no correction of understanding, for instance by means of a comparative procedure. Comparative understanding is the opposite type to this. Schleiermacher elucidates it by reference to the acquisition of language by children: the first beginnings of understanding

> are no different from what happens when children begin to understand what is spoken. How appropriate are our formulae to these beginnings? They do not yet possess language, but are seeking it; however, it is also true that they are not yet aware of the activity of thought, because there is no thought without words: on which side, therefore, do they begin? As yet they have no points of comparison at all: rather, they acquire them gradually as a foundation for a comparative procedure which certainly develops with unexpected rapidity; but how do they establish the first one? Might one not be tempted to say that everyone originally produced both, and either originally, in virtue of an inner necessity, coincides with the way in which the others have created them or else gradually approaches these others as he becomes capable of a comparative procedure. Yet this too, this inner motivation towards one's own creation, but with an original tendency towards receiving from others, is simply the same as what we have referred to by the expression 'divinatory' understanding. This then is the original, and the soul maintains itself here too as totally and truly a surmising being.[14]

In other places, Schleiermacher characterizes divinatory understanding also as guessing, in the sense of an immediate lighting upon the correct meaning, unprepared by any comparative techniques. What is important here is that he relates this pure type of immediate understanding in similar fashion to the grammatical and the psychological domains of understanding, and this demonstrates yet again how false it would be to set aside divinatory understanding as mere psychology; it always requires the 'divinatory boldness' which can be learned from children.

In the ideal case, understanding occupies the middle position between the extremes of both these antitheses and integrates them into itself:

> Just as we can regard immediate and instantaneous understanding as having arisen in one or the other fashion, and us ourselves with our attention as directed towards the productivity of the author or towards the objective totality of language: so we shall be able to express in the same way the methodical procedure in interpretation, if it has completely achieved its goal, and say that now all comparative elements, both on the psychological and on the grammatical side, are so completely together that we no longer need to consider the results of our divinatory procedure, but also *vice versa*, that the thoroughgoing precision of the divinatory makes the comparative superfluous. Likewise, the inner occurrence is by means of a divinatory and comparative procedure so thoroughly perspicuous that, in that what has been so clearly intuited was a thought, but was not thought without words, the whole relation of this production of ideas and formation into language has been completely and simultaneously involved with it; but likewise also the other way round.[15]

At the same time, understanding is thought of by Schleiermacher as a matter of a process and as interminable in principle:

> this business of understanding and interpretation is a constant whole, gradually developing, in the further course of which we more and more give each other reciprocal support, in that each provides the others with points of comparison and analogies; but this begins at every point, over and over again, in the same mode of surmise. It is the gradual self-discovery of the thinking spirit.[16]

Understanding as an 'endless task' is located by means of such formulations in a universal process of communication, which is conceived of, in similar fashion to Hegel, as the coming-to-be of the self-conscious human spirit. This prefigures the extension of general hermeneutics by the added dimensions of history (Droysen) and metaphysics and life-philosophy (Dilthey).

3 Hermeneutics and historics (Droysen)

It has already been shown in an earlier chapter that it was above all the integration of the hermeneutic methods developed by scientific philology into the practice of historiography which led to the development of modern historical science. The significance of Johann Gustav Droysen for the history of the problem of understanding consists in the fact that in his 'historics' he gave a methodological formulation of that factual integration and attempted to give it a theoretical foundation. The effect of such a combination of hermeneutics and historics in return on the theme of understanding consisted in the fact that the concept of understanding itself had to be extended in such a way that it was in a position to move beyond the hermeneutic and philological disciplines and into the methodology of the human sciences, since history, on account of the truth-claims of its assertions, could not be reduced to philology. Only as a result of this extension did the theory of understanding become the foundation of a theory of the human sciences in general, comprising historical *and* philological subjects.

Droysen attributed to 'understanding' the function, essentially, of giving a firm basis to the independence of the historical sciences which, according to Kant, can no longer be given an ontological, but only a methodological, foundation. The opposing conception, that historiography can be raised to the level of a science by attaching itself to the methods of the natural sciences, Droysen found in H. T. Buckle's *History of Civilization in England* of 1859–61, and he even explicitly attacked it in a detailed review of this work.[17] Droysen says in his *Grundriss der Historik* (Outline of Historics), 'According to the objects, and according to the nature of human thought, there are three possible scientific methods: the (philosophically or theologically) speculative, the physical and the historical. Their essence is: to know, to explain and to understand'.[18] It is noteworthy that Droysen does not hesitate to associate knowing with the speculative method, which since Hegel had fallen into universal disrepute. Droysen was one of the few representatives of the Historical School who maintained a non-polemical relationship to Hegel; indeed, he refers favourably to Hegel's philosophy of history in §78 of his *Grundriss*, and in so doing prepares the way for the later Hegel-Renaissance under hermeneutic auspices, which was principally associated with Dilthey and Croce.[19] More important and fruitful, nevertheless, were the connexions which Droysen found between physical method and explanation, on the one hand, and historical method and understanding, on the other. Droysen thereby formulated a model which has been current ever since as a dogma in the theory of science and has correspondingly come under repeated attack: namely, that natural and historical sciences are related to each other as concerned with explanation and understanding respectively. The historical sciences on this view are regarded as paradigms of what were later to be called the *Geisteswissenschaften* or 'human sciences'.

It is also possible to see here how Droysen extended the hermeneutic concept of understanding. If understanding is the basis of historical method, the concept of 'understanding' cannot simply apply to texts – that would be to reduce history to philology: rather, it must be applicable also, and above all, to actions and artefacts. 'Only what the spirit and hand of man has fashioned, marked, touched, only the vestiges of man light us on our way. Impressing his mark, giving form and order – in every manifestation man gives expression to his individual being, his self. Wherever and however such expressions and impressions are present to us, they speak to us and are intelligible to us.'[20] Only what refers to human activity is intelligible to us; only what is a possible object of understanding bears the vestiges of man, and it is clear that such understanding must include more than that of texts.

It is merely an extension of what has been said that the works of industry, the foundations of cities and their fortification, the building of harbours and roads, that justice, law, state, church – in short, all human efforts to impose form on their lives, even if the common will of many created or reshaped them, are of the same sort, expressions of the human spirit and intelligible to the human spirit, just as they come to be empirically observable to it. In a word: nothing which has stirred the human spirit and found sensuous expression could not be understood, nothing can be understood which does not lie in the domain of our common spirit, which we have recognized as belonging to historical experience, in the domain of the ethical world.[21]

Droysen's extension of the concept of understanding, however, does not imply any resurrection of the understanding of phenomena in the Kantian sense in virtue of a faculty of 'understanding' (*Verstand*), still less any reduction to the understanding of language: it remains entirely within the hermeneutic domain. It is the conception of 'understanding meaning' itself which is here applied outside the textual field to actions and artefacts. Historical understanding too is consequently to be thought of as understanding of meaning: 'Our historical understanding is exactly the same as our understanding of those who speak with us.'[22] The possibility of such understanding consists, according to Droysen,

in the congenial nature of the external expressions which are available as historical material. It depends on the fact that the sensuously spiritual nature of man expresses all inner events in sensorily perceptible form, and in all its external expressions reflects inner events. The expression, once perceived, produces by projecting itself into the interior of the perceiver the same inner event. On hearing the cry of fear, we feel the fear of the one who is crying, and so on . . . As far as human beings, human expressions and structures are concerned, we are and we feel ourselves to be essentially of the same kind and reciprocally related, every I accessible to itself, every I disclosing itself to every other in its expressions.[23]

The essential similarity between the one who understands and the one to whose activity what is to be understood refers is, according to Droysen, the third term which mediates between the two others and makes understanding possible: it is the foundation of the 'congenial nature of the external expressions'. At the same time, this quotation makes it clear that in this context understanding is interpreted essentially as understanding of *expressions*: hermeneutic understanding of meaning is simply a special case of this. If what is human expresses itself only in what is a sensorily perceptible externalization of inner events, 'expression' is the fundamental concept of the theory of understanding. In this way, Droysen was preparing the ground for Dilthey's position.

The structure of understanding is indicated by means of the correspondence between expression and perception of expression: 'The individual expression is understood as an external expression of the inner in the inference to this inner event; this inner event is understood in the example of this external expression, as a central force which, in itself one and the same, presents itself both in all its peripheral effects and expressions and in this particular case.'[24] Understanding is accordingly an inference from the external expression to the inner event of which it is an expression; understanding retraces the route by which what is to be understood came into being in the opposite direction. At the same time, however, inner event and external expression stand in a relation of whole and part to each other; thus Droysen can apply the old hermeneutic notion of the circular relation of whole and part to the general understanding of expression as externalization: 'The individual is understood in the whole, and the whole on the basis of the individual. The one who understands, since he, like the one whom he has to understand, is an I, a totality in himself, completes the latter's totality on the basis of the individual expression and the individual expression on the basis of his totality.'[25] This passage makes it clear that Droysen ultimately conceives of historical understanding as an understanding of historical persons and cultural formations in their *totality*, of which the individual expressions and actions are merely indications. Such totalities take the place of complete texts, in relation to which traditional hermeneutics had formerly used the expression 'the whole'. On the logical structure, furthermore, Droysen says: 'Understanding is as much synthetic as analytic, as much induction as deduction.'[26] This is a paraphrase of the idea of the hermeneutic circle, which is here applied to the relations between synthesis and analysis, induction and deduction. In the same way as Schleiermacher had distinguished divinatory and comparative understanding, Droysen asserts on this point: 'The act of understanding is distinct from the logical mechanism of understanding. The act ensues under the conditions described in the form of an immediate intuition.'[27] Understanding, as a procedure which can be subjected to methodological norms, finds its goal in the 'act of understanding', in which understanding is completed. Of understanding in this sense Droysen says:

> Understanding is the most perfect cognition which is possible to us as human beings. Hence it comes about immediately, suddenly, without our being conscious of the logical mechanism which is active in it. Thus, the act of understanding is like an immediate intuition, a creative act, a spark of light between two electrophoric bodies, an act of conception. In understanding the whole spiritual-sensuous nature of man works completely together, giving and taking at the same time, at once generating and conceiving. Understanding is the most human act of human beings, and all truly human activity is based on understanding, seeks understanding, finds understanding. Understanding is the most intimate bond between men and the basis of all ethical being.[28]

The methods of 'inquiring understanding', as Droysen conceived them, cannot be discussed here; what is important is that they include 'heuristics', critique' and 'interpretation'. Heuristics, the business of making the historical material available, and critique, the evaluation of this material in regard to its character as evidence of historical reality, are anyway procedures which cannot be considered apart from the context of understanding. Droysen's discussion of interpretation clearly shows how far removed his conception of understanding is from any methodically uncheckable notions of 'empathy' or mere intuition; the 'logical mechanism of understanding' is very precisely described by him and is governed by very precise norms. Droysen distinguishes pragmatic interpretation, the interpretation of conditions, psychological interpretation and the interpretation of ideas. The last-named model, which originates from Wilhelm von Humboldt, connects Droysen's methodological conception with his material philosophy of history, which has already been discussed in another place.

4 From the 'interpretation of the objectifications of life' (Dilthey) to the 'hermeneutics of *Dasein*' (Heidegger)

Wilhelm Dilthey's importance in the history of the problem of understanding, which it would be difficult to overestimate, is a direct consequence 'of the association which he established between the Kantian critique of reason and the Historical School of the nineteenth century'[29] in the programme of a 'Critique of Historical Reason', which was considered in Section 3. ii of Chapter 2. The linking of Criticism and historicism in Dilthey's foundation of the human sciences also leads to an analogous outcome in the theory of understanding: the unification of Schleiermacher's transcendental approach with Droysen's universalization of hermeneutics. A universalized transcendental hermeneutics, however, does not any longer permit the previous limitation of the problem of understanding to historical knowledge: it necessarily becomes a hermeneutic transcendental philosophy, concerned with *all* forms of consciousness, knowledge and science. The basis for this is that Kant's 'consciousness in general', if it has identified itself as historical consciousness and thus as something historical, is able to comprehend and explicate itself, in exactly the same way as everything historical, by the use of hermeneutic methods. This first became clear in Dilthey: the theme of 'understanding' is only secondarily concerned with methodological questions in the historical and human sciences; it is primarily concerned with the possibility of philosophy itself. This is not because it had at that time sought to escape from its post-Hegelian identity-crisis into the history of philosophy and had thus itself largely become a *Geisteswissenschaft*, but because, as already suggested, in conditions of historical consciousness hermeneutics already includes the critique of reason.

The first steps on the road to a fundamental philosophy of understanding as a self-foundation for philosophy, which led to Heidegger's 'hermeneutics of *Dasein*', had already been taken by Dilthey. Nevertheless, even today Dilthey the philosopher is hidden behind Dilthey the theoretician of science, whose outlines of methodology in the human sciences and psychology so strongly influenced the relevant discussion from the turn of the century onwards that it is possible, with only slight exaggeration, to describe everything since as footnotes to Dilthey: all theoreticians of the human or cultural sciences refer, if often polemically, to him. We must content ourselves in what follows with an outline of some of the stages in the history of the concept of understanding from Dilthey to Heidegger.

i. *Wilhelm Dilthey*

Dilthey's attempt to base the *Geisteswissenschaften* on the connexion of lived experience, expression and understanding, which is itself conceived of as a life-connexion, already shows, even from a purely terminological point of view, his continuity with Droysen. Understanding is essentially understanding of expression, and it is therefore also to the point if one is characterizing the influence of Schleiermacher on Dilthey in this way that in it grammatical understanding is almost completely subordinated to psychological. On the structure of elementary understanding, Dilthey says little that is new as compared with Droysen:

> The given here are always external expressions of life. Appearing in the world of the senses, they are the expression of something spiritual; thus they make it possible for us to know the spiritual. By 'external expression of life' here I understand, not only those expressions which are intended to mean or signify something, but also those which, without such an intention, as expressions of something spiritual make it intelligible for us. The manner and results of understanding differ according to the classes of external expressions of life.[30]

Dilthey then distinguishes three classes: 'concepts, judgments, larger structures of thought', also actions and finally modes of expression of lived experience. The systematic ambiguity of the expression 'expression', which can be applied to facial expressions, postures, gestures, actions and linguistic utterances, is utilized in an ingenious fashion by Dilthey to make his model of understanding apply to anything which is in any way understandable: the concept 'expression' thus acquires the same kind of key function as the concept 'lived experience'. At the same time, Dilthey turns to account the common scope of the words 'expression' and 'externalization'; he philosophizes, as it were, on the basis of etymology. Everything which is understandable is an externalization of something inner, and understanding in its elementary form is a movement from the inner externalized in the expression back to this inner itself: 'an inverse operation to the causal process itself'. This operation is possible because the life-connexion 'lived experience-expression-understanding' includes the one who is externalizing or expressing himself and the one who is understanding in the same fashion. It was Dilthey too who at times affirmed a regular connexion between the individual externalization of life, which he compared to individual letters, and what is expressed in it, and who accepted the description of elementary understanding from the logical point of view as an *analogical inference*. 'The fundamental relationship on which the process of elementary understanding is based is that of the expression to what is expressed in it',[31] which – as the example of fear and posture shows – should not be confused with the relation of cause and effect and also does not suggest any reference to the overlapping totality of a life-connexion.

This reference can be established only by 'higher forms of understanding', which Dilthey formally characterizes on the analogy of *inductive inferences*:

If we sum up the forms of higher understanding which have been mentioned, their common character consists in the fact that they bring the connexion of a totality to understanding in an inductive inference based on given externalizations ... The procedure is based on elementary understanding which, as it were, makes available the elements for the reconstruction ... Understanding always has as its object something individual. And in its higher forms it infers on the basis of an inductive collection of what is given together in a work or a life to the connexion in a work or a person, a life-relationship.[32]

It is noteworthy how Dilthey, with his doctrine of the 'inductive inference from individual externalizations of life to the totality of the life-connexion', seems to have abandoned the idea of the hermeneutic circle, according to which the whole is to be understood on the basis of the individual and at the same time the individual is to be understood on the basis of the whole, in favour of the inductivism of John Stuart Mill which was so popular at that time. In fact, nevertheless, Dilthey sees the limits of such inductivism:

However, we understand individuals in virtue of their affinity to each other, the common elements amongst them. This process presupposes the connexion of the universally human with the individuation which on the basis of it is diffused in the manifold variety of spiritual existences, and in it we are constantly solving in practice the problem of inwardly living through, as it were, this ascent to individuation.[33]

The generality which must always be presupposed in the inductive inference in order that generalization in any respect should be possible, here appears as something which is already previously understood – what would later be called a 'prior understanding' of affinity, community, of the universally human. Probably, Dilthey's doctrine of hermeneutic induction was merely a verbal concession to the dominant inductivist conception of science of the time; in reality, it is an endorsement of the hermeneutic tradition which, since Schleiermacher, had characterized understanding as a circular or spiral movement.

As in the case of the concept of lived experience, Dilthey refuses to limit understanding to the cognitive domain; the part also played by the faculties of emotion and will leads to the characterization of understanding as 'putting oneself in the place of', 'reproducing' and 'reliving'. It is only through the participation of all the forces of life and experience that the one who understands is capable of understanding the individual datum as an objectification of life; thus an active, creative, element comes into play, which Dilthey attributes to 'personal genius'. Droysen's idea of 'congeniality' as the third element between the hermeneutic subject and his object was thus given a subjectivist twist. At the same time, Dilthey sees that personal genius is not a sufficient basis for the tasks which are demanded of understanding in a culture based on historical consciousness in the age of science:

How plainly it is shown in reproduction and reliving of the alien and of what is past that understanding depends on a peculiar personal genius! Since, however, it is an important and continuing task as a basis of historical science, personal genius comes to be a matter of technique, and this technique develops along with the development of historical consciousness. It is bound up with the fact that permanently fixed externalizations of life are present to understanding, so that it can return to them again and again. Such technically developed understanding of permanently fixed externalizations of life we call 'exposition' (*Auslegung*). Since spiritual life finds its complete and exhaustive expression, and so the one which makes objective comprehension possible, only in language, exposition is consummated in the interpretation of those remains of human existence which are preserved in writing. This art is the foundation of philology. And the science of this art is hermeneutics.[34]

Exposition, in the sense of technically developed understanding, requires a scientific foundation, which hermeneutics, a discipline which is always also critical, has to prepare. The current tasks of hermeneutics as a philosophical discipline, as Dilthey sees them, result from this connexion between regulation and critique of understanding on a scientific foundation:

Today hermeneutics enters into a connexion which assigns to the human sciences a new and important task. It has always defended the certainty of understanding against historical scepticism and subjective arbitrariness. It did so, first of all, when it resisted allegorical interpretation, then when it opposed Tridentine scepticism by vindicating that great Protestant doctrine of the possibility of understanding the Biblical Scriptures on the basis of themselves alone, and then again when it gave a theoretical foundation to the advances in the philological and historical sciences made by Schlegel, Schleiermacher and Boeckh, so full of promise for the future, in the face of all doubts. At present, hermeneutics must seek out a relation to the universal task of epistemology, of demonstrating the possibility of knowledge of the connexion of the historical world and discovering the means for the realization of such knowledge.[35]

Even today, it is still a controversial matter in the interpretation of Dilthey to say what the relation is between the psychological and the, in the more restricted sense, hermeneutic portions of Dilthey's foundation of the human sciences. The widespread view that the early, psychological, Dilthey, impressed by the objections of Husserl and Rickert, came close in his later work to a theory of pure understanding of meaning has been modified by Manfred Riedel on the grounds that Dilthey proceeded in a less psychologistic way in his *Einleitung in die Geisteswissenschaften* (An Introduction to the Human Studies) of 1883 than in his writings at the turn of the century; the late *Aufbau der geschichtlichen Welt in den Geisteswissenschaften* (The Construction of the Historical World in the Human Studies) (1905–10), on the other hand, unequivocally distinguishes the hermeneutic foundation of the human sciences from the psychological. But even this picture still seems to be too simple. First of all, it should be remembered that Schleiermacher's psychological understanding, with which Dilthey has points of contact, is a matter of understanding the author and his intentions, and so has little to do with what was attacked as 'psychology' around the turn of the century in the Husserlian and neo-Kantian critique of psychologism: psychological understanding in this sense can be seen as simply a form of understanding of meaning and expression. In this connexion, it is worth noticing what Dilthey says about 'significance' (*Bedeutung*):

> The category of significance denotes the relation of parts of life to the whole, which has its basis in the essential nature of life . . . Significance is the special kind of reference which within life its parts have to the whole. This significance we recognize, like that of words in a sentence, by means of recollections and possibilities for the future. The essence of significance-relations lies in those relationships which in the course of time the configuration of the course of life sustains on the basis of the structure of life in the conditions of the milieu.[36]

The significance-relation is certainly not a brute psychological fact which may be simply affirmed without the work of understanding; even the talk of the 'course of time', which was then repeated in Heidegger in the doctrine of the existential 'temporality' (where there is certainly no suspicion of psychologism) can give no support to this interpretation. Hence it is not a merely superficial parallel which is drawn between this relation and that of words in a sentence: probably the latter relation is even the guiding model for the interpretation of the former, which is conceived from the outset as a hermeneutic relation.

The modern empirical and naturalistic conception of psychology as a 'natural science of the spirit', moreover, was seen by Dilthey from the very beginning as unsuited to be a foundation for the human sciences, and his opposing conception of an 'interpretative psychology' (*verstehende Psychologie*) was itself devised from a hermeneutic perspective, so that between psychology and hermeneutics in Dilthey there is certainly no one-way relationship of grounding. The concept of the 'objective spirit' as the sum of the objectifications of life, to which the purely hermeneutic interpretation of Dilthey usually appeals, was moreover already prepared for in the *Introduction to the Human Studies*, in that the idea constantly recurs there that the specific mode of knowledge of the human sciences (the term 'understanding' is very seldom found in this work) may be included within the boundaries of the psychological. Psychology and anthropology (in a purely descriptive sense) are here merely the basic sciences, which furnish the 'psycho-physical unities of life' in such a way that knowledge in the human sciences can make interpretative contact with them. The later talk of 'objective spirit' seems, therefore, to be not much more than a terminological innovation inspired by Hegel. There is no question that Dilthey at first sought to base psychological understanding in Schleiermacher's sense on an interpretative psychology, but even here it is not clear whether 'psychology' in this context is intended to mean (as in Wilhelm Wundt) merely the comprehensive discipline which marks out the domain of the human sciences, or whether it does not also and in the first instance refer to the medium of the critique of historical reason itself. In the latter case – which finds support in many passages – Dilthey would have been advocating a psychologistic variant of transcendental philosophy, which would then in turn make possible for the first time a grounding of the difference between psychology as a special science and *Geisteswissenschaft* in the hermeneutic sense. In fact, the boundaries between philosophy and psychology in Dilthey are fluid, and he could have argued in his own justification that until well into the nineteenth century psychology, as a science of spirit, was always regarded as a philosophical discipline – indeed, *Geisteswissenschaft* itself can be understood as a translation of 'psychology'. The fact that Dilthey was compelled to move away from psychology can thus be explained only in terms of the history of science: he distanced himself from the discipline which was beginning at that time to gain ground under the name of 'psychology', indeed he attempted to reform it, because it was no longer capable of carrying the weight of the programme of giving an epistemological foundation to the human sciences. Mere allusion to the circular structure of such a foundation, which may be demonstrated in the relationship of philosophy and interpretative psychology, would have had few terrors for the theoretician of the hermeneutic circle: in several passages he himself refers to the fact that his self-confessedly psychological statements also concern the possibility of philosophy, and at the same time there can be no doubt that they are themselves philosophical. It was the South-West German neo-Kantians who first felt this to be a methodological shortcoming and undertook what was claimed to be a purely transcendental-logical grounding for the human sciences (now called the 'cultural sciences'), the anti-psychologistic tendency of which was also followed by their conception of understanding.

ii. Heinrich Rickert

Heinrich Rickert's foundation of the cultural sciences, sketched in Chapter 2, Section 3. iii, can also be seen, from the point of view of the logic of science, as a theory of understanding, although it is in the sharpest imaginable contrast to that of Dilthey. The basis for this is that Rickert undertook to reconstruct the intelligibility of the objects of cultural science without any material preconceptions about this object-domain, solely on the basis of the formal mode of constitution of such objects. To refer back to the life-connexion 'lived experience-expression-understanding' necessarily seemed to him, therefore, to be either pre-Critical metaphysics or a circular borrowing from a psychology which itself had first to be grounded. Even the term *Geisteswissenschaften* was rejected by Rickert on the grounds that it was a Hegelianism which could no longer be justified:

> In so far as the Hegelian terminology has played a part in bringing the word *Geisteswissenschaften* into common use, it is . . . a kind of misunderstanding to refer to those sciences whose objects are psychical entities as *Geisteswissenschaften* and also to count psychology as one of them . . . If one rejects the significance which Hegel gives to the word *Geist* (spirit), one is bound to eliminate from the theory of science also the term *Geisteswissenschaft* as opposed to the science of the merely psychical and so in general. The expression 'psychological discipline' then becomes unequivocal.[37]

The transcendental philosophical principle of the constitution of cultural objects in terms of value-relevance is for Rickert at the same time the principle of intelligibility and of the understanding of cultural objects; he says retrospectively in a debate with Troeltsch and the theoreticians of history:

> The point of our theory lay precisely in this: the proper and central material of historical science, which by its very nature is meaning-charged cultural life, is historically presented in such a way that the values which confer meaning on it at the same time provide the guiding principles of concept-formation with the aid of which the historical sciences appropriate their material.[38]

It is not the physical or psychical status of this material, but the structure of concept-formation, which follows the same principles as the constitution of the object falling under the concept out of that material, which shows object and concept to belong specifically to the cultural sciences. Nevertheless in reality, as Rickert constantly emphasizes, concept-formation and object-constitution are the *same* process. Like Kant, he distinguishes very precisely between material and object and in his theory merely modifies Kant's transcendental principle according to which 'the conditions of the possibility of experience in general' are 'at the same time conditions of the possibility of the objects of experience'. The value-relevance which constitutes both objects and knowledge is however at the same time a meaning-relevance. It is the values which confer meaning on the material of the cultural sciences, so that the comprehension of this meaning and the relevance of objects to such meaning must be thought of as understanding. Psychological empathy, confirmation of something 'inner' and similar psychological procedures cannot be examples of 'understanding' in this sense for the simple reason that psychology itself, as a science, does not conform at all to the model of concept-formation and object-constitution which, according to Rickert, is characteristic of the cultural sciences. Even Dilthey, according to Rickert, failed to recognize, despite making distinctions which were on the right lines, that the difference between the bodily and the mental

is in no way decisive from the methodological point of view: it is essential only in so far as mental life makes it possible to adopt an attitude towards value and meaning and so give oneself a meaningful form, whereas body cannot do this. This circumstance certainly does not suffice to justify the division into the natural and human sciences. The unreal meaningful content of culture, which is found in historical realities, is confused by Dilthey with real psychic being, which factually takes its course in the mental life of separate individuals. Thus it remains hidden that it is not the real spirit (*Geist*) but the unreal meaning which is the truly decisive factor which objectively distinguishes history from all kinds of natural science.[39]

It is in this sense too that understanding is to be interpreted and distinguished from reliving. It is not merely a matter of participating in someone else's psychic reality:

If the word is not to lose its pregnant and methodologically useful meaning, understanding must mean the cognition of a peculiarly formed material of science, which can be expressed, negatively, by saying that it is always a question of something more than a comprehension of real structures which can be described or explained as something merely real. Positively speaking, it means: what neither is nor has value and meaning in any way at all, remains 'impossible to understand' and hence, if it is in general accessible to science, like the value- and meaning-free realities of nature in the widest sense of that word, is merely described or explained.[40]

By understanding in the narrower and precise sense, therefore, is meant 'the *comprehension of an unreal meaning-structure* [my italics – H.S.]'. The understandable meaning of such a meaning-structure is therefore a third term in relation to the dualism of physical and psychical, and it is from this point that there then has to be reconstructed, step by step, the methodical understanding of the cultural sciences, which Rickert, modifying Windelband's principle of the 'idiographic', defines as a cognition by means of an individualizing concept-formation. In opposition to Dilthey's formulation, 'We call "understanding" the process by which we know something inner from signs which are given in external perception', Rickert says: 'The signs which are "externally" given must make it possible to know something more than a real "inner" life. Otherwise they remain impossible to understand.'[41] What is real is 'understood, in so far and to the extent that it is the "bearer" of an unreal meaning'. It is this unreal meaning, also, which represents the third term between one's own lived experience and that of another and so avoids the danger that understanding may become solipsism and a merely private projection of meaning: 'The unreal meaning can build a bridge between one's own real mental life and that of another, because as an unreal meaning it is neither one's own nor the other's.'[42] Dilthey's third term – life, as embracing lived experience, expression and understanding – is rejected by Rickert as pre-Critical and metaphysical. The extraordinary similarity to the theories of meaning of Gottlob Frege and Edmund Husserl, which in both cases belong primarily in the context of a theory of *thought* and not of understanding, should not lead one to overlook the fact that in Rickert the meaning is unreal and derives its 'mode of being' from values, which do not exist but are valid. It is in this way too – and not just by means of the context of a purely transcendental-logical deduction – Rickert believes, that his position can be distinguished from a Platonizing Realism of pure meanings. The central significance of the concept of understanding for the philosophical self-understanding of his time is confirmed in Rickert by the fact that he, along with Windelband and Emil Lask, conceives of philosophy essentially as a theory of values, that is, as a theory of what constitutes the understandability of the understandable in general (see Ch. 6. Sect. 2. ii).

iii. *Other positions*

The inability of Rickert's theory of understanding to win general acceptance, despite its indisputable influence, is connected first of all with its strongly metaphorical character: what exactly is it supposed to mean to say that an understandable reality is a 'bearer' of unreal meaning, because values 'adhere' to it – formulations which Rickert constantly repeats without really clarifying them? The other reason is a certain remoteness from science in the whole body of Rickert's theories, even though they profess to be part to such an extraordinary extent of the 'logic of science': an example of this might be the strict linking of meaning and value, which did not succeed in convincing all those who worked in the field of interpretative science; the domain of the understandable is wider than that of the valuable. This is the explanation of the fact that Dilthey's influence on the self-understanding of the human sciences could not be undermined by Rickert: this can be seen in the fact that the term 'cultural sciences' has never up to now been able to hold its own in competition with *Geisteswissenschaften*. Thus from the beginning of the century onwards the attraction began to be felt of other positions which sought to mediate between the psychologism which Dilthey himself had soon abandoned, and Rickert's radicalism.

The form which these attempts at mediation generally took was to reduce Rickert's comprehension of unreal meaning-structures to the level of a type of understanding subordinate to other types. Particularly influential – and not only in the field of 'interpretative sociology' – was the typology proposed by Max Weber (1864–1920), who distinguished between rational and non-rational understanding and then further subdivided both types of understanding in terms of the properties of being 'direct' and 'explanatory' (or 'motivational'). Direct understanding is related to the intended meaning of actions, including verbal and non-verbal expressions. As an example of direct rational understanding of actions, Weber refers to 'the behaviour of a woodcutter, or someone's grasping a door-handle in order to shut the door, or someone's aiming a rifle at an animal'; here we have immediate rational understanding of what someone is doing. As an instance of direct rational understanding of verbal utterances he gives the understanding of 'the meaning of the proposition "$2 \times 2 = 4$" when we hear or read it: this is a case of direct rational understanding of a thought'; Weber is here close to Frege's and Husserl's theories of understanding. Finally, 'an outburst of anger, manifested in a person's facial expression, exclamations, or irrational movements' is an example of 'direct non-rational understanding of emotional impulses', and it is here that he comes closest to Dilthey's understanding of expressions. Explanatory understanding, on the other hand, is related, according to Weber, both in the rational and in the irrational case, to the complex of meanings 'into which a directly intelligible action fits in virtue of its subjectively intended meaning': the expression 'intended meaning' is used in this connexion even where it is a matter of affective processes.

We understand the action of someone cutting wood or aiming a rifle not only directly but also in terms of motive, if we know certain facts about the action: for instance, if we know that someone is cutting wood for a living or to provide for his own needs or as a form of recreation, these would be examples of rational motivation; on the other hand, if he is simply working off a state of emotional agitation, then this would be an example of irrational motivation. Similarly, if someone fires a rifle because he is ordered to do so in the course of an execution or a battle, this is a rational motive; if he shoots someone for revenge, then this is an affective (and in that sense, therefore, irrational) motive. Finally, we can understand anger in terms of its motives when we know that it springs from jealousy, slighted vanity, or wounded honour, because then we know that it is affectively determined and therefore irrationally motivated.

This understanding of rational and irrational motives is also supposed, according to Weber, to help in answering the question of the causal explanation of the action or utterance to be understood; the understanding of the complex of meaning is, in his view, at the same time to be regarded 'as an explanation of the actual course of the action', though the motivational understanding always leads only to an explanatory hypothesis which stands in need of further corroboration. This is also the origin of Weber's famous definition: '"Sociology" . . . means the science whose object is to interpret the meaning of social action and thereby give a causal explanation of the way in which the action proceeds and the effects which it produces.'[43] The principal concept in all these varieties of understanding is that of 'the interpretative grasp', and Weber is following in this case too the Criticist tendency of his philosophical teacher Rickert, in that he discusses the subjective conditions of the possibility of such a grasp before he classifies the types of interpretative procedure.

The aim of all interpretation of meanings is, like that of science in general, to achieve certainty. This certainty in our understanding of action may take either a rational form (in which case it may be either logical or mathematical) or the form of empathetically re-living the experience in question (involving the emotions and artistic sensibility). Rational certainty is achieved above all in the case of an action in which the intended complex of meanings can be *intellectually* understood in its entirety and with complete clarity. Empathetic certainty is achieved when an action and the complex of feelings experienced by the agent is completely re-lived in the imagination.[44]

The optimal case of logical and mathematical certainty is of virtually no account in regard to the understanding of action; 'the intended complex of meanings' which 'can be *intellectually* understood in its entirety and with complete clarity' can only be in such a case the rational choice of means to achieve already given ends, where there is specific empirical knowledge of causal connexions in the world. 'Every interpretation of a rationally directed purposive action of this kind attains, in the understanding of the means adopted, the highest possible degree of certainty.'[45] In this passage the well-known theory of 'ideal types' is assigned the task of bridging the chasm between real actions, which can be made intelligible with full rational certainty only in limiting cases, and the conditions of the possibility of purely intellectual intelligibility in a controllable fashion. Just as the complete objective rationality of the actions and utterances to be understood scarcely needs to be presupposed in order for it to be possible to classify them as intelligible and to interpret them – a certain approximation to the relevant ideal type is sufficient – so 'the ability totally to re-live' affects and states of mind on the other side is not 'absolutely necessary in order to interpret its meaning. In any piece of behaviour, those elements which can be understood are often intimately bound up with those elements which can not.'[46] Weber's theory of ideal types is a variant, formulated for the purposes of social science, of Rickert's theory of scientific concept-formation; above all, no further claims of a transcendental philosophical kind are raised in connexion with it.

Karl Jaspers (1883-1969), in his conception of an interpretative psychology, combines elements of the theories of Dilthey and Max Weber. Thus, he opposes to sensory perception the 'intuitive making present of the mental' and to causal explanation psychological understanding. At the same time, however, he integrates ideal-typical procedures into his methodology, which he connects above all with 'genetic understanding'. Jaspers further distinguishes between understanding (*Verstehen*) and interpretation (*Deuten*), where the latter seems to be a hypothetical transfer from what is already understood to what is at first impossible to understand. Causal explanations are not excluded from the methodology: they are brought in only in connexion with the cases which cannot be understood: 'Every limit to understanding is a fresh impetus to causal questions.' Jaspers also differs from Max Weber in taking the theme of understanding out of the context of the methodology of the special sciences and restoring it to the heartland of philosophy: in the context of his philosophy of existence, understanding becomes the basic methodological concept of philosophy itself and is there differentiated into spiritual, existential and metaphysical understanding (see Ch. 5, Sect. 3. i)

Eduard Spranger (1882–1963), in his theory of understanding, combines elements of Dilthey and Rickert, in that he regards the understanding of individuals and the individual as possible only by reference to supra-individual overlapping complexes of meaning, which are in turn constituted by means of values: 'The cardinal point of understanding lies therefore in the way in which spirit is governed by laws of value. Understanding means penetration of the peculiar value-constellation of a spiritual complex.'[47] As frequently happens in philosophy in general, the typology of understanding often involves threefold divisions. Spranger distinguishes between 'idiophysical' understanding, which interprets something spiritual on the basis of physical signs, personal understanding and objectively historical understanding. Also worthy of note is the differentiation in the field of understanding proposed by Georg Simmel (1858–1918). After first distinguishing the understanding of what is spoken from that of the speaker and characterizing only the latter as historical understanding, he introduces the difference between cause and reason as the fundamental concepts of the comprehension of psychic processes and psychic contents. Both concepts, however, are insufficient for the understanding of an individual.

What binds together into an intelligible unity the traits of a historical character and the complexes of ideas behind a historical action is, from an epistemological point of view, neither cause nor reason, neither the real law of actual events nor the ideal law of the content, but a very special third term, meaning: that the purely factual elements by means of their individual colouring and arrangement preserve a relation and unity which cannot be determined by means of laws but only empathetically re-lived; so that each hangs together with the other in accordance with its content, but only in so far as it is individually precisely so determined, in the same manner as conceptually universal contents do in virtue of logic. We infer, within historical images, from the kind and degree of the one mental element to the kind and degree of the other – but not in the syllogism, which issues in universally valid conclusions, but in a synthesis of imagination, which has power and right to assign in relation to the merely individual the validity of the rational to the contingency of what merely happens.[48]

Erich Rothacker (1888–1965) classifies understanding itself in terms of a threefold typology and distinguishes it from the two 'rational ways of grasping and explaining'. Grasping means interpretatively replacing something by general concepts, while explanation is derivation from causes. Understanding, on the other hand, makes use of the rational means provided by grasping and explaining, but only for purposes of illustration.

The more deeply the wish to understand penetrates into a matter, the more clearly is that matter shown to be vivified by a personal core: however, this reveals itself not only as an obstacle but precisely as the point from which the essential meaning which lies at its heart radiates. Not as something isolable behind the work, but as something which gives direction, as a centre of the lines of force in the work. It is the last-mentioned which confronts the understanding of great world-views and works of art. And it is precisely the same thing which also confronts the understanding of whole cultures.[49]

Rothacker, who was one of the most influential younger theoreticians of the human sciences in Germany, reveals particularly clearly how the widespread impressionistic way of talking about 'understanding' gave a head-start to the theoreticians of science of the 'other side', that is, the Logical Empiricists with their orientation to the natural sciences and their commitment to their ideals of precision, and thus advanced their ambitions to create a unified science. The blame for the fact that understanding, even today, has to fight for recognition as a scientific method lies not least at the door of the theoreticians of understanding themselves. In the field of hermeneutics, and so indirectly in the domain of the philosophy of philosophy, there is much to do in the way of the theory of science, now as much as earlier. Finally, particular reference should be made to Theodor Litt (1880–1962) because he from the outset discusses understanding in the context of processes of coming to interpersonal understanding; this was a point of contact for Karl-Otto Apel and Jürgen Habermas with their theories of communicative action, which can be regarded as modern variants of theories of understanding: this is in addition to their well-known connexions with Peirce and Wittgenstein.[50]

iv. *Martin Heidegger*

Not least among the factors which allowed Martin Heidegger's *Sein und Zeit* (Being and Time) of 1926 to become an epoch-making work was the fact that it brought together several discussions which were at that time scattered and controversial and seemed to settle them all at once by means of the claim to pose the question at a more radical level. Analogously to his reference of the theme 'history' to the existential 'historicity', Heidegger offers a fundamental-ontological theory of understanding, which promises to go much deeper than any previous attempt. Understanding belongs to the fundamental structure of the 'human being' himself, or *'Dasein'* as Heidegger calls him, and is only at a secondary level a problem in the theory of science. In his peculiar terminology Heidegger says:

Dasein is a being which does not present itself only under other beings. It is rather ontically distinguished in that for this being in its Being this Being itself is *in question*. However, it belongs to this structure of Being of *Dasein* that it has in this Being a relation of Being to this Being. And this in turn means that *Dasein* understands itself in any mode and any form of expression in its Being. It is a characteristic of this being that with and through its Being that Being is disclosed to him himself. *Understanding of Being is itself a determination of the Being of Dasein.* The ontic distinction of *Dasein* lies in the fact that it *is* ontological. [Heidegger's italics].[51]

All understanding, including the philosophical kind, and certainly all theories of understanding, are based on this view in the ontic structure of *Dasein* itself and are primarily understanding of its own mode of Being; all modes of understanding which are not understanding of Being must be seen, to use Heidegger's usual term, as 'descended' (*abkünftig*). In this sense he gives a new interpretation to his teacher Husserl's conception of phenomenology: what in Husserl is seen as a medium of 'first philosophy', simply as a philosophical method, namely, phenomenological description, becomes in Heidegger the *exposition of the meaning of Being*, which for ontic reasons is always in question for the being *'Dasein'* in its Being:

Phenomenology of *Dasein* is *hermeneutics* in the original meaning of the word, according to which it refers to the business of exposition. However, in so far as through the disclosure of the meaning of Being and the fundamental structures of *Dasein* in general the horizon is revealed for all further ontological investigation of beings which are not of the same kind as *Dasein*, this hermeneutics becomes at the same time 'hermeneutics' in the sense of the elaboration of the conditions of the possibility of all ontological enquiry. And finally, in so far as *Dasein* has ontological priority over all beings – as a being in the possibility of existence, hermeneutics in the sense of exposition of the Being of *Dasein* acquires the, philosophically speaking, *primary* sense of an analytic of the existentiality of existence. In this kind of hermeneutics, in so far as it elaborates from an ontological point of view the historicity of *Dasein* as the ontic condition of the possibility of history, lie the roots of what can be called 'hermeneutics' only in a derivative sense: the methodology of the historical human sciences ... Philosophy is universal phenomenological ontology, starting from the hermeneutics of *Dasein*, which, as an analytic of *existence*, has secured the end of the guiding thread of all philosophical questioning at the point from which it *originates* and to which it *returns*.[52]

From this point of view, understanding is a 'fundamental mode of the Being of *Dasein*': an existential, which thus has the same source as the 'situatedness (*Befindlichkeit*) of *Dasein*'. Heidegger says, 'Understanding is the existential Being of the proper capacity for Being of *Dasein* itself, such that this Being in itself discloses the Whereon of Being with itself.'[53] Intuition and thought are then 'both derivatives of understanding, already far removed from it', and not only the methodology of the human sciences, but all forms of pre-scientific and scientific cognitive dealings with the world have their roots here according to Heidegger.

The development of understanding we call *exposition*. In it, understanding understandingly appropriates what it understands. In exposition, understanding does not become something else, but is itself. Exposition is based existentially in understanding: the latter does not arise as a result of the former. Exposition is not the acquisition of knowledge of what is understood, but the elaboration of the possibilities projected in understanding.[54]

The theory of the hermeneutic circle also acquires in this way a foundation in fundamental ontology, for 'all exposition which is to prepare the way for understanding must have already understood what is to be expounded',[55] because it is after all merely an 'elaboration' of a previous understanding. In answer to the objection that this involves a vicious circle Heidegger says,

But to see this circle as vicious and to be on the lookout for ways of avoiding it, indeed even to 'feel' it to be merely an unavoidable imperfection, is fundamentally to misunderstand understanding ... What is crucial is not to escape from the circle but to enter it in the right manner. This circle is not a ring in which any kind of knowledge it chooses moves, but is the expression of the existential *pre-structure* of *Dasein* itself ... A being for which, as Being-in-the-world, its Being itself is in question, has a circular ontological structure.[56]

What this means for the theory of science is this:

Because understanding, according to its existential meaning, is the capacity for Being of *Dasein* itself, the ontological presuppositions of historical knowledge exceed in principle the idea of the rigour of the most exact sciences. Mathematics is not more rigorous than history, merely narrower in regard to the range of the ontological foundations which are fundamental for it.[57]

We can clearly see here the points of contact with Hans-Georg Gadamer's *Wahrheit und Methode* (Truth and Method) of 1960, the hermeneutic philosophy of which must be thought of as a hermeneutic ontology in the sense of a theory of exposition, where 'exposition' means precisely the 'elaboration' of the ontological possibilities of what is understood which are already projected in understanding.

5

Life

Nowadays, 'life' is regarded as the domain of the biological sciences and medicine; we can no longer even remember today how this concept was once the dominant theme of philosophy, and yet the period in which this was so – the decades between 1880 and 1930 – ended only fifty years ago. Georg Simmel stated at that time that 'life' had become a central concept of philosophical thought in the twentieth century in the same way as 'being', 'nature', 'God' or 'ego' had in other ages. Heinrich Rickert, in his book *Die Philosophie des Lebens* (Life-Philosophy) of 1920, attacked life-philosophy as the fashionable philosophy of his time and believed that in so doing he was performing a service for 'the life of philosophy'. It is important that the term 'life' in this connexion does not refer primarily to anything biological. In fact, 'life' is a concept used in the cultural conflict and a watchword, which was meant to signal the breakthrough to new shores. The banner of life led the attack on all that was dead and congealed, on a civilization which had become intellectualistic and anti-life, against a culture which was shackled by convention and hostile to life, and for a new sense of life, 'authentic experiences' – in general for what was 'authentic', for dynamism, creativity, immediacy, youth. 'Life' was the slogan of the youth-movement, of the *Jugendstil*, neo-Romanticism, educational reform and the biological and dynamic reform of life. The difference between what was dead and what was living came to be the criterion of cultural criticism, and everything traditional was summoned before 'the tribunal of life' and examined to see whether it represented authentic life, whether it 'served life', in Nietzsche's words, or inhibited and opposed it.

One reason why life-philosophy, which in its own way was a part of this cult of life, is nowadays forgotten is that it was almost completely absorbed by the philosophy of existence and existentialism, where the impulses derived from it continue to exert their influence even today.

139

But philosophical anthropology also continues the work of life-philosophy, and there is scarcely a single contemporary philosophical tendency which remained uninfluenced by it. Even neo-Marxism after Lukács and the critical theory of the Frankfurt School have taken over the more popular aspects of life-philosophy, its criticism of culture, although they also constantly attempt to make a clear distinction between themselves and the 'irrationalism' of life-philosophy. Metaphysical partisanship for the dynamic and against the static, which conceals only incompletely the opposition of the dead and the living, is here combined with the influence of the Marxian critique of commodity-fetishism, which makes 'reification' the fundamental concept in the critique of culture. The influence of a neo-Hegelianism which itself has features of life-philosophy on Lukács is mingled in this case with the assimilation of Schopenhauer, Nietzsche, Bergson and Freud through Horkheimer and his circle (Adorno, Marcuse, Benjamin, Fromm and others): the effect is that dialectic in general is seen as simply the dynamic and is defended on that basis. In Hegel himself, dynamics was merely a moment of the dialectic and enjoyed no metaphysical priority; particularly in the later Hegel, there is even a clearly discernible preference for what is static, stable, substantial and permanent.[1] At least in the valuation which it gives to what is dynamic, becoming, changing, for which there are remarkable parallels to be found in Heidegger's dismantling of Western metaphysics and the 'forgetfulness of Being' in the name of a Being which is thought of in terms of pure process, critical theory continues to be inspired by life-philosophy.

If the subsequent history of life-philosophy is so little known, and if its revivals, in the form of the Guru-boom, the ideology of the 'Greens' and the 'Alternative Society', and even Paul Feyerabend's anarchistic philosophy, are not usually recognized as such, this is chiefly because life-philosophy is branded with the stigma of irrationalism and of being a precursor of fascism. It is certainly undeniable that the 'heroic realism' of Bäumler, Krieck and Rosenberg, which was once considered to be the official philosophy of National Socialism, was 'inspired' by the traditions of life-philosophy after Nietzsche and above all by Oswald Spengler. 'Fascism' is undoubtedly a term of reproach, but nevertheless it is open to question whether the same holds for 'irrationalism'. The good conscience of modern irrationalisms and their claim to diagnose and cure certain neuralgic points in our culture suggest the question whether it is possible to dismiss them so easily as Georg Lukács does in *Die Zerstörung der Vernunft* (The Destruction of Reason), where life-philosophy, along with the other non-Marxist 'bourgeois' philosophies, is characterized as 'imperialistic' and condemned on that score. Quite apart from the fact that Lukács, as a pupil of Simmel, himself began his career under the influence of life-philosophy,[2] this turns into a tautology if one has already classified the whole age as imperialistic: in that case, every bourgeois philosophy in it is by definition imperialistic, and the corresponding theory of fascism does more than is required to reveal it in addition as pre-fascistic. The use of such labels merely makes it more difficult to be able to pose the question of the truth of irrationalism in general; they thus also exclude from the philosophical field of vision the resurrected life-philosophy of our own day and leave it to its own devices, since it refuses to be intimidated by these criticisms. Why then is 'irrationalism' a reproach? Could it not be the truth?

1 The metaphysics of the irrational

Life-philosophy makes life into a principle. It is not intended as the opposite of academic philosophy, not even as an answer to the 'meaning of life', and certainly not as merely a philosophy of the organic: rather, it is a philosophical position which makes into the foundation and criterion of everything something which essentially stands *opposed* to rationality, reason, concepts or the Idea – life as something irrational. Life-philosophy can thus be described as a *metaphysics of the irrational* and so as irrationalism in a value-free sense.

To make this clearer, I shall return again to the relation of life and spirit in Hegel and Dilthey, to which reference was made in Chapter 2, Section 3. ii. Hegel's dialectic arose in the context of his predominantly theological early writings, in which 'life' was the fundamental category: it stood for what was dynamic, for process, for the organic, for what affirmed itself in contradictions – as opposed to what was fixed, abstract, mechanical, dead. Hegel's closeness to the Romantics is here unmistakable, but that did not prevent life from being seen, at least after the *Phenomenology of Spirit*, as a precursor or anticipation of spirit. The dialectic of the living which introduces the chapter on 'Self-Consciousness' and so the famous chapter on 'Lordship and Bondage', leads to a structure of which Hegel says: 'In that a self-consciousness is the object, it is as much an I as an object. With this, the concept of the spirit is already present for us [i.e. for those who philosophize – H.S.].'[3] The fact that 'life' in itself already exemplifies the spirit is then expressed in the *Science of Logic* by saying that life is the 'immediate Idea' and that the 'soul of life' is the concept. Finally, in the philosophy of nature, life is a form of the Idea in its otherness: spirit in the state of nature. Wilhelm Dilthey, on the other hand, who edited Hegel's early writings and did research into his intellectual development, defines the relation of life and spirit in exactly the opposite way. Life is not a deficient mode of spirit: rather, spirit is an objectification of life. It is only in this way that it is also objective spirit and a possible object of the human sciences. On Hegel's version of 'objective spirit', Dilthey says,

> The assumptions on which Hegel based this concept can no longer be accepted today. He constructed communities on the basis of the general rational will. Today, we have to start from the reality of life: in life, the totality of mental connexions is at work. Hegel engaged in metaphysical construction: we analyse what is given. And present-day analysis of human existence fills us all with the feeling of frailty, of the power of dark instincts, of the passion for darkness and illusion, of the finiteness which resides in everything to do with life, even where the highest forms of communal life arise from it. Thus, we cannot understand objective spirit on the basis of reason, but must return to the structural connexion of the units of life which is continued in communities. And we cannot treat objective spirit as an ideal construction: rather must we take as our basis its reality in history. We seek to understand this reality and to present it in adequate concepts. In that in this way objective spirit is detached from a one-sided foundation in a universal reason which expresses the essence of the world-spirit, and also detached from ideal construction, a new concept of it becomes possible, in which are embraced language, custom, every sort of form of life or style of living as much as family, civil society, state and law.[4]

Life, in the sense of that which is always there to sustain and embrace spirit, culture and also the individual consciousness, is the fundamental notion of life-philosophy in all its different varieties. This metaphysics of the pre-rational, the a-rational, the anti-rational called in question the whole of Western rationalism and compelled it to prove its legitimacy. All of a sudden, it was only those insights which were in accord with this basic idea which were regarded as 'deep', and all other kinds of philosophy were seen as superficial. Along with this there went a basic mood of pessimism amongst philosophers and a marked predilection for the tragic, in comparison with which the optimism about reason which had prevailed in the rationalistic past necessarily seemed merely shallow. No real research has yet been done into the roots in social and ideological history of this basic mood, which was much more an expression of life-philosophy than its cause. There is no doubt that there are connexions with the 'defeat of the bourgeois class' in 1848 and the disenchantment which followed the first euphoria in the wake of industrialization, but these are just conjectures. At all events, any attempt to give an account of the fundamental idea of life-philosophy in terms of the history of ideas must go much further back than such efforts at explanation usually do. In making such an attempt, we can make connexions with the problems discussed in previous chapters, for life-philosophy is a summary of the whole period. It is not just the influence which it had on the most varied philosophical tendencies – an influence which could hardly be overestimated – which vouches for that; its basic metaphysical idea put everything which had gone before into a new context: it was a new metaphysics, which affected everything, and whose history is still continuing.

i. *Life and spirit*

The earlier history of life-philosophy goes back at least as far as German Romanticism, in which 'life' was a concept used in opposition to the rationalism of the Enlightenment and the mechanistic materialism in the conception of nature which was usually equated with it. The reception of Rousseau in Germany, which sparked off the *Sturm und Drang* movement, Hamann, Herder, the young Goethe, Novalis, Friedrich Schlegel, and also the philosophy of intuition associated with Jacobi should be mentioned here; it was in this climate, with its cult of what was living, which Goethe describes in his *Dichtung und Wahrheit* (Poetry and Truth)[5] and which was then also given philosophical articulation by Fichte and Schelling, that the young Hegel began his career: his early writings directly represent this climate. Already, the general contrast was drawn between the dynamic and the static, the living and the dead, the organic and the mechanical, the concrete and the abstract, and intuition, perception, experience and abstraction and the 'mere understanding'.

The history of life-philosophy, however, begins only when 'life' as a principle was opposed to the principles of Idealism, and in the Romantic period this was by no means the case. It was only in Schelling's late philosophy, which developed in opposition to his own system of identity, and above all in the work of Schopenhauer, that the critique of rationalism was transformed into a metaphysics of the irrational: the impact of Schopenhauer was so strong that the history of life-philosophy in essence coincides with that of Schopenhauer's influence. Schopenhauer belongs among the Romantics, and for all his polemics against Fichte and Schelling was greatly influenced by both. Even his theory of knowledge is not very original: he advocates a type of subjective Idealism formulated in psychological and physiological terms, according to which the world is my representation. What is really new is the contrast to the fundamental theses of Absolute Idealism, the affirmation of the identity of being and thought and of the true and the good in the Absolute. It is precisely these theses which Schopenhauer opposes: the Absolute, the thing-in-itself is Will, Will to life, that is, something blind, irrational, indeed evil, for it is only the denial of the Will to life which is good. True being is not 'Being', but impulse, process, the dark, and rationality, meaning, truth, the good do not belong to the essence of the world, but are epiphenomena. This is also how reason is interpreted: the intellect, thought, the understanding arise from the Will and serve the Will as tools for preserving and enhancing life.

From this entirely objective treatment of the intellect and its origins it follows that it is destined for the comprehension of those aims, on the achievement of which individual life and its reproduction depend, and in no way for the representation of the nature in itself of things and the world as it exists independently of the knower. What sensitivity to light is in the case of plants, in consequence of which the growth of the plant tends towards the light, so, in its own fashion, is knowledge in the case of animals, even of men, although according to degree it is enhanced to the extent that the needs of each of these creatures require. In all of them, perception remains a mere awareness of their relation to other things, and is in no way such as to present once again in the consciousness of the knower the genuine and absolutely real essence of these things. Rather, the intellect, arising as it does from the Will, is also destined only to serve the Will, and thus to comprehend motives: it is to this that it is adapted, and so it is entirely practical in its tendency.[6]

In this theory, Schopenhauer created a counter-metaphysics, opposed to the ontological intellectualism of the Western tradition. The thesis of the instrumental character of reason in the service of life has been ever since part of the common store of ideas of the age. Nietzsche's 'psychology' and Freud's psycho-analysis, Heidegger's philosophy of technique and Horkheimer's critique of instrumental reason, and also the whole tradition of philosophical anthropology (Scheler, Plessner, Gehlen and others) play variations on these ideas, as does the Marxist tradition, which, in a use of terms which is certainly not accidental, interprets what Idealism had made into a principle as a 'superstructure' of the 'real processes of life'. All these tendencies differ from each other, not in their diagnosis of the relationship of life and spirit, but only in the consequences to be drawn from it.

In life-philosophy itself, the Schopenhauerian pessimism can be separated only with difficulty from this basic motif – despite Nietzsche's determined turning in the direction of the 'will to power' and his denunciation of pessimism and the ascetic as perversions of this will. The thesis of the ineliminability of the dominance of life over spirit, which is nevertheless a 'destiny', here led to a fundamental mood of tragedy, in which Schopenhauer's premises were once for all given a greater intensity. Nietzsche's idea that spirit, as an instrument of life, could make itself independent and turn against life itself became a watchword which came to be found in the titles of numerous books: *Der Geist als Widersacher der Seele* (The Spirit as Adversary of the Soul) by Ludwig Klages, *Untergang der Erde am Geist* (Decline of the Earth at the hands of Spirit) by Theodor Lessing, *Bewusstsein als Verhängnis* (Consciousness as a Misfortune) by A. Seidel, and so forth. The idea of the self-alienation of life in the spirit was combined, as early as Nietzsche, with cultural criticism based on a theory of decadence, in which a denunciation of rationality was connected in a striking way with an appeal for an awakening to a new culture of life. Theodor Lessing expresses this as follows:

Thus my fundamental idea took firmer and firmer root, the idea that the world of the spirit and its norms are merely the inescapable substitute-world of a life which has fallen sick with humanity, merely the means of salvation for a species which has become questionable in itself and which has, after a short period of waking consciousness, once again been engulfed without trace: it is a species of robber-apes which has been infected with megalomania by science.[7]

Such a philosophy of the 'tragic existence' (Klages) of spirit at the same time has at its disposal certain normative criteria: 'life' is seen as the standard of what is healthy, true and good, while what is to be rejected is usually subsumed under the general concept of the 'sick'. Life-philosophy can be defined simply by the fact that the contrast between 'health' and 'sickness' is the dominant normative antithesis in it. Not all life-philosophers, but most of them, incline towards a glorification of the healthy and the strong, of force and of man as a robber-beast, and all this, together with the idea of the 'blond beast', had its beginnings already in Nietzsche and belongs with the pre-history of fascism.[8] What is problematic in life-philosophy is not the metaphysical irrationalism, which could yet be true, but the valuation of the irrational: even if it were true that the irrational is the essence and rationality a mere epiphenomenon, nothing follows from that about any evaluative priority of the irrational. Why should spirit, as the weaker, not still be the better and the higher?[9]

ii. *Life and world*

The historical influence of life-philosophy coincided with the rejection of history, which was discussed in Section 4 of Chapter 2. Schopenhauer's disgust with history and Nietzsche's escape from historical culture in the name of life-philosophy prepared the way for the counter-movement against historicism, which for a time made biology into the leading science and then, secondarily, led to the production of philosophies of history expressed in terms of life-philosophy. This was given added impetus, as already shown, by the internal crisis of historicism, which was expressed above all in the problem of relativism; as a result, history lost its leading position as a directing influence on culture, and this in turn favoured a general biologism as a view of the world, which was then consolidated into the racial theories of the National Socialists. Historicism, however, had at one time taken on the mantle of Absolute Idealism: 'history' was promoted to the rank of the concept of totality and had dethroned the 'Idea', which had once been regarded as the summation of what was true and obligatory. Now 'history' met a similar fate: 'life' came in life-philosophy to be the concept of totality which philosophy after Idealism and historicism believed to be within its sphere alone. Thus Nietzsche is able to bring history before the forum of life, which for its part cannot be cited before the 'tribunal of reason'. The fact that history, according to Dilthey, itself has its basis in the connexion of lived experience, expression and understanding, which is in turn supposed to be a life-connexion, provides the epistemological foundation for such a change in the hierarchical ordering. The impossibility of going beyond life is a thesis in which rationality claims to become aware of its immanent limits, and at the same time it holds firm in it to a metaphysical idea of totality which gives due credit to it as philosophical rationality. Here too it is advisable to be cautious in making the usual objections of irrationalism, since it could after all be true that the whole is the irrational and only a part of the whole rational; besides, we must face the question of which concept of the whole we have otherwise, and whether it would be rational to renounce the use of such a concept altogether.

The powerful influence which life-philosophy exerted over its age also has important reasons derived from the history of science. In many fields, it was able to feel that it was confirmed by the development of science and the theory of science. Its rise coincided with the vitalistic reaction against mechanism in biology, which also led to a brief revival of Romantic nature-philosophy. It grew stronger in the wake of the anti-Darwinist or neo-Lamarckian tendencies which found their expression in the influential work *Philosophie des Organischen* (Philosophy of the Organic) of 1909 by the biologist and philosopher Hans Driesch. In addition, there was the structural change, discussed in Chapter 3, from science as a system to science as research, which brought with it not only a dynamization of the conception of science but also of its traditional field of objects. The usual historical schemes of systematization, which also led, for example in Wilhelm Ostwald's 'energetism', to a philosophical rejection of mechanism and materialism, confirmed life-philosophy in its Heraclitean ontology of change as what was eternal and permanent: 'What is, becomes not; what becomes, is not' – this was for Nietzsche the great lie of Western metaphysics, and Heraclitus was the only exception which he made. But even in the theory of science themes from life-philosophy (as already discussed in Ch. 3, Sect. 3. ii) were to be found. For Ernst Mach, Richard Avenarius and Hans Vaihinger, concepts, theories, indeed scientific rationality in general, were nothing but servants of life – means of achieving economy and fictions, which had no ontic basis in the flux of appearances. Above all, Avenarius interpreted the principle of intellectual economy in a purely biologistic fashion, because according to him it follows from the principle of the 'smallest unit of energy'. The influence of pragmatism in Germany[10] increased this tendency towards a functionalist interpretation of science, in which scientific rationality was interpreted and valued primarily on account of its functional achievements on behalf of 'life'.

iii. *Life and knowledge*

Dilthey's foundation of the human sciences has already been considered (Ch. 2, Sect. 3. ii). His criticism of traditional epistemology, his initial account of lived experience as a life-process and of the 'willing, feeling, representing' being 'man' and his destruction of Kant's transcendental intellectualism are at least in two respects characteristic of life-philosophy as a whole. First, it is part of the rehabilitation of philosophy as theory of knowledge, in that as a rule it does not present itself directly as an ontology of life, but claims to be able to exhibit the all-embracing life-connexion using the methods of epistemological reflection; as a rule, life-philosophy begins as a philosophy of *consciousness*. Secondly, the premises of life-philosophical epistemology are constituted in such a way that in the light of them subject and object, consciousness and what it is conscious of, are themselves seen as derivative and grounded in an antecedent whole, which it is possible to ascertain only by means of intuition. Pre- and non-objective lived experience, moods, the neutrality of what is experienced are supposed to precede all objectivity; analysis, dichotomization, the hiatus between intuition and concept – all are supposed to come about only by means of secondary exposition of that whole, which up until Heidegger was called 'life'. Usually associated with this is the thesis that only intuition and lived experience, not the abstractive, objectifying understanding, open up a real possibility of access to the world. This theme, according to which scientific rationality counterfeits or dresses up reality rather than illuminating it, is a common topic in that period of philosophy.[11]

It was above all the influence of Henri Bergson's philosophy of the *élan vital*, according to which *durée* and the *évolution créatrice* were presupposed in everything which is objectifiable as time and the temporal, which introduced temporality as a fundamental dimension into the 'Absolute' of life-philosophy. The Heracliteanism of the ontology of life-philosophy was thus given a quasi-epistemological justification. It is astonishing to what degree even those positions which explicitly attacked life-philosophy were affected by it. In the neo-Kantians, Kant's talk of the 'manifold' of sense became a 'heterogeneous continuum', which was founded in the 'immediacy and irrational intuitiveness' of 'experienced life'. In Rickert, philosophy and science are treated as means of rationalizing the irrational and are thus also interpreted in accordance with the perspective of life-philosophy; his critique of life-philosophy is certainly intended to ensure that the field is not left open to it, but it does not touch on the perspective itself. The extent to which the experience of the power of the irrational, as articulated by life-philosophy, influenced Max Weber's conception of science has frequently been discussed. It also affects even the structure of his logic of science, according to which the ideal-types are the conceptual response of scientific rationality to the essentially irrational manifold of social and historical life. Weber is aware of how far removed he is from any 'rationalistic prejudices concerning sociology' or any 'belief that life is in fact dominated by rational considerations'. Finally, the Bergsonian Heracliteanism is obvious in Edmund Husserl's talk about the 'stream of experience'. Via Max Scheler, Nicolai Hartmann and Martin Heidegger it also came to be the basic notion of the new ontology, which believed itself to have gone beyond the philosophy of consciousness (see Ch. 7).

It seems a natural transition to move from a theory of knowledge seen as a theory of lived experience in the medium of the temporal to a metaphysics of life. Already in Dilthey, the life which is revealed in epistemological reflection as what supports and conditions all accomplishments of knowledge had become ontically and normatively primary: 'Life is the fundamental fact which must fashion the outcome of philosophy. It is that which is known from within, that behind which it is impossible to go. Life cannot be cited before the tribunal of reason.'[12] It is then possible without any difficulty to make the connexion with a vitalistic nature-philosophy; Melchior Palágyi writes, 'It is possible to talk of vital facts only because we find life in ourselves. If we could not find it in ourselves, we should not be in a position to look for it anywhere else.'[13] The interpretation of the world on the basis of life, which Dilthey introduced ('Formerly, people sought to comprehend life on the basis of the world. But there is only one route possible, from the interpretation of life to the world. And life exists only in lived experience'),[14] thus went beyond Dilthey to become a universal vitalistic world-view, and it is no accident that in the history of the concept of a 'world-view' or *Weltanschauung*, this term has occasionally been replaced by 'life-view' or *Lebensanschauung*. As a result of its own conceptual premises, life-philosophy tendentiously abolished the traditional difference between nature and culture and thus facilitated the success of the general biologism in the theory of culture, which culminated in National Socialist racism.

2 Types of life-philosophy

The only guidance which it is possible to give in the broad stream of life-philosophy is by an indication of general types. Adapting a proposal of F. O. Bollnow's,[15] I distinguish between metaphysical life-philosophy, life-philosophy as philosophy of history and ethical life-philosophy: this is not meant to rule out the possibility that themes belonging to one of the other types can be found in essence in authors who are here classified as belonging to one of these types.

i. *Metaphysical life-philosophy*

Even in Germany, the most influential example of this type is Henri Bergson's metaphysics of the *élan vital*; but since we are limiting ourselves to the German-speaking world, we shall here concentrate on Ludwig Klages (1872–1956). Even the title of his principal work, *Der Geist als Widersacher der Seele* (The Spirit as Adversary of the Soul) (three volumes, 1929–33), already expresses the one primary insight, of which Klages says that all his scientific discoveries stand to it in the relation of inferences from one proposition: the insight that 'life and spirit are two completely primary and essentially opposed powers, which can be reduced neither to each other nor to any third term'.[16] In the Introduction to *Der Geist als Widersacher der Seele*, this becomes, in more precise terms, the 'thesis' which

has guided all our enquiries for the past three decades or so: that body and soul are inseparably connected poles of the unity of life into which the spirit inserts itself from the outside like a wedge, in an effort to set them apart from each other, that is, to de-soul the body and disembody the soul, and so finally to smother any life which it can attain.[17]

The model for this conception of a whole philosophy as explication and variation of a single idea had already been provided by Schopenhauer in his characterization of his own work.[18] In a yet to be written history of the world-view this will presumably come to be seen as the characteristic feature of thinking in terms of a world-view: a universal pattern of interpretation or explanatory schema, which is applicable to everything and cannot be refuted by anything singular, takes over in a post-Idealist age the traditional role of the philosophical system, both in cognitive and in normative respects. The need for totality is satisfied only by means of a 'view' of the world from a single 'viewpoint', which is also an individual 'standpoint', and the singularity of this point is the only point of unity for the intuition of the totality, the world. Klages himself does not reject the notion of a world-view, but – like almost all philosophers who put forward a world-view – associates it with a universal scientific claim; the subject of his work does not allow any separation of the logical, epistemological, metaphysical, 'soul-study' and 'life-science' domains, and furthermore his work is meant to be 'valued as a contribution to research'. Ludwig Klages was originally a natural scientist, who then became a pupil of the psychologist and philosopher Theodor Lipps and was friendly with Stefan George; he created a system of human characterology and was well-known as a graphologist even outside philosophical circles. Ludwig Klages was regarded as a negative symbol of the irrationalism of life-philosophy in general; Ernst Bloch calls him a 'Tarzan-philosopher'. On the subject of his close relationships with the youth-movement, Klages himself reports,

In 1913, I composed (on request) for the celebratory volume of the Free German Youth (Freideutsche Jugend) on the occasion of the Centenary Festival on the Meissner Heights the essay 'Mensch und Erde' (Man and Earth), in which, on the basis of a terrible analysis of the rape of nature by humanity in the present day, I sought to prove that man, as a bearer of the spirit, has torn himself apart along with the planet which gave him birth.[19]

The duality of life and spirit, thus intensified into an antagonism, remained the fundamental 'tragic' theme of his philosophy, the basic structures of which he himself describes in a series of antitheses:

Spirit and object are the halves of being; life and image the poles of reality – the spirit 'is'; life elapses – the spirit judges; life experiences – judgment is an act, experience a feeling – the spirit comprehends what is; life experiences what comes to be – (pure) being is outside space and time, and so too is the spirit; what comes to be is within space and time, and so too is life – being is fundamentally thinkable, but never directly experienceable; what comes to be is fundamentally experienceable, but never directly comprehensible – the act of judgment needs experiencing life, on which it is founded; life does *not* need the spirit in order to experience – the spirit, as that which inheres in life, signifies a force which is directed *against* life; life, *insofar* as it becomes the bearer of the spirit, resists it with an instinct of defence – the essence of the 'historical' process of humanity (also called 'progress') is the victoriously advancing struggle of the spirit against life, with the logically foreseeable end of the annihilation of the latter.[20]

This metaphysics, which betrays its character as a world-view even in the way the thought is expressed in sweeping, simple alternatives, culminates finally in an eloquent, passionate critique of culture, an indictment of the intellectualization and technical domination of the world, for which, however – unlike Heidegger or critical theory – he makes the spirit itself as a metaphysical principle responsible; as a result, the potential influence of Klages' work on the critique of culture, which could have been considerable in our own present period of ecological, 'green' and alternative ideas, is from the outset forced into an ahistorical and non-political corner.

ii. *Life-philosophy as philosophy of history*

The enormous impression made on his contemporaries by *Der Untergang des Abendlandes* (The Decline of the West) (1918–22), the major work of Oswald Spengler (1880–1936), is something that we today find it hard adequately to imagine. It appeared in the year in which the First World War was coming to an end, and although all its underlying ideas had been formulated long before 1914,[21] it was immediately interpreted in Germany as a kind of beacon-light: the loss of the war ensured for it, simply in virtue of its title, an enormous popularity. Spengler took over a great deal from other writers: the foundation of the human sciences from Dilthey, the metaphysics of power and the diagnosis of nihilism from Nietzsche, Bergson's philosophy, but also the fresh assimilation of Goethe which followed neo-Romanticism and neo-Idealism, vitalism, the whole anti-Idealist critique of culture and much more. Spengler's influence can be explained not least by the fact that he absorbed so much and then, like Klages, structured it in the form of impressive antitheses, as if his motto were: 'The world is complex, the truth completely simple.' Thus, nature is the object of objectifying, mathematico-physical thought; history is the reality of mental becoming. The two are related as outer and inner, what has become (being) and becoming (process). The mechanical is opposed to the organic, and by equating history, the soul, lived experience, becoming and the organic Spengler comes to develop an organistic and ultimately biologistic philosophy of culture, which directly compares the emergence and disappearance of cultures with the life and death of organisms.

In the case of every organism, we know that the tempo, structure and duration of its life and of every detailed expression of life are determined by the characteristics of the species to which it belongs. No one will suppose, of a thousand-year oak, that it is now on the point of beginning the true course of its development. No one expects of a caterpillar, which he sees daily growing, that it may possibly continue to do so for a year or two. In such cases, everyone feels with absolute certainty that there is a limit, and that feeling is identical with the sense of an inner form. Where the history of superior humanity is concerned, however, there prevails an unbridled optimism, disdainful of all historical and so all organic experience, in relation to the course of the future, so that everyone discerns in what happens to be the present the 'beginnings' of a quite remarkably superlative linear 'further development', not because it has been scientifically proved, but because he wishes it to be so. Reliance is placed on boundless possibilities, and no account is taken of a natural end; on the basis of the situation of each moment, a completely naive construction of how things will continue is projected. But 'humanity' has no goal, no idea, no plan, any more than the species of butterflies or orchids has a goal. 'Humanity' is a zoological concept, or else it is an empty word. If we allow this phantom to disappear from the circle of historical form-problems, we shall see emerging an astonishing wealth of real forms. Here there is an immeasurable fullness, depth and movement of the living, which has thus far been concealed by a slogan, by an arid schema, by personal 'ideals'. I see, instead of that bleak picture of a linear world-history, which is accepted only when one closes one's eyes to the overwhelming abundance of facts, the spectacle of a mass of powerful cultures which emerge with primeval vigour from the womb of a maternal landscape, to which each of them is firmly bound throughout the whole course of its existence; each such culture impresses its own form on its material, humanity, each has its own Idea, its own passions, its own life, will, feeling, its own death. Here there are colours, lights, movements which no mental eye has yet disclosed. There are flourishing and aging cultures, peoples, languages, truths, gods and landscapes, just as there are young and old oaks and pines, blossoms, twigs and leaves, but there is no aging 'humanity'. Each culture has its new possibilities of expression, which appear, ripen, fade and never return. There are many kinds of sculpture, painting, mathematics, physics, all completely different in their nature from each other, each with a limited lifespan, each enclosed upon itself, just as each species of plants has its own blossoms and fruits, its own type of growth and decline. These cultures, organisms of the highest class, grow up in an exalted purposelessness, like the flowers in the field. They belong, like plants and animals, to the living nature of Goethe, not to the dead nature of Newton. I see in world-history the image of an eternal formation and re-formation, a marvellous coming-to-be and passing-away of organic forms. The trained historian, however, sees it in the form of a tape-worm which unremittingly 'initiates' epochs.[22]

Further alternatives, to be seen in parallel with these, which determine the ontological and methodological structure of Spengler's philosophy are causality and destiny, extension and direction, space and time, surface and depths, concept and image, knowing and seeing, science and wisdom. Spengler presents himself as a sage, as one versed in expression, a morphologist, a seer, a prophet, who is able to foretell the future of our civilization from the fullness of physiognomically interpreted historical experience. At the same time, he is a 'thinker', who says of himself: 'The appearance of other cultures speaks another language. For other men there are other truths. For the thinker they are all valid or none are.'[23]

Spengler also popularized a topic in the critique of culture which cannot really be adequately expressed except in German: the antithesis of *Kultur* and *Zivilisation* (roughly, 'culture' and 'civilization'). (This was opposed by Sigmund Freud, who 'scorned' to make this distinction at all.) Spengler says,

The decline of the West . . . means nothing less than the problem of *Zivilisation*. One of the fundamental questions of the higher levels of history confronts us here. What is *Zivilisation*, seen as an organic and logical consequence, as a completion and issue of a *Kultur*? For every *Kultur* has its own *Zivilisation*. The two words, which have up to now referred to a vague distinction of an ethical kind, are here considered for the first time in a periodic sense, as expressions for a rigorous and necessary organic succession. *Zivilisation* is the inevitable destiny of a *Kultur*. Thus the culminating point is reached, from which the ultimate and most difficult questions of historical morphology become soluble. *Zivilisation* is the most extreme and artificial condition of which a superior form of humanity is capable. It is a conclusion: it follows becoming as what has become, life as death, development as rigidity, the land and mental childhood, as revealed in the Doric and Gothic styles, as spiritual senility and the petrified, fossilized world-city. It is an end, irrevocable, but it has been attained again and again with inner necessity.[24]

Kultur and *Zivilisation* – that is, Greek soul and Roman intellect, classical Athens and Hellenism, the inhabited land and the world-city which makes all the rest into a province, the 'people which is full of form and has coalesced with the soil' and the 'pure factual man, without tradition and part of a formlessly fluctuating mass'. Products of *Zivilisation* are

'Buddhism, Stoicism and socialism' as 'ultimately valid attitudes to the world . . ., which are able once more to take hold of and reshape an expiring humanity in its entire substance'. But ancient and modern imperialism also belongs to it, for 'pure *Zivilisation* as a historical process consists in a gradual destruction of forms which have become inorganic and extinct'.

Imperialism is pure *Zivilisation*. In the form of this phenomenon lies irrevocably the destiny of the West. The cultured man has his energy on the outside, the civilized on the inside. For that reason, I see in Cecil Rhodes the first man of a new age. He represents the political style of a more distant, Western, Germanic and in particular German future. His dictum, 'expansion is everything', contains in this Napoleonic form the most characteristic tendency of every mature *Zivilisation*. That is true of the Romans, the Arabs, the Chinese. Here there is no choice. Here not even the conscious will of the individual or of whole classes and people decides. The expansive tendency is a destiny, something demonic and monstrous, which seizes on the late humanity of this stage of the world, forces it into its service and uses it up, whether it will or not, whether it knows it or not. Life is the actualization of the possible, and for cerebral humanity there are only *extensive* possibilities.[25]

Structure and prophetic style, metaphysics of the irrational and rhetoric lead in Spengler to the mythologization of history and politics, and thus his writings came to be favoured sources of the National Socialist view of the world. An utterly repellent document in that connexion is his essay 'Der Mensch und die Technik. Beitrag zu einer Philosophie des Lebens' (Man and Technique. Contribution to a Philosophy of Life) of 1931, in which the approach adopted in *The Decline of the West* was supposed to be tested on the 'history of man from his origins'.[26] The result is a parody, with racist overtones, of philosophical anthropology, which was emerging at the same time. Technique is a 'tactic of life', is older than man and has its roots in the character of man as a robber-beast. 'The robber-beast is the highest form of freely-mobile life . . . It confers a high rank upon man that he is a robber-beast.'[27] The robber-beast 'man' rules through the eye and the hand, he has a 'world' and a 'world-picture' as an environment under his sway, a strong 'soul', power and property, where 'property' is supposed to be a 'royal concept'. It was 'hand and tool' which first permitted man to emerge. A state of nature is then postulated, in which the earliest man, with the 'soul of a rebel', in solitude 'built his eyrie like a bird of prey'. 'Weapon in hand', he emerged from the nexus of nature; art came to be the concept opposed to nature and 'every work of man is artificial and contrary to nature, from the kindling of fire right up to those achievements which we in higher cultures designate as properly artistic'.²⁸ But it is just there that the tragedy of man begins,

> For nature is stronger. Man remains dependent upon her, who despite everything includes him himself, her creature. All great cultures are also so many defeats. Whole races remain, inwardly ravaged, broken, having declined into sterility and spiritual disorder, victims on the field of battle. The struggle against nature is hopeless, and yet it will be carried on to the end.²⁹

There then follows the derivation of the *Führer*-principle from the anthropology of the common enterprise, and

> obviously it is natural that there should be those who command and those who obey, subjects and objects of the political or economic process . . . a natural distinction of rank between men, who are born either to rule or to serve, between leaders (*Führern*) and led in life. This is simply the case and is, in healthy times and peoples, instinctively recognized by everyone as a fact, although in centuries of decline most people do their utmost to deny it or not to see it. But the very talk of the 'natural equality of all' itself shows that there is something here which needs further proof.³⁰

There is no need to continue with this account: through the theory of the *Führer*-state and of machine-culture up to the 'Vikings of the spirit in the rise of Faustian culture', to the tragedy of 'Faustian man' incarnated in the 'nations of Nordic blood', there emerges a monstrous and horrifying historical picture, which merges seamlessly into a directly fascistic picture of the present. Imperialism is the only chance of the white nations, but the 'theories of a plebeian rationalism, liberalism, socialism' drive them, along with a civilized boredom with life, towards the 'flight of born leaders before the machine' and to the 'betrayal of technique'. They thus lose the technical monopoly to the 'coloureds' – 'the Russians are here always included' – and so prepare their own unavoidable downfall.

In the face of this fate, there is only one view of the world which is worthy of us, that of Achilles already mentioned: rather a short life full of deeds and glory than a long one without meaning. The peril has become so great, for every individual, every class, every people, that it is pitiful to deceive oneself. Time cannot be held in check; there is no possibility of prudently turning back or cleverly resigning oneself. Only dreamers believe in escape. Optimism is cowardice. We are born into this time and must courageously follow the path to the end, as it is laid down for us. There is no other. To endure to the end on the abandoned positions, without hope, without salvation, is our duty. To endure to the end like the Roman soldier whose remains have been found before a gate in Pompeii, who died because when Vesuvius erupted no one remembered to relieve him. That is greatness, that is what it means to have breeding. This honourable end is the only thing which no one can take from a man.[31]

The possibility of arriving, on the basis of the premises of life-philosophy, at quite different conclusions about the philosophies of history and culture was proved by Sigmund Freud in his later writings, especially in *Das Unbehagen in der Kultur* (Civilization and its Discontents) (1930). Again, it is above all the evaluation of the allegedly fundamental facts of life which also separates the paths followed in life-philosophical philosophies of history. Thus it would be shortsighted to bring proceedings on this question to an end on account of Oswald Spengler and what followed.

iii. *Ethical life-philosophy*

The ethical problem of the appropriate life was from the very beginning the centre of life-philosophy in the work of Friedrich Nietzsche. Life itself becomes in him the *criterion* of what is correct, as should have become clear in Chapter 2, Section 4. ii, and behind that there is in the background the scientific interest in value-free knowledge of the life-sphere. Already in *Die Geburt der Tragödie aus dem Geiste der Musik* (The Birth of Tragedy from the Spirit of Music) of 1871, the contrast between the Apollonian and the Dionysian, the dream and the frenzy, the theoretical and the tragic man is certainly not primarily intended in a historical sense, but as part of a critique of culture, and this was one reason for the bitter rejection which Nietzsche encountered among his professional colleagues in the world of classical philology. Relying on the hint of such alternatives, which Klages, Spengler and many others imitated, Nietzsche immediately proceeded to adopt a more 'hortatory tone':

Yes, my friends, believe with me in the Dionysian life and in the rebirth of tragedy. The age of the Socratic man is past; garland yourselves with ivy, take the thyrsus-staff in your hand and do not wonder if the tiger and the panther lay down fawning at your knees. Only venture now to be tragic men: for you shall be redeemed. You are to lead the festive Dionysian procession from India to Greece! Prepare yourselves for hard struggles, but trust in the marvels of your god.[32]

The Dionysian, the 'life' of the second of the *Untimely Meditations*, becomes after the repudiation of Schopenhauerian pessimism the 'will to power', for 'life itself is a will to power'. In this equation, 'life' in Nietzsche is not only the basis for his critique of the 'behind-world' and of psychological debunking, but immediately becomes the normative foundation of all critique of values in the 'revaluation of all values', as also of the creation of new values by the philosopher who philosophizes 'with the hammer', who in the guise of Zarathustra creates 'new tables':

When I came to mankind, I found them sitting there in their ancient self-conceit: they all fancied that they had known long ago what is good and bad for man. All talk of virtue seemed to them an old and weary matter; and anyone who wanted to sleep well still spoke of 'good' and 'bad' before going to sleep. This indolence I disturbed when I taught: what is good and bad *no one yet knows* – unless it is he who is creative. He it is however who creates a goal for man and gives the earth its meaning and its future: he first *brings it about, that* something is good and bad. And I bade them overthrow their ancient professorial chairs, and wherever that ancient conceit had sat; and I bade them laugh at their great masters of virtue and holy men and poets and world-redeemers. I bade them laugh at their dismal sages, and anyone who had sat on the tree of life uttering warnings like a black scarecrow . . . There it was too that I picked up from the road the word 'superman', and that man is something that must be superseded . . . To redeem the past in man and to transform every 'It was', until the will says: 'But that is how I wanted it! This is how I shall want it' – that is what I called salvation to them, this alone I taught them to call salvation.[33]

Nietzsche's ethical life-philosophy belongs in fact to the history of the problem of 'value' and we shall come back to it again in that context.

3 Life-philosophy and philosophy of existence

Bollnow's thesis that the philosophy of existence developed and thereby superseded the themes of life-philosophy 'in a deeper and more radicalized manner' will now be demonstrated by a consideration of the two most important authors of this philosophical movement – Karl Jaspers and Martin Heidegger. Fritz Heinemann maintains that it was he who coined the term 'philosophy of existence' in his book *Neue Wege der Philosophie* (New Paths in Philosophy) of 1929;[34] according to him, the philosophy of existence went beyond life-philosophy in that it sought a philosophical integration in the concept of 'existence' for the antithesis of life and discursive understanding, the irrational and rationality, but strictly speaking this is true only of Jaspers. In Chapter 2, Section 4. iii and Chapter 4, Section 4. iv, reference has been made to Heidegger's *Being and Time* as the culminating point of the philosophy of history of this period, and also of the theory of understanding; to the extent that Heidegger can be treated as a representative of the philosophy of existence at all – and this is certainly true only of his first great work – his philosophy also draws nourishment from other roots than life-philosophy. Furthermore, the philosophy of existence would be inconceivable without the influence of Kierkegaard; it recapitulates in a different context Kierkegaard's opposition to Hegelian panlogism and thus belongs in the context of anti-Idealism and anti-historicism. What is right about Heinemann's thesis is that the philosophy of existence was at least historically associated with life-philosophy; in the case of Jaspers, this was through a fundamental reinterpretation of 'life' and, in the case of Heidegger, through the notion of 'more radical questioning', through which his existential ontology, as a 'hermeneutic of *Dasein*', was also distinguished from the main hermeneutic tradition of the past.

i. *Karl Jaspers*

Karl Jaspers (1883–1969) began as a doctor and psychiatrist, qualifying in 1913 for an academic career in psychology; in 1921, he became a Professor of Philosophy, though he resigned his Chair for political reasons in 1937; from 1945 to his death, he taught in Basel. He was particularly influenced by Max Weber (after 1909), and then by Kierkegaard (1913) and Kant; but he first came to prominence scientifically with his *Allgemeine Psychopathologie* (General Psychopathology) of 1913, in which he took up suggestions from Dilthey, Husserl and Max Weber, and which is regarded as an epoch-making outline of a *verstehende Psychologie*, or 'interpretative psychology'. In 1919, there followed his *Psychologie der Weltanschauungen* (Psychology of World-Views), which outlined a typology of all possible psychological and philosophical attitudes to the world, and which already contained an anticipation of the theme of 'existence' in the form of the doctrine of the incomprehensibility of the central core of personality. After his influential essay, 'Die geistige Situation der Zeit' (The intellectual situation of our time) (1931), there appeared in 1932 the first comprehensive presentation of his ideas under the lapidary title *Philosophie*. It would be impossible to enumerate here the long series of his books.

Jaspers shares with life-philosophy the conviction of the limited nature of our rational knowledge and of its irrelevance in regard to the really important questions of life, those which concern us in the 'core of personality'. He takes over from Dilthey the criticism of the opposition of subject and object as the starting-point of philosophy; in his case the notion of the 'embracing' (*das Umgreifende*) takes the place of 'life' in this connexion. He follows Dilthey, too, in correcting the cognitivist contraction of the concept of subjectivity; the subject, however, is primarily 'existence', as Jaspers says, making a link with Kierkegaard. In regard to method, also, Jaspers partly associates himself with life-philosophy: it is only individual, 'existential' lived experience, not the discursive understanding or science, which brings us to the place of philosophical truth. It is important, however, that this methodological irrationalism of the 'illumination of existence' does not lead in his case to any devaluation of understanding and science: 'Philosophy of existence is the tendency of thought which makes use of all material knowledge and transcends it, so that man can once again become himself.'[35] The path followed by philosophical activity does not lead to the annihilation, but to the transcendence of rationality in 'shipwreck', through the experience of the 'limit-situation' which brings about the 'suspension of thought', in which man can become aware of his existence and his limitations in the 'embracing' and by means of 'transcendence'. Jaspers says,

The suspension of thought sets free the truly unconditioned. The goal of illumination is not a project of being as such, not the possession of knowledge, not a result, but the methodical awareness of being. Being aware, however, is, as it were, a suspension. In it is achieved release from the ground, in order to reach truer ground, until at last free-floating groundlessness in the world in relation to the basis of the only absolute ground of transcendence is achieved . . . Thus in the end there is no ground, no principle, just a suspension of thought in groundless space. In opposition to solidification and security in the system of ideas in which I hide myself and to which I subject myself, I remain master of my thoughts, in order to be open to transcendence and on that basis to experience the true lack of limits in the world.[36]

Philosophy of existence, conceived of as a critique of the culture of the intellect, here, in token of the concept of 'perceiving' reason (*vernehmende Vernunft*), becomes aware of itself as a philosophy of reason: 'Reason means the perception in the all-combining encounteredness of every being and every possibility, of being and nothingness.'[37] Such 'rational' criticism of the intellect is shared by Jaspers with Heidegger, but also with critical theory, which, however, follows the Hegelian model in associating 'reason' with the self-reflection of the intellect or understanding and not primarily with the perception of the undisguised truth of existence and transcendence. In distinction from critical theory, understanding and reason, world-orientation and illumination of existence remain in Jaspers constrained in a relationship of mere complementarity, which makes his philosophy in many respects into a rather bland programme of contrast to the scientific and technological rationality of our culture of the understanding, without really penetrating it to the heart and calling it in question in its inner core. Jaspers has thus not always avoided the danger of being a kind of philosophical 'Sunday orator'.

ii. *Martin Heidegger*

Heidegger's *Being and Time* also brought life-philosophy to a philosophical end in that it explicitly pronounced the 'existential analytic of *Dasein*' to be this end. Reference has already been made (in Ch. 4, Sect. 4. iv) to the super session of the Diltheyan hermeneutics of life by the 'hermeneutics of *Dasein*'. Other elements taken over from life-philosophy are to be seen in the interpretation of the neutrality of the subject which underlies all objectivity as an existential 'situatedness', as also in the critique of Cartesianism ('being-in', 'being-in-the-world'). Heidegger presents his existential ontology as a result of a more fundamental, more radical kind of ontological questioning in the same direction as that of life-philosophy itself; in it – as with the *cogito* in Cartesianism and the non-objective 'person' in Husserl and Scheler – ' "life" itself ' has not become 'ontologically speaking a problem as a species of Being', while his philosophy poses precisely this question, which lies 'in the rightly understood tendency of all scientifically serious life-philosophy', explicitly as a question about the 'Being of *Dasein*'. The 'analytic of *Dasein*', which is supposed to achieve this and so affirms that it has gone beyond life-philosophy, is governed by the guiding principle: 'The "essence of *Dasein*" lies in its existence.'[38] Here too, if in a fundamentally different way from Jaspers, 'existence' has become philosophically detached from 'life'.

6

Values

As with 'life', so with values: as a philosophical theme, they have become alien to us. Anyone in a philosophical institute who nowadays made any kind of pronouncement about value-theories would either incur the suspicion that he was advocating the old-fashioned ideology of the 'eternal values', or else would appear to many to be a Marx-scholar, promising to unveil the mysteries of the relationship between use-value and exchange-value. But it was not so long ago that 'value' (like 'life') was regarded – as it is called in a representative study from the twenties – as the 'principal and central concept of all more recent philosophy, even, to some extent, of philosophy from other countries.'[1] The neo-Kantians actually defined philosophy as value-theory, and, as a philosophy of values, its aim was to comprehend and provide foundations for all domains of value: from the economic, through the cultural, the ethical and the aesthetic, to theoretical 'truth-value', though it should admittedly be noted that our familiar talk of truth-values is derived from mathematical logic and was introduced by Gottlob Frege. The concept of 'value' was taken over from political economy in the forties of the last century and was made into a fundamental philosophical concept by Rudolf Hermann Lotze (1817–81). All historians of philosophy, however, are in agreement with the contemporaries of the philosophy of values in thinking that it was Nietzsche's provocative slogan of the 'revaluation of all values' which first led to the boom-period of the concept of value; this boom was then further intensified by the value-theoretical interpretation of the cultural sciences in Rickert and Max Weber and also by the debate about value-judgments in the social sciences. Nowadays, on the other hand, the first thing which has to be done is to clarify the problem of value as the fundamental question of philosophy, which is how it was considered in the second half of our period.

1 'Value' as a philosophical problem

An interpretation of this state of affairs purely from the point of view of the history of ideology would not be sufficient to make it intelligible. T. W. Adorno says,

> The economic concept of value, which served as a model for the philosophical conceptions of Lotze, the South-West Germans, and later of the debate about objectivity, is the original phenomenon of reification, the exchange-value of the commodity. It was of it that Marx gave his analysis in terms of fetishism, which deciphered the concept of value by showing it to be a reflection of a relationship between human beings which presented it as if it were a property of things.[2]

Adorno interprets the problem of value on analogous lines, as a problem of reification, which could arise only in the reified bourgeois world, while it can be exhibited in a dialectical critical theory of society as 'falsely posed'. Such a genetic analysis, however – even if it is true – is not a *philosophical* criticism of the whole way of posing the problem and therefore can be no substitute for a philosophical solution, if it should be the case that what we are dealing with here is not merely a pseudo-problem. We must, therefore, apply ourselves to the philosophical genesis of the problem of value and enquire into the conditions in the history of philosophy which made it possible for it to appear at least from the time of Nietzsche to the thirties of our own century as a fundamental problem in philosophy.

i. *Is and ought*

In Section 3 of the Introduction, Absolute Idealism was characterized by means of three theses, the second of which was the affirmation of the identity of the true and the good in the Absolute. (The 'true' is here understood both as true being *and* as true knowledge of being.) This revival of the Scholastic doctrine, *ens et bonum convertuntur*, came to an end, philosophically speaking, with the resurrection of the 'philosophy of reflection', to which Hegel had once objected on the grounds of its opposition of 'is' to 'ought' and which had since seemed to be finished. The return to Kant in the middle of the century then confirmed the Kantian way of posing the problem, on which Fries and Herbart had stubbornly insisted,[3] as generally obligatory, thus creating the background against which the rejection of the 'naturalistic fallacy' has come to seem so obvious to us today. The philosophical results of the loss of the convergence between *ens* and *bonum* are described by Helmut Kuhn in these terms:

In metaphysics, the good proves to be a concept of the highest systematizing power. This constructive capacity results from its close connexion with the concept of being. With the disintegration of the metaphysical concept of being, the concept of the good also collapses, and each of its component parts develops the tendency to seek to represent the whole good. In this process of division the general term loses its status. In part, it becomes a term enclosed within an ethics which thinks of itself as an autonomous discipline; in part, it is released into the freedom of everyday language and is thus abandoned to poetic and practical usage. The loss of status which the good suffers ultimately leads to an attempt by a substitute word to occupy its place. The notion of 'value', imported from political economy, is the *caput mortuum* of this once living concept. The good, torn apart from being, ontologically uprooted, no longer, as with the Platonists, beyond existence, but rather beneath existence, only 'having validity' (*geltend*), in the same way that we say of the dollar or the mark that they are valued (*gelten*) at such-and-such – this is what it amounts to, this concept of value which has risen to a short-lived position of philosophical honour.[4]

If being, thus stripped of its being good, and so reduced to mere facticity, is no longer able to provide a basis for the 'ought', then neither, contrariwise, can any good which in any way 'is' or 'exists'; but value is thought of as such a non-existent good. 'The existent is, values have validity' as it was then formulated by Lotze and the neo-Kantians. At the same time, values were supposed, however, to be something objective; they were supposed to be given, though not in the manner of existing things. In this way, the value-problem was burdened from the outset with the ontological dilemma of objects which were supposed to have objective validity without existing: they were supposed merely to have objective validity. (Max Scheler later coined the expression 'states of value' (*Wertverhalte*), on the analogy of 'states of affairs' (*Sachverhalte*).) The parallel with Russell's criticisms of Meinong's theory of objects cannot be avoided, and one of the reasons why philosophers have forgotten the problem of value is the 'linguistic turn' in philosophy, which has made such ontological problems into a favourite field for the analytic dismantling of problems and has even eliminated what was left of the problem of value by philosophical scepticism.

The fact that the problem of the objectivity of values was posed, after Lotze, in the form of a question about an object-domain of 'values'. existing in-itself, thus reflects, first of all, the fact that, in a post-metaphysical, post-Idealist age, no 'is' or 'exists' is any longer in a position to furnish an objective basis for the 'ought'; *ontology* must therefore be supplemented by *axiology*. (This is the source, in terms of the history of metaphysics, of the principle of value-freedom: anyone who transgresses that principle is conjuring up an obsolete metaphysics.) The claim to objectivity, however, is, in the post-metaphysical interpretation of science of the time, simply one of the fundamental claims involved in being scientific. Hence, the significance of the concept of value relates to the problem of an objective 'ought', in this sense of 'objective' science, and thus to the question of ethics in a scientific age: ethics seen as *value-ethics* (as Max Scheler calls it) is the philosophical response to this situation. This object-oriented concept of objectivity which is presupposed here also explains why Kant's ethics, which were orientated not to objects, but to intention and will, were regarded so universally as formalistic and appeared to be in need of supplementation by a value-theory: they were so regarded even amongst neo-Kantians. The philosophy of value thus came to be the basis of *practical* philosophy, indeed tended to coincide with it once the material themes of the old *philosophia practica universalis* (action, law, economy, state, history and so on) had migrated, along with the historical and social sciences, out of the sphere of philosophical systematics and had been monopolized by these latter disciplines. After that, philosophers believed that they were no longer able, within their proper sphere of reflective competence, to work in these areas. This is also the answer to the question which might be raised, why there has been so little discussion in this presentation of the period of social theory: after Hegel, the history of social theory, despite all dependencies and cross-references, no longer coincides with that of philosophy.

ii. 'Is' and 'has validity'

The reason for the fact that, in the philosophy of value, it is not the 'ought' which occupies the foreground, but the concept of 'validity' is that, according to it, every ought refers to a value, but it is not true that conversely every value is the foundation for an ought; apart from ethical values, for which this is the case, 'there are' also theoretical values (truth) and aesthetic ones (beauty). Thus, 'ought' is not a concept by means of which it would be possible to give a general characterization of the 'mode of being' of values; the philosophy of value therefore operated after Lotze instead with 'having validity': something can have validity in that it is true, good or beautiful, whereas only from 'X has validity in being good' does it follow that X ought to exist. Rickert then added the observation that a common feature of what has validity is the contrary character of its opposite, whereas in what exists the result of negation is a contradictory opposite: 'true – untrue', 'good – bad/evil', 'beautiful – ugly' – but 'exists – does not exist'. The turn of phrase 'X has validity in being . . .' further indicates the way in which a more detailed characterization of the relation of existence and having validity should be given. J. E. Heyde distinguished in this connexion between 'something is a value' and 'something has a value', and spoke in the first case of an 'object-value' (*Objektwert*) and in the second of a 'value-object' (*Wertobjekt*). It follows that what has validity is either itself a value, or is something existent which, to the extent that it has a value, exemplifies a value or to which – as Rickert put it – a value 'attaches'. The existent itself, on the other hand, without any value-reference, is mere facticity, which does not fall under such 'differences of validity'[5] as a result of itself alone, but only in the light of values which may be presupposed, and is only in general subject to possible assessment in that light.

The philosophy of value maintains that only what is assessable is intelligible in terms of meaning; only what can be true, good or beautiful, that is, what is potentially related to values and thus has validity, is a possible object of meaningful understanding. This association of value and meaning, validity and understanding (*Verstehen*) is something which Rickert unceasingly emphasizes: 'The problem of value remains fundamental for any scientific work on the meaning-problems of life or on a general world-view ... Properly understood, meaning-problems always lead to problems of value, for to interpret the meaning of life is to bring to consciousness the values which endow it with meaning.'[6] 'Meaning', however, is not to be confined to the 'meaning of life': all meaning-structures, and in particular those which are hermeneutically interpretable, are according to Rickert constituted as bearers of meaning by their value-relevance; this point has already been discussed in Chapter 2, Section 2. iii and Chapter 4, Section 4. ii. It is the connexion of value and meaning, and *not* primarily that of value and the ought, which is also from the historical point of view the root of the problem of value: the ethical theme is secondary in comparison. The philosophy of value arose in Lotze, not as a reaction to the disintegration of the unity of 'is' and 'ought' in the Absolute, but as a response to the loss of the identity of being and meaning which had been affirmed by Absolute Idealism. If Hegel, in his *Lectures on the Philosophy of World-History*, attributes the possibility of understanding history as rational to the fact 'that reason rules the world, that the course of events in world-history has therefore also been rational', this is simply a variation on the more general thesis of the identity of subjective and objective reason in the Absolute Idea, which one must have already grasped in philosophy in order also to be able to recognize it as the absolute goal of world-history. This 'understanding-as-rational' of history, however, is what was later called by historicists *Verstehen* or 'understanding'; in making the goal and purpose of history intelligible, it also made its meaning accessible, as philosophers after Hegel put it. (Hegel himself preferred the expressions 'goal', 'final goal' and 'destination'; the expression 'value' also occurs only occasionally in his writings: 'The rational is that which exists in and for itself, by means of which everything has its value.'[7]) The understanding of the meaning of the world on the basis of its goal, however, was given up after Idealism; what in Hegel looked like a mere new version of objective teleology had to be philosophically abandoned. That meant that the *ens*, which no longer coincided with the *verum*, *bonum* and *pulchrum*, as a value-free facticity fell under general suspicion of meaninglessness, and it was against that above all that the philosophy of value after Lotze brought the concept of value into play. Values were supposed to help to resolve the question of meaning, of which Helmut Kuhn says: 'The modern question about 'meaning' – a word which first acquired the force which is familiar to us as a result of Nietzsche – is at bottom the question of the good, formulated in a situation of ontological perplexity.'[8] The neo-Kantian interpretation of the old ontology as a combination of ontology and axiology indicates the new philosophical situation after Hegel, in which ontology, as the philosophy of what is – to the extent that it was still considered to be in general possible – had from the outset to do with a value- and meaning-*free ens*; values, which did not exist and so, however, had validity, were required to close the systematic gap which thus resulted.

iii. *An excursus on 'nihilism'*

The modern question about meaning, in the form in which Nietzsche posed it, is the problem of nihilism. 'What is meant by nihilism? *That the highest values are devalued*. There is no goal. There is no answer to the question "Why?"'[9] Nihilism as a 'psychological condition' occurs

when we have looked for a 'meaning' in all that happens which is not to be found there: so that the seeker finally loses heart... What has happened at bottom? The feeling of *valuelessness* has been attained when one grasps that the total character of existence may be interpreted neither by means of the concept '*purpose*', nor by that of '*unity*', nor by that of 'truth'. Nothing is attained or achieved in that way; there is no overlapping insight into the multiplicity of what happens: the character of existence is not 'true', it is *false* . . ., there is absolutely no reason any longer to persuade oneself of a *true* world . . . In short: the categories of 'purpose', 'unity', 'being', by means of which we have applied a veneer of value to the world, are once again *abolished* by us – and now the world is seen as *valueless* . . .[10]

It is apparent here that the diagnosis of nihilism no longer primarily concerns the *moral* values, which Nietzsche had generally presented, since the time of *Beyond Good and Evil*, as the central core of all values; what loses value in this nihilistic disillusionment are simply the *metaphysical* values: being, truth, unity, purpose, meaning – all prove to be results of our own evaluations. Thus Nietzsche conceives of

> the evaluation, 'I believe that such-and-such is the case' as the essence of truth. In evaluations, conditions of self-preservation and growth are expressed. All our cognitive organs and senses are developed only in view of the conditions of self-preservation and growth . . . The necessity for the existence of a number of beliefs, the need for judgments to be made, the absence of doubt in regard to all essential values – these are preconditions for all that is living and for its life. Therefore, what is necessary is that something must be regarded as true – not that anything should actually be true. 'The *real* world and the world of *appearance*' – this antithesis is reduced by me to *value-relationships*. We have projected *our* conditions of self-preservation as *predicates of being* in general. We have to be stable in our beliefs in order to prosper. From that we have fashioned the view that the 'real' world is not one of change and becoming, but of *being*.[11]

Nihilism *is* just this insight: 'That there is *no truth*; that there is no absolute constitution of things, no "thing-in-itself". *This itself is simply nihilism, indeed nihilism of the most extreme kind.*'[12]

The 'ascent of nihilism', which Nietzsche prophetically spoke of as the 'history of the next two centuries', is an inevitable fate: 'for necessity itself is here at work'. It is the immanent dynamics of values themselves which is here manifesting itself:

> For why is the ascent of nihilism now *necessary*? Because it is our previous values which are arriving at their ultimate conclusion in it; because nihilism is the logic of our great values and ideals, thought through to the end, – because we must first experience nihilism in order to get to the bottom of it, which was, properly speaking, the value of these 'values'.[13]

The momentum of this dynamic is explained by Nietzsche in terms of the concept of truth: '*Truth is the sort of error*, without which a particular kind of living being cannot live. It is the value for *life* which ultimately decides.'[14] The 'value for life' refers genetically to evaluations in the service of life, which is itself merely a 'will to power': 'All evaluations are merely consequences and narrower perspectives in the service of this *one* will: the evaluation *itself* is merely this *will to power*.'[15] Here Nietzsche's diagnosis of nihilism coincides with his ethical philosophy of value, from which results his 'fundamental objection' 'to all philosophico-moral cosmodicies and theodicies, against all "*whys*" and *supreme values* in previous philosophy and philosophy of religion. A form of *means has been misunderstood as an end*: while conversely *life and the increase in its power* have been *reduced to a means*.'[16] The factual dominance of evaluations by the will to power was positively valued by Nietzsche to the extent that it conformed to the will of the one who evaluated and posited values himself, and this is the normative foundation of the 'revaluation of all values'. The metaphysical disillusionment associated with nihilism was thus celebrated by Nietzsche as 'the *great alleviation* of our burden, – as a result of it, we no longer *have* to be pessimists';[17] at last we can create our values ourselves, for 'what is good and bad *no one yet knows* – unless it is he who creates them'.[18]

2 Three types of philosophy of value

It is possible to find one's way in the broad stream of the philosophy of value only by classifying general types. The classification used must have some relation to the problem of value itself. Initially, Heyde's distinction between 'object-value' and 'value-object' is useful, if the discussion is generally about 'value'. Where the ontological status of values is concerned, it is advisable to go beyond the difference of 'being' and 'having validity' and to make a clear distinction between the pairs of concepts 'real–ideal' and 'objective–subjective'. Values are real, if they are present in reality, and they are ideal, if they exist only in consciousness. This is not to be confused, however, with the difference between 'objective' and 'subjective', which simply has to do with the question whether the values which have real or ideal existence exist independently of the consciousness which apprehends them or not. Even what exists in consciousness can be experienced as independent of consciousness; an objective Idealism with regard to values is just as conceivable as a subjective Realism which asserts that there really are values, but makes their nature and intensity dependent on the valuing subject: this is a difficult position, but nevertheless a conceivable one. A further distinction is brought to bear if one poses the gnoseological question of the way in which values are apprehended: is it by means of intellectual cognition or intuitive feeling? Accordingly, one can introduce intellectualism and intuitionism about values as a further typological antithesis, which came once again to play a role in the discussions between cognitivists and emotivists in meta-ethics. As a result, we have a whole spectrum of useful pairs of concepts:

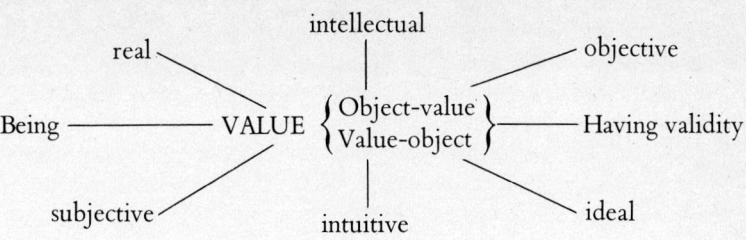

In the account of the philosophy of value which follows, which will make use of these concepts, only those positions will be referred to which explicitly distinguish themselves from the psychology of value and so conceive of themselves as philosophical positions in the narrower sense. In the nineteenth century, psychology was regarded as no longer philosophical, but as an empirical scientific discipline; accordingly, those philosophical theories of value which differentiated themselves from 'psychologism' also did not understand themselves as empirical theories, but independent of experience. This concentration on *a-priorism* in regard to values means that the great part played by psychologizing theorists in the philosophy of value of the period (such writers as Meinong, Ehrenfeld, Münsterberg, Stern and others) will not be taken into account here.

i. *The reinterpretation of Idealism in terms of value-theory (Lotze)*

Hermann Lotze (1817–81) is a key figure in the history of philosophy in the nineteenth century. His significance extends far beyond that of being the founder of the philosophy of value. In his life and work, Lotze brought the rejection of Hegel and Absolute Idealism within the bounds of academic philosophy. As a pupil of Christian Hermann Weisse (1801–66), one of the principal representatives of 'speculative theism', which was one variety of late Idealism, he also studied medicine at the same time, which convinced him of the untenability of the Idealist and Romantic philosophy of nature. Throughout his life he remained convinced of the necessity to integrate philosophical speculation and modern natural science and attempted to allow for such integration, especially in his much-read *Mikrokosmos* (Microcosm), which appeared in three volumes between 1856 and 1864. However, Lotze remained a systematic philosopher and resisted the reduction of philosophy to epistemology or theory of science. In his teaching activity as an *Ordinarius* at Göttingen, which lasted more than thirty-five years, and by his publications he exercised a lasting influence on the philosophy of his time, though without founding any 'school'. His most important pupil was Wilhelm Windelband (1848–1915), who reshaped Lotze's essays towards a transcendental philosophy of value. Through Rudolf Eucken (1846–1926), the famous neo-Idealist of the Wilhelmine era, Lotze also influenced Max Scheler, who advanced the philosophy of value on the basis of Edmund Husserl's phenomenology. In 1882, Wilhelm Dilthey became Lotze's successor in Berlin.

The philosophy of value arose in Hermann Lotze, not in the context of ethical reflection, but as an answer to the problem of reality. (It was Nietzsche's critique of morality which first brought together value-theory and moral theory in the way which seems so obvious to us today.) The point of departure was the Leibnizian problem of the relation between truths of reason (*vérités de raison*) and truths of fact (*vérités de fait*). Reason tells us what is possible, and there are infinitely many possible worlds. The question why this particular possible world is the actual world is answered in Leibniz's metaphysics by reference to the divine will, which singles out, wills and actualizes this world from among the infinity of worlds made possible by the divine understanding, and because God's will is infinitely good, Leibniz is able to derive a theodicy: God has willed and created the best of all possible worlds. Kant formulates this question of the reality of the world in analogous fashion as a question about the purpose of the world. It must be possible for that which we, as moral beings, are unconditionally obliged to do, to be realized by us in this world in the way in which it factually exists. Thus, the objective purpose of the world must ultimately coincide with the purposes of our existence and our action as moral agents, which we have an unconditional obligation to realize in virtue of the Categorical Imperative. This leads Kant to propose an ethico-theological proof of the existence of God, which alone makes an explanation of this possible, but which, as distinct from Leibniz, has only practical validity.[19] The facticity and the purpose of the world, which in Kant are brought together only in reflective thought, Absolute Idealism then sought to bring together in cognition, and Hegel's work has repeatedly been cited as an illustration of this. Lotze's differentiation of his own position from Hegel's, on which the most decisive influence was that of Herbart, provides the most important reason for saying that the links of the philosophy of value are not with Hegel, but with Fichte. Fichte's ethical Idealism affirms the moral both as the final purpose of the world and also as the ground of its being, so that the theory of morality is immediately transformed 'into a theory of being (into a theory of true being, of genuine reality)'. The 'given world' is thus 'merely the visible aspect of the moral, of freedom'. This interpretation of the world by reference to the moral, the recognition of the 'divine Idea' and the attempt to live in it, is the task of philosophy, and it alone raises philosophical awareness above imprisonment in the 'world of sense'. In the *Wissenschaftslehre* (Theory of Science) of 1813, the expression 'sense' was used to designate this reference of the world of facts to the moral: 'The root and the innermost essence of the organon for philosophy is precisely that you are required to have sense for sense as something absolutely other than everything possible which is taken in a sense.'[20] In the light of this sense, the impenetrability of the mere fact of 'chance and good luck' disappears for philosophy. It is certainly quite wrong to suggest that Fichte 'first elaborated this concept of "sense" in conceptual clarity and determined its systematic position';[21] 'sense' as 'sensorium' is by no means clearly distinguished from 'sense' as 'intelligible meaning'.

The world of the new sense and thereby the sense itself is provisionally clearly defined: it is the seeing of the premises on which the judgment 'It is something' is grounded: the ground of being, which just because it is this, does not itself once more *exist* and have a being. The new world elevates and extends itself to something beyond being.[22]

To interpret this 'beyond being', which in Fichte is the cognitive correlate of the new philosophical sense (*sensus*),[23] as 'sense' in exactly the same sense as that of later philosophy of value is a projection. This is all the more true in that it was only after his move away from Hegel, Weisse and Absolute Idealism as a whole that Lotze again saw, with regard to the metaphysical problem of reality, how it necessarily presented itself in the conditions of the philosophy of reflection. The given and the concept, existence and purpose, facticity and sense, had to be brought together without any a priori borrowing from an Absolute, if the aims of metaphysics, to which Lotze always adhered, were to be achieved. The 'question of meaning', as a problem which was not merely hermeneutic, but metaphysical, which was a matter of such intense concern to post-Idealist philosophy, does indeed, as already shown, have its roots in Idealist philosophy itself, but it was only in the post-Idealist situation that it came to be simply a metaphysical problem.

The genesis of the metaphysical need for meaning and meaning-giving may be followed, by way of example, in Lotze. Already, in his famous encyclopaedia article of 1843, 'Leben und Lebenskraft' (Life and Life-energy), which is connected with his medical dissertation of 1838 'De futurae biologicae principiis philosophicis' (On the philosophical principles of future biology), Lotze opposed all efforts at vitalistic or teleological interpretation in natural science; for Lotze, the only kind of explanation which can be given in science in general is causal and mechanical, and this is true even in the case of psychology, anthropology and historical science. This mechanistic view of the world, however, leaves a metaphysical vacuum, which Lotze undertook to fill, though no longer, like Kant, by means of reflective judgment in a practical regard, but by means of his philosophy of value. In the Introduction to his *Metaphysik* (Metaphysics) of 1841, Lotze defined the essence of philosophy in terms of the basis which 'philosophical enquiries' have in the 'requirements and situation of immediate mental life'. The decisive factor is, first of all, the need to go beyond what is already known and given in the direction of something as yet unknown and not given, but determinable, and this is the common root of philosophy and science. Philosophy goes beyond the sciences in not merely seeking this non-given, but investigating, as a 'universal science', the 'relation in which the non-given stands to the given, through which it becomes the necessary completion of the latter'. It takes as its theme the basis of the necessity of such a completion:

> Thus, we are not just able to seek out those determinate completions which the feeling of the incompleteness of our immediate thought-content in relation to any circle of individual appearances requires us to presuppose, but the demand for such completions in relation to all appearances is itself a universal completion of the course of our thought, the more detailed content of which needs to be investigated.[24]

Philosophy seeks in this way, not the laws of the appearances themselves, but 'those laws in accordance with which it is in general possible for it to happen, in relation to every possible content, that a non-given stands in a necessarily complementary relation to a given'. The fact that in general there exists the need for the elucidation of these laws is interpreted by Lotze as an indication that

> we have in ourselves an indwelling criterion, a truth, in comparison with which the inadequacy of our perceptions is revealed . . . The presence of that truth in the mind, which forces us to go beyond what is given, is the situation which makes philosophy possible and in favourable circumstances actual, that is to say, when other movements of the mind compel it to examine itself and consciously to investigate what it is compelled unconsciously to employ.[25]

By talking in this way of the 'truth' which is present in the mind, Lotze gives his a-priorism from the outset a Platonic twist, which helps to shape his whole philosophy of value.

The philosophy of value itself, however, is brought into play in that Lotze characterizes these 'requirements of mental life' by no means simply in cognitive terms; they concern the whole field of human experience and aspiration – the 'formation' (*Bildung*) of the 'soul' (*Gemüt*).

First, the appearances of the world in its course pass, changing and varying, before the unprejudiced soul and form the material for reflections which undertake, by a comparison of particulars, to distinguish the essential from the inessential, the constant from the transitory, the valuable from the indifferent; and so we see precipitated, out of the experience of life, as the outcome of that sensory observation, the *formation* which acquires from a certain sum of experiences a content of the truly existent which is comparatively constant and is determinable by thought.[26]

This quotation epitomizes Lotze's early metaphysics. He shares the extension of 'mind' or 'spirit' beyond the cognitive with Schelling's notion of the 'whole spirit', for which Lotze had already in his early aphorisms invented the term *Gemüt* or 'soul'. The programme at that time was a philosophy thought of as a 'phenomenology and critique of the soul', which was to lead to a 'world-view of the soul'. The 'unprejudiced soul', of which Lotze speaks in the passage just quoted, does not merely distinguish the constant from the transitory, but also the essential and the valuable from the inessential and the indifferent. The value-aspect, therefore, enters into Lotze's metaphysics in that, in common with the whole Platonic–Aristotelian tradition, he holds firm to the view that *ens et bonum convertuntur*. In Lotze's psychologistic style of expression, which became still more marked in his article 'Seele und Seelenleben' (The soul and its life) of 1846, the extension of 'mental life' comes as a result to concern emotive, voluntative and evaluative elements and activities. It was then possible for Dilthey's life-philosophy to take up this comprehensive concept of the mind (see Ch. 4, Sect. 3). Lotze, however, remained this side of life-philosophy, since he did not make the transition to a metaphysics of the irrational. At the same time, he remained a metaphysician, because he refused to understand the talk of the truth which was present in the mind in a merely epistemological sense; for him, knowledge itself is a relation of being, which it is necessary first of all to elucidate metaphysically. The difference between the valuable and the indifferent, however, supplied the catchword with which the reinterpretation of traditional Idealist metaphysics by the philosophy of value commenced.

What is the truly existent? Philosophy as metaphysics is the effort 'to bring unity into the material of the formation'.

In order to make the various contingent views of the formation comparable with each other, we must emphasize that element in that concept of the truly existent which is alone common to all of them. But this is the moral weight which is placed on this concept, and which certainly has a content which is different from the determination of that concept from another quarter. Anyone who speaks of the truly existent desires to know what is valuable in and for itself, not what is indifferent. This antithesis is at the basis of that concept; it is by it that the concept must be knowable, just as also the contingent formation undertakes to define it by means of the predicates of the necessary or the free.[27]

The last clause refers to Lotze's differentiation of his own position from that of Hegel and the late Schelling: his objection was to their identification of the truly existent with the necessary or the immemorially free, without taking into account the valuable as its principle. The fundamental idea of Lotze's philosophical programme is the antithesis of the valuable and the indifferent as itself the basis of the concept of the truly existent. To philosophy – which, in harmony with the research-centred conception of science of the period, he thought of as an unfinished project – he assigned the task of enquiring 'whether there is a point at which the claim to a value which exists in and for itself coincides with a form of being'. The answer to this question is Lotze's 'teleological Idealism', which is in fact an Idealism of values, and from which the whole later philosophy of value developed.

The methodical route to this position is described as follows:

The requirement to transform that knowledge which is present even in the immediate mind in the form of fluctuating intimations and to lead it out in that way beyond the transitoriness of our impressions has led us to enquire, in a metaphysical science, into the universal assumptions which must be made, not merely by us in our individual mode of thought, but also by the universal mind concerning the nature of what exists.[28]

These universal assumptions are developed in the first part of the *Metaphysics* under the title of 'The Theory of Being'. To that is attached 'The Theory of the Appearance', which treats of the themes of Kant's Transcendental Aesthetic, but corresponds in systematic terms to Hegel's Logic of Essence. The third part contains the Theory of Categories, and it too represents a peculiar intermediate position between Kant's Transcendental Analytic and Hegel's Logic of the Concept. Like Hegel, Lotze affirms the unity of logic and metaphysics, but he differentiates himself from Absolute Idealism in interpreting metaphysics essentially as a formal discipline, which must have no pretensions to be able to reconstruct the whole content of the world out of itself. The last section of the Theory of Categories bears the title 'Deduction of the Categories'. This 'Deduction' contains the explicit transition to 'teleological Idealism', which, however, in distinction from German Idealism from Kant to Hegel, involves no essential reference any longer to a transcendental or absolute subject. The Deduction of the Categories is no longer a variant on the 'Transcendental Deduction of the Pure Concepts of the Understanding'; rather, it attempts, by means of an objective concentration on the truth which is 'present' in the mind, to show that we are compelled to refer to an objective 'ought' as a necessary presupposition of the existent and the categories of the existent, and indeed that we do this by means of an interrogation of the categories themselves as the formal determinants of the necessarily existent with regard to their necessity.

How shall we justifiably concede to these formal determinants, which are not in themselves the truly existent, that all-governing necessity? We shall affirm that the metaphysical categories are certainly not the true content of the world as it ought to be, but just as little that they exist of themselves as an incomprehensible necessity, as an absolute *prius*, in order to permit, as the possible result of their entry into appearance, the truly existent as something which came into being later. Rather, they are the system of principles which the true content of the world as it ought to be requires, in accordance with its own determination, in order to actualize itself by means of the cooperation of existents in accordance with those principles.[29]

Leibniz's problem of the specification of reality is thus to be resolved on the basis of a deduction of the categories of reality from the 'true content of the world as it ought to be' itself.

The categories are not what is first in the world, rather, the moral content is the substance of what happens, and is there without categories; but it calls forth in the mind as a purpose these categories themselves as the principles in accordance with which alone the unknown mechanism of reality produces it itself . . . the fact that the true content of the world is that which ought to be, which possesses this apodicticity of existence in virtue of what it is, is the formal metaphysical determination of this same content.[30]

Lotze continues: 'Apodicticity of existence can be granted only to the good. Metaphysics requires that everything which happens and thus its inherent determinations depends on, and is derived from, that which in virtue of its content belongs to the metaphysical category of the absolute purpose.'[31]

The conclusion of the *Metaphysics* of 1841 reads: 'The beginning of metaphysics lies not in itself, but in ethics.'[32] Acceptance of an 'ought' as a metaphysical basis of the 'is' was also the principle of Fichte's ethical Idealism. What distinguishes Lotze's teleological Idealism from Fichte's version is the fact that the 'good', the 'absolute purpose', the 'thing which ought to be' is not understood merely in a moral or ethical sense, but as something which provides the basis for the more general priority of what is aimed for as valuable in general. This shift to a general and univocal value-theoretical point of view was then in the later writings also given terminological expression; in his polemic against I. H. Fichte, Lotze described his metaphysics as the defence of the conviction 'that the world of values is at the same time the key to the world of Forms'.[33] Lotze sets himself apart from pure Platonism by his methodical claim to attain to that 'world of values' by pure categorial analysis, treating them as necessary presuppositions of knowledge of reality itself. It is important here that this solution of the Leibnizian problem in terms of the philosophy of value is added as a complement to the purely causal-mechanical knowledge of reality, the causal structures being regarded as a medium for the realization of the valuable and obligatory. The truly existent is 'the purpose fulfilled by its causal means'. 'When efficient causes come together in such a way as to produce the effected existent in accordance with the determinations of the principle which lie in them through the process of causality, the decisive moment for this cannot be itself in its turn a cause, but must be conceived of, in another mode of being, as the effective purpose.'[34]

As a result of this relationship of complementarity between the causal and the final nexus, Lotze's metaphysics comes to stand in a complementary relation to science in general; his teleological Idealism thus comes to look like an 'Idealist world-view' which is added on to scientific Realism. The Realist view

affirms that the only premise required for the explanation of appearances is the recognition of the factual existence of a world of real things, to the content of which, although it can ultimately be characterized only by means of ideal determinations, nevertheless belongs irrevocably and once and for all that absolute, unchangeable and hence relationless existence . . . Everything which happens and appears thus results only from the nature of that which is, but that which is is absolute, and completely underivable from anything else . . . As against that, Idealism accepts the premise that that which happens is indeed to be explained first of all on the basis of that which is; but that which is does not stand on its own feet, but receives the form and value of its existence only from that which is contemporaneous and ought to be because of its inner value, or, in other words, from that whose existence we are called upon to accept, not only as a result of some demand of experience, but also as a result of the dignity of its inherent content.[35]

This Idealism is nothing but a particular ideal perspective, in which the real world is seen, and its justification lies essentially in the satisfaction of the requirements which are not satisfied by the Realist world-view. Lotze himself emphasizes

> that this Idealist view is certainly based on an aesthetic or ethical requirement which affords, for the unprejudiced understanding, a broad foundation adequate to bear the load . . . The fundamental presupposition which is expressed in an Idealist view is that in the world in general reason rules, that it is not the indifferent which exists, but only that which is characterized by means of its value, that in general the substratum, the subject, to which a position of existence belongs, can be comprehended, not by means of theoretical concepts of a quality or the like, but only by means of the sense of a content which is valuable in itself, by means of aesthetic Ideas.[36]

Lotze's metaphysics is the attempt to justify the 'Idealist view', which knows itself to be in harmony with the requirements of the 'unprejudiced understanding', against the overwhelming objections of modern scientific Realism; the mere existence of these requirements is, however, no 'foundation adequate to bear the load' of their legitimation and fulfilment. 'Teleological Idealism' may therefore be summarized as the thesis

> that the concept of a real thing, little as it in general satisfies our longing for an ultimate immutable principle, possesses equally little inner force by means of which it could contribute anything to the necessary Forms of what happens, or offer resistance to the commands of the Idea; the real everywhere effects as much as it is commissioned to do. The world of nature is a dependent reflection of a world of grace.[37]

This allusion to Leibniz at the same time makes clear the context into which the Leibnizian problem of the specification of reality is here being placed. Lotze is certainly the first metaphysician of the 'metaphysical requirement', that is, the quest for a metaphysical completion of that modern scientific interpretation of the world which seems to have no further need of philosophy. His value-theoretical Idealism is no longer presented as an answer to problems within science, but seeks to satisfy requirements of the 'soul' which are ignored by the sciences. These requirements, which Lotze himself characterizes as ethical and aesthetic and which have their basis in the 'sense of a content which is valuable in itself', do not however relate primarily to a normative orientation or to the possibility of also experiencing aesthetically the causally explained world; they are above all requirements for a meaning of the world, for 'giving sense to the senseless' (T. Lessing). Already, in his *Metaphysics* of 1841, Lotze was posing the question of the connexion between processes of being and knowledge as a question of the meaning of this connexion. Do both processes, the objective and the internal sequences of the whole subjectivity, take place alongside each other, merely guided by chance, or is it a content which ought to be which generates both this duality in the branches of the process and the determination of what happens in the subjectivity, the metaphysical Forms? Does it have a meaning that the universal subjectivity reacts, and reacts in this way, to stimulation by the real process, or is this merely the way it is?[38]

Since Lotze, 'Idealism' has essentially been a matter of conferring meaning: a higher 'world-view' than that of science, which allows us to recognize from the 'standpoint of the ideal' (F. A. Lange) what is the meaning of all that which science can certainly explain, but cannot interpret. It is not 'is and ought', but 'existence and meaning', which indicates the situation of tension in which Lotze's teleological Idealism stands and the philosophy of value in general originates. Lotze's 'Idealist world-view' thus belongs at the same time to the history of the world-view, which can in general be understood only on the basis of the history of the metaphysical problem of meaning, and it is the first form of an Idealist world-view. Philosophy of value and the notion of a world-view are in general inseparable.

Lotze's metaphysics no longer belongs to 'speculative theism', for what was later termed 'value' – the 'good', the 'absolute purpose', the 'thing which ought to be' – was not thought of by him in personal terms. His Idealism is distinguished from that of Kant and Fichte in that it contains no essential reference to the Ego; it can thus be characterized as an Idealism without a subject. There is also, however, no question of Hegel's Absolute Idea: to the extent that there is any talk of an 'Idea' at all, it refers to something valuable which possesses a peculiar kind of objectivity. Thus, Lotze's Idealism, despite its tendency towards a Platonism of values, is not a mere new version of the Platonic theory of Ideas, since the being of the world of values is supposed to be of a different type from that of reality. Values are objectively ideal, but they do not exist in the way that the real does: rather they have validity.[39] To the extent that this ideal is not simply a particular class of the existent, this Idealism of values with validity may also be characterized as an Idealism without Ideas, which is completely in accordance with the reduction of the Idealist systems to an 'Idealist world-view'. At all events, it was the neo-Kantians who were the first really to make a complete distinction between ideal being and irreal validity (see Ch. 6, Sect. 2. ii).

The further development of Lotze's theory of value is interesting because, besides the beginnings of a Platonism of values, there is also an anticipation of the two other principal positions of the later philosophy of value – psychologism about values and objectivism about values; they remain, however, in the context of his philosophy as a whole and are therefore not elaborated and defended independently. Hence (and on account of the manner of his philosophy – cautious and continually considering alternatives) almost all later philosophers of value have appealed to Lotze. Lotze first turns from the question of the individuality *of* the world to the problem of individuality *in* the world, and for this it is necessary – if the constitutive relation between value and reality is to be maintained here too – to abandon the original value-monism of the early writings in favour of a theory of individual values and of the value-individualities which are determined by them. Lotze thus shifts to a theory of values and valuation and he makes connexions in doing so with his early conception of a 'phenomenology and critique of the soul'. The concept of value was here for the first time conceived of as the essential concept of individuality in general – an idea which was later developed in Windelband into a theory of the idiographic sciences. At the same time, his confrontation with the problem of the beautiful in art and his psychological and anthropological enquiries compelled him to develop a theory of the value-judgment, for which his critique of the soul supplied the theoretical framework. Valuation, assessment, criticism in the light of evaluative points of view, are not mere intellectual activities: they concern other psychic strata of the 'soul' as well, of which Lotze selects pleasure for special emphasis. In this way, however, the problem of the objectivity of values arises – that objectivity which is threatened by their reference to valuations by a subject. This is the point of contact for the psychologistic and subjectivist philosophies of value. Although Lotze himself undertook to secure this objectivity by reference to a 'universal subjectivity' (what Windelband later called 'normal consciousness') and so suggested the later transcendental philosophy of value, the structural premises of his philosophy themselves do not allow of a pure subjectivism about values. In Idealist terms, 'value' is the highest synthesizing concept in Lotze's philosophy. That means that values are not just the ground of being of the valuable, but also the ground of knowledge of the valuable as valuable; the identity of the 'conditions of the possibility of experience with the conditions of the possibility of the objects of experience' (Kant) is represented, in Lotze's subject-less Idealism by values themselves, and this is true not only of the cognitive access of philosophy to reality, but *a fortiori* of its evaluative dealings with it. Lotze's principled critique of the Criticist thesis that epistemology is the fundamental discipline of philosophy – in this regard Lotze remained a Hegelian all his life – does not allow of any recourse to the neo-Kantians' transcendental subject; hence the 'universal subjectivity' is always in his work defined in terms of the world of values. Lotze, however, never evaded the problems of the theory of knowledge, but always devoted considerable space to them in his works. For instance, in his later years he undertook to provide an epistemological guarantee of the objectivity of values. He thus arrived at an objective a-priorism about values, which, in contrast to the Platonism about values of his earlier years, sought to exhibit the valuable as something a priori demonstrable in the value-objects themselves. Already in his essay 'Über Bedingungen der Kunstschönheit' (On the conditions of beauty in art) of 1847 Lotze was saying, 'Pleasure itself is not just a state of well being in the enjoying mind, but at the same time a recognition of the objective beauty, excellence or goodness of that which occasions it.'[40] In this respect, the phenomenological value-theories of Max Scheler and Nicolai Hartmann could salute Lotze as their precursor.

ii. *Transcendental philosophy of value (Wilhelm Windelband, Heinrich Rickert)*

This fairly detailed account of Lotze's philosophy of value ought to have made it clear how great is the difference between its historical influence and the degree of its present-day familiarity. The tendency in histories of philosophy always to treat Lotze as simply a founder and precursor (and usually as a founder and precursor of the positions which one is oneself currently defending) is chiefly to be explained by the fact that neo-Kantianism and phenomenology still exert an undiminished influence even today and still constitute the mainstream of the German academic philosophical tradition. The belief that the 'Critical path alone is still open' and that it cannot be followed by using psychological methods is a conviction which has forced ontological and psychological discussions into the background, and not just in the philosophy of value. Even in phenomenology, where at times there has been an anti-subjectivist turn, expressed by the slogan 'To the things themselves!', so that the way has been prepared for the 'rebirth of metaphysics', the conviction of the primacy of the transcendental has ultimately remained dominant. 'Transcendental' here means nothing more than a preliminary discussion of the subjective conditions under which in general it is possible for something to become a philosophical object; the famous, and not always entirely clear, question of the 'conditions of the possibility of' has come to be adopted as a philosophical formula for this purpose. Lotze's idea that the knowledge-relation between subject and object is itself a relation of being and can be presented only in a philosophy which already appears as a metaphysic, despite various attempts at revival,[41] has by contrast not managed to gain acceptance. Thus, in the philosophy of value too, we are again treading on familiar ground if we consider the transcendental tradition.

From a historical point of view, the acceptance of the methodological primacy of the transcendental question coincides with the influence of neo-Kantianism, the 'South-West German' variety of which, clearly diverging from Kant, elevated the problem of value to the rank of the fundamental problem of philosophy. Its founder was Wilhelm Windelband (1848–1915), a pupil of Hermann Lotze, who retained the most important of his basic orientations and gave them greater terminological precision, but at the same time consistently placed them in a frame of reference derived from transcendental philosophy. The existent and values were now seen as objects of ontology and axiology: these philosophical subdisciplines were no longer distinguished primarily in terms of the classes of objects with which they deal, but in accordance with the difference between judgments and valuations. Despite their similar grammatical form, there was a *logical* distinction between the two, which provided the foundation for the division between ontology and axiology and also between their objects. According to Windelband, judgments relate predicates to a subject (in the logical sense), and consciousness therefore adopts to what is so related a purely theoretical, that is, contemplative, attitude. Valuations, on the other hand, bring consciousness (the epistemological subject) into play as the adopter of an evaluative position, where not only cognitive, but also emotional and voluntative aspects are significant, and it is on this basis that the meaning of the expression 'value' is to be elucidated:

In the first place, every value signifies something which satisfies a need or occasions a feeling of pleasure. It follows that valuableness (naturally, in the negative sense of a disvalue as well as in the positive sense of a value) never belongs to objects in themselves alone, as a property, but always only in relation to an evaluating consciousness which in willing satisfies its needs or in feeling reacts to the influences of the environment. If willing and feeling were removed, there would no longer be any values.[42]

The conviction that a pure objectivism about values was untenable was shared by Windelband with the Lotze of the middle period and with the psychological theories of value; the solution for the problem of objectivity was thus sought by him, not in the objectivity of *values*, but in the objectivity of *valuation*, which in turn, quite in accordance with the Kantian pattern, was referred to the universal validity of valuations (evaluations, assessments, value-judgments). The question of the universal validity of valuations led to second-order valuations, 'valuation of valuations', and it was only problems on this meta-level of valuation – as we should say nowadays – which belonged to philosophical value-theories: 'It is here that the philosophical problem arises, in the form of the task of comprehending and grounding such a valuation of valuations.'[43] It seems most obvious to evaluate such valuations as universally valid if 'they express or presuppose a relation to a universally valid value',[44] but Windelband shows that this route necessarily leads to relativism about values. All those things which one might seek to bring into play in theoretical, psychological discussions – even conscience, as 'the voice of the common consciousness in the individual consciousness' – always concern only facts, which by themselves (without evaluation) are unable to answer the question '*quid iuris?*' The question of value is a question of criteria, which also cannot be resolved by reference to a factual recognition of criteria: 'Custom too is ultimately merely something factual, and the quantitative superiority which it has in its validity over individual feeling and willing never amounts to a right. Rather do we know that custom too is just as capable of falling into error with its valuations as the individual.'[45] Historical and ethnographic materials could supply us with sufficient illumination on that score. If one wishes to avoid relativism about values and arrive at 'absolute values', then, according to Windelband, one must follow the transcendental direction in one's questioning, and ascend above the level of factually universal consciousness to a 'normal consciousness', which Kant had already had in mind in his notion of transcendental 'consciousness in general' and which may be demonstrated in the theory of knowledge as a necessary 'postulate'. This normal consciousness, as an evaluating consciousness, constitutes, according to Windelband, what is called in the ontological mode of speech 'absolute values'; only for *this* consciousness are there absolute values, and to postulate it is the only viable alternative to relativism. On Windelband's interpretation, Kant regarded the thing-in-itself as a correlate of 'consciousness in general'; in a completely analogous way, values-in-themselves could then be seen as correlates of the evaluating normal consciousness.

The reinterpretation of the teleological value-relevance of reality which Lotze had taught as a relation of transcendental constitution in which value stood to valuation was at the same time applied by Windelband in such a way that the evaluating normal consciousness became the basis of both axiology *and* ontology. Teleological Idealism was transformed into a universal *second*-order axiology: philosophy as a whole was therefore seen as philosophy of value. The reason, according to Windelband, was that not only valuations but also judgments in theoretical thinking must be evaluated in the light of the normal consciousness, so that transcendental axiology itself was seen as a foundation of the theory of knowledge. It is important in this connexion that 'truth' was also thought of as a value-concept; truth was thus seen as a *theoretical* value, and accordingly the traditional division of philosophy into logic, ethics and aesthetics was then given a foundation in value-theory: these disciplines concerned themselves with the true, the good and the beautiful and thus followed the 'division of the universally valid values'. The synthesis of these values in a comprehensive world-order can, as a correlate of a normal consciousness which can only be postulated, itself only be postulated. According to Windelband, it is a necessary concept, which leads to a postulational philosophy of religion: according to it, God is the normal consciousness conceived of as real, that is, absolute reason itself.

Windelband's pupil, Heinrich Rickert (1863–1936), first came to prominence as a systematizer of the 'South-West German School' and did not extend his teacher's circle of ideas in any essential way; he made their premises more precise, radicalized them in several regards and, in his famous early works *Der Gegenstand der Erkenntnis* (The Object of Knowledge; first edition, 1892) and *Die Grenzen der naturwissenschaftlichen Begriffsbildung* (The Limits of Concept-Formation in the Natural Sciences; first edition, 1896–1902), worked out their possible applications in the theories of knowledge and science. Rickert in these works always continued to accept as his basis 'consciousness in general' in an axiological interpretation, that is, transcendental philosophy with a value-theoretical twist. Later, Rickert went beyond these limits in the direction of a neo-Idealism based on trans-subjective values which had validity in themselves, which made it possible to treat Windelband's sharp distinction between transcendental and metaphysical philosophies of value as more fluid. It was no longer the difference between judgments and valuations which was the guide to the distinction between ontology and axiology, but the differentiation between existence and having validity, in the sense of pure modes of 'being', without any essential reference to a subject.

From a historical point of view, this change can be explained principally in terms of Rickert's intensive debate with life-philosophy. He seems to have realized that recourse to a 'consciousness in general' was not sufficient to oppose to a life-philosophy which he had classified as a 'relapse into barbarism', especially since the theory of consciousness had itself come to be the province of life-philosophy. Rickert saw that life-philosophy itself advocated 'life', not just as an ontic principle, but above all as a principle of value, and that theories of life-enhancement and decadence and even a biology which proceeded in a teleological way could not on their own form the basis of any axiology. Hence, the 'life' which life-philosophy presented as a criterion of value must already be a life which is interpreted as valuable – 'Vegetating is not the highest of goods.'[46] This proof of an unexpressed value-reference is the heart of the Rickertian critique of the 'fashionable biologistic philosophy'. Again and again he emphasizes that the fact that all values and goods have life as a condition should not be confused with a grounding of valuableness by means of the principle of 'life'. What goes beyond the mere facticity of life and transcends it is culture (*Kultur*), which is in general constituted only by means of a value-relevance and so has always already left mere life behind it.

Systematically speaking, Rickert in his later works starts from the assumption that philosophy is a 'universal science or theory of the world-whole'. There is no longer any talk of a Criticist self-limitation of philosophical enquiry to the 'conditions of possibility'; Rickert seems to have gone back to the Lotzean roots of his tradition. The world of values is attained, on this basis, by a two-stage process of elimination. The 'universe' (*Weltall*) is not exhausted by what really (physically or psychically) exists; there are also ideal existents, e.g. mathematical objects. But even this ideal being is still not all that there is to make up the totality of the world: there are, according to Rickert,

> yet other unreal objects, which do not exist even ideally . . . The non-existent includes everything of which we say that we 'understand' it, like a true sentence! What is so understood we call the sense of the sentence . . . The sense of a true sentence is unreal, indeed it does not exist at all in the previously understood meaning of the word.[47]

According to Rickert, the true sense of our sentences about what exists – which therefore cannot exist in the same sense as that which it is about – is an unreal value-structure: something unreal to which the value 'truth' is attached. In this thesis, Lotze's and Windelband's axiological theory of truth is retained; at the same time, however, it is associated with an objectivism which functions as a kind of radicalization of the Husserlian distinction between noesis and noema and like the result of an ontologization of the noematic (see Ch. 7, Sect. 2). The decisive difference from Husserl and the phenomenologists, however, consists in the fact that Rickert employs the concept of 'validity' in order to show how it is possible to speak meaningfully of there being ideal non-existents: they have validity. The opposition of existing and having validity was first really accomplished in Rickert; Lotze was criticized for having associated the valid still with the ideally-existent, and Windelband's talk of 'factual validity', which seems unproblematic to us today, was put in its place with the suggestion that all valuation and validity presuppose an unreal sphere of value. Rickert's linking of sense, value and validity, to which repeated reference has already been made, was supposed to receive its philosophical foundation as follows: the sense (of sentences) is supposed to be something unreal, which 'is' in virtue of the fact that what has sense (the sentences) is related to values, which themselves do not really exist, but have validity; only through this reference of the really existent (sentences) to the value-sphere, which has validity, is an unreal sense constituted. For this theory the distinctions between the real and the unreal and between the really-existent and the ideally-existent are fundamental: these distinctions are then joined by the difference between being and having validity in such a way that everything unreal which 'there is', is supposed to have validity, that is, to be valuable. Rickert's completion of these distinctions by means of the pairs of concepts 'subjective–objective' and 'theoretical–untheoretical values', and his attempt to rethink, under the title of the 'Third Realm', Windelband's idea of a unity of existence and validity, reality and world of values, is less important in this connexion than the anti-subjectivist turn given to Critical philosophy, which underlies everything. Here too (as in Windelband) philosophy is seen as a theory of value, which is supposed, on the basis of the constellation which is presented of reality, truth and value, to underlie all theories of reality. (Thus metaphysics too, as a theory of the Absolute, can be based only on value-theory.) It is no longer the reference to an all-constituting subjectivity, but only the distinction between the dimensions of 'existence' and 'validity', which separates this objective a-priorism from pre-Critical metaphysics. Again, the objective world of values is no longer the correlate of a transcendental normal consciousness, as in Windelband, but vice versa: Kant's 'transcendental apperception' is interpreted as an ideal subjective correlate of an objective, but unreal, domain of values, which real subjects cannot found, but can only exemplify. It thus becomes clear how greatly overrated the differences usually are between late neo-Kantianism and the phenomenologically based objectivism about values which is now to be discussed.

iii. *Phenomenological philosophy of value (Max Scheler, Nicolai Hartmann)*

The existence, alongside South-West German neo-Kantianism, of another anti-psychologistic and rigorously a priori philosophy of value is the achievement of Max Scheler (1874–1928), who was a pupil of the neo-Idealist Rudolf Eucken and became familiar with Husserl's phenomenology only after his habilitation. He wilfully re-directed its methodological tendency, saying that it was useful as a basis for an allegedly 'rigorously scientific and positive foundation of philosophical ethics with regard to all the essential fundamental problems which come into question for it'. One important difference between the neo-Kantian and the phenomenological philosophies of value is thus indicated; in Scheler, the theme of value belongs from the outset in the context of ethics: 'The existence of an objective material hierarchy of values, which makes it possible for us to become discerning' is supposed to make possible the grounding of a 'rigorous ethical absolutism and objectivism'.[48] The other important distinction is that, according to Scheler, values are, exist, and do not merely have validity. (Nicolai Hartmann later called this 'ideal being-in-itself'.) The values which exist in-themselves, independently of any subject, can be grasped and exhibited, because they 'appear' in that which is valuable. This idea of grasping, exhibiting, allowing to appear what is independent of the subject is what gives methodological solemnity to the phenomenology of Husserl's middle period, which claimed to present 'philosophy as a strict science' and, adopting an anti-subjectivist stance, declared itself to be an a priori science of essences. The two methodological devices which were supposed to make this possible were the phenomenological and the eidetic reductions. The phenomenological reduction, also described as the *epoché*, was held to make it possible to isolate what was given in the 'stream of experience' in consciousness purely as such, as a mere phenomenon without any material or causal interpretation; in this way, a field of enquiry for philosophy was to be opened up which is not further reducible and is given in indubitable evidence. The eidetic reduction then consisted in throwing into relief, in what was phenomenally given, the essential content, the purely qualitative in it or its mere *Sosein*, or 'being-so', as Scheler called it; as a result of it, phenomenological enquiry was further defined as phenomenological *Wesensschau*, or 'inspection of essences'. Max Scheler's attempt to develop a 'material ethics of value on the broadest basis of phenomenological experience' involved at the same time a claim to move within the 'limits of what is demonstrable in rigorously a priori ideas of essence and essential connexions'. He writes,

We call 'a priori' all those ideal units of meaning and sentences which, without regard to the nature of the position of the subjects who think them and their real natural constitution, and without regard to the nature of the position of an object to which they are applicable, come to self-givenness by means of the content of an immediate intuition. Thus, every kind of position is to be disregarded, including position in the sense of 'real' or 'unreal', 'apparent' or 'real' and so forth. Even where, for example, we are mistaken in assuming that it is something living, there must be given to us in the content of the mistake, nevertheless, the intuitive essence of 'life'. If we call the content of such an 'intuition' a 'phenomenon', the 'phenomenon' therefore has not the slightest connexion with 'appearance' (of something real) or with 'illusion'. Intuition of this kind, however, is *Wesensschau* or – as we prefer to say – 'phenomenological intuition' or 'phenomenological experience'. The 'what' which it gives cannot be given to a greater or lesser degree – as we can 'observe' an object more or less closely, or 'observe' now these, now those, of its features – rather, it is either 'seen' and so given 'itself' (without remainder and without deduction, neither by means of an 'image' nor by means of a 'symbol') or else it is not 'seen' and hence not given.[49]

The application of Husserl's phenomenological programme to ethics presupposes a twofold extension of the original conception. First, not only states of affairs (*Sachverhalte*) but also 'states of value' (*Wertverhalte*) must be taken into account phenomenologically, and it is possible, according to Scheler, to demonstrate in them 'genuine and true value-qualities, which represent a special domain of objects'. Values, as 'material qualities' of states of value are to be thought of as phenomena in the same sense in which Husserl speaks of phenomena: as objects which are comprehensible purely a priori, they are supposed, according to Scheler, to make possible a rigorous a-priorism about values. Values, as material qualities or 'essences' of things and phenomena are supposed also to be a priori in the sense that they are the reason why valuable things and phenomena can be experienced as valuable. Values are not goods, but qualities (or essences) of goods – to that extent, Scheler advocates an ethics not of goods but of values – and they may be isolated purely as such by means of the eidetic reduction.[50] The second extension of the Husserlian programme concerns method. If value-qualities are also made into objects of phenomenological enquiry, then cognitive modes of access to the phenomena are no longer sufficient. The phenomenology of value must begin with the '*feeling* of value' and is possible only as a 'phenomenology of the *emotional* life'. Scheler begins with a corresponding reinterpretation of the phenomenological reduction, which he describes as an emotional *epoché*, that is, as a suspension of everyday impulsive dealings with the valuable and as itself an ethically motivated adoption of a purely theoretical, intuitive attitude towards it. Scheler then follows the Husserlian distinction between the act and the content of consciousness (noesis and noema) and outlines a typology of emotional acts – states of feeling, feelings of . . ., preferring, loving and so on – with the aim of isolating, by means of an eidetic reduction of their intentional, that is, meant, content, a spectrum of a priori value-qualities which would be independent of both feeling and object. In this way a double a priori was supposed to be demonstrated in the experience of value: an a priori of value-noeses and one of value-noemata. In this way the anti-subjectivist point of the whole exercise was supposed to be achieved by means of the thesis that the a priori modes of the value-intentions were regulated in accordance with the essential quality of the intentional objects, and not vice versa: as in Plato, it was to be the values of love and hate which determined love and hatred, whereas the empiricist or psychological value-theories elevated the subjective dispositions of loving and hating into the foundation of the qualitative determination of what was loved and hated.[51] The next step in the method is then the proof that the value-qualities thus isolated possess an a priori structure and are arranged in a hierarchy. An important role in the thesis of the structure of value-qualities is played by the principle of emotional contradiction: that it is impossible to love and not to love something at the same time, or to will it and not will it, is supposed to be a principle which possesses a truth derived from the same source as that of logical contradiction and independent of it. The elaboration of the rank-ordering of value-qualities leads to the hierarchy of 'agreeable – noble – beautiful/right/true – holy', together with their respective opposites. The highest values, according to Scheler, are the values of the *person*, and this leads to a characterization of his own position in the philosophy of value as a value-theoretical 'personalism'. Taken together, these structures and hierarchical arrangements are the foundation for what Scheler calls 'moral knowledge', which in turn first makes it possible in general to find a basis for moral willing and action. The thesis that it could not be the form of the moral will, but only the content of moral knowledge, which could provide the basis for ethics then also became the foundation of Scheler's criticism of Kant, which takes up a large part of his principal work *Der Formalismus in der Ethik und die materiale Wertethik* (Formalism in Ethics and the Material Ethics of Value) (1913–16). Scheler's apriorism in principle excludes any formalist, subjectivist and so transcendental interpretation.

Nicolai Hartmann (1882–1950), in his *Ethik* (Ethics) of 1926, took up and systematically carried out Scheler's programme. Once detached from the context of the criticism of Kant in which it was put forward in Scheler, the phenomenology of value here appears as a systematic part of a comprehensive ontology:

> Knowledge of value is genuine knowledge of being. In this regard, it is entirely in line with every kind of theoretical knowledge. In relation to the subject, its object is as much an independent existent as are spatial relations for geometrical knowledge and things for the knowledge of things. To 'grasp' values – however different its character may be in other respects – is as much a transcendent act as any other genuine act of knowledge, and all the difficulties of the epistemological problem of transcendence reappear in it. In this 'inspection', the subject is purely receptive, passive. It sees itself determined by its object, the value which exists in itself; it itself, however, for its part determines nothing. The value remains as unaffected by the inspection of value as any object of knowledge is by becoming known.[52]

Values, as 'ideal beings-in-themselves', belong to the stratum of 'ideal being', and Hartmann goes beyond Scheler above all in characterizing the 'mode of being of values' more precisely in the context of his whole ontological project. We shall return to this ontology in the chapter on 'Being'.

3 Remarks on the later fate of the philosophy of value

Life-philosophy developed, for the most part, into the philosophy of existence, and some of its biologistic and racist varieties which flowed directly into Nazi ideology were compromised once and for all along with it. The philosophy of value, on the other hand, enjoyed a fresh boom after the Second World War: the appeal to values seemed to be the only thing which could be opposed to the barbarism through which people had just lived. It is significant in this connexion that it was above all Scheler's style of material value-theory which attracted adherents; neo-Kantianism, even in Rickert, had not managed to produce a systematic theory of value, and even in the twenties the influence of Max Weber had far outstripped that of his teacher Rickert. In Max Weber, however, the gulf between science and a universally binding value-orientation is uncrossable, 'because the different orderings of value in the world stand in irreconcilable conflict with each other'. Science, in a rationalistically disenchanted world, cannot decide between them, and so the famous demand for value-freedom in science follows from the ethos of intellectual honesty. As far as values are concerned, 'polytheism' is the final word: 'The many ancient gods, disenchanted and so in the form of impersonal forces, rise from their graves, strive for power over our lives and begin once again their eternal conflict between each other.'[53]

Why could not Max Scheler succeed against Max Weber? Martin Heidegger had already answered this question in 1935 with a diagnosis of the philosophy of value to which very little needs to be added:

> Values have validity. But the term 'validity' all too readily suggests being valid for a subject. In order to give support again to obligation once it has ascended to the level of values, one attributes a being to the values themselves. Here being means basically nothing more than a property belonging to what exists. It is just that this does not exist in the same rough and ready way as tables and chairs. In regard to the being of values, the maximum amount of confusion and uprooting is achieved. Nevertheless, the expression 'value' is gradually excluded as outworn, and values are now called 'wholes'. But this just amounts to a change in the letters. Certainly it is easy to see in these wholes what they basically are, namely, halves. In the domain of essences, halves are even more ominous than the Nothing which is so much feared. In 1928, there appeared Part I of a complete bibliography of the concept of value. 661 writings on the concept of value are listed in it. Probably since then the number has reached a thousand. All this calls itself philosophy.[54]

The values which were supposed systematically to replace the Kantian and Fichtean 'ought' took up a precarious intermediate position between 'is' and 'ought', facts and norms; in order to avoid abandoning them entirely to the relativism of subjective valuation, a peculiar kind of 'being' was attributed to them, though it had to be distinguished from the being of other existents. It was precisely this that was the reason for the 'halves' of the philosophy of value, which were worse than the Nothing and its philosophy, nihilism. Thus Heidegger, in his lectures on Nietzsche (1936–40), was able to formulate the point like this: 'Value and the valuable have become the positivist substitute for the metaphysical.' The circle is completed: Lotze's post-Idealist incantation of values as a metaphysical domain with its own positivity has shown itself, in a positivist age, to be unstable. Not just in the case of 'being', but also in that of values, '*it is no go*'. The controversy between the neo-Kantian and the phenomenological philosophies of value already reflected precisely the hopeless situation of values between the ontological and the deontological. On the other hand, our scepticism has in the meantime received fresh nourishment from the meta-ethics of analytic philosophy. How can values have validity when they do not exist? (In Rickert's sentence, 'There is an ideal non-existent', what is meant by 'There is . . .', and what ontology does he want to commit us to?) And conversely: can values be verifiable qualities, if they are not found at all in judgments, but only in evaluation? Even if values exist, can one base an 'ought' on the 'is' of values? Analytical meta-ethics, however, is connected with the psychological theories of value and continues their work by other means; the pluralism[55] of its principles supports Max Weber against Max Scheler. Thus it is only in our own day that philosophical a-priorism about values has come to an end.

7

Being

The necessity to write the history of German philosophy in the century after Hegel's death as essentially the history of an identity-crisis results from the fact that that which is, the existent, reality, had come to belong completely to the domain of 'science', in a sense of that word in which it was distinct from philosophy. The question whether there could be a knowledge of objects which was independent of experience and the empirical sciences had already been posed, and answered in the negative, by Kant as the problem of the possibility of metaphysics or synthetic judgments a priori; in so far as metaphysics and such judgments are possible, they must be confined to the domain of possible experience. When philosophy then, in the face of the claim of the empirical research-sciences to universality, again considered Kant, it had at first no use for his positive version of the concept of 'metaphysics'. As a result of the reinterpretation of the transcendental question as psychological (Fries) and physiological (Schopenhauer, F. A. Lange, Helmholtz and others), empiricism took over generally even in the 'theory of knowledge', and when later – principally in Marburg neo-Kantianism – there was a critical counter-movement and some consideration of the non-empirical elements in the Kantian theory, they could be perceived only in the form of logical determinations of knowledge. Epistemology, reinterpreted in this empiricist or logicist spirit, seemed finally to have marked the end of philosophy as metaphysics; the idea that it could offer a knowledge of reality which was independent of the empirical sciences was regarded as ruled out in principle.

After the turn of the century, however, there was talk of the 'rebirth', the 'reawakening', the 'resurrection' of metaphysics; it took shape, actually, as an attitude of protest against 'the absence of content of declining neo-Kantianism, positivism and psychologism in the concept of our century'.[1] It is important that this revived metaphysics essentially understood itself as ontology, that is, as a philosophical knowledge of being, which had finally liberated itself from the reduction of philosophy to epistemology and logic. The other meanings associated with 'metaphysics' in the tradition withdrew almost entirely into the background. If the old ontology, as a *metaphysica specialis*, had taken as its theme simply the existent in general and in so far as it is existent, the newer ontology abandoned such restrictions: everything existent, or simply 'reality', was once again an object of philosophical knowledge. Metaphysics, reawakened as ontology, took up the counter-attack against the occupation of reality by the empirical sciences, and so against a philosophy which seemed, in its self-limitation to logic and theory of knowledge, to have surrendered without a struggle to the invaders. In general, the newer ontology had a passionate concern with content. 'The absence of content of declining neo-Kantianism, positivism and psychologism' was generally attributed to the concentration of philosophical enquiry on the forms or formal conditions of knowledge, in the course of which, in a way which was in no sense self-evident, the pairs of concepts 'concept–form' and 'being–knowledge' were treated as parallel: an ontology can also be formally rich and a theory of knowledge rich in content. The positive evaluation of content and the negative view of the formal, which is still to be found in almost all philosophical camps in Germany even now – in accordance with the schema, 'dry form and rich content' – is certainly always a symptom of that 'hunger for being' which found a voice in the resurrected metaphysics of our century. The myth of a philosophical vacuum between Hegel and Heidegger, still so common in our text-books, is also essentially a product of the new ontology, the representative name for which is that of 'Heidegger'; without much exaggeration, it can be described as a self-justificatory ideology for a philosophical tendency which sees itself as a rehabilitation of philosophy in general after its 'decay' as a result of enfeeblement by empiricism, epistemology and formalism. The fact that, even today, several philosophers who are otherwise far from the new ontology still advocate this view does not prove the truth of this myth, but rather its extraordinary effectiveness.

The rebirth of metaphysics as ontology is more than a mere renaissance of classical ontological theories. Certainly, the age of historicism produced, along with many other revivals, several neo-positions in philosophy: the neo-Aristotelianism of Trendelenburg (1802–77) and his school; neo-Thomism, which was essentially a confessional movement; the revival of links with Leibniz, stimulated by Bernhard Bolzano (1781–1848) and still influential, through Franz

Bretano (1838–77), on Husserl and Meinong; and mention should also be made of the renaissance of Wolff in the work of Hans Pichler. However much these tendencies – to which neo-Idealism and neo-Romanticism should also be added – may have influenced the new ontology, it is nevertheless not a product of them. An important reason for this is the fact that what it rejected was itself something which had appeared in the form of a renaissance: theory of knowledge, seen as either neo-Kantianism or in the form of a positivism which was a revival of classical empiricism and sensualism (especially Hume). The period of the new ontology was at the same time that of the 'crisis of historicism' and of the rediscovery of actually-lived reality, which historical culture had taught to understand in a merely historical way; in art and literature, this trend was represented by the *Jugendstil* and the 'New Objectivity' (*neue Sachlichkeit*). It also runs right through philosophy. Ontology, as the knowledge of what always is and exists unchanging behind the façade of change, itself takes an anti-historicist direction, which it shares, for instance, with life-philosophy.[2] That rules out any possibility that current philosophical activity might interpret itself simply as a revival of what had already been thought. Husserl's call 'To the things themselves!', which essentially marked the beginning of ontological philosophy, was the motto of a new direct relation to things, indeed of the 'New Objectivity' in philosophy itself, in which the 'thing' – the most general structures of that which is – was defined in an anti-historicist sense as an object of ontological philosophy.

If, in what follows under the general title of 'Being', we are to give an outline of the rebirth of metaphysics as ontology, we cannot avoid giving an account in detail of the various ontological projects of that time. What is to be clarified can be described as a rehabilitation of the 'problem of being' as a genuinely philosophical problem. This 'problem of being' must obviously be posed in such a way that it cannot be solved by any of the procedures of the empirical sciences; otherwise, any philosophical theory of being would be superfluous. On the other hand, the 'problem of being' should also not be reducible to the problem of knowledge, as the whole of Criticism had taught, since then the attempt to break out of the epistemological ghetto would fail. A third general condition, accepted by all the new ontologists, is that modern ontology should not proceed in a dogmatic fashion in Kant's sense; this also rules out simple reference back to pre-Kantian traditions. The rehabilitation of philosophy as theory of knowledge also remains decisive for the new ontology, to the extent that it regards an epistemological self-justification as absolutely indispensable. The priority of the question of being over that of knowledge, which is the general characteristic of the new ontology, should itself be seen as the result of epistemological reflection: since the time of Lotze, the argument that the subject is himself an existent and the knowledge-relation a relation of being had played a central role in that connexion. In Hegel's words, the new ontology saw itself as an immanent critique of epistemology, not as its simple opposite. The success of this critique was then felt as the great liberation 'to things themselves'.

1 Remarks on the history of ontology after Kant and Hegel

The history of post-Hegelian ontology has not yet been written, and it could even be seen as impossible to do so, if one follows Kant, who maintained that 'The haughty name of an ontology, which presumes to afford synthetic knowledge a priori of things in general in a systematic theory, . . . must make room for the modest name of a mere analytic of the pure understanding.'[3] Does not that mean that any ontology which respects Kant's dictum, 'The Critical way alone is still open' – and the new ontology claims to do so – is doomed to failure? Any answer to the question whether there was after Kant in general any ontology which was more than a dogmatic conservation of positions which had already been superseded will depend on what one understands by an 'ontology'. In the widest sense, the word means (at least since Quine) the sum of convictions at any given time with regard to 'what there is'. Every science, and also every kind of everyday consciousness, implies on this view an ontology, that is, a prior understanding of what must in principle be counted as a possible object – whether it be elementary particles or witches on broomsticks. To explain and justify such 'ontological commitments' is a philosophical activity which can likewise be called 'ontology', and which has always been so called up to the present day. Even if one confines oneself to this broad concept of ontology, it is obvious that there has always been ontology, even after Kant: almost all philosophers have expressed their views on the ideas and prejudices of everyday and scientific consciousness of the world concerning what there is, usually in a critical vein. Kant's own Analytic of the Pure Understanding is meant to be at the same time a theory of the possible objects of this understanding, and so includes an 'ontology' of objects as appearances, but for historical reasons he called this, not 'ontology' any longer, but 'transcendental philosophy'.

It would be impossible here to give an account of the ontology of German Idealism; a few indications may be sufficient at this point. For Fichte, all being is essentially posited by the Ego, and this is also true of the Ego itself: 'That whose being (essence) consists merely in the fact that it posits itself as existent is the Ego as absolute subject. As it posits itself, so it is; and as it is, so it posits itself . . . To posit oneself and to be are, when used of the Ego, completely the same'.[4] Because he conceives of the integration of that being which is not the Ego into the Ego as the moral task of the Ego, in him theory of morality and theory of being (or ontology) merge into each other; Lotze's teleological Idealism and the later philosophy of value were able to make contact with this kind of ontology. Hegel's ontology is contained in the first book of his *Science of Logic* under the title of 'The Theory of Being'; its first result is 'Pure being and pure nothing are therefore one and the same'[5] and its last reads 'Being is an illusion'.[6] Hegel's 'Theory of Being', as a positive part of the total system which, as an absolute system, terminates in the unity of being and thought in the Absolute, is thus at the same time a critical destruction of all ontology in the pre-Critical or metaphysical sense. Whereas in his early and middle periods Schelling thought of 'true being' as a point of indifference between Ego and Non-Ego, subject and object, his later, 'positive', philosophy denied that the 'immemorial That' of being could in general be grasped in concepts; he described the Idealism of Fichte and Hegel as a 'negative' philosophy, because it remained attached to the logical, which was the mere 'negative of existence'. Logic and ontology (even in the Hegelian sense of a 'Theory of Being') could according to him be only a formal science – theories about the mere forms of what is and what can be thought, without attaining to reality itself.[7] This idea of the non-reducibility of true reality to what is conceptually explicable influenced not only late-Idealist metaphysics (H. C. Weisse, I. H. Fichte, Hermann Lotze); it also became the foundation of Feuerbach's critique of Hegel and thus of the whole of post-Hegelian materialism, in so far as it was inspired by Feuerbach. It was thus also the foundation of the Marxist tradition in philosophy. This dualistic ontology – the view that there was an unbridgeable divide between thought and being – gave further support to the philosophical rehabilitation of the empirical sciences as against Idealist pretensions to totality, and in this respect too almost all tendencies are united, including the disciples of Hegel and the late-Idealists; indirectly it also prepared the way for the general return to Kant. Finally, in Kierkegaard, the application of this theme to one's own self led to the primacy of existence over everything which was conceptually explicable; thus from this root there grew the philosophy of existence, which did not merely absorb life-philosophy into itself, but, in Heidegger, in association with Husserlian phenomenology, helped to produce the new ontology itself.

In the multiplicity of philosophical systems after Hegel, almost all of which maintained the non-reducibility of being to thought (or of ontology to logic), one can find one's way only by considering general types; from this point of view, one can say that the 'other of thought' was conceived of as the material, the sensuous, the irrational or the existential. All four types of ontology always refer also at the same time to positions which endeavour to transform the dualistic metaphysics of a distinction between thought and being into a new monism of being which reduces thought to the ontic element which is subordinated at any given time to true being. This monistic trend is, however, less marked than in earlier modern metaphysics, and it usually goes no further than the reduction of thought to a mere epiphenomenon of being. Obviously, Kant's model of a critique of knowledge was still influential enough largely to exclude the naïve Realism of a thought which was forgetful of itself in this way.

The ontology of materialism says: 'Everything which is is material being.' The physicalistic or biologistic vulgar-materialism of the middle of the century, which attempted to interpret thought itself as a directly material process, did not long survive the rehabilitation of philosophy and was soon forced into the position of a mere world-view.[8] Feuerbach's materialism, on the other hand, was a philosophy of sensuousness, and not primarily in the epistemological sense: rather, it was an anthropology of the real human being as a sensuous and bodily being. The reality which this being is and which it 'has' in sensuous knowledge is true being, and not the abstract conceptual realm of the Hegelian system. (The connexions between this and the sensualist and existentialist type of ontology cannot be ignored.) In Marx's 'sociologization' of the Feuerbachian anthropology, according to which the essence of human beings 'in its reality' is 'the ensemble of social relations',[9] Feuerbach's sensuous or bodily reality of man is changed into 'real history', that is, the material life-process of the species in history and society, the substratum of which is the 'material exchange with nature' in 'activity directed towards objects'. Its non-reducibility to mere thought is the central argument which Marx and Engels opposed to Hegel and the historical Idealism of the Young Hegelians. Their materialism is essentially a historical materialism, and their familiar thesis that being determines consciousness and not the other way around should not be understood in the sense of the vulgar-materialists whom they opposed throughout their lives.[10] The further development of historical materialism into dialectical materialism, in the sense of a closed 'world-view' or 'ideology of the working class', by Engels and Lenin was possible only at the cost of copious borrowing from the metaphysical materialism of the eighteenth and nineteenth centuries. It is important that the ontology of historical materialism does not have in mind a reductionist theory of the relation between thought and being, but rather a dialectical one (in Hegel's sense), in which the difference between the two, and above all their antagonism in the phenomenon of ideology, is to be explained on the basis of the contradictions in the material 'base' itself.

The conception of the 'other of thought' as the sensuous is the fundamental theme of a tradition which can be characterized by its ontology of the sensuously-given. (Feuerbach's part in it was only marginal.) Its links were with pre-Kantian empiricism and sensualism and, as in their case, that which is was identified with what is accessible to our senses and was reconstructed out of it. This ontology is not simply identical with epistemological Idealism, since the Critical reminiscence of the difference between the thing-in-itself and appearance does not involve any denial of the mere existence of the thing-in-itself and thus this Idealism of the 'world as representation' can be associated in Schopenhauer with the metaphysics of the irrational, that is, the world as Will. The whole of the neo-Kantian tradition, from F. A. Lange to Rickert, which from the time of Lange's *Geschichte des Materialismus* (History of Materialism) proclaimed itself to be essentially a critique of the materialist ontology, always contained elements of a sensualist ontology as well, but the difference between this given and the object of knowledge made it impossible to reduce that which is (and what there is is for science to tell us) to the sensuous. The ontology of the sensuously-given was fully realized only in the 'immanence-positivism' of the turn of the century, while the empirio-criticism, with its principle of economy, which Lenin attacked principally on epistemological grounds, always laid claim to structural elements, capable of a quasi-transcendental or conventionalistic interpretation, which were not reducible to the sensuous. As long as reality, in Kantian terms, was still conceived of as what is constituted in the collaboration of sensibility and understanding, the understanding itself could not be reduced to sensibility and no monistic sensualist ontology existed.

We have already considered the metaphysics of the irrational in Section 1 of Chapter 5, 'Life'. Schopenhauer, Nietzsche and the whole tradition of life-philosophy belong, despite their anti-Idealist metaphysics, to the history of post-Hegelian ontology, since what they elevate into a principle – the Will, the will-to-power, life – is at the same time that which is in reality, while the rational is supposed to be a mere epiphenomenon. It is important that a general dynamism, described above as 'Heracliteanism', is associated with this ontology of the enemies of reason. The two motifs are independent of one another: Schopenhauer's idea of conceiving of the difference between thought and being as a distinction between rationality and irrationality and presenting Kant's thing-in-itself, which had once marked that difference, as the Will, still does not imply that the domain of the rational is to be thought of as the static and that of the irrational as the dynamic. The real connexion of the two ideas was only achieved in Nietzsche, whose early *Geburt der Tragödie* (Birth of Tragedy) already distinguished the 'Apollonian' and the 'Dionysian' in this sense; in Nietzsche's later work, this then became the basis for his critique of the whole of Western ontology. The principle 'What is, *becomes* not; what becomes, *is* not' was for Nietzsche a 'prejudice', indeed an 'idiosyncrasy' of philosophers:[11] where the real manifests becoming, alteration, change, they bring into play the difference between reason and sensibility and make the deceptiveness of the senses responsible for the semblance of becoming. Nietzsche then says,

> I mention with great reverence the name of *Heraclitus*. If the rest of the tribe of philosophers objected to the evidence of the senses, because they revealed multiplicity and change, he objected to their evidence, because they revealed things as if they had duration and unity. Even Heraclitus did the senses an injustice. They do not lie either in the manner that the Eleatics believed, nor in the way he believed – in general, they do not lie at all. It is in what we *make* of their evidence that the lie comes in, for instance, the lie of unity, of thinghood, of substance, of duration . . . The 'reason' is the cause of our falsification of the evidence of the senses. In so far as the senses reveal becoming, passing away, change, they do not lie . . . But Heraclitus will be for ever in the right in saying that being is an empty fiction. The 'seeming' world is the only one: the 'true world' is merely a *deceitful addition*.[12]

The 'true world' of previous philosophy was merely a 'moral optical illusion', born of the 'instinct of defamation, disparagement and accusation of life'. The history of this philosophy is the 'history of an error', in which 'the "true world" finally came to be a fable' and its end is in sight: 'We have abolished the true world: which world still remains? The seeming world perhaps? . . . But no! *Along with the true world we have also abolished the world of seeming*! (Noon; moment of the shortest shadows; end of the longest error; high-point of humanity; INCIPIT ZARATHUSTRA.)'[13] By means of such formulations Nietzsche achieved in the field of the metaphysics of the irrational a new monism, since the difference between the true and the seeming worlds is, according to him, the basic dualism from which all further dualisms can be derived; what stands behind it is always the will-to-power:

> There is neither 'spirit', nor reason, nor thought, nor consciousness, nor soul, nor will, nor truth: all are fictions which are useless. It is not a matter of 'subject

and object', but of a particular kind of animal, which flourishes only when there is a certain relative *rightness*, and especially a *regularity* in its perceptions (so that it can capitalize on experience) . . . Knowledge works as an *instrument* of power. Thus it is obvious that it grows with every increase of power . . . *The necessity of preservation* – *not* any abstract theoretical need not to be deceived – stands as a motive behind the development of the organs of knowledge . . ., they develop in such a way that their observation suffices to preserve us. To put it differently: the *extent* of the will to know depends on the extent of growth of the *will-to-power* of the species: a species apprehends as *much* reality *as it can become master of, as it can take into its service*.[14]

Reference has already been made to the roots of the existentialist interpretation of the 'other of thought' in the later philosophy of Schelling; it can be understood as the outcome of an introjection of the 'immemorial That'. The being of the subject – his 'existence' – retains in Kierkegaard the status of something prior, incapable of being overtaken by any thought and always already presupposed in it. That even this philosophy and its tradition, which really only begins with Jaspers' philosophy of existence, belongs to the history of post-Hegelian ontology is confirmed by the fact that Heidegger, in *Being and Time*, presents the 'Hermeneutics of *Dasein*', whose essence is held to lie in its existence, as an 'Existential Ontology' or 'Fundamental Ontology'. The notion that with existence something is thought which, being presupposed in the difference between subject and object, cannot be treated as an object, but only expounded as the 'essential' and at the same time lived or accomplished, is certainly a theme which was anticipated in life-philosophy, but which also belongs amongst the fundamental ideas of Max Scheler's 'personalism'. It was Heidegger's achievement to connect this with the 'question of being', as a result of which a critical reconstruction of the history of ontology as a whole was also initiated which, as in Nietzsche, terminated in its destruction. Heidegger's later 'turn' then also gave rise in the 'existentialist' ontology to the monism of unobjective or pre-objective Being.[15]

In this typology of post-Idealist ontologies, we ought not to forget, however, the type which defines the 'other of thought' as itself thought, Idea or spirit: that is, neo-Idealism in its various forms. What is involved here is a genuine renaissance of Absolute Idealism itself, and so with an attempt to interrupt the course of later developments by Absolute Idealist means. If the Marburg School of neo-Kantianism concluded from the fact that everything which is is only as a result of thought that, strictly speaking, it is also nothing but thought, then this 'logical Idealism' is closer to Fichte than to Kant and hence is appropriately mentioned here. Neo-Fichteanism and neo-Hegelianism moreover had close connexions with life-philosophy: the conviction that everything is 'spirit' is not incompatible with irrationalism, if the irrational is located in the spirit itself. There are marked elements of life-philosophy, too, in the later philosophy of Scheler, whose ontology connected the idea of the primacy of spirit with that of its ontic feebleness or even impotency. The philosophies of 'ideal being' and 'ideal validity' (Lotze, Eucken, Rickert and many others) should also be recalled; they too conceive of thinking in terms of various objects, existing in themselves, which are considered as purely spiritual, and so belong amongst the objective-Idealist ontologies. Some of them even formed curious associations with parapsychology,[16] in which the boundary between the philosophy of spirit and the philosophy of spirits was overstepped. The ontological monism of 'spiritual being' revealed itself in such cases particularly blatantly as a mere parody of the classical Idealist systems of the past.

In what follows, the concept of 'ontology' will be further circumscribed; obviously, all post-Hegelian philosophies imply a particular ontology, but what concerns us here is those philosophical positions which explicitly thought of themselves as a 'rebirth' of ontology in the traditional sense. In the remainder of this discussion, only those positions will be called 'ontologies' which use the concept of 'being' as a basic notion and deny its derivability from other concepts – for example, those of thought or cognition. That this means also that 'the question of being is prior to that of knowledge'[17] is a consequence which follows naturally from the character of the method of these philosophies. What makes the newer ontologies really into the *new* ontology is itself nothing but this method, which was supposed at the same time to satisfy the most advanced claims of the critique of knowledge. Its source was the phenomenology of Edmund Husserl.

2 Ontology and phenomenology (Husserl)

The re-foundation of ontology by phenomenology, which eventually led to the primacy of the question of being over that of knowledge, has historical roots in the theory of knowledge: in reconstructing this prehistory, as in the business of finding one's way in the field of post-Idealist ontology by means of typological classification, the relation of being and thought provides a useful guiding thread. It is essentially the history of a redefinition of 'thought' in the post-Hegelian situation, which deserves a monograph to itself. This redefinition travelled along the line of 'Austrian railway-stations', as Bolzano, Brentano, Meinong and Husserl were referred to in Oxford in the twenties,[18] to which there should at least be added one Saxon (Lotze) and one Mecklenburger (Frege). This new concept of 'thought' defined thinking, in opposition to Kant and the Fichtean Idealism of generation, no longer as an index of the 'spontaneity of the understanding', but as a receptive *'apprehension of . . .'* The idea that thinking is not merely a matter of certain operations (acts of the understanding, synthesis, logical functions, positing) was formulated by Brentano, on behalf of the whole neo-ontological tradition, in the form of his principle of intentionality: like all consciousness, thinking too is always a thought of something which is not entirely comprised in the act of consciousness and thought itself. The principle of intentionality, however, did not demarcate thinking itself from sense-perception and other acts of consciousness, but initially affirmed merely the structural equivalence of thought and perception implied in the interpretation of thought as 'apprehension of . . .' Indeed, it even confirmed the empiricist reduction of thought to sense-perception which was widely accepted at that time, and which was then fully accomplished in 'immanence-positivism' (see Ch. 3, n. 90). It is only possible to make this distinction when a definition of thought as apprehension of non-empirical objects or states of affairs is achieved. The foundations for this were laid by Bernhard Bolzano in his *Wissenschaftslehre* (Theory of Science) of 1837, in which he aligned himself with Leibniz and explicitly attacked Fichte and Hegel. 'The thought of a thing and the thing itself which comes to be as a result of this thought are, in my opinion, always distinct; even in the case where the thing of which we are thinking is itself a thought.'[19] To the distinction between thought and thing-in-itself, on this view, should be added that between thinking and thoughts, propositions or truths-in-themselves: 'Only if one believes that, besides things-in-themselves and our thought of them, there is no third element, namely, truths-in-themselves, which we merely apprehend by means of our thought, does it become intelligible how someone could be inclined to regard the logical forms as something which merely adheres to our thought.'[20] Here we already see the outline of the idea of a critique of psychologism in logic – that is, of the interpretation of logical rules as empirical laws of thought: it was the realization of this critique in Frege and Husserl which greatly increased the plausibility of the re-definition of thought as non-empirical receptivity. It was Gottlob Frege, above all, who found the classical formulation for this idea: according to him, thinking is essentially 'the grasp of a thought', and thoughts are what can be true or false independently of our apprehension of them and so possess a being in themselves.[21] The idea that thought always has to do with something independent of thought and not produced by it then came to be – whether in an intentionalist version (as in Brentano or Meinong) or in a Platonist version (as in Frege) – the foundation of the new ontology in general, to the extent that it was more than a merely revivalist position.

The thesis of the structural homogeneity of thought and perception was also the fundamental methodological idea of philosophy conceived of as phenomenology, an idea which Edmund Husserl shared with the positivism of the period. As is generally known, he nevertheless distinguished his conception of phenomenology from all empiricist positions by means of the idea of the 'phenomenological reduction' (*epoché*), and thus first created the epistemological basis for a 'pure' (that is, a priori) logic. In this connexion, Husserl explicitly reintroduced the concept of 'ontology', which had been generally discredited by the philosophical Criticism of the second half of the century. First of all, Husserl emphasized that in the phenomenological reduction all 'transcendent being', understood in the normal sense as true being, was excluded or 'bracketed'.

What is to remain is simply and solely 'consciousness itself' in its own essence, and, in place of transcendent being, the 'intended being' of the transcendent and with it all kinds of correlates, objects-as-intended, noemata ... We thus retain perception and the perceived as such (in so far, that is, as we can evidently assert, *after* exclusion of the real being of the perceived, that according to its essence the perception is precisely perception *of* this or that object, it intends it or is consciousness of it); we retain recollection and the recollected as such, thinking and what is thought as such, in short, noesis and noema.

To this reduction, which must be applied even to the sphere of the psychic itself, '*are subject ... all ontologies*' [Italics mine – H. S.].[22] As a result of the completion of the phenomenological reduction by the *eidetic*, which brings to light universal essential connexions in the material presented in the phenomenological attitude, the categorial fundamental determinations of everything which can in general be an object of consciousness are arrived at, and these are nothing less than the 'fundamental concepts and axioms' of all possible ontologies. 'Ontology' here is meant precisely in the sense of Meinong's 'theory of objects', that is, as a science of the most general characteristics and structures of what can in general be an object, but it also coincides with what was described at the beginning as ontology in the wider sense. An important qualification results in Husserl, however, from his theory of 'eidetic existential judgments', which does not merely base ontology in his sense on propositions about essences, but over and above that is supposed also to allow for the adoption of a positive or negative attitude *vis-à-vis* the existence of the eidetic itself. (Meinong's theory of objects applies, in Husserlian terms, to noemata in general.) In order to present itself as an ontology, phenomenology first has to separate the essential determinations and connexions of what is intended in the phenomenological attitude, that is, the noemata, from the noemata themselves and then has to decide whether the 'eidos' of the noema in question exists or not; only positive existential propositions provide a basis for the 'fundamental concepts and axioms' of the ontology in question, while negative existential propositions have the 'function' of 'excluding invalid concepts and meaningless expressions'.[23] As an example, Husserl cites the 'round square': as something thought, as a noema, it exists as much as other noemata, but the essence (eidos) 'round square' does not exist; in order for that judgment to be possible, the essence of the noema 'round square' must, however, have been fixed beforehand. This makes it clear that, according to Husserl, it is not the results of the eidetic reduction, but only the existential judgments which are to be passed on it, which constitute ontology: it is here that we have developed the phenomenological judgment on noemata into ontological judgments on the eidetic. Ontology is more than merely a clarification of ontological concepts: in it what is involved is 'grounding the *validity* of these concepts, the being of essence and the validity of judgments of essence (the veracity of essential states of affairs)'. On the basis of his theory of significance and knowledge, Husserl can present this grounding only in the form of existential propositions.

The 'eidetic existential judgments' of phenomenological ontology furnish, according to Husserl, the valid fundamental concepts of any regional science: 'number', 'space', 'thing', 'motion' and so on. 'Every simple intuition "conceals within itself" the essence of the region which corresponds to it and the regional categories which belong to it, which undergo their eidetic positing in the corresponding ontology, and further conceals in itself all axioms of the relevant ontology.'[24] It becomes clear here why Husserl constantly – and in plain distinction from the tradition – speaks of 'ontolog*ies*' (in the plural): each ontology is regionally defined, that is, it is comprehensible only in terms of the general phenomenological perspective, which is always already articulated according to fields of investigation, and so there is an ontology of the mathematical, of the psychical, the physical and so forth. Husserl also introduces a further differentiation in the form of his distinction between formal and material ontology: material ontologies are the regional ontologies already mentioned, while formal ontology, as an 'eidetic science of the object in general', reveals the fundamental formal structures of any material ontology. Formal ontology comprised Husserl's 'theory of the object' before the transcendental turn in his thought.

Despite Husserl's rehabilitation of the concept of 'ontology', it should not be forgotten that what he dealt with under that heading still remained completely in the domain of the philosophy of consciousness; his ontology remained phenomenological in the sense that the phenomenological reduction was always presupposed in it. 'Absolute' being belongs to consciousness alone, and every other existent always stands within its horizon. It was Husserl's own pupils who attempted to free the conception of formal and regional ontologies from this transcendental or (in the epistemological sense) Idealistic context of its introduction and to press forward to a new *real* ontology' (Hedwig Conrad-Martius). Names to be mentioned here include those of the Munich Phenomenological Circle (Geiger, Pfänder, Reinach and others) and Max Scheler, who, strongly influenced by the 'Munichers', lent great weight, especially because of his well-known ethics of value, to anti-transcendentalist ontology, which sought to take over from Husserl his eidetic reduction, without the phenomenological. (In Scheler himself, the idea of the *epoché* was reinterpreted in such a way that it no longer came into conflict with the Realist intention.) It was Scheler, too, who prepared the way for and gave impetus to the other great ontological 'reform' of phenomenology – that of Heidegger. The 'rebirth' of ontology thus began, not with Husserl himself, but only with his pupils. It can be seen as an attempt to release the ontology which Husserl had reawakened from the clutches of subjectivism and to enable it to stand on its own feet. An account of these events published in 1933, and influenced by this picture, presents it as follows:

Like all pure philosophy of consciousness, Husserl's phenomenology is so incurably introverted that, despite all apparent attempts at an objectivist realignment, it is completely impossible for it to understand the opposite mental attitude, even simply in terms of its 'meaning'. It has annexed to itself the traditional ontology, with which it is itself associated in terms of its presuppositions. But it has neutralized the force of its motives. It has twisted the intention of this ontology into its opposite. The further development of modern ontology is thus anything but a consistent realization of phenomenological principles. It is – in the form which it has maintained in Scheler and Heidegger – a radical transformation of phenomenology, nourished from other sources.[25]

3 Fundamental ontology (Heidegger)

Heidegger's transformation of Husserl's project, on the other hand, does not consist in a Realist reinterpretation of phenomenology, but in the inversion of its relation to ontology. To be sure, in *Being and Time* there is the remark, quite in Husserl's sense, that 'ontology is possible only as phenomenology', but 'phenomenology' is used here merely as a *methodological* concept and no longer also, as in Husserl, as a definition of a field of *objects*:

> 'Phenomenology' neither refers to the object of its investigations, nor characterizes the title of their content. The word gives information only about the *how* of the way in which *what* is to be treated in this science is exhibited and treated. A science 'of' phenomena means a comprehension of its objects of *such* a kind that everything which is part of the discussion of them must be treated in a direct exhibition and a direct demonstration.[26]

Anything which is a 'phenomenon' in the sense of an object of phenomenology must be such as to allow of 'direct exhibition' and 'demonstration': 'The phenomenological concept of a phenomenon means *the Being of a being as self-showing* [italics mine – H. S.], its meaning, its modifications and derivatives.'[27] From this it follows that 'From the point of view of its content, phenomenology is the science of the Being of beings – ontology.'[28]

This sounds like real ontology and must be understood in that sense as long as one does not take into account the peculiarities of Heidegger's concept of ontology: the connexion of the ontological with the subject, seen as the place at which alone that 'self-showing' can show itself, and the asociated interpretation of the 'question of Being' as a question about the '*meaning* of Being'. Heidegger is closer to Husserl than the Munich Circle, Scheler and Nicolai Hartmann, in that he does not simply gloss over the subjective conditions of the possibility of ontology or, like Hartmann, reinterpret them in the manner of objectivist ontology; he finds these conditions fulfilled in the mode of Being of that being who is alone capable of pursuing science or ontology: *man*. In this way, the transcendental conditions of knowledge are also given an ontological interpretation – that is, as aspects of the mode of Being of the knower – but precisely not an objectivist one. Heidegger's term for the subject of knowledge, who is to be characterized only in terms of his mode of Being, is '*Dasein*':

> The *Dasein* is a being which does not present itself only under other beings. It is rather ontically distinguished in that for this being in its Being this Being itself is *in question*. However, it belongs to this structure of Being of *Dasein* that it

has in this Being a relation of Being to this Being. And this in turn means that *Dasein* understands itself in any mode and any form of expression in its Being. It is a characteristic of this being that with and through its Being that Being is disclosed to him himself. *Understanding of Being is itself a determination of the Being of Dasein.* The ontic distinction of *Dasein* lies in the fact that it *is* ontological.[29]

It is not only the subject of ontology, but also the discipline of 'ontology' itself which is thereby given an ontological (in Heidegger's sense) reinterpretation, as a mode of Being of *Dasein*. The Being of the being of *this* mode of Being, that is, of the *Dasein* which always has the capacity for self-understanding, Heidegger calls 'existence' (*Existenz*), and its general determinations he calls 'existentials' (*Existenzialien*). The clarification of this domain in the 'existential analytic of *Dasein*' which is 'indicated with regard to its possibility and necessity in the ontic structure of *Dasein*', is a 'fundamental ontology' which is prior to all regional ontologies:

Sciences are manners of Being of *Dasein*, in which it also is related to a being which it does not itself need to be. It essentially belongs to *Dasein*, however, to be in a world. The understanding of Being which appertains to *Dasein* thus affects, with a common source, the understanding of such a thing as a 'world' and understanding of the Being of the beings which are accessible within the world. The ontologies which have as their theme beings of a type of Being different in character from that of *Dasein* are accordingly founded and motivated in the ontic structure of *Dasein* itself, which comprises in itself the determination of a pre-ontological understanding of Being. Hence, the *fundamental ontology* from which alone all others can be derived must be sought in the *existential analytic of Dasein*.[30]

The way in which the 'ontic distinction' of *Dasein* is thus made more precise by means of the 'understanding of Being' as a 'determination of Being' of *Dasein* itself also makes it possible to understand why Heidegger's fundamental ontology is presented as a 'hermeneutics of *Dasein*' and so made part of the tradition of the philosophy of *Verstehen* (understanding). If the relation of *Dasein* to its own Being, that is, to existence, is already a matter of *understanding*, and ontology follows in its method this ontic indication, the phenomenological procedure, which Heidegger interprets as '*légein tà phainómena*' (letting what shows itself be seen), can also be conceived of simply as an 'exposition' (*Auslegung*):

The methodological sense of phenomenological description is *exposition*. The *lógos* of the phenomenology of *Dasein* has the character of *hermeneúein*, by means of which the understanding of Being which belongs to *Dasein* itself is *informed* of the true meaning of Being and the fundamental structures of its own Being. Phenomenology of *Dasein* is *hermeneutics* in the original meaning of the word, according to which it refers to the business of exposition.[31]

This also makes it clear why Heidegger treated the 'question of Being' as a question about the '*meaning* of Being': the hermeneutic character of his ontology suggested this interpretation. What are customarily called 'ontology' or 'hermeneutics' – theory of being and methodology of the human sciences – are thus merely modes of the understanding of Being which is grounded in the ontic structure of *Dasein* itself, and as such are derivative and dependent on the original meaning of those expressions. Heidegger says of philosophy,

> Ontology and phenomenology are not two different disciplines among others which belong to philosophy. The two titles characterize philosophy itself according to its object and its manner of treating it. Philosophy is universal phenomenological ontology, starting from the hermeneutics of *Dasein*, which, as an analytic of *existence*, has secured the end of the guiding thread of all philosophical questioning at the point from which it *originates* and to which it *returns*.[32]

The historical influence of the Heideggerian ontology lies outside the period to be discussed in this book: two references to it must therefore suffice. The replacement of the traditional conception of essential ontology, the last representative of which was Husserl, by an existential ontology, represented in the proposition 'The "essence" of *Dasein* lies in its existence', led to *existentialism*, though Heidegger sharply distinguished his own position from it in his *Brief über den Humanismus* (Letter on Humanism) of 1946. The transformation of ontological hermeneutics into a hermeneutic ontology, brought about by Heidegger's 'turn' itself, resulted in Heidegger's works on the philosophy of language, but especially in Hans-Georg Gadamer's *Wahrheit und Methode* (Truth and Method) of 1960: the reversal of the relation of ontology and hermeneutics expressed in the phrase 'hermeneutic ontology' is there taken to imply the replacement of the 'hermeneutics of *Dasein*' as a fundamental discipline of philosophy and the substitution for it of a 'more original' kind of thinking, reflecting on the 'Being of beings' itself and expounding its linguistic presence. Gadamer's *Truth and Method* accordingly merged into an 'ontological turn in hermeneutics following the guiding thread of language'.[33] Here too a post-Hegelian ontological tradition ended in monism – that of Being.

4 Critico-realist ontology (Nicolai Hartmann)

The history of the new ontology in Germany is characterized by the rivalry between the phenomenological conception in Heidegger's version and its alternative in the work of Nicolai Hartmann (1882–1950). Most accounts make a direct connexion between his ontology and 'Critical Realism', and they are right to the extent that Hartmann himself time and time again placed great value on the characterizations of his philosophy as 'Critical' and 'Realist'; nevertheless, to refer to it directly as 'Critical Realism' runs the risk of identifying it with an epistemological tendency of the same name, which certainly opposed Idealistic neo-Kantianism from the end of the nineteenth century onwards, but did not, unlike Nicolai Hartmann, aspire to a new ontology. 'Critical Realism' (E. von Hartmann, O. Külpe, A. Messer, and also W. Wundt and A. Riehl) can be thought of as a philosophical position which, while respecting the achievements of Kant in the critique of knowledge, undertakes to justify the Realism of everyday consciousness and the sciences, that is, to refute the Idealist interpretation of the world as a mere representation. Starting from the 'given' and taking into account the results of the special sciences, the aim was to demonstrate the possibility in principle of arriving at assertions about the most general structures of a reality that was independent of consciousness. In so far as this philosophy was completed by a metaphysics, it was largely identical with the programme of an 'inductive metaphysics' achieved by a 'synthesis of the sciences'.

Nicolai Hartmann's route to ontology took a different direction. A pupil of Hermann Cohen and Paul Natorp, he achieved his habilitation in Marburg in 1909 with a thesis on 'Plato's Logic of Being'. It was only later, under the influence of Husserl, Scheler and the Critical Realists, that he turned against the logicist neo-Kantianism of his own origins; he did so, however, not by proposing an alternative theory of knowledge, but by radically reversing the relationship of epistemology and metaphysics itself, which made it possible to replace the Criticist logic of knowledge in the neo-Kantian style by a 'metaphysics of knowledge'. The *Grundzüge einer Metaphysik der Erkenntnis* (Main Features of a Metaphysics of Knowledge), which he published in 1921, were the origin and justificational basis of an ontology, in the sense of a programme of philosophical work to which Nicolai Hartmann then devoted his life. Although he himself constantly presented it as a 'New Ontology', it was thought of at the same time as regaining an area of investigation which had been overwhelmed by Kant and what came after him. Hartmann himself refers to the lasting impression made on him by the neo-Wolffian Hans Pichler and his attempt to restore the problem of being to philosophy. Even in his *Zur Grundlegung der Ontologie* (On the Foundations of Ontology) of 1935, Nicolai Hartmann speaks of the return to ontology as a process to which stood opposed 'the pressure of habits of thought which have been established for at least a hundred and fifty years and acquired the solidity of a tradition'.[34] What differentiates him, nevertheless, from the advocates of historicist revivals is the conviction that this return is not merely historically required at this time, but is objectively necessary.

To prove this necessity is the task set for itself by his 'metaphysics of knowledge'. The first assumption which he makes in this regard is stated in the first sentence of that work: 'The following investigations proceed from the conception that knowledge is not a creation, generation or production of the object, as Idealism in both old and new styles seeks to teach us, but a grasping of something which is present before all knowledge and independently of it.'[35] This conception is not as yet that of metaphysical Realism, but simply the natural attitude of knowledge in the everyday and scientific consciousness of the world – every knower believes or hopes that he can grasp something in-itself, independent of himself – and there is room for dispute only at the level of interpretation, explanation or justification of this conception. Hartmann characterizes it as

> a state of affairs in the phenomenon of knowledge which is prior . . . to all discussion of points of view. The natural conception of the phenomenon of knowledge is characterized by precisely this notion of 'grasping'; it coincides with that 'empirical Realism' which even extreme transcendental Idealism cannot avoid upholding, indeed expressly justifying in its own way.[36]

The Realism of the natural and scientific attitude to knowledge is thus for Hartmann both a phenomenon and a problem at the same time, for, as the history of the problem of knowledge shows, philosophy cannot simply acquiesce in that phenomenon; it has to take it up 'prior to all discussion of points of view', that is, 'this side of Idealism and Realism'. (The key-words 'phenomenon', 'problem' and 'freedom from points of view' already indicate his conception of method.) Hartmann then affirms that the phenomenal content of the problem thus posed itself shows that the question of knowledge must be posed as a metaphysical question,

> for whether, in pursuing the problem further, we shall find that it is still the case that knowing is grasping something in-itself or that we have to return to some

form of 'production', can change nothing in the content of the problem. In both cases, the proposition which forms the fundamental thesis of all further discussion still stands: 'The problem of knowledge is neither a psychological nor a logical one, but at base *a metaphysical problem*.' It cannot be dealt with by the methods of psychology, nor by those of logic, but only by those of a *metaphysics of knowledge* specifically designed for this purpose. Whether it is possible to solve it in this way, and how far, is another question, the answer to which will also concern, amongst other things, the following investigations.[37]

In another place Hartmann says,

There is no problem of knowledge without a problem of being. For there is no knowledge the whole meaning of which does not consist in being a knowledge of being. Knowledge is simply a relatedness of consciousness to something which exists in-itself. Theory may subsequently prove that this in-itself is not in-itself at all. But the phenomenon of the relation itself is not thereby removed from the world . . . A theory of knowledge which disputes that is not a theory of knowledge at all. That which it deals with is certainly not knowledge.[38]

Since the problem of knowledge, being a metaphysical problem, can be dealt with only in a metaphysics, every theory of knowledge, according to Hartmann – even and especially the Criticist theory – implies the adoption of a metaphysical position towards this problem: that is, it implies a metaphysics of knowledge. To be sure, it should not be uncritical: 'Kant's thesis, that there is no metaphysics without a critique, remains in force. Only the thesis must be set against its natural antithesis: no critique without a metaphysics . . . Epistemology presupposes metaphysics as much as metaphysics presupposes theory of knowledge: they mutually limit one another.'[39]

For all that, the two relations of limitation are not of equal value: the 'Critical theory of knowledge' which is a 'prolegomenon to all metaphysics' in Kant's sense and the 'Critical metaphysics' which is a 'prolegomenon to theory of knowledge' are situated on different levels. Hartmann first really advances beyond the 'metaphysics of knowledge' towards 'Critical ontology' when he points to the *philosophia prima sive ontologia* as systematically prior to all epistemology. In his late work, *Neue Wege der Ontologie* (New Ways in Ontology), of 1942–9 Nicolai Hartmann once again retrospectively brought together the most important arguments for this view. First, theory of knowledge itself already presupposes the possibility of philosophical knowledge and the knowledge of the sciences; it cannot therefore arrive at any position prior to knowledge, but must take it up as already a phenomenon and a problem. Secondly, knowledge is never a mere phenomenon of consciousness like beliefs, representations, etc., but a 'transcendent act', that is, a relation in which one stands to something independent of consciousness in an 'ontological attitude', and this is also true of theory of knowledge as a 'reflection of knowledge on itself'. Thirdly, the 'knowledge-relation' between subject and object, 'to which the transcendence of the act is attached' is '. . . at base a relation of being, and indeed a real one; indeed, it is merely one of many real relations by which consciousness is bound to the surrounding real world.'[40] The proof of this third thesis in Hartmann is the fundamental justification of posing the problem of knowledge, not merely as a metaphysical problem, but as an ontological one, and thus according to ontology the systematic primacy over the theory of knowledge: ontology and epistemology are related to each other, according to him, as *ratio essendi* to *ratio cognoscendi*. His philosophy as a whole is thus an ontology in the narrower sense of the word, referred to at the beginning of this account, and it is so in the most consistent way by comparison with many other recent ontologies.

What nevertheless distinguishes Nicolai Hartmann's ontology from the ancients' *prima philosophia sive ontologia* is its Critical pretensions. Kant's thesis that there can be no metaphysics without a critique is supposed to remain in force, and so no mere repetition of pre-Critical ontology is possible. The explanation for the fact that Hartmann's development of the problem of knowledge nevertheless did not lead him back to a transcendental philosophy, in the sense of an 'analytic of the pure understanding' is that he understood by 'critique' something essentially different from Kant and only partially went along with Kant's 'Critical road'. First, the Critical and the subjectivist elements were to be separated, since the latter already implied support for Idealism.

If one gives in to subjectivism, on the other hand, then to be sure it is possible to derive quite a different consequence from the tendency of the critique: the consequence that it is precisely the *metaphysical* element in the problem of knowledge which is to *receive Critical treatment*. As long as only what is founded on subjective principles is called 'Critical', such treatment contains a contradiction within itself. But if one understands by a 'Critical' treatment one which takes into account all elements of a problem with which one is confronted, giving them all equal value, whether or not they transcend the subject, in such a way that *the critique as such never functions as a court of appeal against the content of the problem*, but only against premature attempts at a solution, this contradiction collapses of its own accord. A Critical theory of knowledge can very readily be metaphysical. And it must be so, since its problem is metaphysical. What is uncritical is precisely the denial of the metaphysical where it is present.[41]

The Critical attitude, as opposed to the dogmatic, is thus synonymous with a methodical abstinence from the adoption of particular points of view, as long as the object of enquiry does not itself suggest them; this variant of the Husserlian *epoché* thus means simply freedom from preconceptions and presuppositionlessness. Critical ontology in this sense is thus always in the first instance critical sifting of a problem-field and argumentative rejection of over-hasty and unfounded assertions relating to it. On the other hand, the element of critique which Nicolai Hartmann takes over directly from Kant and to which he reduces Kantian Criticism, as to its rational core, is the distinction between thing-in-itself and appearance: 'The thing-in-itself is the true Critical motif in the "Critical Philosophy"; its abandonment in the post-Kantians and in neo-Kantianism was in itself the abandonment of the Critical position.'[42] The idea of the thing-in-itself

distinguishes the Critical ontology from the Wolffian. Wolff's *philosophia prima* was rationalistic; the Kantian thing-in-itself, however, is not rational, it is intelligible but not sensible, thinkable but not intuitable, and so not cognizable. For that reason, Kant called it a 'noumenon in the negative sense'. But it remained positive in the sense of its existence.[43]

Hartmann then interprets Kant's Critical philosophy as a negative ontology of an 'endless object' of knowledge as an 'endless task', and he infers from this that 'the negative ontology of Kant must be transformed into a positive ontology'.[44]

This 'positive ontology', because of its Critical self-understanding, can be characterized only by its methodology, and it must in other respects justify itself in terms of its results. 'It is therefore not a matter of characterizing ontology from the outset as Realism.'[45] Here Nicolai Hartmann makes explicit his links with Husserl and Aristotle. If the fundamental attitude of critical analysis is to be connected only by association with the phenomenological *epoché*, nevertheless, in describing the initial stage of ontological work, explicit reference is made to Husserl's phenomenology, though of course only to its eidetic aspect.

The phenomenon of knowledge must be described in such a way that the connexion of its essential features is perspicuous as a whole and so at the same time offers a guarantee that they are complete. We possess the method for such a description of essences today in the procedure of phenomenology. This still young philosophical science has already provided an abundance of important analyses of essence, but in the area of knowledge has so far confined itself almost exclusively to the logical and parts of the psychological aspects of the phenomenon. Up until now there has not existed a *phenomenology of knowledge* in the sense of an essential analysis of the *metaphysical* element in the phenomenon of knowledge. It must first be designed anew from the foundations upwards.[46]

Hartmann's own efforts in this direction

endeavour to follow the natural attitude of the knowing consciousness and to comprehend the phenomenon of knowledge (always in the sense of the narrower problem of knowledge) as widely and completely as possible. This preliminary analytical work in principle stands, not merely on this side of all conceptions based on particular points of view, but also on this side of all genuine formulation of the questions themselves, *on this side of all problem-formation*, that is, of all selection of perspectives and points of interest. It deals with the pure *quaestio facti*.[47]

Phenomenology is seen here as a description and analysis of phenomena with the methods of the eidetic reduction; that is why it is called 'analysis of essences'. (It is plain that the metaphysical interpretation of the domain of phenomena and essences belonging to such an analysis is the chasm which separates Nicolai Hartmann from Husserl.) The second methodological step in Hartmann's conception is the analysis of the problem, which he calls, following Aristotle, '*aporetic*', where Aristotle also serves him as a model. The third step is theory-formation itself, which Hartmann does not conceive of directly as construction of a system, but as a further argumentative elaboration of the objective problem. If one surveys these four steps – *epoché* of specific points of view, analysis of essences (phenomenology), analysis of the problem (aporetic), theory-formation – then it becomes clear how great the distance is between Nicolai Hartmann and Husserl, and how questionable it would be to regard this ontology as a mere continuation of phenomenology by other means, as it occasionally has been; it is more correct to say that Hartmann believed that he could use the phenomenological method 'untroubled by the philosophical grounding which it had received in Husserl, as if it were an ownerless instrument'.[48]

It is impossible here to give an account of Nicolai Hartmann's ontology; a few characteristic features must suffice. It has already been said that it thinks of itself as a new ontology, because it thinks of itself as a *Critical* ontology. But it aims to avoid the defects of the old ontology, not only in regard to method, but also in what concerns the content of its teaching. These defects can be traced back, according to Hartmann, to a fundamental error: the identification with each other of thought, ideal being and the structures of real being, whereas in reality what we have to do with here is a 'triad of structures which are in their essence completely distinct'.

What, however, is it which is defective in this ontology? . . . It lies precisely in the identity of logical form and form of being which is presupposed. According to this assumption, there cannot be anything alogical in the real; logic rules the world of things completely, even as far as particularization, concretion, individuation. And this first thesis of identity is joined by a second, the equation of logical structure and pure thought, reason (*ratio*). That too is an obvious assumption, but an arbitrary one. It involves a failure to recognize the fact that there is a realm of ideal structures and laws which subsists independently of thought and is already presupposed in thought itself as subsisting in-itself. Such laws as the Principle of Identity or of Contradiction, the *dictum de omni et nullo* and the laws of the figures of the syllogism are of this kind.[49]

Whereas the first error leads ontology to an unjustifiable rationalization of the world, the second implies a subjectivization of the logical, which makes the problem of ontological knowledge completely insoluble. Nevertheless, there must, according to Hartmann, exist a partial identity between these three domains: if the real were completely alogical, if it were not rationally cognizable, and if the logical form of reality as an ideal being were not at the same time at least partly comprehensible in thought, there would be no a priori knowledge of reality. In terms of method, it follows from this that ontology must proceed inductively (in the Aristotelian sense, but also on the model of 'inductive metaphysics') – 'The categories with which the new ontology deals are acquired, neither by means of a definition of the universal nor by derivation from a formal table of judgments, but pick up without a break the real relationships.'[50] It also follows that it must avoid the mistake of regarding everything universal as directly a matter of principle: 'It is certainly true that everything which is a principle is universal, but it does not follow from that that everything which is universal is also a principle.'[51] This mistake was, in Hartmann's view, the reason for the emergence of the deductivist metaphysics of substantial forms, of which the old metaphysics believed that they determined real being a priori; the new ontology cannot therefore present itself as a pure essential ontology.

This line of argument at the same time indicates two further features of Nicolai Hartmann's ontological theory. First, rational cognition and the rationally cognizable are regarded ontologically as an island in the sea of the irrational, where by 'irrational' is chiefly meant only what evades reason. The opposition to a 'panlogism' in Hegel's sense which originates in that traditional identification of the logical, the ideal and the real was shared by Nicolai Hartmann with contemporary life-philosophy and philosophy of existence, despite all his emphatic affirmations of the difference between his position and such tendencies. The other feature which comes to the fore in Hartmann's critique of the old ontology is the tendency to think in spatial metaphors – levels, domains and strata. Hartmann's philosophy is quasi-geographical; his theory of categories, the centre of which in turn is his modal analysis, is put forward, essentially, as an ideal topology of concepts. It is important nevertheless that these categories are principles of *being* which for their part certainly indicate the *Aufbau der realen Welt* (Structure of the Real World) (1940), but do not completely determine it. Hartmann's well-known theory of *strata* (physical, organic, psychic (*seelisch*) and mental (*geistig*) being) is thus not simply deducible from the theory of categories; here too a quasi-empirical element enters.

If one compares Nicolai Hartmann's ontology with that of Heidegger from a present-day perspective, one is bound to say that Hartmann certainly affected his own epoch, but did not, like Heidegger, make an epoch. Various reasons, both external and internal to philosophy, can be given for that. Only one extra-philosophical reason will be mentioned here, derived from the history of science: Hartmann's claim to give a scientific demonstration of the principles and strata of being itself brought him into competition with the empirical natural sciences – a competition which he was bound to lose. His theory of strata in particular forced him, for instance, to adopt positions towards the theory of evolution, and also towards psychological questions, which were empirically untenable. The most important intra-philosophical reason for the fact that Nicolai Hartmann has become a historical figure in Germany lies in the influence of analytical philosophy, which had the effect here of a rebirth of Criticism under more rigorous conditions involving the critique of meaning and language. The new ontology as a whole found it difficult to withstand critical arguments of this kind.

5 Ontology today?

The way in which one assesses the possibility and necessity of ontology at present will depend, not only on what one understands by 'ontology', but also on how one sees its 'rebirth' in our century. After a brief survey of the various uses of the word 'to be' Wolfgang Stegmüller says, 'Failure to attend to this multiplicity of meanings and thoughtless substantival use of this auxiliary verb have produced a disease which began to spread like an epidemic in Middle-European philosophy more than a hundred years ago and whose culminating point has perhaps now been passed: the being-plague ("the Being of beings" and so on).'[52] Nicolai Hartmann would hardly feel himself to be affected today by this diagnosis, since he wanted 'ontology' to be understood precisely *not* as philosophizing on the basis of word-meanings, but as a science of the *real*. On the other hand, it is the standard objection to Heidegger that he has wretchedly mistreated the word 'to be': but his philosophy can be called 'ontology' only in a limited sense and one which is radically changed as compared with the tradition. It is certainly this change of meaning above all which has conferred such an influence in the history of thought on this 'ontology' which is a philosophy of an unobjective Being: it consists in the *reinterpretation of ontological knowledge as hermeneutics*. (Nicolai Hartmann always opposed this.) Thus it is above all Heidegger's influence in the science of literature and art, and also in theology, which is responsible for the expanding influence enjoyed today by Heidegger's thought in the form of Gadamer's hermeneutic ontology, while the esoteric thought of Heidegger's later writings has remained largely inaccessible. Many social scientists and historians expected Gadamer's hermeneutics finally to provide the philosophical foundations of their disciplines which Heidegger himself had scorned to give; conversely, Gadamer's historical and philological interests strengthened the hermeneutical aspects of Heidegger's thought, so that such expectations (disappointed in this case too) were understandable.

What will ultimately decide the further destiny of ontology in the narrower sense of a philosophy which grants the question of being primacy over the problem of knowledge are, as already indicated, not primarily arguments derived from the critique of knowledge, but considerations based on the critique of meaning. Against Hartmann it could be objected that the real relation between subject and object which, according to him, knowledge must be interpreted as involving is in no case objectively statable and describable: there simply *is* no such phenomenon as this real relation, it is a metaphorical, spatializing interpretation of what we understand by the word 'knowledge'. It seems reasonable, therefore, to suspect Hartmann's 'metaphysics of knowledge' in general of a '*mingling of types of discourse*': it is plain that explicative discourse is here masked as descriptive discourse and the impression is given that what is contained in the meaning of concepts can be grasped by means of a description of phenomena. There seems to be a mingling of types of discourse of the opposite kind when Heidegger defines 'phenomenological description' as 'exposition', and thus presents description as explication. The authorization for this is already to be found, however, in Husserl's understanding of phenomenology, for there, as later in Hartmann and other ontologists, the explication of concepts is itself presented as description, so that in fact Heidegger seems to deserve the credit for revoking this move. For Husserl, the noemata are at once meanings, as what is intended in the noeses or acts of consciousness, *and* something phenomenologically describable in the *epoché*, whereas Heidegger, by means of his version of fundamental ontology as a 'hermeneutics of *Dasein*', again characterizes such noemata (e.g. the existentials) as something to be expounded. Probably this is also one reason for his criticism of all attempts to think of Being as an object and so as a being. Nevertheless, this does not prevent him from then once again speaking of Being in a quasi-descriptive fashion: that it conceals itself, while being present, that it is 'itself' and so on.[53] A consistently explicative ontology, which made no further descriptive knowledge-claims, could no longer be brought into connexion with the old and with the resurrected ontology: as a pure science of concepts, it would be a part of semantics.[54] To associate objective knowledge-claims with it would mean attributing an objective 'being' to the denotata of the concept-words, and this would require, not merely a refutation of nominalism, but also a reference theory of meaning, which identified the meaning of an expression with the object to which it referred. Neither of these are to be had, and so it seems that Kant's dictum about the 'haughty name of an ontology' turns out to be true once again today in our changed situation.

8

Epilogue: Man

Any account of German philosophy in the nineteenth century would remain incomplete if it failed to mention a phenomenon which caused a stir as a German peculiarity at the end of the period: philosophical anthropology. At first sight, this looks like a matter of a mere curiosity (perhaps a typically German one): the creation of a *mésalliance* between the established special science of anthropology and the tradition of philosophy. At first glance, such an alliance would seem only to be beneficial to both partners: the empirical science of man could thus also satisfy philosophical claims, and the purely philosophical attempt to answer the question 'What is man?' would finally receive in return a reliable basis in empirical science. This supposed possibility of empirical science's becoming philosophical and philosophy's becoming empirical in fact explains part of the fascination exercised by philosophical anthropology after Max Scheler's *Die Stellung des Menschen im Kosmos* (The Position of Man in the Cosmos) of 1928, and which Heidegger felt it necessary, as early as his book on Kant of 1929, to oppose:

Anthropology today, and for a long time past, is no longer the name for a discipline; rather, the word signifies a fundamental tendency in the present-day position of man in relation to himself and in the totality of beings. According to this fundamental position, something is known and understood only when it has found an anthropological explanation. Anthropology does not merely seek the truth about man, but now claims to decide what it is possible for truth itself to mean.[1]

Heidegger's argument here is directed more against a tendency in the spirit of the times than against the founder of philosophical anthropology himself, who had conceived of it as certainly a fundamental discipline of philosophy and the human sciences, but also as merely an introduction to metaphysics, and never advocated the reduction of philosophy to anthropology which Heidegger feared. In Heidegger, too, is to be found the most obvious objection to the success of that association, which seemed so fashionably attractive to contemporaries: that of 'anthropologism', that is, of a new version of the circular relationship between philosophy and special sciences, already familiar from the cases of psychologism, sociologism, biologism and also historicism.

Seen in this way, philosophical anthropology appears to be not much more than one of the numerous attempts to escape from the post-Idealist identity-crisis in philosophy: a further variant of the 'rehabilitation of philosophy as a science', and this in fact is part of the explanation of its influence. That this does not exhaust its significance results from the fact that it also bears witness to another identity-crisis: that of the philosophers themselves. Philosophical anthropology belongs to the history of the crisis caused by the 'collapse of Idealism' for the traditional self-interpretation of man, and it forms in a certain sense the terminating point of that history. The post-Hegelian revolution of consciousness under the banner of history and science, and its consequent problems, which I have attempted to present in the preceding chapters by following the guiding thread of 'six great themes', may thus once again be retrospectively considered in the form of the question of man.

1 'Philosophical anthropology'

The question, 'What is man?', has been one of the central questions of philosophy since its beginnings, so that, strictly speaking, the expression 'philosophical anthropology' must be considered as a pleonasm. Kant even asserts that metaphysics, morality and religion can 'at base . . . be counted as belonging to anthropology', because the guiding questions, 'What can I know?', 'What should I do?' and 'What may I hope?' are related to the question 'What is man?',[2] and he seems in so doing to be an early advocate of the reduction of philosophy to anthropology. The need felt in our own century for a further specification of anthropology as philosophical in general shows that the question of the nature of man has for a long time no longer been considered as *self-evidently* philosophical. The charge of reductionism against Kant is unjustified, because it was only after Hegel that philosophy and anthropology separated in such a way that the reference of those fundamental questions to the anthropological question could seem like a reduction to something extra-philosophical. Between anthropology as a subdiscipline or fundamental discipline of philosophy and the philosophical anthropology of our own times lies the rise of the empirical sciences of man – human biology or the Anglo-Saxon 'cultural anthropology' (which in Germany is called '*Völkerkunde*' or 'study of peoples'). It was only secondarily, after their separation from philosophical systematics, that these could once again be brought into connexion with philosophical questions. This is also the explanation for the reactive and essentially assimilative character of philosophical anthropology. Because all material knowledge of man was available only in the form of empirical scientific knowledge, those who were interested from a philosophical point of view could no longer obtain and justify such knowledge by merely philosophical means, as had still seemed to be the case in Hegel. But that also meant that the philosophical element in philosophical anthropology had become a problem.

Arnold Gehlen cut the Gordian knot, without untying it, when he professed to pursue philosophy itself as an empirical science; the predicate 'philosophical' then simply has the function of indicating that the new empirical science of man is ready to concern itself with the same questions which were once regarded as philosophical in the traditional sense. Max Scheler did not go so far; he wanted to regard philosophical anthropology as a philosophical discipline because it posed questions of essence which the empirical sciences neglected to pose. Helmut Plessner, on the other hand, whose *Die Stufen des Organischen und der Mensch. Eine Einleitung in die philosophische Anthropologie* (The Degrees of the Organic and Man. An Introduction to Philosophical Anthropology) of 1928 represents the second basic work of philosophical anthropology, largely independent of Scheler, criticizes this fixation on questions of essence – which he also finds in Jaspers and Heidegger – and characterizes the philosophical element in this new science of man as a result of a 'partial overlapping' of a 'comprehensive philosophy' with a 'comprehensive anthropology'. The 'peripheral discipline' which thus emerged nevertheless had central philosophical tasks to fulfil: for instance, that of normative guidance in concept-formation in the human sciences. Plessner's answer to the question of the philosophical character of philosophical anthropology is superior to that of Scheler, because it starts from the character of the questions to which this discipline seeks to provide an answer, whereas Scheler can only allow certain answers – namely, those which contain assertions about essences – to be counted as both philosophical and anthropological. Moreover, Scheler, by giving this definition, lays himself open to the charge of adhering to an outmoded model of science as a 'science of essences' and trying to revive it anew under philosophical auspices. To what extent, however, is 'What is man?' in general a philosophical question?

If the question is understood as an enquiry about the 'essence', the essential or species-characteristics, the fundamental life-functions of *homo sapiens*, together with his most important characteristic differences from the rest of the organic world, then the answer can lie only in the empirical field: in that of human biology and behavioural science. Even Kant's distinction between physiological and pragmatic anthropology – 'The physiological study of man is concerned with the investigation of what nature makes of man, the pragmatic with what he, as a freely-acting being, makes of himself, or can and ought so to make'[3] – does not really help here, since the 'pragmatic study of man' has long been regarded as scientific and monopolized by the social sciences, and they at all events are possible only as empirical disciplines. (Besides, the presupposition here of a 'freely-acting being' is somewhat suspicious, and anyone who takes its claims too strictly and is ready to follow Kant must reduce pragmatic anthropology to an appendix to ethics, in which alone, if only in a practical regard, it is possible to talk of free agents; but by doing this, one would also be sacrificing the empirical character of the science.) The question, 'What is man?', can, however, also be understood in a different sense: not as a question about the characteristic features of the species *homo sapiens*, but as a question about our inherent identity. 'What is man?' could then be paraphrased as 'Who are we?' This the human sciences alone are unable to tell us; the empirical knowledge about ourselves, which is scientific and so which we can derive only from the human sciences, must be supplemented by the work of *interpretation*, which alone makes that knowledge understandable in the light of this question about our identity. Understandability in this area is achieved when, having understood a good deal of empirical information about ourselves, we also know *what* we can *understand* ourselves as being. This reflexive self-certainty has been, since Descartes, a basic theme of modern philosophy: that it cannot be attained primarily by the methods of the knowledge of objects, but only by the interpretation of what is known in the knowledge of objects – above all, the explicative clarification and criticism of primary assumptions – results from the structure of the discourse, which is the form in which philosophical reflection in the traditional sense can be reconstructed. It is in *this* area that the philosophical element in philosophical anthropology is to be sought.

This is confirmed by the founder of philosophical anthropology himself. The question of the essence of man appears in Scheler as a *descriptive* question only because of the influence of phenomenological eidetics on him; the context shows that it is intended *interpretatively*:

In no age have views about the essence and origin of man been more uncertain, more indefinite and more various than in our own . . . We are, in the approximately ten thousand years of history, the first age in which man has become fully and absolutely problematic to himself; in which he no longer knows what he is, but also knows at the same time that he does not know it.[4]

It is obvious that Scheler here is not speaking of ignorance in the sense of a lack of empirical knowledge, but of a loss of identity. Scheler then relates his own philosophical anthropology to the 'history of man's self-consciousness', which according to him exhibits the tendency to a 'growing increase' in this self-consciousness, and he sets the new discipline the task of interpreting this state of affairs:

It is one of the most fundamental questions for a philosophical anthropology to decide what is in truth the meaning of these increases in human self-consciousness by leaps and bounds. Putting the question in the form of a sharp antithesis: do they mean a process in which man gains a deeper and deeper, and truer and truer, understanding of his objective position and situation in the totality of being? Or do they mean an increase and advance of a perilous illusion – a symptom of an increasing sickness?[5]

It is clear that mere empirical generalizations of what we know about our species cannot answer such questions of interpretation; the anthropological question of essence is therefore, in Scheler too, to be understood as an expression of the need for interpretative self-certainty in the light of the empirical knowledge about ourselves. This is still clearer in Plessner; he requires of philosophical anthropology 'a theory of man with a philosophical purpose, based on his essential dubitability'. This 'dubitability' has historical causes; the idea of man has 'become ... endangered'.

When its ancient metaphysical and ontological guarantees are no longer regarded as beyond question, then man and humanity become a problem from the moral point of view. The formal unity of man as a biological species, with the various characteristics of upright gait, the developed hand, language, the invention and use of tools and so on, the possibility which is thereby given for the members of our species to come to understand one another and so to produce in the element of spontaneous work that which nature has already indicated to them, – all this is not sufficient to encourage man to be a man. He can lose himself in the most precise sense of the word, he can decline from a historically responsible level of existence if he no longer recognizes any worth in this responsibility. This worth can today no longer be guaranteed to man on the basis of an unquestioned tradition. Thus if he takes such doubts about this disrupted tradition as seriously as they can be taken, his humanity, as a fact and as a task, has become a problem for him. And if we regard it aright, a problem of such an extent and such depth that no further growth in it is possible. It is no longer a matter of questions about how God's creature could become sinful or how finite and sinful man can conceive of the infinity of God's essence, but of whether and how man, subject as he is to causal laws, asserts his freedom in the face of their determination. It is a matter of humanity as such and also of the rightness of his theoretical limitations and practical obligations, of the question, what it means and how it is possible to be a man.[6]

As a 'method for man to *rediscover* himself by *taking risks* [my italics – H. S.]', we have available, according to Plessner, only 'unrestrained scepticism', and that is a matter for philosophy; but this scepticism can accomplish this 'only as a philosophical anthropology realized with the methods of scientific criticism'. This makes it intelligible in what sense Plessner locates this new discipline in the zone of overlap of two traditional sciences: in fact, what it amounts to is a project for an empirical science of man with an interpretative, meaning-establishing and identity-securing purpose, and it is only in this sense that philosophical anthropology is philosophical.

Thus, if one characterizes philosophical anthropology as an answer to the question, 'Who are we?', in which, for reasons derived from the history of science, empirical and interpretative knowledge enter into a particular constellation, it becomes clear how the identity-crisis of philosophy and the identity-crisis of philosophers coincide in it: the scepticism with regard to the traditional self-image of man, from which Scheler, Plessner and many of their contemporaries start, is accompanied by scepticism with regard to all attempts to resolve the 'crisis of the Ego' with the traditional philosophical or reflexive self-certainty; hence the precarious connexion of the philosophical with the empirical elements in the concept of a philosophical anthropology.

2 From the 'existing concept' to the 'defective creature'

This interpretation of philosophical anthropology as a final stage in a historical crisis can appeal to Max Scheler himself, who, in his *Mensch und Geschichte* (Man and History) of 1926, sought to understand the change in man's self-interpretation by typological means and presented the outcome as 'a small section from the introduction to a comprehensive anthropology'. Although he did not make any historical claims for this and claimed equal present-day actuality for his five types of human self-image, it is nevertheless clear that they stand to each other in a relation of historical succession. The 'religious anthropology', which interprets man as God's creation, is, in Scheler's own words, 'entirely meaningless in every sense for an autonomous philosophy and science'. The second type, '*homo sapiens*', was, according to Scheler, 'a discovery of the Greeks, of the Greek city-state: one of the most potent and momentous discoveries in the history of man's assessment of himself, which the Greeks, and only they – not any other human cultural group – made'. The basis of this image of man is reason (*lógos, ratio*), which was regarded as at the same time a principle of the world and of its ordering, and it was man's participation in this reason which marked him out from the rest of nature.

Especial value is placed here on four more detailed determinations: 1. Man has therefore a divine agency in himself, which the whole of nature does *not* subjectively contain; 2. this agency and that which eternally forms and shapes the world into the world (which rationalizes Chaos, or 'matter', into Cosmos) are ontologically, or in terms of their principle, *the same*; and so they are also truly equal to the knowledge of the world; 3. this agency, as λόγος (the realm of '*formae substantiales*' in Aristotle), and as human reason, has force and power, even without the impulses and sensibility (perception, μνήμη etc.) which man shares with animals, to realize its ideal contents ('power of the spirit', 'inherent power of the Idea'); 4. this agency is historical, racial and, in relation to social groups, absolutely constant.[7]

Scheler goes on to emphasize 'that almost the whole specifically philosophical tradition of anthropology, from Aristotle to Kant and Hegel – so momentous is the change – did not alter anything essential in these four features of a theory of man',[8] and 'that this theory of "*homo sapiens*" took on for the whole of Europe the most dangerous character which any idea can acquire – that of being self-evident'; it was Nietzsche and Dilthey who first saw it as problematical. Scheler's third type is '*homo faber*': 'the naturalistic, "positivist", and later also pragmatist theory' of man, which recognizes only gradual distinctions between him and the animals, starts from the assumption of an essentially similar instinctual endowment in all living creatures and regards human intelligence as a mere development of natural mental capacities which are already present in the animals too.

What is man, primarily, on this view? He is 1. the symbolizing animal (language), 2. the tool-using animal, 3. a creature with a brain . . . Even symbols, words, so-called concepts are in this view merely tools – they are simply refined mental tools. Just as, in terms of organs, morphology or physiology, there is nothing in man which is not to be found, potentially, also in the higher vertebrates, so also there is nothing mental or noetic.[9]

Scheler leaves no room for doubt that this type, despite its roots in the heterodox tradition of Democritus and Epicurus, has triumphed in modern times over the second and for the time being is regarded as the truly scientific self-portrait of man. Scheler's fourth and fifth types represent conceptions which remained essentially limited to Germany: the anthropology of life-philosophy and that of 'postulatory atheism'. For the anthropology of the 'Dionysian man', the species *homo sapiens* is not just one evolutionary cul-de-sac among others, but 'the cul-de-sac of life in general'. 'The spirit as adversary of the soul' (Klages) is regarded at the same time as a sickness, as simply a decadence of life; 'life-values' are thus ranked more highly than all those things by which *'homo sapiens'* had once taken his bearings, and the logical consequence is the demand for the superman. (Scheler here provides an impressive genealogy and interpretation 'of this monstrous pan-romanticism of an uncouth vitalistic value-theory'.) The anthropology of 'postulatory atheism', finally, is seen by Scheler as the result of a rational underpinning of the theory of the superman. This theory, advocated by D. H. Kerler and Nicolai Hartmann, regards the assumption of the existence of a God as incompatible with the idea of a free and responsibly acting being called 'man'. This 'denial of God', as the 'most extreme conceivable intensification of responsibility and sovereignty', at the same time implies, from the ontological point of view, the exclusion of all objective teleology which sets limits to the instrumental use of the causal connexions in the world by man in any direction whatsoever.

This typology shows how the founder of philosophical anthropology assessed the theoretical situation to which his own work was meant to be a response. It is certainly clear that not everything which has been said about man from a philosophical point of view forms part of philosophical anthropology in the sense established by Scheler. For all that, it is not the novelty which it at first took itself to be. Odo Marquard has shown, in his investigations in conceptual history, that at least where philosophy emphatically understands and presents itself as anthropology the roots of modern philosophical anthropology can be traced.[10] The mere history of the term, which can clarify at what point the theory of man which had always implicitly existed began to be called 'anthropology' is insufficient for that purpose. The term 'philosophical anthropology' in the narrower sense ought to be used only where the theory of man acquires a fundamental significance or a key-role for the whole of philosophical activity. Philosophical anthropology, so understood and writ small, belongs to the prehistory of the philosophical anthropology (writ large) of our own century.

Marquard defends the thesis that philosophical anthropology, for which Kant's *Anthropology with a Pragmatic Intent* was the first model, arose because of the 'turn to the life-world' and the 'turn to nature as a result of the renunciation of the philosophy of history'. The 'turn to the life-world' is seen by him as a 'renunciation of the philosophy of "traditional School-metaphysics", on the one hand, and of "mathematical natural science", on the other', and he demonstrates this in an impressive manner. Philosophical anthropology in the sense of 'life-world philosophy' terminates, methodologically speaking, in a renunciation of the abstract reason of principles and an empiricization of the whole of philosophy. Anthropology as a counter-movement against the philosophy of history can be identified, as Marquard shows, in the area of Romantic nature-philosophy and its influence on Feuerbach and Schopenhauer. In fact, the emphasis on the anthropological in philosophy after the end of Idealism nearly always terminated in an anti-historicist strategy, and the charge of being 'unhistorical' has been a standard objection to it from Marx to Horkheimer. All the same, Marquard's thesis requires differentiation; its second part, at least, runs the risk of being applicable only to those anthropologies which explicitly present themselves as against the philosophy of history, and then it is only the anti-historicist anthropologies which are anti-historicist, that is, the thesis becomes trivial. Moreover, the picture of anthropology, as should have become clear in the previous section, is by no means as unified as Marquard presents it. Marx's thesis against Feuerbach, 'The human essence is not an abstraction inhering in the isolated individual. In its reality it is the ensemble of the social relationships', is also an anthropological proposition, and the belief that man has a history, because he is 'open to the world' has become a commonplace in the philosophical anthropology of our own day. The 'turn to nature', as a renunciation of the philosophy of history, cannot therefore mean the opposition of anthropological thought to historical in general; rather, it must concern a particular constellation of naturalistic and historicist motifs in anthropological thought and the question of the primacy of these motifs.

To characterize this constellation more precisely, it is useful to recall Hegel's use of 'anthropology': as a name for that part of the system in which the 'subjective spirit . . . in itself or immediately', or as 'soul or natural spirit', is an object of enquiry.[11] (Marquard has made a plausible case for saying that Hegel wanted to use this as a terminological device in his opposition to the wave of Romantic anthropology in the form of nature-philosophy.) However, if one wants to discover in Hegel what man is, one cannot limit oneself to the section called 'Anthropology', which deals only with the natural features of the human spirit; the *Phenomenology of Spirit* and the *Philosophy of Spirit*, taken as a whole, give the answer. This answer, however, may be concentrated, in an abstract form, in the thesis that man is essentially an 'Ego', and that 'Ego' is the existing concept:

> The concept, in so far as it has advanced to such an existence, which is itself free, is nothing other than Ego or pure self-consciousness. I certainly have concepts, that is, determinate concepts; but I, or Ego, is the pure concept itself which as a concept has come to existence. Hence, when one considers the fundamental determinations which constitute the nature of the Ego, one should assume that something known, that is, something familiar to the representation, is being considered. Ego, however, is this primary pure unity, relating itself to itself, and this not immediately, but in that it abstracts from all determinacy and content and in the freedom of unbounded identity returns to itself. Thus it is universality; a unity which is a unity with itself only by means of that negative procedure which appears as abstraction and thereby contains all determinacy dissolved in itself. Secondly, Ego is equally immediately, as the negativity relating itself to itself, individuality, absolute determinacy, which opposes itself to the other and excludes it: individual personality. That absolute universality, which is also immediately absolute individuation, and a being in- and for-itself, which is simply a posited being and is only this in- and for-itself through unity with the posited being, constitutes the nature of the Ego as well as of the concept; of the one as of the other, nothing can be understood if the two moments just indicated are not comprehended both in their abstraction and in their perfect unity.[12]

Hegel's 'concept' is the dialectical version of the Western *lógos*, and his theory of man, that is, of the Ego as the existing concept, formulates once again, at the end of the great metaphysical tradition, the anthropology of the *animal rationale*. The separation of philosophical consciousness from Absolute Idealism in the name of history and science, since it was a farewell to metaphysics, necessarily also meant a farewell to that anthropology of the *animal rationale* in the traditional sense. What took its place was at first, in this field also, a turn towards the empirical: the reality of man, his conditions of life, as presented to our gaze by 'real' history and the research-disciplines which modelled themselves on the example of natural science, would show us who we are, not metaphysical speculation. It is important that in the first decades after Hegel's death the historical sciences and the natural sciences competed with each other in their claims to be leading sciences. The watchword was not 'anthropology versus philosophy of history'; rather, it was a matter of rivalry between a historicist and a naturalistic self-image of man, in which, as shown above, the historicist party was at one with the naturalistic in repudiating 'philosophy of history'.

The naturalistic self-image of man presently being discussed was not at all represented by the kind of Romantic nature-philosophy which was indebted to Schelling, and was represented only with qualifications by Feuerbach, who was independent of it. When Feuerbach says, 'The new philosophy makes man, including nature as the basis of man, into the exclusive, universal and highest object of philosophy – and this anthropology, including physiology, into the universal science',[13] 'nature' is meant primarily as the real which is perceptible with the senses, as opposed to the Hegelian Idea, and not as the object-domain of post-Hegelian natural science. ('Physiology' was at that time still the name for a purely phenomenological discipline.) The naturalization of the image of man under the influence of natural science was the work of the materialist movement of the middle of the century. It was here, already (for example in Moleschott), that the leading-role of biology was outlined: it later seemed to be confirmed once and for all by the invasion of Darwinism. Naturalization then meant, essentially, biologization of anthropology, and that proved to have extremely important consequences for the other sciences of man: for psychology, the organicist and social-Darwinist theories of society, but above all for racial ideology, which ultimately merged into National Socialism and there brought about a fateful 'assurance of identity'.

The great contrasting programme to these attempts to infer the identity of man from his physical organization was indicated by the historicist creed that what man is is to be discovered from history. Droysen says, 'What their species-concept is to the animals and plants . . . that history is to man . . . History is the becoming-conscious and the consciousness of man in regard to himself.'[14] In Dilthey it is put as, 'What man is, only history tells him.'[15] Since the opposition of nature and history is made epistemologically parallel to that between explaining and understanding, man can comprehend himself only by means of understanding: hence in this tradition, up to Heidegger, it is hermeneutics which is the key to man. Even the young Marx, whose critique of Feuerbach can be seen as a re-Hegelianizing of anthropology, refers the philosophical question of man to history, with the result that philosophy seems to disappear into historical science:

Where speculation ceases, in real life, there begins, therefore, real, positive science, the description of practical activity, of the practical process of human development. The phrases of consciousness cease, real knowledge must take their place. An independent philosophy loses its medium of existence once reality is described. In its place there can be at most a synthesis of the most general results which can be abstracted from the consideration of the historical development of man. These abstractions in themselves, divorced from real history, have absolutely no value. They can serve only to facilitate the ordering of the historical material and to indicate the sequence of its individual strata. But they in no way furnish, like philosophy, a recipe or schema according to which the epochs of history can be arranged.[16]

Here for the first time the opposition between anthropological and historical thought is so pronounced that one seems to exclude the other.

An interesting intermediate position between naturalism and historicism is taken by Hermann Lotze, who presents his best-known work, *Mikrokosmos. Ideen zur Naturgeschichte und Geschichte des Menschen* (Microcosm. Ideas on Natural and Human History) of 1856, as 'an essay towards an anthropology'. His aim is reconciliation 'between the needs of the soul and the results of human science'. The 'needs of the soul' refer to the demand to understand what, in the light of the indisputable results of the causal-analytical knowledge of nature and of man, we 'have to honour as the true meaning of existence, what we have to do and what to hope for'. The sciences cannot bring this about, even though they themselves originate from this demand. To a philosophy seen as anthropology thus falls the task of incorporating the 'restless advances of natural science', 'the sublime development of the knowledge of nature', which, as a 'mechanical science', does not even pause before the 'microcosm of the human being', into a meaning-establishing view of the world-whole, in which those 'needs of the soul' would be satisfied. This is the anthropological origin of the theme of 'values' and the later philosophy of value.

For history to be able to be so radically opposed to nature as it is in historicism, but also in Marx and Engels, history must be conceived of as the domain of those things which man in freedom determines of himself. This ontology of the historical, which Droysen sums up in the sentence, 'The life-pulse of historical movement is freedom',[17] was the basis for the philosophy of history of the Historical School, the position from which they carried on their polemics for many decades against naturalism, materialism, the methods of natural science, even against theory-formation in historical science. Even Marx shared this ontology when he characterized the stage of social development in which men made their history without consciousness as mere 'pre-history'. Objections to this linking of history and freedom, and of nature and necessity, were first raised by the metaphysics of the irrational discussed in the chapter on 'Life', which brought about a revolution, not only in metaphysics, but also in anthropology. In Schopenhauer, this metaphysics is associated with the Romantic nature-philosophy and thus greatly increased the continuing historical influence of the latter in anthropology. Certainly, even according to Schopenhauer, 'history is to be regarded as the rational self-consciousness of the human race', but, like reason in general, this self-consciousness is also merely on the surface: an objectification of the Will to life.

The true philosophy of history consists, that is to say, in the insight that, in all these endless changes and their disorder, one is yet confronted always only with the same, identical and unchangeable essence, which has the same concerns today as yesterday and always: it should therefore recognize the identical in all events, of ancient as of modern times, of the Orient as of the Occident, and, in spite of all differences in the special circumstances, of costume and of customs, everywhere discover the same humanity. This identical element, which persists amid all change, consists in the fundamental qualities of the human heart and head – many bad, a few good.[18]

Jacob Burckhardt speaks as a follower of Schopenhauer when, in opposition to the Historical School from which he came, he assigns to history as its object 'suffering, striving and acting man, as he is and ever was and will be.[19]

The philosophical anthropology of the second half of the century, as well as that of our own century, is essentially characterized by the confluence of the naturalistic anthropology which was given great impetus by the rise of the human sciences and the metaphysics of the irrational. The traditional rationalist self-portrait of man was regarded no longer merely as shallow or superficial, but simply as unscientific. Scheler's types *'homo faber'* and 'Dionysian man' were, anthropologically speaking, in the ascendant; life-philosophy and evolutionary theory with all their strength classified the species *homo sapiens* as part of the continuum of all living things. It is astonishing to see the way in which this antihistoricist tendency established itself in the centre of historicism, in Dilthey. Certainly, it is only, according to him, through history that we know what man is, but at the same time history tells him 'that the nature of man . . . is always the same'.[20] Life-philosophy, as a metaphysics of the irrational, disparages in this case too the historical, reducing it to an epiphenomenon, and absorbs the historicist metaphysics of freedom; the narration of the changeable, according to it, remains on the surface, while only the typology of what is always the same permits comprehension of the essential. The 'crisis of historicism' greatly intensified this trend. It would be impossible here to enter into the complexity of the relationship between Nietzsche's theory of the superman and his metaphysics of the 'eternal recurrence of the same'. Nietzsche's anthropology combines Schopenhauer's metaphysics of the Will, to which he gives a positive turn, with motifs taken from evolutionary theory, which he transforms, in an explicit criticism of Darwin, into a model of active self-alteration of man by means of 'breeding'.[21] The anthropology of the superman is at the same time a theory of man as a 'transition', as something to be overcome, and this idea was then, under the influence of empirical investigations in human biology, reinterpreted as the theory of man as a 'defective creature', which is characteristic of all more recent philosophical anthropology. Man is here seen as a creature which must compensate for its natural deficiencies in the area of organic and instinctual endowment by *action* and can survive as a species only by that means. Consciousness, language, reason, mind – all are then reinterpreted functionalistically. This completes a circle which had its origin in the anti-rationalist anthropology of the Romantics – the expression 'defective creature' can already be found in Herder – and seems to bid a final farewell to the rationalist self-image of man, since it is equipped with the authority of science. The protests against it in the name of values and of being – for example, Rickert's value-theoretical philosophy of culture or the new ontology of Scheler and Nicolai Hartmann, which brought into the field against such naturalism 'spirit' and 'ideal being' – have proved so far completely ineffective against it.

3 On post-anthropological philosophy

Helmut Plessner has remarked that the antithesis of naturalistic and historical consciousness of man has long been obsolete.[22] The history of later historicism, foreshortened for the sake of the *télos*, and the nature of living things, given dynamism by the theory of evolution, approximate so closely to each other that the contours grow blurred: what distinguishes the purposeless succession of events in both sequences from each other, if the human sciences have once and for all dissolved the historicist ideology of freedom? The question which then obtrudes itself is whether, with the crisis of historicism and the obsolescence of the antithesis between naturalism and historicism, philosophical anthropology itself has not become obsolete too. Walter Schulz has recently proposed precisely this diagnosis, though on a somewhat different basis; he speaks of 'the way in which the fundamental features of philosophical anthropology have become a matter of increasing indifference'.[23] This phenomenon was already evident towards the end of the period here under discussion. Heidegger's statement, 'The essence of *Dasein* lies in his existence', is no longer an anthropological proposition in the narrower sense, since he asserts nothing further about the essence of man than his existence and explicates its features then in the form of existentials, which are no longer supposed to concern the *concrete* man, but only the man who *exists* as *Dasein*. Heidegger's attempt to distance himself from anthropology can be seen as the result of a questioning which is more radical than the anthropological kind; thus, anthropology can no longer be, as it was in Scheler, the fundamental philosophical discipline. Jaspers' philosophy of existence, too, and even more Sartrean existentialism, have, according to their own claims, abandoned anthropology, where by 'anthropology' is understood the definition of man in terms of a fixed and qualifiable essence. As a result of Heidegger's 'turn', a paradigm of *post*-anthropological philosophy was introduced. Heidegger sought to go beyond the modern anthropocentrism, still followed by philosophical anthropology, by means of a new 'thinking of Being'. Man as *Dasein* thus became the '*Da des Seins*' (there of Being), a form of 'clearing of Being' (*Lichtung des Seins*), and man could not have Being at his disposal in his actions:

Man is rather 'thrown' by Being itself into the truth of Being, that he may, by ek-sisting in this manner, take care of the truth of Being, so that in the light of Being a being, as the being that it is, may appear. Whether and how it appears, whether and how God and the gods, history and nature enter the clearing of Being, are present and absent, is not decided by man. The arrival of a being depends on the destiny of Being. For man, however, the question remains whether he finds what is appropriate in his essence, which corresponds to this destiny; for in accordance with this he, as the ek-sistent, has to take care of the truth of Being. Man is the shepherd of Being . . . Yet Being – what is Being? It is itself. To discover this and to say it is what future thinking must learn to do.[24]

In Gadamer's later hermeneutic ontology, the theme of Being was linked, following Heidegger, with that of language, and language thus appears 'as a horizon of a hermeneutic ontology' which is concentrated in the sentence: 'Being that can be understood is language';[25] the process of language, as a process of meaning, is prior to all subjectivity, since the 'action of the thing itself is the true speculative movement which takes over the speaker'. This 'action of the thing' Gadamer characterizes at the end of *Truth and Method* as the 'play of language itself which addresses us, proposes and withdraws, asks and in the answer fulfils itself'. From here to Wittgenstein's 'language-games', in which rules, but not players, play an essential part, is but a small step. Wittgenstein's anti-subjectivism, which already in the *Tractatus* assigned transcendental status to the logic of language itself,[26] is certainly the reason why his later philosophy has been received by hermeneuticists with so much liveliness and agreement.

The tradition of *critical theory* can also be interpreted as a form of post-anthropological philosophy. If what man really is is a utopia, and the human status quo is so corrupted by domination, instrumental reason and reification that only the 'completely other' can save us, then here too man, as we can know him, has been removed from the centre of philosophy; the sciences of man, whether anthropologically or sociologically orientated, can enlighten us about our identity at best in a critical regard. The points of agreement between Heidegger and critical theory are slowly beginning to penetrate a philosophical consciousness which has thus far been fascinated by their opposition. To give an account of them would be out of place here. Both philosophical tendencies belong, however, to the history of the rejection of modern anthropocentrism, which philosophical anthropology accelerated rather than retarded.

Notes

Introduction

1 Thus e.g. Karl Löwith, *Von Hegel zu Nietzsche. Der revolutionäre Bruch im Denken des neunzehnten Jahrhunderts.* Zurich, 1951/Stuttgart, 1958.
2 The 'end of the Idealist period in Germany' and the 'collapse of German Idealism' have repeatedly been linked with the July Revolution of 1830 in France, but for contemporaries Hegel's death was the prominent event, since it initiated the battles over the Hegelian inheritance and thus the 'process of dissolution of the Hegelian School', of which Friedrich Engels retrospectively speaks in *Ludwig Feuerbach und der Ausgang der klassischen deutschen Philosophie* (Ludwig Feuerbach and the End of Classical German Philosophy, in Marx–Engels, *Selected Works*, Moscow, 1951), Ch. 1. On this view, Idealism was simply equated with Hegel's philosophy and other positions were no longer considered worthy of mention.
3 G. W. F. Hegel, *Wissenschaft der Logik*, Vol. I, Leipzig, 1934–51, (*Hegel's Science of Logic*, trans. A. V. Miller, London, 1969); Hegel says here about the 'identity of identity and non-identity': 'This concept could be regarded as the first and purest, that is, most abstract, definition of the Absolute.'
4 Hegel, *Enzyklopädie der philosophischen Wissenschaften* (1830), § 214 (ed. F. Nicolin/C. Pöggeler), Hamburg, 1959, p. 183. (The *Enzyklopädie* contains: the 'Lesser Logic' (trans. J. N. Findlay, *Hegel's Logic*, Oxford, 1975) the Philosophy of Nature (trans. M. J. Petry, *Hegel's Philosophy of Nature*, London, 1970) and the Philosophy of Spirit (trans. W. Wallace and A. V. Miller, *Hegel's Philosophy of Mind*, Oxford, 1971).)
5 Ibid., Preface to the 2nd edn of 1827, p. 7.
6 Ibid., § 235, p. 193.
7 Theodor W. Adorno, *Negative Dialektik*, Frankfurt, 1966, p. 33 (*Negative Dialectics*, trans. E. B. Ashton, London, 1973).
8 Hegel himself comes to terms with the general hostility to philosophy in various of his Prefaces and Introductions; this is not just a matter of the rejection of the claims of a Romantically toned culture of the feelings, but more of the criticism of an empiricist interpretation of the ideal of science, which was brought into action against 'philosophy'; cf. the first sections of Hegel's *Philosophy of Nature* (trans. M. J. Petry, London, 1970), the Preface to the 2nd edn of the *Enzyklopädie*, esp. pp. 4f. in the Nicolin/Pöggeler edition, and *Die Vernunft in der Geschichte* (ed. Hoffmeister), Hamburg, 1955, esp. pp. 28ff. (*Reason in History*, in *Lectures on the Philosophy of World-History*, trans. H. B. Nisbet, Cambridge, 1975).

9 The classic example of this type of criticism of Hegel is Rudolf Haym, *Hegel und seine Zeit* (1857), whose account of the *Philosophy of Right* as a justification of Prussian absolutism and the Carlsbad Decrees relies entirely on the Preface; the effect and the influence of this work even now can hardly be overestimated.

1 Sketch of an Age

1 Thus Jacob Burckhardt and Friedrich Nietzsche agree in warning against regarding the German victory over France and the foundation of the *Reich* as evidence of the superiority of German culture. Cf. J. Burckhardt, *Weltgeschichtliche Betrachtungen*, Stuttgart, 1955, pp. 202ff.; F. Nietzsche, *Unzeitgemässe Betrachtungen*, First Essay, in Werke (3 vols., ed. K Schlechta), Vol. I, Munich, 1960, pp. 137ff. (*Untimely Meditations*, trans. R. J. Hollingdale, Cambridge, 1984).
2 Reinhart Koselleck, 'Staat und Gesellschaft in Preussen 1815–1848', in H. U. Wehler (ed.), *Moderne deutsche Sozialgeschichte*, Cologne, 1976, p. 72.
3 Thus Wolfgang Zorn, 'Wirtschafts- und sozialgeschichtliche Zusammenhänge der deutschen Reichsgründungszeit (1850–1879)', in Wehler (ed.), *Sozialgeschichte*, p. 269.
4 Heinrich Heine, *Sämtliche Werke* (ed. H. Kaufmann), Vol. IX, Munich, 1964, p. 241.
5 Ibid., p. 250.
6 Ibid., pp. 282ff.
7 Karl Marx, *Zur Kritik der Hegelschen Rechtsphilosophie*, in Marx, *Die Frühschriften* (ed. S. Landshut), Stuttgart 1953, p. 213 (*A contribution to the Critique of Hegel's Philosophy of Right*, in *Early Writings*, Harmondsworth, Middx, 1975).
8 Ibid., p. 216
9 Friedrich Albert Lange, *Geschichte des Materialismus und Kritik seiner Bedentung in der Gegenwart* (1875) ed. A. Schmidt, Frankfurt, 1974, pp. 529ff.
10 Plessner, *Die verspätete Nation*, Frankfurt, 1974, p. 12.
11 Ibid., p. 14.
12 Cf. ibid. pp. 40f.
13 Cf. Wilhelm von Humboldt's petition for discharge, in *Werke* (5 vols., A. Flitner/K. Giel eds.) Vol. IV, Darmstadt, 1964, pp. 247f.
14 Hippolyte Taine, quoted in H. Schelsky, *Einsamkeit und Freiheit*, Düsseldorf, 1971, p. 34.
15 The expression is Plessner's, in 'Zur Soziologie der modernen Forschung und ihrer Organisation in der deutschen Universität' in Plessner, *Diesseits der Utopie*, Frankfurt, 1974, p. 133; cf. also Arthur Schopenhauer's mockery of the 'philosophy of the professors of philosophy' in 'Über die Universitäts-Philosophie', *Parerga und Paralipomena*, Leipzig, n.d., Vol. I, Part 3 (*Parerga and Paralipomena. Short Philosophical Essays*, trans. E. F. J. Payne, 2 vols, Oxford, 1974).
16 Max Weber, *Wissenschaft als Beruf*, in *Gesammelte Schriften zur Wissenschaftslehre (GSW)*, Tübingen, 1973, p. 585.
17 Ibid.
18 Immanuel Kant, *Der Streit der Fakultäten* (1798), A6f.
19 Ibid., A8f.
20 Ibid., A15f.
21 The separation of the Faculty of Natural Sciences in Tübingen in 1863 was remarked on by contemporaries as a decisive event. In the newly founded Reichsuniversität of

Strassburg (1872), a Faculty of Natural Sciences was instituted from the outset. Up until the middle of the century, its independence was normal in the German universities. In Switzerland and Austria, there still exist even today Philosophical-Natural Scientific Faculties alongside Philosophical-Historical Faculties. Cf. F. A. Lange, *Geschichte des Materialismus*, pp. 592ff. and 728ff.
22 Humboldt, *Werke*, Vol. IV, p. 257.
23 Ibid., p. 256.
24 Ibid., p. 258.
25 Ibid., p. 191.
26 Cf. Plessner, *Die verspätete Nation*, pp. 65ff.
27 Quoted from K. Vondung (ed.), *Das wilhelminische Bildungsbürgertum*, Göttingen, 1976, p. 34.
28 Max Weber, *Wissenschaft als Beruf*, in *GSW*, p. 591.
29 Ibid.
30 Cf. Nietzsche, *Unzeitgemässe Betrachtungen*, First Essay.
31 F. Paulsen, *Die deutschen Universitäten und das Universitätsstudium*, Berlin, 1902, p. 109.
32 Ludwig Curtius, *Deutscher und antiker Geist*, Stuttgart, 1950, pp. 335f.
33 Ibid., p. 332
34 Cf. H. Heimpel, *Schuld und Aufgabe der Universität* Göttingen, 1954.

2 History

1 In Prussia, the assumption of power by Friedrich Wilhelm IV in 1840 was also seen as a corresponding revolution in cultural policy; official sympathies no longer went to Hegelianism, but to the Historical School. At the same time, in 1840 Schelling was called to Berlin by the king; he was intended to destroy the 'dragon-seed of Hegelianism'. The conservative constitutional lawyer (and pupil of Schelling), Friedrich Julius Stahl (1801–41), was also summoned to Berlin in the same year to counter the influence of the Hegelian philosophy of law. The philosophical climate in Prussia was dominated thenceforth by historicism and speculative theism. This makes it clear once again how absurd is the objection to Hegel of being a 'Restoration philosopher'. The higher value set on the historians by the powerful was also expressed in the memoranda of Leopold von Ranke, by which Friedrich Wilhelm IV allowed himself to be advised in the years 1848–51. King Maximilian II of Bavaria invited Ranke in 1854 to give private lectures 'on the epochs of recent history', and this was with the aim of getting political advice. The science of history seemed to have taken over the role of political philosophy. Droysen then openly expressed this, 'Historical study is the basis for political education and formation. The statesman is the practical historian' (Johann Gustav Droysen, *Grundriss der Historik (GdH)*, § 93, ed. R. Hübner, Darmstadt, 1974, p. 365).
2 Droysen, *GdH*, §§ 83 and 86, pp. 357f.
3 What follows is a condensed version of the corresponding sections in my essay, *Geschichtsphilosophie nach Hegel. Die Problem des Historismus*, Freiburg/Munich, 1974, pp. 19ff.
4 This was particularly emphasized by Ernst Troeltsch in his great works on historicism; cf. E. Troeltsch, *Der Historismus und seine Probleme, Gesammelte Schriften*, 3, Tübingen, 1923–64. Classical formulations of this culturalism are to be found above all in Droysen: 'Only what the spirit and hand of man has formed, shaped, touched,

only the traces of man light us further on our way' (*GdH*, § 7). 'The field of the historical method is the cosmos of the moral world' (§ 45). 'The life-pulse of historical movement is freedom' (§ 75).
5 This is described in detail in Friedrich Meinecke, *Die Entstehung des Historismus*, 2 vols. Munich/Berlin, 1936; Meinecke is the most important representative of the positive valuation of historicism.
6 The expression 'Romantic School' first appears in Heinrich Heine, in the essay of the same name of 1836 (in *Sämtliche Werke*, Vol. IX, Munich, 1964).
7 On the history of the term, see J. Ritter (ed.), *Historisches Wörterbuch der Philosophie*, Vol. III, col. 211ff.
8 See H. Schnädelbach, 'Über historistische Aufklärung', *Allgemeine Zeitschrift für Philosophie*, 4, 2, 1979.
9 Since Lukács' *Geschichte und Klassenbewusstsein*, Berlin, 1925 (*History and Class Consciousness*, London, 1971), the thesis of the opposition between Enlightenment and historicism has become a commonplace of the neo-Marxist interpretation of the nineteenth century. For a correction of this thesis, cf. E. Cassirer, *Die Philosophie der Aufklärung*, Tübingen, 1932. (*The Philosophy of Enlightenment*, trans. F. C. A. Koelly and J. P. Pettegrove, Princeton, N. J., 1969).
10 This is the central argument used by Savigny against the Natural Law theories. References to historical origins formed part of the standard repertoire of Enlightenment criticism. Savigny merely uses such a reference here against one of the bases of the bourgeois Enlightenment movement itself.
11 This is an argument of Edmund Burke's against the ideologues of the French Revolution which was constantly repeated in Germany.
12 In Germany, sociology did not develop simply by following the models of Comte and Spencer, which were rather subjected to criticism, but – as the examples of Max Weber and Georg Simmel show – with a primarily historical and philosophical orientation; in particular, the strictly culturalist tendency and the conception of sociology as a human science which had to use the procedure of *Verstehen* remained dominant for a long time and were only driven back gradually as the Anglo-Saxon conception of empirical social enquiry took over.
13 Droysen *GdH*, § 82, p. 357.
14 Marx/Engels, *Das Kommunistische Manifest*, in S. Landshut (ed.) *Die Frühschriften*, Stuttgart, 1953, p. 539 (*The Communist Manifesto*, Harmondsworth, Middx, 1967).
15 Jacob Burckhardt, *Weltgeschichtliche Betrachtungen* (ed. R. Marx), Stuttgart, 1955, p. 4.
16 Ibid., pp. 3f.
17 Ibid., p. 5.
18 This is the meaning of Ranke's famous dictum, 'Every age is immediate to God'.
19 The expression is Savigny's.
20 The idea that to understand something is the same as to understand how it came to be can be described as a methodological premise of historicism in general.
21 Hegel, *Die Vernunft in der Geschichte* (ed. Hoffmeister), Hamburg, 1955, pp. 20f.
22 Thus Hegel was for example never called to the Berliner Akademie der Wissenschaften, the majority of whose members were theologians and historians.
23 On this cf. Ch. 4, Sect. 3.

24 Ranke was criticized by his own pupils for his lack of involvement in political and moral questions, and Burckhardt says of himself, 'Freedom and the state have not lost much in me. With men such as I am no state can be built.'
25 Droysen says of the objectivity of the non-partisan, 'for us the question of objectivity, of lack of partisanship, of the much-prized point of view outside and above things has been set aside. Of course, I shall not wish to solve the great problems of historical presentation on the basis of my subjective caprice, my little petty personality. In that I treat of past events from the standpoint, from the ideas of my people and state and my religion, I stand far above my own ego. I *think*, as it were, from the viewpoint of a higher ego, in which the dross of my own petty personality has been melted away.' *GdH*, p. 287.
26 The theory that great historical personalities are agents of the *Weltgeist* or 'world-spirit' was, in various formulations, a common theme of the Historical School up until Burckhardt and Treitschke, shared by them with Hegel.
27 The criticism of 'abstract' cosmopolitanism also forms a historicist tradition in which Hegel had a decisive share. It was thus no accident that the internationalist Social Democrats, despised in the Wilhelmine era for being 'comrades without a fatherland', found their way back to Kant.
28 Erich Rothacker, *Einleitung in die Geisteswissenschaften* (1919), reissue of 2nd edn, Darmstadt, 1972, p. 46.
29 On this point there is astonishing agreement also between Marx and Engels and the Historical School, except that the former are concerned, not with identification with state and nation, but with the class-interests of the proletariat.
30 Hegel, *Die Vernunft in der Geschichte*, pp. 28 and 29.
31 The expression is Rothacker's, *Einleitung*, p. 68.
32 On this cf. G. G. Iggers, *Deutsche Geschichtswissenschaft*, Munich, 1971.
33 Kant, *Critique of Pure Reason*, B 884.
34 Cf. H. Schnädelbach, *Geschichtsphilosophie nach Hegel*, Part II and bibliography.
35 Droysen, *GdH*, § 16, p. 331.
36 Ibid., § 18, p. 331.
37 Ibid., § 8, p. 328.
38 Ibid.
39 Ibid., § 1, p. 323.
40 Ibid., § 19, p. 332.
41 Droysen, *Historik* (Lectures), p. 10; the *GdH* formulates the point as follows, 'What their species-concept is to animals and plants ... history is to man' (§ 82, p. 357).
42 *GdH*, § 94, p. 365.
43 Wilhelm Dilthey, *Einleitung in die Geisteswissenschaften, Gesammelte Schriften*, Vol. I, Stuttgart/Göttingen, 1959, p. xvi; Wilhelm Dilthey, *Der Aufbau der geschichtlichen Welt in den Geisteswissenschaften* (ed. Manfred Riedel), Frankfurt, 1970, p. 135. *Einleitung* (henceforth cited as *EG*) and *Der Aufbau* (henceforth *AGW*) are distinguished above all in that *EG* starts from the broadly presented fact of the human sciences and undertakes to analyse them, while *AGW* claims synthetically to lead towards this fact.
44 *EG*, p. xviii.
45 *AGW*, pp. 177f.
46 The consistent limitation of theory of knowledge to the logic of knowledge for anti-

psychologistic reasons was first demanded by Hermann Cohen, *Das Prinzip der Infinitesimalmethode und seine Geschichte* (1883) (ed. W. Flach), Frankfurt, 1968, pp. 47ff.
47 Wilhelm Windelband, *Geschichte und Naturwissenschaft*, in his *Präludien II*, Tübingen, 1924, p. 143.
48 Ibid., pp. 144f.
49 The thesis that history (*historia*), being an account of the particular, was incapable of being a science goes back as far as Aristotle (cf *Poetics*, 1451 a 36ff.; similarly, *Metaphysics* A, 981aff.) and was handed down unchanged at least until Kant.
50 Schopenhauer, *Die Welt als Wille und Vorstellung*, Vol. II, Ch. 38, *Sämtliche Werke*, Vol. III, Leipzig, n.d., p. 427 (*The World as Will and Representation*, 2 vols., London, 1967).
51 Ibid., p. 431.
52 Ibid., pp. 432f.
53 Friedrich Nietzsche, *Werke* (3 vols., ed. K. Schlechta), Vol. I, Munich, 1960, p. 210.
54 Ibid., p. 209.
55 Ibid., p. 277.
56 Ibid., p. 219.
57 Ibid., p. 250.
58 Ibid., p. 247.
59 Martin Heidegger, *Sein und Zeit* (1926), pp. 72ff. (*Being and Time*, trans. J. Macquarrie and E. Robinson, Oxford, 1967).
60 The phrase is Jürgen Habermas', cf. *Theorie und Praxis*, Frankfurt, 1971, p. 235 (*Theory and Practice*, trans. J. Viertel, London, 1974).
61 Cf. Kant's essay, *Ideen zu einer allgemeinen Geschichte in weltbürgerlicher Absicht* (1784). This placing of the philosophy of history in the context of philosophical systematics was again recalled, after the abandonment of the speculative phase, above all by the neo-Kantians. Via the neo-Kantian socialists (Karl Vorländer, Max Adler and others) this also made its way into neo-Marxism and critical theory. The massive re-Hegelianization of Marxism by Lukács did not cause this Kantian motif to disappear altogether. Thus, Jürgen Habermas in 1960, in the course of his debate with Marx, conceived of an 'empirical philosophy of history with practical intent', in *Theorie und Praxis*, pp. 244ff.

3 Science

1 Helmut Plessner, 'Zur Soziologie der modernen Forschung und ihrer Organisation in der deutschen Universität', in *Diesseits der Utopie*, Frankfurt, 1974, p. 130.
2 Ibid., p. 121.
3 Ibid., pp. 122f.
4 Ibid., p. 125.
5 Ibid., pp. 126f.
6 Ibid., p. 132.
7 See Wolf Lepenies, *Das Ende der Naturgeschichte. Wandel kultureller Selbstverständlichkeiten in den Wissenschaften des 18. und 19. Jahrhunderts*, Frankfurt, 1978, pp. 16ff.
8 Interpretative psychology was conceived of by Wilhelm Dilthey, Karl Jaspers, Eduard Spranger and others; the programmatic work *Ideen über eine beschreibende und*

zergliedernde Psychologie appeared in 1894; cf. also Erich Rothacker, *Logik und Systematik der Geisteswissenschaften*, Bonn, 1947. 'Interpretative' sociology was the idea of Max Weber in the famous (1) of his 'Soziologische Grundbegriffe' 'Sociology . . . means the science whose object is to interpret the meaning of social action and thereby give a causal explanation of the way in which the action proceeds and the effects which it produces.' Max Weber did not, however, advocate a conception of sociology as a pure *Geisteswissenschaft* as did Othmar Spann, and others, where hermeneutical procedures are frequently associated with phenomenological. The theoretician of this association was Alfred Schütz.

9 The idea that psychology is a 'science of the soul' was explicitly rejected by Wilhelm Wundt in *Grundriss der Psychologie*, § 1, Leipzig, 1896–1922, p. 1; on psychology as a 'basis of the human sciences' see ibid., § 2, p. 16.
10 Hermann von Helmholtz, *Über das Ziel und die Fortschritte der Naturwissenschaft*, Innsbruck, 1869, in his *Philosophische Vorträge und Aufsätze*, Berlin, 1971, pp. 153ff.
11 *Das Denken in der Medizin*, 1887, in *Philosophische Vorträge*, pp. 219ff.
12 Psychophysics (Fechner, *Elemente der Psychophysik*, 1860) was the first form of psychology as a natural science; the programme of a physiological psychology was formulated by Wilhelm Wundt in 1874.
13 Thus Lange wrote, 'If one considers simply Hegel's influence on historiography, however, and especially on cultural history, one is bound to confess that this man in his own fashion powerfully promoted the sciences too' (*Geschichte des Materialismus und Kritik seiner Bedeutung in der Gegenwart*, ed. A. Schmidt, Frankfurt, 1974, p. 515). The importance of Hegel for the human sciences is not seriously disputed by anyone and was to be the important theme of the neo-Hegelianism inspired by Dilthey.
14 *Geschichte des Materialismus*, p. 517.
15 His work *Kosmos* (1845ff.) was one of the most widely read scientific works of the nineteenth century and a standard work in German education.
16 E.g. by Helmholtz, *Über Goethes naturwissenschaftliche Arbeiten* (1853) and *Über das Verhältnis der Naturwissenschaften zur Gesamtheit der Wissenschaft* (1862) in *Philosophische Vorträge*, pp. 95ff. and 19ff.
17 Fechner (1801–87), the teacher of Wilhelm Wundt, who formulated the famous thesis of 'psycho-physical parallelism', belongs, philosophically speaking, to speculative late Idealism.
18 See Lange, *Geschichte des Materialismus*, pp. 544ff.
19 Schleiden, for example, looking back in 1863, called Schelling a 'Cagliostro of philosophy', because he constructed out of 'unspoken equations a system of naturephilosophy in which he demonstrated his pitiful scraps of real ignorance as a philosophical necessity. This superficial tittle-tattle did not touch at all on astronomy or mathematical physics, but confused the organic natural sciences for a long time' (quoted in D. von Engelhardt, *Hegel und die Chemie*, Wiesbaden, 1976, p. 25).
20 Heinrich Heine, *Zur Geschichte der Religion und Philosophie in Deutschland*, in *Sämtliche Werke* (ed. H. Kaufman), Vol. IX, Munich, 1964, pp. 274f.
21 See Schelling, *Einleitung zu dem Entwurf eines Systems der Naturphilosophie. Oder über den Begriff der spekulativen Physik und die innere Organisation eines Systems dieser Wissenschaft* (1799), in *Werke* (ed. M. Schröter), Vol. II, pp. 271ff. According to K. E. Rothschuh, the principles of Schelling's nature-philosophy decisively influenced

thinking in German physiology from 1800 to 1820; he gives the following summary characterization of its fundamental ideas: 'The whole of nature is the arena of an unconsciously creative spirit. At their source, in the Absolute, nature and spirit are identical. Only for our experience does the Absolute divide into the various phenomenal forms of nature. Nature is spirit in the course of becoming. Man can recognize behind the appearances of nature the unfolding of original Ideas, because in man spirit attains to consciousness of itself. And if the understanding is itself a product of the nature which unfolds itself in natural phenomena, and thus itself a part of nature, the laws of nature must be found in consciousness and the laws of consciousness must allow of being proved to be laws of nature. Hence the thinking spirit may, in a creative construction, generate the Idea of nature, from itself. Nature and empirical reality are thus merely arenas and façades for the Ideas which are at work behind them.

'It is easy to recognize them, if one knows the key which unlocks them, and if one knows the universal and constantly recurring principles involved in the unfolding of spirit in nature. According to Schelling there are two main principles: first, the principle of *polarity*, secondly, the principle of *analogy*. The first affirms that nature maintains itself only by means of polar oppositions, so that it is the first duty of the student of nature to look for polarity and dualism everywhere. The second way, the analogical inference, is justified because, in virtue of a third principle, that of the structuring of existents into stages of increasing perfection, similar, related phenomena must be demonstrable by comparison at all stages of nature. Finally, in that nature transforms itself, by means of continuous changes, into higher stages of perfection, the application of the principle of metamorphosis must always lead to fresh insights. The application of these principles makes it possible both to see nature as a unity and to grasp in its variety the stages of unfolding of the original unity – spirit in the course of becoming – as a unity and also at the same time in the manifold of the multiplicity of appearances' (K. E. Rothschuh, '*Zur Entwicklung der Methodologie in der Physiologie seit dem Beginn des 19*. Jahrhunderts, in A. Diemer (ed.), *Beiträge zur Entwicklung der Wissenschaftstheorie im 19. Jahrhundert*, Meisenheim, 1968, 121f.).

22 I do not know of any thorough account and interpretation of the Hegelian Philosophy of Nature; there is a good introduction in Charles Taylor, *Hegel*, Cambridge, 1975, pp. 350ff.
23 Cf. Hegel, *Naturphilosophie*, in *Enzyclopädie*, pp. 29ff. (*Hegel's Philosophy of Nature*, trans. M. J. Petry, London, 1970).
24 For instance, the Anthroposophical Society as a foundation of Rudolf Steiner, known for his edition of Goethe's writings on natural science, and the *Deutsche Monistenbund* (German League of Monists) founded in 1906 under the honorary presidency of Ernst Haeckel, the disciple of Darwin and author of the work *Welträtsel*, of which over 400,000 copies were sold and which aimed at popularizing the monist world-view. In the debate between mechanism and energetics after 1895, the famous chemist and creator of physical chemistry Wilhelm Ostwald came to be known as a protagonist of energetics, advocating an 'energetic conception of the world'. Ostwald, again, gave (probably the first) 'lectures on nature-philosophy' (Leipzig, 1902).
25 The chief advocate of neo-vitalism and a corresponding philosophy was Hans Driesch, in *Die Philosophie des Organischen* (1909).
26 Kant, *Metaphysical Principles of Natural Science*, A VI.

27 Ibid., A VIII.
28 Hegel, *Phänomenologie des Geistes* (ed. J. Hoffmeister), p. 12. (*Hegel's Phenomenology of Spirit*, trans. A. V. Miller, Oxford, 1977).
29 Hegel, *Wissenschaft der Logik,* Vol. I, Leipzig, 1934–51, pp. 6f. (*Hegel's Science of Logic*, trans. A. V. Miller, London, 1969).
30 Hegel, *Naturphilosophie*, p. 37.
31 Ibid., p. 44.
32 The formulation of the principle *De singularium non est scientia* originates from Duns Scotus.
33 Kant, *Metaphysical Principles of Natural Science*, A IVf.
34 The view that the empirical sciences must certainly be recognized, but that one must go beyond them and empiricism in general from a philosophical point of view was a commonplace advocated also by many non-Hegelians: names to be mentioned include Schopenhauer, Fechner (n. 17 above) and the late Idealists (I. H. Fichte, H. C. Weisse), Lotze (see Ch. 6, Sect. 2. i) and also F. A. Lange, who, in a similar fashion to the later philosophy of value, complemented the empirical scientific interpret ation of the world with a 'standpoint of the ideal' (cf. *Geschichte des Materialismus*, Vol. 2, pp. 981ff.). In general after Hegel, Idealism was no longer a philosophical impulse which sought to permeate everything – Hegel's *Philosophy of Nature* is a document of the failure of this effort – but came to be a 'higher world-view' (Lotze), a 'higher plane' than one based on a realistic scientific civilization, shaped by empiricism and threatened by nihilism: a mere 'Weltanschauung'. This can also be seen in the titles of numerous books of which the most striking example was certainly Otto Braun, *Hinauf zum Idealismus!*, Leipzig, 1908.
35 On the interpretation of positivism as a scientistically inclined version of empiricism, see Jürgen Habermas, *Erkenntnis und Interesse*, Frankfurt, 1968/73, pp. 88ff. (*Knowledge and Human Interests*, trans. J Shapiro, London, 1972), and Herbert Schnädelbach, *Erfahrung, Begründung und Reflexion. Versuch über den Positivismus*, Frankfurt, 1971.
36 The translation of J. S. Mill's *Logic* by Schiel, inspired by Justus von Liebig, appeared in 1849 and was very widely read.
37 Helmholtz referred to Mill in 1869 as the one who had finally introduced methodological norms into procedure in the natural sciences (in *Über das Verhältnis der Naturwissenschaften zur Gesamtheit der Wissenschaft*, in *Philosophische Vorträge*, pp. 16 and 22). Friedrich Albert Lange held a Chair of 'Philosophy of the Inductive Sciences' in Zurich from 1870; Ernst Mach's Chair in Philosophy (1895) was dedicated to the 'history and theory of the inductive sciences'. 'Inductive metaphysics' was the philosophical programme of Wilhelm Wundt (see Ch. 3, Sect. 3.iv) and Eduard von Hartmann (1842–1906).
38 H. Hertz, *Prinzipien der Mechanik*, Leipzig, 1894, p. 1.
39 See on Wittgenstein and Hertz George Pitcher, *The Philosophy of Wittgenstein*, Englewood Cliffs, 1964, pp. 79 and 194. Popper even classifies Hertz at one point as an 'instrumentalist' (*Conjectures and Refutations*, London, 1963, p. 99), and thus does not count him as one of his own ancestors. But despite all his scepticism about a picture-theory of knowledge, there are marked points of agreement between Popper and Hertz.
40 The basic work is the book by Gustav Robert Kirchhoff, *Vorlesungen über mathematische Physik* (1876); for an account see E. Cassirer, *Das Erkenntnisproblem in der Philosophie und Wissenschaft der neueren Zeit*, Vol. IV, new ed., Darmstadt, 1973,

pp. 96ff. (*The Problem of Knowledge, Philosophy Science and History since Hegel*, trans. W. H. Woglom, New Haven, Conn., 1950).
41 Avenarius interpreted the principle of economy in a more naturalistic fashion than Mach, who gave it a rather conventionalistic twist.
42 The atomic theory was regarded as a myth for decades by philosophically minded physicists; under the pressure of empirical evidence, even the energetist Ostwald had to admit defeat in 1909 and recognize the atomic theory (reference in Cassirer, *Erkenntnisproblem*, p. 109). The debate about atomism brought Boltzmann and Planck into the arena against Mach and phenomenological physics, and here too Mach had finally to admit defeat: experiments convinced him of the 'existence of the atom'. On the history of the atomic theory, see van Melsen/Dolch, *Atom – gestern und heute*, Freiburg/Munich, 1957.
43 See Edmund Husserl, *Philosophie als strenge Wissenschaft* (1911), published in book form, Frankfurt, 1965
44 Hegel says, 'The familiar is in general, simply because it is familiar, not known' (*Phänomenologie des Geistes*, ed. Hoffmeister, p. 28).
45 Hegel says, 'The history of philosophy is the history of the disclosure of thoughts about the Absolute, which is their object' (*Enzyklopädie*, Preface to 2nd ed., ed. Nicolin, Hamburg, 1959, p. 10). On the relation of this process to that of the self-unfolding of the Absolute, cf. ibid., §§ 575–7.
46 Hegel, Preface to the *Rechtsphilosophie* (ed. J. Hoffmeister), Hamburg, 1955, p. 16 (*Hegel's Philosophy of Right*, trans. T. M. Knox, Oxford, 1942).
47 This dictum from the *Phänomenologie* (ed. Hoffmeister, p. 12) sets, in a very traditional fashion, aspiration to knowledge and 'real' knowledge in an opposition which, from the point of view of 'research-science' simply must not exist (cf. Ch. 3, Sect. 2). The self-interpretation of the Hegelian philosophy as a successful conclusion of a long love for knowledge, to which contemporaries soon responded with a mere shrug of the shoulders, has been shared in the nineteenth and twentieth centuries almost only by Marx, Engels and various Marxists, though with the qualification that they believed Hegel to be an insurmountable peak and conclusion of 'bourgeois' philosophy. Engels even says, 'With Hegel philosophy in general comes to an end' (*Ludwig Feuerbach und der Ausgang der klassischen deutschen Philosophie*, Berlin, 1960, p. 12).
48 Wilhelm von Humboldt, *Werke* (eds. Flitner/Giel), Vol. IV, Darmstadt, 1964, p. 257.
49 On the 'yearning for the spurious infinite', see Plessner, *Moderne Forschung*, p. 127.
50 Kant even brings together in his thought a statically conceived metaphysics of nature and an advance in empirical knowledge of nature which is in principle endless; the relation of the two is a central theme of the *Opus Postumum*.
51 On the 'fear of error' as a 'fear of truth', cf. Hegel, Introduction to the *Phänomenologie* (ed. Hoffmeister, pp. 64f.); cf. also Hegel's interpretation of empiricism and the Critical philosophy, in *Enzyklopädie*, §§ 37ff., pp. 64ff.
52 Karl R. Popper, *Logic of Scientific Discovery*, London, 1959, § 85, pp. 276ff.
53 Nietzsche says: 'Truth is the kind of error, without which a certain kind of living being could not live. What ultimately decides is value for life' (*Werke*, ed. Schlechta. Vol. III, Munich, 1960, p. 844); in Hans Vaihinger (1852–1933) these lines of thought, which ultimately, by way of Nietzsche and F. A. Lange's physiological interpretation of Kant, refer back to Schopenhauer, were developed into a 'fic-

tionalism': Hans Vaihinger, *Philosophie des Als-Ob. System der theoretischen, praktischen und theologischen Fiktionen der Menschheit aufgrund eines idealistischen Positivismus*, Berlin, 1911.

54 Even in 1900, Husserl could still formulate the point as follows: 'It belongs to the essence of science ... that there should be a unity in the interconnexions of its foundations, in which the foundations themselves involve a systematic unity with the individual items of knowledge and the higher complexions of foundations, which we call theories, also involve a systematic unity with them' (*Logische Untersuchungen*, Vol. I, Tübingen, 1900, p. 15; *Logical Investigations*, trans. J. N. Findlay, London, 1970). Among the neo-Kantians, Bruno Bauch was the first to allow the idea of system to recede into the background in favour of the procedural characterization of science: science, according to him, is 'founded knowledge'; in science, it is a matter of 'how in general it is necessary to proceed, in order that scientific knowledge should be attained, so that science should be the foundation of science and in the founded knowledge truth should be achieved' (*Wahrheit, Wert und Wirklichkeit*, Leipzig, 1923, p. 312)

55 Friedrich Schiller was already bemoaning, in 1800, the 'prevailing hatred of philosophers' (from G. Hennemann, *Naturphilosophie*, p. 43).

56 Cf. Eduard Zeller (1814–1908), *Die Philosophie der Griechen in ihrer geschichtlichen Entwicklung* (3 vols.), 1844ff. (Zeller was later a neo-Kantian); Johann Eduard Erdmann (1805–92), *Versuch einer wissenschaftlichen Darstellung der Geschichte der neueren Philosophie* (6 vols.), 1834ff. (Erdmann remained a Hegelian all his life); Kuno Fischer (1824–1907), *Geschichte der Philosophie* (10 vols), 1854ff.

57 The most important representative of neo-Aristotelianism was Adolf Trendelenburg (1802–72), who taught in Berlin for almost 40 years; particularly influential was his critique of Hegel in his *Logische Untersuchungen* of 1840. The founder of neo-Thomism is regarded as being Joseph Kleutgen, S. J., (1811–83). Bernhard Bolzano (1781–1848), who, through Brentano, influenced Husserl, sought to return to Leibniz. On neo-Kantianism, see Ch. 3, Sect. 3. iv. The neo-Idealism of the very influential Rudolf Eucken (1846–1926), who won the Nobel Prize in 1908, was neo-Fichtean in character. The central figure of neo-Hegelianism was Georg Lasson (1862–1932), but the influence of Benedetto Croce should also be mentioned. Neo-Marxism began as a movement directed against the monopolistic claims of Soviet Marxism, and only after the end of the Second World War; nevertheless, Lukács' *Geschichte und Klassenbewusstsein* (1923) must be regarded as the first foundational work of neo-Marxism.

58 In his book *Kant und die Epigonen* of 1865, which introduced neo-Kantianism, Otto Liebmann ended every chapter with the battle-cry 'Thus we must return to Kant!'

59 The founder of the neo-Friesian school was Leonard Nelson (1882–1927); Hans Pichler (1882–1958) was a neo-Wolffian.

60 The chief representatives of 'immanence-positivism' were Ernst Laas (1837–85) and Wilhelm Schuppe (1836–1913).

61 Jacob Moleschott, *Der Kreislauf des Lebens*, 1887, pp. 26.

62 See Wilhelm Ostwald, *Die Überwindung des wissenschaftlichen Materialismus*, Leipzig, 1895.

63 See Ernst Haeckel, *Die Welträtsel. Gemeinverständliche Studien über monistische Philosophie*, Bonn, 1899; (see also n. 24 above).

64 In 1929, the Vienna Circle of Logical Positivism brought out a publication which bore the title *Wissenschaftliche Weltauffassung* (Scientific Conception of the World). Viktor Kraft makes it clear, in his well-known account *Der Wiener Kreis. Der Ursprung des Neopositivismus* (Vienna, 1950) (*The Vienna Circle, the Origins of Neopositivism*, London, 1953), that this 'Conception of the World' did not include the political domain (Neurath), but was 'purely philosophical' (see n. 3); thus, neopositivism can no longer be regarded as a world-view in the older style, which fact, in my view, is expressed, not by chance, in the self-description 'Conception of the World'. The emergence of the Nazi ideology as a 'radical world-view' finally discredited the term 'world-view' in Germany. A scientific world-view survives today only in the form of the 'Marxist–Leninist world-view' of 'scientific socialism'.

65 Ludwig Feuerbach, *Grundsätze einer Philosophie der Zukunft* (1843), § 54.

66 Cf. Karl Marx, *Die Frühschriften* (ed. S. Landshut), Stuttgart, 1953, p. 346.

67 Ibid., p. 235, where communism is described as the 'solved riddle of history'; on the identity of 'human science of nature' and 'natural science of man', cf. p. 246.

68 Ibid., p. 350; Marx says 'Furthermore, in this conception of the matter . . . all profound philosophical problems resolve themselves quite simply into empirical facts' (p. 352).

69 Nietzsche, *Jenseits von Gut und Böse, Werke* (ed. Schlechta), Vol. II, Munich, 1960, pp. 586f. (*Beyond Good and Evil*, trans. R. J. Hollingdale, Harmondsworth, Middx, 1973).

70 Cf. e.g. Bertrand Russell, *Problems of Philosophy*, Oxford, 1959, pp. 149ff.

71 Even Edmund Husserl, as a disciple of Franz Brentano, still followed psychologism in his *Philosophie der Arithmetik* (1891); his turning against this position, to the criticism of which almost the whole of *Logische Untersuchungen* I (1900) is devoted, was principally the result of Gottlob Frege's review of this first work. Husserl quotes Goethe's dictum, 'There is nothing towards which one is stricter than errors once set aside' (*Logische Untersuchungen*, p. viii) (*Logical Investigations*, trans. J. N. Findlay, London, 1970). Frege is referred to with agreement on p. 169 and the earlier criticism of his anti-psychologism is formally withdrawn. Husserl himself, moreover, appeals to Leibniz, Kant, Bolzano, Herbart and Lotze. Frege's review appeared in the *Zeitschrift für Philosophie und philosophische Kritik*, 100, 1894, pp. 313–32.

72 Since Aristotle's *De anima*, psychology had been part of philosophy, and Hegel still gave this name to one of the parts of his system (*Enzyklopädie*, §§ 440–82); it was not until the eighties of the nineteenth century that it began to form itself into an independent science. It was only this development which made psychologism into a philosophical problem; previously, psychology had simply been identical with philosophy and so the psychological procedure had been a recognized procedure of philosophy – thus there was also no 'circle' in psychologism.

73 The word '*Geisteswissenschaften*' was first really naturalized as a result of Dilthey's *Einleitung in die Geisteswissenschaften* (1883), but had already been used in Schiele's translation of Mill's *Logic* (1849) as an equivalent for 'moral sciences': the 'moral sciences' were, however, referred by Mill to psychology as their foundation. It was as a result of this, too, and not only as a result of Dilthey's 'psychologism' that the thesis of the psychological basis of the *Geisteswissenschaften* came to be a commonplace. The antipodes to this conception were not only the later, hermeneutic, Dilthey and Heidegger as a disciple of Husserl, but above all the South-West German

neo-Kantians who based the special position of the cultural sciences no longer on psychology, but on philosophy of value. (cf. Ch. 4, Sect. 4 and Ch. 6, Sect. 2.ii).

74 Helmut Plessner, *Die verspätete Nation*, Frankfurt, 1974, pp. 144ff.
75 The Right-Left division amongst Hegelians was already mentioned by David Friedrich Strauss in 1837. His *Das Leben Jesu, kritisch bearbeitet* (1835) was certainly the most important cause of that division, which was connected with the dispute over the interpretation of Hegel's philosophy of religion. See also Karl Löwith, *Von Hegel zu Nietzsche. Der revolutionäre Bruch im Denken des neunzehnten Jahrhunderts*, Zurich, 1951/Stuttgart, 1958, pp. 65ff.
76 Cf. Ludwig Feuerbach, *Vorläufige Thesen zur Reform der Philosophie* (1842).
77 Cf. e.g. Karl Marx, *Kritik der Hegelschen Rechtsphilosophie. Einleitung*, in *Die Frühschriften* (ed. Landshut), pp. 207ff.
78 Marx, *6. These über Feuerbach*, ibid., p. 340. (Feuerbach Thesis No. VI, in *The German Ideology*)
79 Cf. Marx, *Deutsche Ideologie*, ibid., p. 350. (*The German Ideology*).
80 The basic text is Max Horkheimer's 'Traditionelle und kritische Theorie', in A. Schmidt (ed.), *Kritische Theorie*, Vol. II, Frankfurt, 1968, pp. 137ff. (*Critical Theory: Selected Essays*, New York, 1972); cf. also Herbert Marcuse, 'Philosophie und kritische Theorie' (1937), now in Marcuse, *Kultur und Gesellschaft 1*, Frankfurt, 1965, pp. 102ff. Jürgen Habermas writes as a result of his critique of Marx in 1968: 'Philosophy is preserved in science as critique. The social theory which makes claims to being a self-reflection of the history of the species cannot simply negate philosophy. The mantle of philosophy is rather passed on to the attitude of the critique of ideology, which is defined by the method of scientific analysis. But, apart from its role as critique, no rights are left to philosophy. In the measure in which the science of man is a material critique of knowledge, philosophy too, which, as pure theory of knowledge, had deprived itself of all content, indirectly regains its access to material questions. As philosophy, however, the universal science which it sought to be falls victim to the destructive judgment of criticism' (*Erkenntnis und Interesse*, Frankfurt, 1968/1973, p. 86 (*Knowledge and Human Interests*, trans. J. Shapiro, London, 1972)).
81 This assertion, more frequently made as an objection, is given a socio-economic derivation by Herbert Marcuse in *Der eindimensionale Mensch* (trans. A. Schmidt), Neuwied/Berlin, 1967, pp. 16f. (*One-Dimensional Man*, Boston, 1964).
82 See above all Søren Kierkegaard, *Unwissenschaftliche Nachschrift zu den Philosophischen Brosamen*, Cologne 1959/Munich 1976.
83 Cf. Arthur Schopenhauer, '*Über die Universitätsphilosophie*', in *Parerga und Paralipomena 1*, Leipzig n.d., pp. 127ff.
84 Nietzsche, *Werke*, Vol. II, p. 571.
85 The more recent interpretation of 'criticism' which no longer equates the concept with Kantianism, stems from Alois Riehl, *Der philosophische Kritizismus und seine Bedeutung für die positiven Wissenschaften*, 1876ff. in several editions.
86 Helmholtz, *Philosophische Vorträge*, pp. 46f.
87 Cited from Cassirer, *Erkenntnisproblem*, p. 13.
88 Ibid.
89 See e.g. Heinrich Rickert, *Die Grenzen der naturwissenschaftlichen Begriffsbildung*, Tübingen, 1921, pp. 10f.
90 'Positivism' was at that time a fairly vague collective term, still standardly defined in

relation to Comte; seen from the present day, a series of tendencies which did not describe themselves in these terms also belonged under that heading, e.g. Ernst Laas, *Idealismus und Positivismus* (1876): also empirio-criticism (Mach, Avenarius), Schuppe's immanence-philosophy, the philosophy of Eugen Dühring (familiar from Engels' polemics), and also Vaihinger's fictionalism, with its integration of idealistic, positivistic and pragmatist elements.

91 Wundt was Lange's successor in F. A. Lange's Chair of 'Inductive Philosophy'.

4 Understanding

1 Cf. Wittgenstein, *Philosophical Investigations*, § 199: 'To understand a language means to be master of a technique.'
2 Quoted from K. O. Apel, 'Das Verstehen (eine Problemgeschichte als Begriffsgeschichte)' in *Archiv für Begriffsgeschichte*, 1, 1955, pp. 142ff., 152.
3 In Kant, explanation presupposes understanding (in his sense); he says, 'We can explain nothing save what we can refer back to laws, whose object can be given in any possible experience' (*Groundwork of the Metaphysics of Morals*, BA 120).
4 Kant, *Reflexionen*, No. 395.
5 The interpretation of the understanding of phenomena itself as an understanding of meaning has a long history, which manifests itself for example in the metaphor of the 'book of nature', which according to Galileo is written in a mathematical language; it can be traced back as far as Augustine.
6 Quoted from M. Frank, Introduction to F. D. E. Schleiermacher, *Hermeneutik und Kritik*, Frankfurt, 1977, p. 13.
7 Hegel, *Vorlesungen über Geschichte der Philosophie, Werke* (ed. Glockner), Vol. XVIII, pp. 102f. (*Hegel's Lectures on the History of Philosophy*, trans. E. S. Haldane and F. H. Simpson, London 1896).
8 Hegel, *Die Vernunft in der Geschichte* (ed. Hoffmeister), Hamburg, 1955, p. 28.
9 Hegel, Preface to the 2nd ed. of the *Enzyklopädie der philosophischen Wissenschaften*, p. 28.
10 A thesis first effectively represented in Germany by Hamann, in his criticism of Kant, *Metakritik über den Purismum der Vernunft* (1784).
11 Schleiermacher, 'Autobiographische Notiz', in his *Hermeneutik und Kritik* (ed. M. Frank).
12 Schleiermacher 'Über den Begriff . . .', ibid., p. 315.
13 Ibid., p. 328.
14 Schleiermacher, 'Über Begriff und Einteilung der philologischen Kritik', in *Hermeneutik und Kritik* (ed. Frank), pp. 326f.
15 Ibid.
16 Ibid., p. 328.
17 Cf. Droysen, *Grundriss der Historik* (*GdH*), ed. R. Hübner, Darmstadt, 1974. pp. 386–405.
18 Ibid., § 14, p. 330.
19 Dilthey's *Die Jugendgeschichte Hegels* (1905) is regarded as the beginning of neo-Hegelianism.
20 Droysen, *GdH*, § 7, p. 328.
21 Ibid., p. 24.
22 Ibid., p. 25.
23 Ibid., § 9, p. 328.

24 Ibid., § 10, p. 329.
25 Ibid.
26 Ibid.
27 Ibid., § 11, p. 329.
28 Ibid., p. 26.
29 Manfred Riedel, Introduction to Dilthey, *Der Aufbau der geschichtlichen Welt in den Geisteswissenschaften* (*AGW*), Frankfurt, 1970, p. 67.
30 Dilthey, *AGW*, p. 252.
31 Ibid., p. 255.
32 Ibid., p. 261.
33 Ibid., p. 262; on the criticism of Mill, see, *Einleitung in die Geisteswissenschaften* (1883) (*EG*), *Gesammelte Schriften*, Vol. I, Stuttgart/Göttingen, 1959, p. 108.
34 *AGW*, p. 267.
35 Ibid., pp. 268f.
36 Ibid., pp. 288f.
37 Heinrich Rickert, *Die Grenzen der naturwissenschaftlichen Begriffsbildung*, Tübingen, 1929, p. 181; on page 136 he even accuses Wundt and Dilthey of spiritualism.
38 Ibid., p. 540.
39 Ibid., p. 543.
40 Ibid., p. 560.
41 Ibid.
42 Ibid., p. 578.
43 Max Weber, *Soziologische Grundbegriffe*, § 1; all the passages previously cited are to be found in Notes 1–6 to this §
44 Ibid., Note 3.
45 Ibid.
46 Ibid., Note 2.
47 Apel, 'Das Verstehen', pp. 178f.
48 Georg Simmel, *Die Probleme der Geschichtsphilosophie*, Berlin, 1907, pp. 39f. (*The Problem of the Philosophy of History*, West Drayton, Middx, 1977).
49 Apel, 'Das Verstehen', pp. 182f.
50 On Litt, see Apel, 'Das Verstehen', p. 185.
51 Heidegger, *Sein und Zeit*, Tübingen, 1957, p. 12.
52 Ibid., pp. 37f.
53 Ibid., p. 144.
54 Ibid., p. 148.
55 Ibid., p. 152.
56 Ibid., p. 153.
57 Ibid.

5 Life

1 According to Hegel, philosophy imparts 'the insight that nothing is real but the idea. What matters is to recognize, in the appearance of the temporal and transient, the substance which is immanent and the eternal which is present.' The eternal and the temporal are related to each other as 'kernel' and 'outer husk': *Rechtsphilosophie* (ed. Hoffmeister), Hamburg, 1955, p. 15.
2 See Lukács, *Die Seele und die Formen* (1911) and *Die Theorie des Romans* (1916), (*Soul*

and Form, trans. A. Bostock, London, 1974; *Theory of the Novel*, trans. A. Bostock, London, 1971).

3 On the dialectic of living cf. Hegel, *Phänomenologie des Geistes* (ed. Hoffmeister), Hamburg, 1952, pp. 133ff.; the quotation is from p. 140.

4 Dilthey, *Der Aufbau der geschichtlichen Welt in den Geisteswissenschaften* (*AGW*), Frankfurt, 1970, p. 183.

5 See Goethe, *Dichtung und Wahrheit, Werke* (ed. E. Trunz), Vol. IX, Hamburg, 1955, pp. 490ff. (*Autobiography*, trans. J. Oxenford, Chicago, 1975).

6 Schopenhauer, ch. 22 of the second volume of *Die Welt als Wille und Vorstellung*, *Sämtliche Werke*, Vol. III, Leipzig (n.d.), p. 272.

7 Quoted from Philipp Lersch, *Lebensphilosophie der Gegenwart*, Berlin, 1932, p. 82.

8 A philosophical history of the concept 'sickness' in the nineteenth and twentieth centuries has not yet been written; it would presumably prove that this concept essentially belongs to life-philosophy and the philosophy of existence (cf. Kierkegaard's *Sickness unto Death*). Nietzsche's work is shot through with the theme of sickness: from the 'historical sickness' of the second *Unzeitgemässe Betrachtung* to his later work, which e.g. refers to 'bad conscience' as 'the most fearful sickness which has yet raged amongst men'. The theme of 'sickness and art' was also the theme of a number of variations by Thomas Mann and was then applied to the philosophers themselves, for example in *Doktor Faustus*, while cultural criticism as a diagnosis of a collective sickness is a central idea of Sigmund Freud (e.g. *Civilization and its Discontents*) and of the Freudians up until the present day.

9 Max Scheler defended such a position and for that reason should not be treated as belonging to life-philosophy. See *Die Stellung des Menschen im Kosmos*, Darmstadt, 1928.

10 It began in 1908 with the translation of William James' *Pragmatism* (1907). Since then, pragmatism has been a favourite object of criticism for almost all philosophical tendencies in Germany: from Logical Positivism via neo-Kantianism (esp. Rickert), and critical theory up to Heidegger. This results from the fact that the 'typically American' movement of pragmatism is essentially known only through this translation of James. It was only the influence of Peirce in the fifties and sixties (Jürgen von Kempski, Karl Otto Apel, Klaus Oehler and others) which corrected the picture.

11 Here too it is easy to point to a 'Great Coalition' of several, otherwise very different, tendencies; I mention only the traditional mistrust of the Frankfurt critical theorists for empirical '*social research*' and Gadamer's *Truth and Method*, which tends very strongly towards *Truth versus Method*.

12 Dilthey, *Gesammelte Schriften*, Vol. VII, Berlin/Leipzig, 1927, p. 359.

13 Quoted from P. Lersch, *Lebensphilosophie der Gegenwart*, p. 6.

14 Dilthey, *Gesammelte Schriften*, Vol. VII, p. 291.

15 Cf. F. O. Bollnow, *Die Lebensphilosophie*, Berlin, 1958, pp. 16ff. and 39ff.

16 Ludwig Klages, *Der Geist als Widersacher der Seele*, Vol. I, Leipzig, 1929, p. vii.

17 Ibid., p. 7.

18 Schopenhauer's first volume of *Die Welt als Wille und Vorstellung* begins as follows, 'I have sought here to suggest how this book should be read in order that it should be understood as much as possible. What is meant to be communicated by it is a single thought. Nevertheless, notwithstanding all my efforts, I was unable to find a shorter way to communicate it than this whole book. I regard that thought as the one which

has been sought for a very long time under the name of philosophy' (Preface to the First Edition, 1818).
19 Klages, *Der Geist*, p. xix.
20 Ibid., p. 68f.
21 Oswald Spengler, *Der Untergang des Abendlandes. Umrisse einer Morphologie der Weltgeschichte*, Munich (new one-volume edition), 1980, pp. ixf. (*The Decline of the West*, trans. C. Atkinson, London, 1934).
22 Ibid., pp. 28f.
23 Ibid., p. 34.
24 Ibid., p. 43.
25 Ibid., p. 51.
26 Munich, 1931, p. v.
27 Ibid., p. 12.
28 Ibid., p. 24.
29 Ibid., p. 25.
30 Ibid., p. 36.
31 Ibid., pp. 61f.
32 Nietzsche, *Werke*, Vol. I, p. 173.
33 *Also sprach Zarathustra, Dritter Teil: Von alten und neuen Tafeln*, *Werke*, Vol. II, pp. 443ff. (*Thus Spoke Zarathustra*, trans. R. J. Hollingdale, Harmondsworth, Middx, 1973, Third Part: 'On Old and New Tablets').
34 Fritz Heinemann, *Existenzphilosophie lebendig oder tot?*, Stuttgart, 1954, p. 11.
35 Karl Jaspers, *Philosophie* (1932), quoted from Heinemann, *Existenzphilosophie*.
36 Ibid., p. 65.
37 Ibid., p. 80.
38 Heidegger, *Sein und Zeit*, p. 42.

6 Values

1 Joachim Ernst Heyde, *Wert. Eine philosophische Grundlegung*, Erfurt, 1926, p. 7.
2 T. W. Adorno, Introduction to Adorno, Dahrendorf et al., *Der Positivismusstreit in der deutschen Soziologie*, Neuwied and Berlin, 1969, p. 74 (*The Positivist Dispute in German Sociology*, trans. G. Adey and D. Frisby, London, 1976).
3 In the first half of the century Jakob Friedrich Fries (1773–1843) and Johann Friedrich Herbart (1776–1841) were among the most tenacious and effective opponents of the integration of 'is' and 'ought', reality and value.
4 Helmut Kuhn, Article 'Das Gute', in Krings et al. (eds), *Handbuch philosophischer Grundbegriffe*, Munich, 1973, pp. 671f.
5 The expression is Hans Wagner's, cf. his *Philosophie und Reflexion*, Basel, 1967, esp. pp. 29ff.
6 Heinrich Rickert, *System der Philosophie I*, Tübingen, 1921, p. 142.
7 Hegel, *Die Vernunft in der Geschichte*, (ed. Hoffmeister), Hamburg, 1955, p. 29.
8 Kuhn, 'Das Gute', p. 672.
9 Nietzsche, *Nachlass*, *Werke*, Vol. III, p. 557.
10 Ibid., pp. 676 and 678.
11 Ibid., p. 556.
12 Ibid., p. 557.
13 Ibid., p. 635.

14 Ibid., p. 844.
15 Ibid., p. 680.
16 Ibid., p. 586.
17 Ibid., p. 588.
18 Nietzsche, *Also sprach Zarathustra, Werke*, Vol. II, p. 444.
19 Cf. Kant, *Critique of Judgment*, § 83ff.
20 Fichte, *Nachgelassene Werke* (ed. I. H. Fichte), Vol. I, p. 137.
21 As does Fritz Bamberger, *Untersuchung zur Entstehung des Wertproblems in der Philosophie des 19. Jahrhunderts*, Halle, 1924, pp. 13f.
22 Fichte, *Nachgelassene Werke*, p. 16.
23 On 'sense' in Fichte, cf. *Transzendentale Logik* (1812), in *Werke* (6 vols), Vol. VI, pp. 271 and 275ff.
24 Hermann Lotze, *Metaphysik*, Leipzig, 1841, p. 4.
25 Ibid., p. 5.
26 Ibid., p. 8.
27 Ibid., p. 13.
28 Ibid., p. 19.
29 Ibid., p. 323.
30 Ibid.
31 Ibid., p. 324.
32 Ibid., p. 329.
33 Quoted from G. Misch, 'Einleitung zu Lotzes Logik', in Lotze, *Logik*, Leipzig, 1928, p. xxiii.
34 Ibid., p. xxxiv.
35 Lotze, *Seele und Seelenleben, Kleine Schriften*, Vol. II, Leipzig, 1886, pp. 174f.
36 Ibid., p. 175.
37 Ibid., pp. 176f.
38 Lotze, *Metaphysik* (1841), p. 326.
39 This is also the nature of the correction which Lotze believed it necessary to make to the traditional understanding of Plato: cf. *Logik*, esp. pp. 513ff.
40 Lotze, *Kleine Schriften*, Vol. I.
41 The most important revival of this idea in our own century is to be found in Nicolai Hartmann: see Ch. 7, Sect. 4.
42 Wilhelm Windelband, *Einleitung in die Philosophie*, Tübingen, 1914, p. 253.
43 Ibid., p. 252.
44 Ibid., p. 245.
45 Ibid., pp. 252f.
46 'Lebenswerte und Kulturwerte', *Logos* II, 1911–12, p. 152. In this polemical essay Rickert was already attacking (pp. 137ff.) the idea of human breeding which emerged from the biologistic form of the philosophy of culture, and anticipated in the medium of criticism precisely the later S.S. institution of the 'spring of life'. Rickert ascribed these ideas, not to any particular author, but to the whole tendency.
47 Rickert, *System der Philosophie*, Vol. I, Tübingen, 1921, p. 109.
48 Max Scheler, *Der Formalismus in der Ethik und die materiale Wertethik*, Halle, 1913–16/Bern, 1954, pp. 13–14.
49 Ibid., pp. 67f.
50 According to Scheler, values are also not aims or purposes, since in his view only the valuable is aimed for: see pp. 61ff.
51 It is possible to see in this theory the secondary influence of Franz Brentano, trans-

mitted through Husserl's mediation; the idea of the intentionality of everything mental is expressed by him as follows: 'Every psychic phenomenon contains something as an object in itself, though not in every case in the same manner. In the representation something is represented, in the judgment something is accepted or rejected, in love something is loved, in hatred hated, in desire desired, and so forth ...' (Franz Brentano, *Psychologie vom empirischen Standpunkte*, Vienna, 1874 (*Psychology from an Empirical Standpoint*, ed. L. McAlister, London, 1973)). Scheler, however, tends, like the Husserl of the middle period, towards the ontologization of the intentional object, which is not the case in Brentano.
52 Nicolai Hartmann, *Ethik* (1926), Berlin, 1935, p. 134.
53 Max Weber, *Wissenschaft als Beruf* (1919), in *Gesammelte Aufsätze zur Wissenschaftslehre*, Tübingen, 1973, p. 605; Weber refers, in connexion with his choice of the word 'polytheism', to Mill's dictum that if one starts from the realm of pure experience, one comes to polytheism (p. 603).
54 Martin Heidegger, *Einführung in die Metaphysik*, Tübingen, 1966, pp. 151f. (*Introduction to Metaphysics*, trans. R. Manheim, New Haven, Conn., 1959). This book contains the text of the Freiburg lectures delivered in 1935. The passage quoted is followed by this sentence: 'The philosophy which is bandied about today everywhere as a philosophy of National Socialism, but which has not the slightest to do with the inner truth and greatness of this movement (namely, with the encounter of planetary technology and the man of the new age), makes its haul in these muddy waters of "values" and of "totalities"', (p. 152). Here the philosophy of value is seen as a politically influential evil. How to explain the fact that Heidegger has once again since 1953 allowed this sentence to be printed unchanged – whether as an affirmation of what was said at that time or as a refusal to rewrite his biography at a later date – is difficult to decide. On this, cf. his posthumously published *Spiegel* interview, in *Der Spiegel*, No. 23, 1976, pp. 85ff.
55 Meta-ethics, as is well known, advocates an ethical neutralism, that is, it maintains that as a meta-theory it does not prejudice any substantive ethics.

7 Being

1 Nicolai Hartmann, *Zur Grundlegung der Ontologie*, Berlin, 1935, p. v.
2 The parallels and connexions between recent ontology and life-philosophy are much more numerous than is generally accepted; an important common feature is the general 'Heracliteanism', that is, the tendency to interpret what exists in reality as dynamic and ultimately irrational. Scheler, Nicolai Hartmann, and Heidegger participated in this in their different ways.
3 Kant, *Critique of Pure Reason*, B 303.
4 Fichte, *Grundlage der gesamten Wissenschaftslehre* (1794), Part I, §§ 1, 7 and 9.
5 Hegel, *Wissenschaft der Logik*, Vol. I. (ed. G. Lasson), Hamburg, 1963, p. 67.
6 *Logik*, Vol. II (ed. Lasson), p. 9.
7 See Schelling, *Das Wesen der menschlichen Freiheit* (1809), new edition by H. Fuhrmans, Düsseldorf, 1950 (*Of Human Freedom*, trans. J. Gutmann, La Salle, Ill., 1977). This essay marked the beginning of Schelling's later phase.
8 The classic example of this is the 'League of Monists'; see Ch. 3, n.24.
9 Marx, *Theses on Feuerbach*, No. VI.
10 Cf. Marx/Engels, *Die heilige Familie* (The Holy Family), chapter on 'Kritische Schlacht gegen den französischen Materialismus' (1844–5), in *Frühschriften* p. 325;

here are to be found already all the essential arguments which were later brought into play, mainly by Engels, against 'vulgar materialism': especially in *Anti-Dühring* and in the *Dialektik der Natur*.

11 Nietzsche, *Jenseits von Gut und Böse*, Werke II, p. 567.
12 Ibid., pp. 957f.
13 Ibid., p. 963.
14 Nietzsche, *Nachlass*, Werke, Vol. III, p. 751.
15 The central document of this 'turn' is Heidegger's essay *Über den Humanismus* (1946), Bern, 1947/Frankfurt, n.d. (translated in *Basic Writings*, London, 1975).
16 E.g. Traugott Oesterreich, who in his account devotes a whole paragraph to 'parapsychology' and 'parapsychophysics': *Die deutsche Philosophie*, Berlin, 1923, § 59, pp. 617ff. Rudolf Steiner's anthroposophy should also be mentioned here: see Rudolf Steiner, *Wie erlangt man Erkenntnisse der höheren Welten?* Berlin 1909 (*Knowledge of the High Worlds, How is it Achieved?*, trans. C. Davy and D. S. Osmond, New York, 1977).
17 Nicolai Hartmann, *Neue Wege der Ontologie*, Stuttgart, 1949, p. 7.
18 Quoted in Rüdiger Bubner (ed.), *Sprache und Analysis. Texte zur englischen Philosophie der Gegenwart*, Göttingen, 1968.
19 Bolzano, *Wissenschaftslehre*, § 394.
20 Ibid., § 7.
21 Gottlob Frege, *Einleitung in die Logik* (1906), in his *Nachgelassene Schriften* (eds Hermes/Kambartel/Kaulbach), Hamburg, 1969; also, Frege, 'Der Gedanke' (1918), in his *Logische Untersuchungen* (ed. G. Patzig), Göttingen, 1966, pp. 30ff. (*Logical Investigations*, trans. P. T. Geach and R. H. Stoothoff, Oxford, 1977).
22 Husserl, *Ideen III*, new edition, The Hague, 1952 (Husserliana V), p. 76 (*Ideas*, trans. Gibson, London, 1931).
23 Ibid., pp. 85f.; cf. the whole of § 16.
24 Ibid., p. 91.
25 Gerhard Lehmann, *Die Ontologie der Gegenwart in ihren Gestalten*, Halle, 1933, pp. 11f.
26 Heidegger, *Sein und Zeit*, Tübingen, 1957, p. 35.
27 Ibid.
28 Ibid., p. 37.
29 Ibid., p. 12.
30 Ibid., p. 13.
31 Ibid., p. 37; '*légein tà phainomena*': p. 34.
32 Ibid., p. 38.
33 H. G. Gadamer, *Wahrheit und Methode*, Tübingen, 1965, p. 361 (*Truth and Method*, New York, 1975).
34 Nicolai Hartmann, *Zur Grundlegung der Ontologie*, Berlin/Leipzig, 1935, pp. 1f.
35 Ibid.
36 Ibid., p. 2; cf. also pp. 94ff.
37 Ibid., p. 3.
38 Nicolai Hartmann, 'Wie ist kritische Ontologie möglich?' in *Festschrift für Paul Natorp* (1924), now in *Kleine Schriften*, Vol. III, Berlin, 1958, p. 269.
39 Hartmann, *Zur Grundlegung*, pp. 6f.
40 Hartmann, *Neue Wege der Ontologie*, Stuttgart, 1949, p. 107.
41 Nicolai Hartmann, *Grundzüge einer Metaphysik der Erkenntnis*, Berlin, 1921, p. 28.

42 Ibid., p. 142.
43 Ibid., p. 148.
44 Ibid., pp. 148 and 142.
45 Ibid., p. 152.
46 Ibid., p. 30.
47 Ibid.
48 Lehmann, *Ontologie der Gegenwart*, p. 24.
49 Hartmann, *Wie ist kritische Ontologie möglich?*, pp. 272f; on what follows, see pp. 273ff.
50 Hartmann, *Neue Wege*, p. 13.
51 Ibid., p. 11.
52 Wolfgang Stegmüller, *Probleme und Resultate der Wissenschaftstheorie und Analytischen Philosophie*, Vol. I, Berlin/Heidelberg/New York, 1969, p. 5.
53 See Martin Heidegger, 'Über den Humanismus': 'Yet Being – What is Being? It is itself. To experience this and to say it is what future thinking will have to learn. "Being" is not God and not the ground of the world. Being is further than all beings and is nevertheless closer to man than all beings, whether a field, an animal, a work of art, a machine, whether an angel or God. Being is what is closest ...' (pp. 19f.).
54 This is the central critical thesis of Ernst Tugendhat, which he attempts to prove in the course of his argument with tradition: ontology has always been the same as formal semantics: cf. *Vorlesungen zur Einführung in die sprachanalytische Philosophie*, Frankfurt, 1976 (*Traditional and Analytical Philosophy*, trans. P. A. Gorner, Cambridge, 1982).

8 Epilogue: Man

1 Heidegger, *Kant und das Problem der Metaphysik* (1929). Frankfurt, 1951, p. 189.
2 Kant, *Logik*, A 26; Heidegger agrees completely with this Kantian thesis, to which Scheler laid claim: see Heidegger, *Kant*, pp. 188ff.
3 Kant, *Anthropologie in pragmatischer Hinsicht*, A III.
4 Scheler, '*Mensch und Geschichte*', in *Philosophische Weltanschauung*, Munich, 1954, p. 62.
5 Ibid., p. 65. See also pp. 63ff.
6 Helmut Plessner, 'Die Aufgabe der philosophischen Anthropologie' (1931) in *Zwischen Philosophie und Gesellschaft*, Frankfurt, 1979, pp. 141f.
7 *Mensch und Geschichte*, p. 69.
8 Ibid.
9 Ibid., p. 74.
10 Cf. Odo Marquard, 'Zur Geschichte des philosophischen Begriffs "Anthropologie" seit dem Ende des achtzehnten Jahrhunderts', in Marquard, *Schwierigkeiten mit der Geschichtsphilosophie*, Frankfurt, 1973, pp. 122ff.
11 Hegel, *Enzyklopädie*, § 387, p. 317.
12 Hegel, *Wissenschaft der Logik*, Vol. II (ed. G. Lasson), Hamburg, 1963, pp. 220f. Heinrich Heine remembers Hegel's thesis thus: 'At some moments, especially when my spinal cramps are rumbling only too painfully, the doubt flashes across my mind as to whether man really is a god on two legs as the late Professor Hegel assured me twenty-five years ago in Berlin.' (H. Heine, *Sämtliche Werke* (ed. H. Kaufmann),

Vol. XIV, Munich, 1964, p. 104).
13 Ludwig Feuerbach, *Grundsätze der Philosophie der Zukunft* (1843), § 54, in Feuerbach, *Kleine Schriften* (ed. M. G. Lange), Leipzig, 1950, p. 167.
14 Droysen, *Grundriss der Historik (GdH)*, §§ 82 and 83 (ed. R. Hübner), Darmstadt, 1974, p. 357.
15 Dilthey, *Gesammelte Schriften*, Vol. VIII, p. 224.
16 Marx, *Deutsche Ideologie, Frühschriften*, ed. S. Landshut, p. 350.
17 Droysen, *GdH*, § 75, p. 354.
18 Schopenhauer, *Die Welt als Wille und Vorstellung*, Vol. II, ch. 38, *Sämtliche Werke*, Leipzig, n.d., pp. 431f.
19 Jacob Burckhardt, *Weltgeschichtliche Betrachtungen*, new ed., Stuttgart, 1955, pp. 5f.
20 Dilthey, *Gesammelte Schriften*, Vol. V, p. xci.
21 In general Nietzsche criticizes Darwin because his principle of selection in the struggle for survival works 'to the disadvantage of the strong, the privileged, the fortunate exceptions'; then he continues, 'Species do not grow in perfection: the weak become masters of the strong over and over again – that is because there are more of them, and also they are cleverer . . . Darwin has forgotten the spirit (how English!), the weak have more spirit . . . One must also have spirit in order to acquire spirit – one loses it when one does not need it any more. Someone who has strength gives up the spirit ("let it go!", people think nowadays in Germany "the *Reich* will still be left to us" . . .). By "spirit" I mean how one sees prudence, patience, deceit, hypocrisy, great self-mastery and everything which is "*mimicry*" (to the latter belongs a large part of so-called virtue)' (*Götzendämmerung, Werke*, Vol. II, p. 999 (*Twilight of the Idols*, trans. R. J. Hollingdale, Harmondsworth, Middx, 1969), see also *Nachlass, Werke*, Vol. III, pp. 748f.). Along with this hidden compliment for the English there is also an overt one for the contribution of the English nobility towards the solution of the 'European problem, as I understand it . . . the breeding of a new ruling caste for Europe' (*Jenseits von Gut und Böse, Werke*, Vol. II, p. 718).
22 Helmut Plessner, 'Immer noch philosophische Anthropologie?', in *Diesseits der Utopie*, p. 235.
23 Walter Schulz, *Philosophie in der veränderten Welt*, Pfullingen, 1972, p. 461; cf. also pp. 457ff.
24 Heidegger, *Über den Humanismus*, Bern 1947/Frankfurt, n.d., p. 19.
25 Hans-Georg Gadamer, *Wahrheit und Methode*, Tübingen, 1965, p. 450.
26 'Logic is transcendental' (*Tractatus* 6.13).

Select bibliography

This includes a number of the more general background references on the period which readers may be interested to consult. For a full list of the German references used readers are directed to the German edition of the book, *Philosophie in Deutschland 1831–1933*, Suhrkamp, 1983.

History of Philosophy

T. K. Oesterreich, *Die deutsche Philosophie des XIX. Jahrhunderts und der Gegenwart* (Pt IV by F. Überweg, *Grundriß der Geschichte der Philosophie*), 12th edn, Berlin 1923

G. Lehmann, *Die Philosophie des neunzehnten Jahrhunderts*, Vol. I/II, Berlin 1953

Die Philosophie im ersten Drittel des zwanzigsten Jahrhunderts, 2 vols., Berlin 1957–60

F. A. Lange, *Geschichte des Materialismus und Kritik seiner Bedeutung in der Gegenwart,* Book II (1875), new edn Frankfurt 1974 (important presentation of events after 1831)

W. Stegmüller, *Hauptströmungen der Gegenwartsphilosophie. Eine kritische Einführung*, Vol. I, 4th edn, Stuttgart 1969 (deals with Brentano, Husserl, Scheler, Heidegger, Jaspers and Nicolai Hartmann)

Political History

B. Gebhardt, *Handbuch der deutschen Geschichte* 3/4, Stuttgart 1962

G. Mann, *Deutsche Geschichte des 19. und 20. Jahrhunderts,* Frankfurt 1958 (*The History of Germany Since 1789*, London 1968)

Social History

H. U. Wehler (ed.), *Moderne deutsche Sozialgeschichte*, 5th edn, Cologne 1976

H. Plessner, *Die verspätete Nation*, Stuttgart 1959/Frankfurt 1974

K. Vondung (ed.), *Das wilhelminische Bildungsbürgertum. Zur Sozialgeschichte seiner Ideen*, Göttingen 1976

University History

F. Paulsen, *Die deutschen Universitäten und das Universitätsstudium*, Berlin 1902

H. Schelsky, *Einsamkeit und Freiheit*, 2nd edn, Düsseldorf 1971

A. Busch, *Die Geschichte des Privatdozenten*, Stuttgart 1959

History

F. Wagner, *Geschichtswissenschaft*, Freiburg 1951

G. G. Iggers, *Deutsche Geschichtswissenschaft*, München 1971

M. Asendorf (ed.), *Aus der Aufklärung in die permanente Restauration. Geschichtswissenschaft in Deutschland*, Hamburg 1974 (important as a collection of documents)

H. Schnädelbach, *Geschichtsphilosophie nach Hegel. Die Probleme des Historismus*, Freiburg/München 1974

Science (history and theory of science)

E. Cassirer, *Das Erkenntnisproblem in der Philosophie und Wissenschaft der neueren Zeit*, Vol. IV, new edn Darmstadt 1974 (*The Problem of Knowledge. Philosophy, Science and History Since Hegel*, New Haven, Conn. 1950)

A. Diemer (ed.), *Beiträge zur Entwicklung der Wissenschaftstheorie im 19. Jahrhundert*, Meisenheim 1968ff.

W. Lepenies, *Das Ende der Naturgeschichte. Wandel kultureller Selbstverständlichkeiten in den Wissenschaften des 18. und 19. Jahrhunderts*, Frankfurt 1978

G. Hennemann, *Naturphilosophie im 19. Jahrhundert*, Freiburg/München 1959

H. Plessner, *Zur Soziologie der modernen Forschung und ihrer Organisation in der deutschen Universität* (1924), in *Diesseits der Utopie*, Frankfurt 1974, 121ff.

Understanding

J. Wach, *Das Verstehen. Grundzüge einer Theorie der hermeneutischen Wissenschaften im 19. Jahrhundert*, 3 vols., Tübingen 1926–33

K. O. Apel, *Das Verstehen. Eine Problemgeschichte als Begriffsgeschichte,* in *Archiv für Begriffsgeschichte* 1 (1955)

H.-G. Gadamer, *Wahrheit und Methode. Grundzüge einer philosophischen Hermeneutik*, Tübingen 1960 (*Truth and Method*, New York 1975)

Life

Ph. Lersch, *Lebensphilosophie der Gegenwart*, Berlin 1932

G. Misch, *Lebensphilosophie und Phänomenologie* (2nd edn 1931), new edn Darmstadt 1975

F. O. Bollnow, *Die Lebensphilosophie*, Berlin 1958

Values

J. E. Heyde, *Wert. Eine philosophische Grundlegung*, Erfurt 1926
A. Messer, *Wertphilosophie der Gegenwart*, Berlin 1930
F. Bamberger, *Untersuchungen zur Entstehung des Wertproblems im 19. Jahrhundert*, Halle 1924

Being

G. Lehmann, *Die Ontologie der Gegenwart in ihren Grundgestalten*, Halle 1933
H. Pichler, *Nicolai Hartmann, der Denker und sein Werk*, Göttingen 1952

Man

O. Marquard, *Zur Geschichte des philosophischen Begriffs 'Anthropologie' seit dem Ende des achtzehnten Jahrhunderts*, in *Schwierigkeiten mit der Geschichtsphilosophie*, Frankfurt 1973, 122ff.
A. Gehlen, *Anthropologische Forschung*, Reinbek 1961

Index

Absolute, the 5, 6, 10, 89, 101, 144, 148, 162, 165, 171, 185, 196
Absolute Idealism 5, 6, 9, 10, 11, 143, 146, 162, 165, 169ff., 174, 200, 228
Academic freedom 22ff.
Adorno, Theodor 101, 140, 162
Aestheticization of philosophy 95
Aesthetics 36, 106, 107, 161, 177f., 183
Alienation 101
Analytic philosophy 191, 216
Anthropologism 220
Anthropology, historical 37
Anthropology, philosophical 11, 64, 74, 97, 101, 128, 140, 154, 197, ch. 8 passim
Apel, Karl-Otto 136
Apollonian/Dionysian contrast 156, 199
Aristotle 23, 60, 64, 66, 72 81, 84, 87, 173, 225
Art 36, 61, 63, 73, 95, 102, 154, 179, 180
Atomism 87
Avenarius, Richard 87, 100, 147
Axiology 163, 166, 181, 182, 183, 184

Barth, Karl 2
Bauer, Bruno 101
Being 59, 65, 137, 139, 140, 144, 151, 152, 162, 167, 171, 173, 181, 183, 189, 190, ch. 7 passim, 233
Benjamin, Walter 140
Bergson, Henri 140, 148f., 151
Berlin University 22, 89, 170
Biologism 99f., 146ff., 152, 184, 197, 220
Biology 75f., 99, 139, 146, 171, 184, 222f., 229
Bloch, Ernst 150
Bollnow, F.A. 149, 157
Boltzmann, Ludwig 87

Bolzano, Bernhard 193, 201f.
Börne, Ludwig 12f., 19
Brentano, Franz 194, 201f.
Büchner, Georg 12
Büchner, Ludwig 78, 96f.
Buckle, H.T. 119
Buddhism 154
Burckhardt, Jacob 40, 41ff., 59, 62, 231

Cambridge 22
Cartesianism 160
Cassirer, Ernst 87
Categorical Imperative 170
Chemistry 76, 82
Classical philology 44, 111, 156
Classicism 3, 18, 111
Cohen, Hermann 105, 209
Comte, Auguste 52, 85
Conrad-Martius, Hedwig 205
Conservatism 36
Critical Realism 106, 209
Critical theory 1, 65, 101, 140, 151, 159, 234
Criticism (Kantian philosophy) 103, 123, 133, 179f., 184, 185, 195, 203, 209ff., 216
Critique of ideology 10, 18
Croce, Benedetto 119
Culturalism 36, 37
Cultural sciences 58, 73, 129ff., 161
Culture (*Bildung*) 21ff., 71, 78, 145
Culture (*Kultur*) 58, 130, 148, 151, 152, 153ff., 184
Culture, historical 34ff., 37, 68, 71, 145f.
Culture, philosophy of 10, 29, 58, 152, 156
Curtius, Ludwig 21, 31

INDEX

Darwin, Darwinism 59, 76, 77, 81, 91, 96, 100, 146, 229, 231
Dasein 64, 122, 123, 137ff., 158, 200, 206f. 218, 232f.
Deductivism 85, 90
Democritus 225
Descartes, René 81, 222
Dialectical materialism 99, 106, 197
Dilthey, Wilhelm 37, 50, 54ff., 99, 116, 118, 119, 121, 122ff., 130f., 132, 134, 141, 146, 147f., 151,158, 159, 170, 173, 225, 229, 231
Dionysian man 226, 231
Driesch, Hans 146
Droysen, Johann Gustav 9, 34, 39, 42, 43, 46, 50ff., 61, 91, 112, 118ff., 123, 124, 125, 229, 230

Eidetic reduction 186ff., 203, 204f., 213
Einstein, Albert 75
Eleatics 199
Emotivism 168
Empathy 112, 117, 122, 130, 133
Empiricism 85ff., 192, 193, 198, 202, 203
Empiricists 54, 188
Empirio-criticism 100, 198
Energetics 75, 100
Energetism 96, 147
Energy, conservation of 75
Engels, Friedrich 2, 3, 39, 65, 92, 96f., 99, 101, 102, 197, 230
Enlightenment 20, 22, 36, 37, 40, 45, 65, 79, 90, 112, 143
Enlightenment, historicist 37ff., 53
Epicurus 225
Epistemology 50, 51, 65, 86, 103, 105f., 107, 109, 126, 143, 147ff., 150, 169, 173, 180, 182, 183, 189, 192, 194f., 197, 198, 201, 203, 205, 209ff., 211f.
Epoché 107, 186, 187, 203, 205, 213, 218
Essence 86, 186ff., 203f., 213, 221f.
Essentialism 86
'Ethical forces' 46, 47
Ethics ix, 7, 99, 106, 107, 149, 156f., 161, 163, 164, 175, 183 186ff., 222
Eucken, Rudolf 170, 186, 201
Evolution 59, 84, 91, 96, 216, 231
Existential philosophy 64f., 95, 102, 134, 136ff., 139, 157ff., 189, 197, 200, 207, 208, 215, 233
Expression 55ff., 123ff.

Fechner, Gustav Theodor 78
Feuerbach, Ludwig 3, 65, 96, 97, 101, 196f., 227ff.

Feyerabend, Paul 140
Fichte, I.H. 176, 196
Fichte, J.G. 3, 5, 17, 22, 79, 80, 95, 143, 171, 175, 178, 190, 195f., 200ff.
Fischer, Kuno 94, 105
Frankfurt School 65, 140
Frege, Gottlob 74, 99, 131, 161, 202
Freud, Sigmund 2, 74, 95, 140, 142, 144, 153, 156
Fries, J. 95, 105, 162, 192

Gadamer, Hans-Georg 138, 208, 217, 233
Gehlen, Arnold 144, 221
Geisteswissenschaften 36f., 50ff., 93, 94, 119, 123, 127, 128, 129, 132ff *see also* Human sciences.
Geometry 85, 189
George, Stefan 150
Goethe 3, 72, 77, 78ff., 90, 143, 151, 153
Goethe, Age of 3, 72, 77f., 96
Gogarten, Friedrich 2
Göttingen University 22, 169
Grotius, Hugo 112

Habermas, Jürgen 136
Haeckel, Ernst 96
Halle University 22
Hamann, J.G. 36, 45, 143
Hartmann, Eduard von 107, 209
Hartmann, Nicolai 1, 148, 180, 186 188f., 206, 209ff., 216, 226, 232
Hauptmann, Gerhart 14
Hegel, G.W.F. 2, 3, 6, 7, 8, 9, 10, 17, 18, 30, 32, 33, 34, 37, 41, 42, 43, 44, 47, 48, 49, 50, 51, 56, 60, 61, 64, 65, 66, 72, 76, 77, 78, 80, 81, 82, 83ff., 94, 99, 100, 101, 102, 104, 105, 109, 113, 118, 129, 140, 141, 142, 143, 158, 164, 165, 166, 169, 170, 174, 178, 179, 192, 193, 195, 196, 197, 198, 202, 215, 220, 225, 227ff.
Heidegger, Martin 1, 53, 59, 64, 65, 88, 99, 102, 122ff., 127, 136ff., 140, 144, 147, 148, 151, 157, 159, 160, 190, 193, 196, 200, 206ff., 216, 217, 219, 221, 229, 232ff.
Heimpel, Hermann 32
Heine, Heinrich 12, 16ff., 18, 79f.
Heinemann, Fritz 157
Helmholtz, Heinrich von 75, 85, 87, 192
Helmholtz, Hermann 103f., 107
Heraclitus 147ff., 198
Herbart, J.F. 105, 162, 170
Herder, J.G. 28, 36, 45, 143, 232
Hermeneutic circle 53, 121ff., 128, 138

INDEX

Hermeneutic philosophy 7, 9, 52, 53
Hermeneutic problem 45
Hermeneutics 111, 112f., 114ff., 136f., 158, 171, 200, 207f., 217, 218, 229, 233
Hertz, Heinrich 75, 86
Heyde, J.E. 164f., 168
Historical School 9, 36, 39, 41ff., 119, 122, 231
Historicism 34ff., 54, 56, 66, 85, 95, 100, 109, 112, 123, 146, 158, 165, 193, 220, 227f., 230
Historicity 136f.
Historicization
   of history 37
   of man 38
   of philosophy 94f.
   of understanding 112f.
'Historics' 51ff., 118ff.
History 9, ch. 2 passim, 82, 89, 97, 109, 112, 118ff., 130, 136ff., 145f., 152f., 172, 197, 217, 220, 227, 230ff.
History, Philosophy of 9, 40ff., 56ff., 59, 60f., 64f., 77, 146, 149, 151ff., 157, 226ff.
Holbach, Baron 79
Holism 46f
Horkheimer, Max 101, 140, 144, 227
Human sciences 36ff., 64, 73f., 76, 109, 119, 123, 126ff., 136, 138, 151, 208, 219, 221f., 231, 232, see also *Geisteswissenschaften*
Humboldt, Alexander von 77
Humboldt, Wilhelm von 22, 26ff., 32, 34, 42, 52, 89, 96, 113
Humboldt-University 21ff., 67, 68, 92
Hume, David 54, 95, 194
Husserl, Edmund 1, 74, 87, 99, 107, 126, 131, 132, 137, 148, 158, 160, 170, 184, 186ff., 194, 196, 201ff., 206, 208, 209, 213, 214, 217

Idea, the 6, 7, 18, 42, 48, 90, 113, 141, 146, 165, 170, 177f., 200
Idealism 3, 5ff., 9, 10, 11, 17, 18f., 28, 33, 35, 41, 43, 48, 49, 62, 66, 76ff., 85, 86, 90, 92, 93, 94, 100, 101, 103, 104, 109, 113, 144, 146, 150, 158, 163, 165f., 168, 169, 170, 173, 174, 175, 176, 177f., 179, 182, 183, 190, 195, 196, 197, 198, 200f., 205, 209, 210, 212, 220, 227
Ideal types 134, 148
Idiographic sciences 57f., 131, 179
Inductivism 85, 90, 124f.
Immanence positivism 95, 198, 202

Intentionality 202
Irrationalism 10, 46f., 140ff., 198f., 201
'Is' and 'ought' 7, 10, 162ff., 190
'Is' and 'has validity' 164ff., 185, 190

Jacobi, F.H. 143
Jaspers, Karl 2, 102, 134f., 157ff., 200, 221, 233
Jugendstil 194

Kaiser-Wilhelm-Gesellschaft (Max-Planck-Gesellschaft) 24
Kant, Immanuel 3, 5, 17, 25f., 34, 40, 50, 53, 54, 74, 79, 80, 82, 84, 85, 86, 89, 91 94, 95, 97, 104ff., 109, 110, 112, 114, 115, 119, 122, 123, 130, 147, 158, 162, 164, 170, 172, 172, 174, 180ff, 188, 189, 190, 192, 195f., 197, 199, 200, 202, 209ff., 218, 219, 220, 222, 225
Kautsky, Karl 39, 99
Kierkegaard, Soren 2, 3, 92, 95, 102, 158, 159, 196, 200
Klages, Ludwig 145, 149f., 156, 226
Koselleck, Reinhart 15
Kuhn, Helmut 162, 166
Külpe, O. 106, 209

Lange, Friedrich Albert 18f., 77, 79, 98, 105, 107, 178, 192, 198
Language, philosophy of 208
Lask, Emil 131
Lavoisier, Antoine 75
Law 39
Laws, historical 38
Left-Hegelians *see* Young-Hegelians
Legal theory 36
Lessing, G.E. 28
Leibniz, G.W. 22, 69, 78, 95, 170, 175f., 177, 193, 202
Lenin, V.I. 86, 99, 106, 197
Lessing, G.E. 28
Lessing, T. 145, 177
Liebig, Justus 19, 103
'Life' 10, 56, 62, 63, 124ff., 131, ch. 5 passim, 184, 198
Life-philosophy 10, 11, 55, 60, 62, 63, 65, 75, 95, 100, 118, ch. 5 passim, 173, 183f., 189, 194, 196, 198, 201, 215, 226, 231
Life-world 67, 226
Lipps, Theodor 150
Litt, Theodor 136
'Lived experience' (*Erleben*) 55, 123, 125, 129, 131, 147, 148

INDEX

Locke, John 54, 112
Logic 57, 74, 76, 79, 85, 98, 99, 105, 133f., 135, 148, 150, 161, 181, 183, 192f., 196, 197, 203, 209, 215
Logical Empiricists 136
Logicism 85, 192, 209
Lotze, Hermann 107, 161, 163, 164, 165, 166, 169ff., 180, 181, 182, 190, 195, 196, 201, 202, 230
Lukács, Georg 1, 65, 101, 140, 141
Luther, Martin 19

Mach, Ernst 87, 100, 147
Marburg School 105, 192, 200
Marcuse, Herbert 101, 140
Marquard, Odo 226f.
Marx, Karl 2, 3, 9, 13, 18, 37, 39, 65, 90, 92, 95, 96ff., 99, 99, 101, 107, 161, 196f., 227, 230
Marxism 39, 65, 95, 97, 99, 140, 144, 196
Materialism 18, 19, 34, 75, 78, 86f., 96, 103f., 143, 147, 196f., 229, 230
Mathematics 74, 76, 78, 81, 83, 85, 133, 138, 151
Mayer, Robert 75
Mechanism 74f., 87, 96, 143, 146f.
Meinecke, Friedrich 37
Meinong, Alexius 163, 169, 194, 201f.
Messer, A. 209
Meta-ethics 168, 182, 191
Michelet, K.L. 77
Mill, J.S. 85, 99, 125
Moleschott, Jakob 78, 96, 229
von Müller, Johannes 97, 104
Munich Circle 205f.
Münsterberg, H. 169

National Socialism 4, 21, 29, 31, 100, 140, 146, 149, 154, 189, 229
Natorp, Paul 209
Naturalism 36, 37, 59, 228ff.
Natural law 39, 68
Natural rights 36, 39
Natural sciences 19, 51, 52, 57f., 72, 73, 74, 76f., 78, 83, 85, 103f., 130, 150, 169, 172, 216, 227, 228, 230
Nature philosophy 17, 43, 76ff., 95, 104, 146, 169, 227ff., 230
Neo-Aristotelianism 193
Neo-Hegelianism 140, 200
Neo-Idealism 151, 170, 194, 200
Neo-Kantianism 1, 57ff., 65, 100, 105ff., 127, 128, 148, 161, 163, 164, 166, 178, 180, 181, 185, 189, 190, 192, 193, 198, 200, 209, 213

Neo-Marxism 99, 102, 140
Neo-Romanticism 81, 139, 151, 194
Neo-Thomism 106, 193
Neo-vitalism 81
Neo-Wolffianism 210
'New Objectivity' (*Neue Sachlichkeit*) 194
Newton, Sir Isaac 74, 80, 84, 104, 153
Nietzsche, Friedrich 2, 3, 10, 30, 34, 40, 62ff., 92, 98, 100, 102, 139, 140, 144ff., 151, 156, 161, 162, 166ff., 170, 190, 198ff., 225, 231f.
Nihilism 10, 40, 151, 166ff., 190
Noesis/noema 203f., 218
Nominalism 218
Nomothetic sciences 57
Normative ethics 39, 40
Novalis, F. 45, 143

Ontology 10, 53, 109, 144, 147, 148, 158, 160, 163, 166, 168, 180, 181, 182, 183, 184, 189, 190, ch. 7 passim, 226, 232
Organicism 46f.
Ørstedt, H.C. 75, 77
Ortega y Gasset 32
Ostwald, Wilhelm 96, 147
Oxford 22, 202

Palágyi, Melchior 149
Paulsen, Friedrich 30
Peirce, C.S. 71, 136
Personalism 188, 200
Pessimism 142, 168
Phenomenological reduction 186ff., 203, 205
Phenomenology 1, 87, 107, 137, 170, 179, 180, 184, 186ff., 196, 201ff., 207, 213f., 217, 222
Philology 111, 126
Philosophy of nature *see* Nature-philosophy
Philosophy of spirit 8, 37, 47, 56
Physics 75f., 152
Picture-theory of meaning 86
Pichler, Hans 194, 210
Planck, Max 87
Plato 60, 172f., 188, 209
Platonism 176, 178ff., 203
Plessner, Helmut 20f., 28, 67ff., 88, 99f., 144, 221ff., 232
Popper, Sir K.R. 86, 90
Positivism, positivists 1, 35, 106, 190, 193, 194, 225
Practical philosophy 65
Pragmatism 147
Progress 42, 62, 151
Psychologism 56, 74, 98f., 127f., 132, 169, 179, 186, 193, 202, 220

INDEX

Psychology 37, 55, 56, 57, 73ff., 98f., 102, 107, 116, 117, 123, 126ff., 134, 144, 150, 158, 168f., 179, 180, 182, 188, 216, 229

Quantum theory 74
Quine, W.V.O. 195

Ranke, Leopold 9, 34, 41, 42, 46
Rationalism 36, 37, 69, 111f., 142, 155
Realism
   scientific 176, 197, 210, 213
   Platonic 131
Relativism 35, 40, 54, 56, 58, 93, 146, 182, 190
Relativity, theory of 75, 76, 85, 87
Religion
   history of 37
   philosophy of 100, 106, 113, 167, 183
Rhodes, Cecil 154
Rickert, Heinrich 51, 57ff., 105, 126, 129ff., 132, 133, 134, 139, 148, 161, 165, 180, 183ff., 189, 190, 191ff., 198, 201, 232
Riedel, Manfred 126
Riehl, A. 209
Romanticism 3, 18, 37, 43, 45, 76ff., 92, 112, 143, 146, 169, 227ff., 230, 232
Rothacker, Erich 47, 185f.
Royal Society 23
Russell, Bertrand 163

Sartre, Jean-Paul 233
Scheler, Max 1, 99, 144, 148, 160, 163, 170, 180, 186ff., 191, 200, 201, 205, 206, 209, 219, 221ff., 232, 233
Schelling, F.W. 3, 5, 17, 18, 22, 77, 78, 79f., 82, 104, 143, 174, 196, 200, 229
Schiller, F. 19
Schlegel, F. 28, 36, 126, 143
Schleiermacher, F.D.E. 22, 53, 111f., 114ff., 123, 125, 127f.
Schopenhauer, Arthur 3, 34, 42, 59ff., 92, 97, 100, 102, 105, 140, 143ff., 150, 156, 192, 198, 227, 230f.
Schülz, Walter 232
Science 3, 7, 8, 9, 10, 11, 19, 21ff., 26, 27ff., 33f., 35, 36, 37, 40, 43, 44f., 48, 49, 50, 52, 59, 60, 63, 64, 65, ch. 3 passim, 109, 133, 146, 147, 148, 153, 159, 164, 176f., 189, 192, 194, 195, 198, 209, 219, 224, 228, 229, 232
Scientism 68, 93, 96, 103
Seidel, A. 145
Semantics 218
Simmel, Georg 65, 99, 102, 154, 155

Socialism 39, 99, 102, 154, 155
Social science 64, 134, 161, 164, 217, 222
Sociologism 98f., 220
Sociology 39, 52, 64, 73ff., 133, 148
Sociology of knowledge 99
Solipsism 131
Sosein 186
South-West German School 57ff., 105f., 128, 162, 181, 183, 186
Spengler, Oswald 100, 140, 151ff., 156
Spinoza, Benedict 94, 112
Spinozism 80
Spirit 45, 46, 56, 57, 109, 128, 129, 142ff., 149f., 199, 200f.
Spirit, Absolute 37
Spirit, objective 37, 45, 56, 128, 142
Spirit, subjective 37, 227
Spranger, E. 135
Stegmüller, W. 216
Stirner, Max 101
Stoicism 154
Strauss, D.F. 101
Sturm und Drang 79
Subject, the 6, 7, 48, 54, 158, 180f., 183, 196, 199, 206, 212
Substance 87, 199
System 5, 8f., 10, 33, 42, 48, 49, 78, 88ff., 146, 150, 164, 169, 214

Teleology 7, 43
Temporality 127, 148
Theism, speculative 169, 178
Theology 36, 43, 111
Thomas Aquinas 95
Tillich, Paul 2
Toynbee, Arnold 19
Transcendental philosophy 53, 55, 56ff., 123, 129, 170, 174f., 179, 180ff., 195, 205, 212
Troeltsch, E. 129
Tübingen School 36

Understanding *see Verstehen*
University system, German 21ff.

Vaihinger, H. 147
Value 7, 10, 29, 58, 107, 130ff., 157, ch. 6 passim
Value-freedom 29, 35, 40, 156, 163, 189
Value-philosophy 10, 11, 58, ch. 6 passim, 196, 230
Value-relevance 58, 129f., 135, 165, 184
Verstehen (understanding) 9, 43, 52, 55, 56, ch. 4 passim, 146, 158, 165, 207, 229

Vienna Circle 1, 98
Vitalism 95, 146, 149, 171, 226
Vogt, Carl 96, 103
Volkelt, J. 106
Voltaire, F.M.A. de 30, 99

Wagner, Richard 62
Wagner, Rudolf 103
Weber, Max 24f., 28f., 32, 40, 44, 68, 71, 132ff., 148, 158, 161, 189, 190
Weisse, C.H. 169f., 196
Wesensschau 186

Whewell, W. 85
Will (Schopenhauer) 144, 198, 230f.
Will to power (Nietzsche) 98, 144f., 156, 167, 198f.
Windelband, Wilhelm 57ff., 105, 107, 131, 170, 179, 180ff., 184, 185
Wittgenstein, Ludwig 1, 86, 110, 136, 233
Wolf, F.A. 53, 111, 114
Wolff, Christian 78, 95, 194, 213
Wundt, Wilhelm 99, 107f., 128, 209

Young-Hegelians 8, 9, 37, 65, 100ff., 197

Wang 307-0970